FINAL REPORT
Classical Music Consumer Segmentation Study

How Americans Relate to Classical Music and Their Local Orchestras

October 2002

Commissioned by the John S. and James L. Knight Foundation and 15 American Orchestras:

Brooklyn Philharmonic Orchestra
Charlotte Symphony Orchestra
Colorado Symphony Association
Detroit Symphony Orchestra Hall
Fort Wayne Philharmonic Orchestra
Kansas City Symphony
Long Beach Symphony Association
Louisiana Philharmonic Orchestra
New World Symphony
Oregon Symphony Association
The Philadelphia Orchestra Association
Saint Louis Symphony Orchestra
Saint Paul Chamber Orchestra
Symphony Society of San Antonio
Wichita Symphony Society

John S. and James L.
Knight Foundation

Second Printing, April 2003

ISBN 0-9740748-0-2

ABOUT
The Study

Abstract

Orchestras are adrift in a sea of classical music consumers who rarely, if ever, attend live orchestra concerts. With more than 25,000 interviews with potential classical consumers and orchestra ticket buyers in 15 cities, the Classical Music Consumer Segmentation Study offers a sweeping view of an art form in transition and an orchestra field increasingly detached from its potential customers.

The study paints a detailed picture of how consumers fit classical music into their lives — listening to classical radio and recordings in their automobiles and homes, and attending live concerts in churches, schools and traditional concert venues. Roughly 10 percent to 15 percent of Americans have what might be termed a close or moderately close relationship with classical music, and again as many have weaker ties. Across the 15 study cities, approximately one in four adults are prospects (i.e., potential orchestra ticket buyers). But only half of those who express the very highest levels of preference for attending classical music concerts actually attend, even infrequently.

On a tactical level, the study produced a long list of ideas for new and refined marketing strategies. Subscription marketing, the study suggests, is an increasingly dysfunctional marketing paradigm that is often at odds with the goal of attracting younger audiences. From a strategic standpoint, increasing attendance — or at least staving off a decline in attendance — may require a loosening of the definitional boundaries around "classical music" and structural changes to the concert experience that recognize the underlying values and benefits that consumers seek from listening to classical music and attending live concerts.

Study Team

Audience Insight LLC
P.O. Box 423, Southport, Conn. 06890
Telephone 203-256-1616
Email: info@audienceinsight.com

Alan S. Brown, Project Director
Steven A. Wolff, Principal
Andrew J. Fish, PhD, Research Director
Mary Beth Fenlaw, Project Manager
Chris Lorway, Analyst
Erik Swenson, Analyst

Audience Insight is the research affiliate of AMS Planning & Research Corp.

ACKNOWLEDGEMENTS

The consultants are grateful to entire study team for their support and encouragement throughout the study.

Knight Foundation Staff

- Penelope McPhee, Vice President and Chief Program Officer

- Larry Meyer, Vice President of Communications

- Lisa Versaci, Director of National Venture Fund

- John Bare, Director of Program Development and Evaluation

- Gary Burger, former Arts & Culture Program Director

Expert Panelists

Two marketing experts assisted the study team in formulating the research plan:

- Joanne Scheff, Adjunct Associate Professor of Arts Management, J.L. Kellogg Graduate School of Management, Northwestern University, and Principal, Joanne Scheff Arts Management

- John H. Mather, Professor of Marketing, Graduate School of Industrial Administration, Carnegie Mellon University

Study Advisory Group

The Study Advisory Committee provided guidance and feedback to the study team with the overall goal of keeping the study relevant to the day-to-day issues and challenges facing orchestras. The group included administrators, board members and a musician.

- Ed Cambron, Dir. of Marketing and Patron Services, Philadelphia Orchestra

- Julia Kirchhausen, Former Dir. of Marketing, St. Paul Chamber Orchestra

- Don Roth, Past President and Executive Director, St. Louis Symphony Orchestra

- Christopher Stager, Former Dir. of Marketing, Brooklyn Philharmonic Orchestra

- David Tang, Associate Conductor, Charlotte Symphony Orchestra

Our heartfelt thanks go to each of the current and former staff members of the 15 orchestras whose assistance and cooperation made the study possible. We are especially indebted to the Charlotte Symphony Orchestra for serving as the test site for the various methodologies.

TABLE OF
Contents

INTRODUCTION

Magic of Music has been one of the major funding initiatives of the Knight Foundation since 1994. In its first phase, nearly $6 million in grants was awarded to a select group of 12 orchestras with the overall goal of strengthening the bond between musicians and audiences in the concert hall. A number of innovative programs were designed and tested, ranging from informal performances at unusual locations to abbreviated programs and "informances" as entry points for new and younger audiences.

Knight Foundation's trustees funded a second phase for Magic of Music in December 1999, involving 15 orchestras. In addition to further work in the areas of program innovation and audience development, the second phase included a significant investment in market research. Each orchestra was required to participate in the research project in order to be eligible for a program grant.

All 15 orchestras applied to participate in the research initiative, and all were granted a share of the funds necessary to participate. Each orchestra contracted separately with Audience Insight LLC to conduct a standardized program of market-specific research.

To begin the research initiative and to set the stage for the local studies, Knight Foundation contracted with Audience Insight to conduct a national study of classical music consumers, which included both qualitative and quantitative components.

The study is unique in scope, focus and design. More than 11,300 random sample telephone interviews were fielded in 15 markets corresponding to the areas served by the 15 orchestras (approximately 750 interviews in each market). The local surveys were preceded by a national telephone survey of 2,200 adults. In addition, 1,500 orchestra ticket buyers were surveyed by mail in each market (750 subscribers and 750 single-ticket buyers, each), yielding just over 10,000 responses.

At the end of the two-year study the 15 orchestras were able to compare national results with market-area results and results for their own ticket buyers — along a wide range of variables relating to classical music participation.

Thanks to a combination of resources from Knight Foundation, the orchestras and a broad array of professional expertise in marketing, market research and consumer behavior, this initiative represents the most comprehensive discipline-specific audience study ever undertaken in the United States.

KEY THEMES
And Observations

"Sometimes I think that people who know too much don't enjoy things because they're looking for the mistakes and they're honing in on that so hard that they don't relax and enjoy what's going on." — Focus Group Participant, November 2000

Orchestras are adrift in a sea of classical music consumers who rarely, if ever, attend live orchestra concerts. Roughly 10 percent to 15 percent of Americans have what might be termed a close or moderately close relationship with classical music, and again as many have weaker ties. Yet only half of those who express the very highest levels of preference for attending classical music concerts actually attend, even infrequently.

Results from the Classical Music Consumer Segmentation Study paint a detailed picture of how people fit classical music into their lives and offer a sweeping view of an art form in transition and an orchestra field increasingly detached from its potential customers.

As part of its Magic of Music initiative, the John S. and James L. Knight Foundation commissioned the Classical Music Consumer Segmentation Study in 2000, inviting its 15 U.S. orchestra partners to join the research. The study involved a national telephone survey as well as a series of comparable research efforts in each of the 15 orchestras' communities. In each market, data gathering included an analysis of the orchestra's customer data file, a general population telephone survey of 750 adults, and a postal survey of orchestra ticket buyers. Additionally, focus group discussions were held with various groups of prospects and ticket buyers in Charlotte, St. Paul and Detroit. At the conclusion of the study, the consultants traveled to each city to present and discuss the research results with board and staff members of each orchestra.

Altogether, the Classical Music Consumer Segmentation Study represents that largest discipline-specific arts consumer study ever undertaken in the U.S., with nearly 25,000 completed interviews and surveys.[1]

....
Radio is the dominant mode of consumption of classical music, followed by recordings and then live concerts.
....

---

[1] *The data are public available and may be accessed through the electronic catalog of the University of North Carolina's Odum Institute for Research in Social Science at www.irss.unc.edu.*

Connections to Classical Music

Consumers experience classical music — both live and recorded — in a variety of settings and venues. Nationally, the most common setting for experiencing the art form is the automobile, followed by the home. Live classical concerts, including chamber music concerts, recitals, choral concerts as well as orchestra concerts, are heard in a range of formal and informal settings. In addition to formal concert venues, consumers attend classical concerts in schools, houses of worship, outdoor amphitheatres and private homes.

Radio is the dominant mode of consumption of classical music, followed by recordings and then live concerts. Six in 10 orchestra ticket buyers listen to classical music on the radio daily or several times a week. The typical orchestra subscriber owns 105 records, tapes and CDs, compared to 63 for single-ticket buyers. While some consumers think of classical radio programming as a substitute for live concerts (particularly those with modest levels of knowledge about classical music), most do not. Generally, classical consumers sustain and enhance their interest in the art form through radio and recordings.

The study reveals a symbiotic, long-term relationship between live attendance and consumption via electronic media. If listening to classical radio and recordings at home and in the car is how consumers grow and sustain a love for classical music, then these are primary arenas for long-term audience development. Increasing the availability and quality of classical music on the radio, and increasing ownership, exchange and use classical recordings is strategic to the long-term vitality of the orchestra field.

Attitudes and Self-Perceptions

In addition to consumption patterns, the study also investigated attitudes about classical music, including self-reported knowledge levels and levels of interest in learning more. Nationally, just 6 percent of the large base of potential classical consumers[2] self-identified as being "very knowledgeable" about classical music, while 44 percent said that they are "somewhat knowledgeable." Similarly, 13 percent of potential classical consumers reported that they are "very interested" in learning more about classical music, while 53 percent said that they are "somewhat interested."

Overall, just 10 percent of potential classical consumers think of themselves as "critical listeners" (self-defined), while 78 percent consider themselves "casual listeners" and 11 percent say that they are "uninterested listeners." Thus, the vast majority of potential customers for orchestras are casually involved with the art form.

> **The vast majority of potential customers for orchestras are casually involved with the art form.**

---

[2] *Potential classical consumers were defined as a subset of adults who qualified for a lengthier interview based on their responses to an initial series of questions about arts activities. In the national study, 59 percent of adults qualified as potential classical consumers. In the 15 local studies, 52 percent qualified as potential classical consumers, on average.*

"Casual listeners" also dominate the audience base. Across the 15 orchestras, 42 percent of subscribers think of themselves as "critical listeners," while 57 percent say that they are "casual listeners." For single-ticket buyers, the figures are 28 percent for "critical listeners" and 68 percent for "casual listeners."

On balance, the study finds a range of sophistication levels in the audience and the prospect base. While most everyone understands this intuitively, the study provides new insight, clarification and impetus for action. What does it mean to an orchestra that a third of its ticket buyers are more sophisticated about classical music and two-thirds are less sophisticated about classical music, by their own definitions? If a majority of ticket buyers have a limited classical music vocabulary and don't know enough to select programs based on artists and repertoire, then on what basis are they making decisions?

Connections to the Local Orchestra

The study illustrates the broad impact that some orchestras have had in their communities, and it exposes large numbers of classical enthusiasts in each of the 15 cities. The Saint Louis Symphony Orchestra, for example, has touched a third of adults in the St. Louis area, on a cumulative basis. Similarly, the Wichita Symphony Orchestra, Fort Wayne Philharmonic, Detroit Symphony Orchestra and Oregon Symphony have reached at least a quarter of adults in their respective markets, on a cumulative basis.

By any measure, these are impressive figures. They also point to the fact that orchestras have accumulated large numbers of inactive, former buyers — people who have attended a concert at some point in their lives but who do not attend now with any regularity.

On average, 22 percent of potential classical consumers say that they are "very interested" in attending a concert by their local orchestra, while 71 percent say that they are "open to attending, but it's not a high priority." That's a lot of wishful thinking but nevertheless a very raw measure of interest.

On a cumulative basis, the Saint Louis Symphony Orchestra has touched a third of adults in its market area.

The study produced a large amount of data on respondents' frequency of attendance at all live performing arts events, frequency of attendance at classical music concerts, and frequency of attendance at concerts by a specific local orchestra. On average, orchestra subscribers in the 15 cities reported that classical music accounts for 58 percent of their total "diet" of performing arts activities, compared to 41 percent for single-ticket buyers. The average Brooklyn Philharmonic subscriber attended 31 performing arts events over the preceding year, while the average Charlotte Symphony subscriber attended 15.

Within the realm of classical music, individual orchestras account for the lion's share of their ticket buyers' concert-going activity, but not all of it. In cities like

Charlotte and Fort Wayne, the orchestras supply upwards of 80 percent of all of the live classical concerts that their ticket buyers attend in a given year. The Saint Paul Chamber Orchestra, in contrast, accounts for just 41 percent of its single-ticket buyers' concert-going activity.[3]

While most orchestras use similar, if not identical marketing strategies and tactics — relying heavily on subscription marketing as the primary means of selling tickets — ticket buyers in these cities experience their orchestras quite differently. Single-ticket buyers to the Brooklyn Philharmonic could not look more different than single-ticket buyers to the Fort Wayne Philharmonic, in terms of sophistication, experience level and frequency of attendance, yet the marketing tactics used to attract them are strikingly similar.

Social Context

The power of social context in driving orchestra attendance and arts attendance, generally, is a major theme of the study. Nationally, six in 10 potential classical consumers have close friends or immediate family members who attend classical concerts. This compares to eight in 10 orchestra ticket buyers.

Different people like different amounts of social activity before, during and after concerts. For some, the social opportunity itself is what triggers consent to attend. An attractive social context, from a consumer behavior perspective, lubricates the purchase decision process.

A serious examination of the large base of potential classical consumers reveals that for many, if not most, a relationship with the orchestra is contingent on an external social stimulus — an invitation. Across the 15 markets, 16 percent of potential classical consumers self-identify as "Initiators" — people who instinctively organize cultural outings for their friends, but 52 percent identify themselves as "Responders" — people who are much more likely to attend cultural outings if someone else invites them.

Indeed, the study paints a picture of a largely invisible "shadow audience" for most orchestras — people who've attended concerts but who did not buy their ticket and may not have participated in the purchase decision process. Results from the public telephone surveys in each of the 15 markets indicate that, on average, 40 percent of those who've ever attended a concert by their local orchestra did not (and have never) purchased a ticket.

....

*On average,
40 percent of those
who've ever attended
a concert by their
local orchestra did
not (and have never)
purchased a ticket.*

....

....

[3] *The Saint Paul Chamber Orchestra, Brooklyn Philharmonic, New World Symphony and Long Beach Philharmonic all operate in markets with other major orchestras. Results of the ticket buyer surveys are orchestra-specific and are not representative of other orchestras' ticket buyers.*

Focus group research suggests that the absence of social context is a major barrier to attendance. Consider a married couple with divergent musical tastes; one likes classical music and the other doesn't — a phenomenon we call "taste dissonance." Or, consider a single person who is new to an area and has yet to develop a social network with shared values about concert going. In both cases, the potential demand for classical concerts remains latent without a social context for attending.

Orchestras and other arts groups spend a great deal of time and money trying to convert Responders into active buyers. The data suggest, however, that indirect selling to Responders (through their respective Initiators) might be more effective in activating their interest in classical music, and other marketing strategies that leverage the potent currency of social context are likely to unlock additional demand for arts programs.

All of this raises an urgent question for orchestras: What defines the customer? Is a customer someone who buys tickets, or is a customer someone who enjoys the concert? The difference is important. If the definition of "customer" is expanded to include people who enjoy concerts but won't attend without an invitation, then a fundamental realignment of marketing strategy is implied — a shift toward strategies that create and facilitate attendance in small social groups.

The Prospect Universe for 15 Orchestras

Cluster analysis was employed to create two new consumer models — a model that reflects the range of relationships that people have with classical music and another model that reflects the range of connections that consumers have with a specific local orchestra. At the end of the study, the two models were merged to create a third "orchestra prospect model" that represents a new framework for understanding both current and prospective audiences.

All told, the prospect universe for the 15 orchestras, on average, is 27 percent of adults.

On average, the 15 orchestras attract roughly 4 percent of adults in their communities on any sort of a regular basis — they are "Captured Prospects." Across the 15 markets studied, another 15 percent of adults, on average, are "Low Frequency Alumni" of the orchestra, and another 8 percent are "Uninitiated Prospects" — people with a close art-form relationship who have never attended a concert by the local orchestra included in the study. All told, the prospect universe for the 15 orchestras, on average, is 27 percent of adults. The figure ranges from a low of 16 percent (Brooklyn Philharmonic, New World Symphony) to a high of 35 percent (Wichita Symphony Orchestra, Saint Louis Symphony Orchestra).

Not all of these people, of course, are ready to subscribe or buy single tickets to orchestra concerts. But they all share one of two important characteristics: either they have already been to a concert by the local orchestra at some point in their lives, or their level of interest in classical music is high enough that they must be considered to be prospects in the eyes of the local orchestra.

Difficult Questions, Difficult Answers

Two-thirds of Americans would accept a free ticket to a classical concert by a symphony orchestra, if offered by a friend or family member. So, why are some orchestras having difficulty filling their halls? What's keeping orchestras from attracting the next 2 percent or 3 percent of adults in their communities? Among others, these are some of the most difficult questions addressed in the study.

Can better marketing renew the constituency for classical music?

When pressed, some orchestra managers acknowledge that more and better marketing is only part of the answer to declining attendance. This study produced a long list of ideas for new and refined marketing tactics — including concert clubs (much like book clubs), thematic packaging, more clever sales messages, broad-based prospect campaigns, low-threshold trial experiences, cooperative marketing with other arts groups, and many other ideas that deserve to be tested and evaluated.

The study also raised questions about mission and strategy. Subscription marketing is a conundrum for orchestras and an increasingly dysfunctional marketing paradigm. While a great number of classical music lovers enjoy subscribing, only 8 percent of potential classical consumers are highly inclined to subscribe. This is especially true for younger people who attend orchestra concerts. Among ticket buyers in the 18-34 age cohort, 15 percent are highly inclined to subscribe, compared to 56 percent of those aged 75 and older.

Subscription campaigns generate the cash flow and sales volume that orchestras need to survive and are efficient from a marketing standpoint (i.e., a relatively low marketing cost-per-ticket). Single-ticket marketing, in contrast, is expensive on a cost-per-ticket-sold basis. Orchestra marketers do their job well by selling out on subscription and are rewarded for doing so.

Notwithstanding the benefits of subscription marketing, this study brings to light two of its major flaws. First, subscription marketing acts as a filter on an orchestra's constituency that runs counter to the goal of attracting younger audiences. About half of subscribers across the 15 markets are 65 or older, and 17 percent are 75 or older. Subscribers are almost twice as likely as single-ticket buyers to be retired (45 percent vs. 24 percent, respectively) and are significantly more likely as single-ticket buyers to have incomes above $150,000 (25 percent vs. 16 percent, respectively). Moreover, subscribers are half as likely as single-ticket buyers to have children in the household (12 percent vs. 23 percent, respectively).

The other major problem with subscription marketing is that the lion's share of prospects for these orchestras — including many of those who are highly knowledgeable about classical music — are simply not interested in making subscription commitments. Less than 10 percent of "Uninitiated Prospects" are

....

Only 8 percent of potential classical consumers are highly inclined to subscribe.

....

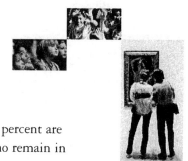

highly inclined to subscribe. Within the base of single-ticket buyers, 36 percent are former subscribers who have opted out of subscription packaging but who remain in the audience.

We do not suggest that there is anything conceptually flawed with subscription packaging or that orchestras summarily abandon subscription marketing. What the study does illustrate, very clearly, is that subscription marketing comes at a price and that trade-offs are being made that are not always consistent with some of the orchestras' own goals or the larger ideals for community cultural involvement espoused by funders.

In the marketing area, perhaps the biggest challenge facing the orchestra field is defining other customer relationships or "involvement opportunities" that do not require advance commitment or large, lump sum payments — and then finding new ways to build loyalty among single-ticket buyers, even those who may attend just two or three times a year. There are no easy answers here, but the study points to many ideas. Perhaps, with the advent of e-mail marketing, we are actually approaching a time when the cost of selling a single ticket is not ten or twenty times the cost of selling a subscription seat.

Orchestras are constrained by a financial model that is largely dependent on subscription sales. There is little room to experiment — no "R&D" capacity, like other industries — and even less room to fail. Until this equation fundamentally changes, subscription marketing will continue to be the sweet honey that sustains orchestras and a slow-acting poison that impedes their long-term sustainability.

A much more difficult, complex and strategic proposition — and the larger part of the answer to declining attendance — is what to do differently onstage.

Each of the 15 orchestras draws about 80 percent of its ticket buyers from the geography within by a 25-mile radius around the performance venue.

Where can orchestras find customers?

More to the point, how can orchestras help people find meaning in classical music in the places like churches, schools, cars, private homes and especially on the radio — places where they actually experience the art form on a daily basis? Can orchestras leverage these different settings and mediums into audience development opportunities? A cold look at the data begs the question of why orchestras (and opera companies, for that matter) don't own or operate classical radio stations in their markets.

Analysis of the customer files of the 15 orchestras revealed a clear picture of the geographical draw of these orchestras, and it points to a close relationship between drive time and frequency of attendance, particularly with respect to subscribers.

There are some interesting variations, but each of the 15 orchestras draws about 80 percent of its ticket buyers from the geography within by a 25-mile radius around the performance venue. In some cities, suburban sprawl continues to reposition the base of high quality prospects farther away from the urban center. Meanwhile, more consumers place a premium on convenience and are disinclined to negotiate traffic for any number of reasons. Some orchestras will have increasing difficulty capturing the market potential around the periphery of their market areas without finding new venues in which to perform. The Charlotte Symphony, the Saint Paul Chamber Orchestra and several other orchestras now offer series of concerts at multiple secondary venues around their market areas. Several of the orchestras have had success breaking up into smaller ensembles and performing in numerous venues, but these tend to be educational programs, not regular concerts.

How can orchestras adapt to changing market conditions?

Not long ago, orchestras were the dominant, if not sole providers of classical music in their communities. Now, consumers integrate classical music into their lives in many settings and for many reasons. They see orchestra concerts along a continuum of arts and entertainment offerings that are commercial and nonprofit, professional and nonprofessional. These offerings range from light entertainment to more educational and spiritual experiences.

Orchestras operate in a highly dynamic consumer-marketing environment and compete with well-capitalized entertainment conglomerates like Disney and Clear Channel for leisure time and consumer "mind share." When artistic planning occurs in a vacuum of consumer information, orchestras risk growing detached from their audiences and potential audiences. The product must be a variable in the marketing mix, eventually, or the market for classical orchestra concerts will slowly — and in some cities not so slowly — shrink, as the definition of the art form itself evolves and melds with other genres of music, and as the demographic and cultural landscape around classical music shifts.

This is not to suggest that consumer preferences should replace artistic vision as the impetus behind orchestras' programming decisions. The two may co-exist productively; artistic choices can be informed by consumer information, and consumers can be influenced by artistic vision. Looking at the concert experience through the consumer's lens can only help orchestras enhance their level of service and relevance to the communities they serve.

If 10 to 15 percent of Americans have a moderate to close relationship with the art form, why don't orchestras perform special concerts once or twice a year in large concert venues, where so many people go regularly for other types of music? The event phenomenon took hold in the musical theatre world with *Phantom of the Opera* and then *Riverdance*, *Lord of the Dance*, and *Spirit of the Dance*. Museums weighed in with blockbuster exhibitions like *King Tut*, *Monet* and others. The opera world got

turned on its ear by Three Tenors and, more recently, Three 'Mo Tenors and The Irish Tenors. What is the orchestra field's answer to this consumer phenomenon? People go in droves. Why can't orchestras self-produce large-scale concert extravaganzas in stadiums and arenas that might attract 10,000 or 15,000 people at a time?

How can the concert experience be enhanced?

Each orchestra will have a different answer that depends on how it interprets its mission, how it understands the art form, and especially how its board members, funders, musicians and artistic leadership can be engaged in a productive dialogue about what's happening offstage, not only in the audience but in the daily lives of classical consumers.

Both quantitative and qualitative results from the study indicate that structural changes to the concert experience and a loosening of definitional boundaries around the art form will help orchestras attract and retain more ticket buyers. Some orchestras, especially those in the large metropolitan markets, may rededicate themselves to traditional symphonic repertoire, scale themselves appropriately and find plentiful demand for the foreseeable future. Other orchestras may choose to re-organize as music organizations with a somewhat broader mission to present and produce a wider range of programs across various genres of music, drawing on the talents of their own musicians, perhaps, in new ways. This will require a great deal more flexibility in the services of musicians.

Discussions with "casual listeners" suggest that some, if not most, want to be able to appreciate the music a little more and want help negotiating other aspects of the concert experience. They want to become better listeners but can't do it by themselves. Pre-concert lectures and annotated program notes appeal mostly to those who are already knowledgeable about the art form. These devices are not long-term solutions to "experience enhancement" for causal listeners.

Beyond marketing, the study's findings suggest that some orchestras, especially those in smaller cities, might reexamine how they define their constituencies and how they select, package and deliver their musical products. During several of the site visits that followed the study, discussions revolved around possible structural changes to the concert experience on certain performance nights that would provide less sophisticated concertgoers with a more interesting, less intimidating and generally more rewarding concert experience. The tactics discussed included greetings from the stage, short introductions of pieces by musicians or a classical radio host, longer intermissions to allow for more "social processing time," less formal attire for the musicians, thematic lighting, decorations and various other program content and ambience enhancements. While some audience members would abhor such informalities, the data suggest that more than not would enjoy them.

FIGURE 1: LAYERS OF VALUE AROUND CLASSICAL MUSIC AND THE CONCERT EXPERIENCE

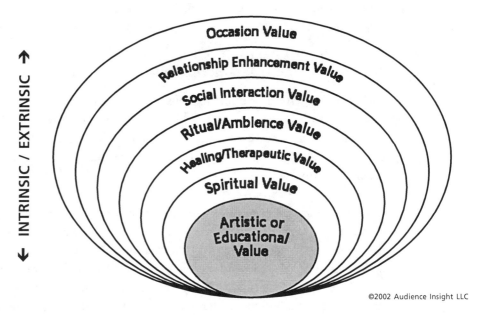

©2002 Audience Insight LLC

Why do people attend orchestra concerts?

A large part of this question has to do with why people attend live concerts — what benefits and utilities they seek and what aspects of the experience they value. This topic was a focus of the ticket-buyer surveys and yielded a great deal of insight. In sum, classical consumers derive "layers of value" around the concert experience that don't always relate to what's happening onstage (see Figure 1).

Some people use classical concerts to entertain visiting friends and family members ("occasion value"), while others use concerts as a means of nurturing and sustaining their personal relationships ("relationship enhancement value"). In focus groups, classical consumers quickly start talking about the "healing and therapeutic value" of classical music and the "spiritual or transformational value." These layers of benefits and values surround the actual artistic and educational experience, which is what orchestras sell.

Respondents to the ticket-buyer surveys highly rate the "ritual/ambience" value of the concert experience. What can orchestras do to enhance the visual and emotional value of the concert setting and otherwise make the concert experience more interesting to watch? In focus groups, audience members talk about closing their eyes and retreating into the unlimited visual possibilities of their imaginations during concerts. While one can debate whether this sort of self-induced hallucination is a healthy, creative activity, the point is that some people find the visual aspect of the concert experience uninteresting, at best.

The analysis suggests that many people in the audience are there for reasons other than (or in addition to) the music.

While it might seem distasteful to some, the analysis suggests that many people in the audience are there for reasons other than (or in addition to) the music. Understanding, interpreting and selling back the complex values which consumers construct around the concert experience may help to stimulate demand among those who are already predisposed to attending orchestra concerts.

What is "classical music," and whose definition matters?

If anything, results from the study point to a divergence, with consumers' definition of classical music differing from the definition of classical music idealized by orchestras, music directors and musicians.

Respondents to the various surveys were allowed to self-define classical music. Like the NEA Surveys of Public Participation in the Arts, no definition of the art form was provided at the beginning of the protocol. Instead, respondents who reported attending at least one classical music concert were asked to describe the last concert they attended (i.e., name of ensemble, type of program) in an open-ended follow-up question. Results provide a broad overview of the types of live concerts considered to be "classical music." The large majority of respondents who answered this question cited classical and pops concerts offered by symphony orchestras. Other types of concerts mentioned included community band and orchestra concerts, choral music concerts, instrumental and vocal recitals, chamber music concerts, opera performances, holiday performances of *Nutcracker and Messiah*, and the occasional mention of a musical theater performance (e.g., *Phantom of the Opera*). One respondent cited a performance by Cirque du Soleil as a classical music experience.

Similarly, respondents were allowed to self-define "classical music on the radio" and "classical music recordings." In the realm of commercial recordings, where consumer demand is a daily reminder of just how far the definition of classical music has evolved, a quick review of Billboard magazine's Top 40 "Classical Crossover" recordings paints a clear picture of "what is classical music" in the daily lives of consumers. Artists like Yo Yo Ma, James Galway, Erich Kunzel, Joshua Bell, Wynton Marsalis, Denyce Graves, Vanessa Mae and of course the ubiquitous Three Tenors have effectively and lucratively tapped into an expanded definition of classical music that resonates with a larger public.

A new age of appreciation for classically-influenced vocal music has dawned, led by classically-trained singers like Andrea Bocelli, Charlotte Church, Josh Groban, Russell Watson, Britain's notorious "Opera Babes" and the singing New York City firefighter, Daniel Rodriguez. Each of these artists, in recent years, has enjoyed a rapid ascent to popularity that has been out-of-the question for classical artists until now. (Imagine if Maria Callas had a web site.) Increasingly, crossover also happens in the other

Engaging classical consumers in many settings and at different levels of sophistication is implied as a broad strategy to address some of the findings of this study.

direction, with pop artists like Paul McCartney, Billy Joel, Joni Mitchell, Sting, Elton John, Celine Dion and Bobby McFerrin composing classical music, incorporating classical references into their music, and performing with classical artists and ensembles.

Advances in digital recording and broadcast technologies have accelerated the diversification and fragmentation of musical tastes globally. A worldwide television audience watched in hushed silence on Feb. 8, 2002, when Yo-Yo Ma and Sting performed a moving rendition of "Fragile" at the Opening Ceremonies of the Olympic Winter Games in Salt Lake City, assisted by the Mormon Tabernacle Choir and the Utah Symphony. The plaintive strains of Ma's cello echoed around the globe in counterpoint to Sting's verse. For five minutes, the boundaries between popular music and classical music all but dissolved.

Classical music is all around us — at musical theater performances, in the orchestra pit at ballet performances, in film scores, and in the sound tracks to television advertisements for everything from mortgages to laxatives. To the horror of some and the glee of others, some cellular telephones can be programmed to ring to the tune of Beethoven's *Für Elise*. Classical music — broadly defined — has been so thoroughly appropriated by mass culture that it has all but disappeared for its ubiquity.

Conductors and orchestra musicians, quite naturally, are most interested in performing challenging symphonic and chamber music repertoire in acoustically suitable venues. Meanwhile, consumers have embraced a radically different, much broader and rapidly evolving definition of classical music that bears little resemblance to the fine programs offered by most orchestras season after season.

Orchestral pops concerts were conceived as an answer to attracting younger audiences by embracing a wider range of musical styles. But some orchestras' pops audiences (e.g., Detroit, Saint Louis), ironically, are now older than their classical counterparts.

While orchestra attendance is relatively flat or declining in some cities, classical music is alive and well — in a new sense — and touching people in ways that no one could have imagined 20 years ago. In the end, whose definition of classical music matters?

Summary

The study is both reassuring and challenging to orchestras. On the one hand, the constituency for the art form — broadly defined — looks healthy. On the other hand, orchestras are hard pressed to adapt to a rapidly evolving cultural landscape and to respond competitively to marketing challenges and social pressure for more intense leisure experiences.

Engaging classical consumers in many settings and at different levels of sophistication is implied as a broad strategy to address some of the findings of this study. This does not necessarily involve compromising artistic standards, at least from the audience's perspective, but it does mean taking risks — both financial and artistic — on both sides of the stage. Consumers derive benefits and values from classical music on many levels; one man's anesthesia is another man's revelation.

The primary theme of the study is that orchestras are part of a larger "classical music system" in their communities that includes other professional and nonprofessional ensembles, radio programming, personal libraries of classical and classical crossover recordings, church music programs, music education programs and private instruction. On average, 74 percent of orchestra ticket buyers have played a musical instrument or performed vocal music at some point in their lives.

Does an orchestra's prospect base renew itself more or less naturally, or should orchestras and other classical music presenters concern themselves with a much larger picture? Can orchestras depend on other players in their "classical music system" to nurture and cultivate tomorrow's audience? Surely, this proposition is too capital intensive for one institution to tackle. But orchestras are not alone in their desire to regenerate a constituency for classical music. A comprehensive response to long-term audience development must involve a range of community partners including funders and other stakeholders in different corners of the classical community.

Stimulating creative expression and enrichment through classical music and other art forms is a quality-of-life issue for communities. The art form cannot survive without musicians, conductors, composers, donors, civic leadership, teachers, students, record labels, radio hosts and listeners — and, of course, audiences for live concerts.

> *"My sound system can't duplicate what goes on in the concert hall."* —
> *Sophisticated Low-Frequency Single-Ticket Buyer, July 2002*

RESEARCH GOALS
and Methodologies

Research Goals & Objectives

Statement of Purpose

The overall purpose of this study is to advance participating orchestras' knowledge of their audiences and markets and to develop a conceptual model that will assist the orchestras in understanding prospects and in capturing additional market potential.

General Goals

1. To provide orchestras with high-quality market research data on their audiences and market areas as general marketing support

2. To better understand the potential for increased attendance in each of the 15 markets

3. To apply some of the theoretical constructs of consumer behavior to the marketing of classical music concerts

4. To develop a general conceptual framework or "market model" for classical music consumers for use in developing more effective marketing strategies, with a focus on defining and profiling different types of prospects

5. To stimulate the participating orchestras to design and test new marketing strategies based on the research results

Eight specific research objectives and a number of research questions relating to each are detailed in the first section of the Appendix.

The Central Hypothesis

The central hypothesis for this study emerged from discussions with orchestra managers and on a synthesis of previous models of cultural participation drawn from the research literature on the subject. In spring 2000, a Study Advisory Committee gathered with the consultants and Knight Foundation staff in New York City to discuss potential directions for the research. Committee members, when asked how the study could be most useful, voiced a clear preference for a focus on prospects (i.e., who is not coming that might come) rather than current audiences (who is already coming). Based on this input, the research team set out to define a central hypothesis and conceptual approach that would substantially address "prospects" for the 15 local orchestras and, by implication, the orchestra field.

Are orchestras reaching the lion's share of classical music lovers in their markets? If not, how can we quantify and characterize the prospect base for each of the 15 orchestras? Until now, these questions have not been systematically addressed through scientific research. They are difficult questions to answer, but their implications are wide ranging for the 15 orchestras, the orchestra field and the larger arts industry in general.

Our central hypothesis, illustrated in Figure 2, posits that there are many adults with connections to classical music who do not regularly attend concerts by their local orchestra.

We understand this hypothesis in a two-dimensional conceptual space where consumers exist along related continua. The first continuum recognizes that consumers have a relationship with classical music that ranges from none (no relationship) to a very sophisticated and complex relationship, and that this relationship exists apart from their relationship with any specific institution such as an orchestra.

FIGURE 2: Central Hypothesis

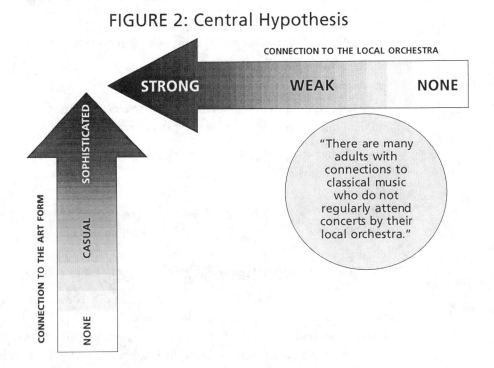

CONNECTION TO THE LOCAL ORCHESTRA

STRONG   WEAK   NONE

CONNECTION TO THE ART FORM

SOPHISTICATED

CASUAL

NONE

"There are many adults with connections to classical music who do not regularly attend concerts by their local orchestra."

The second continuum recognizes that consumers may or may not have a relationship with their specific local orchestra, and that this relationship also ranges from none (no relationship) to very strong. There are milestones along the way (e.g., ever attended a concert, ever subscribed), but the relationship is, more or less, a continuum of involvement that stretches from unaware to high-frequency subscriber.

In this two dimensional conceptual space, our "hypothesis area" is the upper right hand quadrant. The study was designed to deconstruct these two relationships,

build consumer models for each, and then merge them into a final prospect model that reflects both. In this manner, we set out to test the hypothesis.

A similar hypothesis might be investigated for theater, opera and dance companies, performing arts presenters, different types of museums and other types of cultural organizations with constituencies relating to one or more art forms or genres.

Our hypothesis builds on the work of numerous other researchers, foundations and arts agencies, without which this study would not have been possible. In particular, we have drawn heavily form the cumulative body of research commissioned by the National Endowment for the Arts, including the 1997 Survey of Public Participation in the Arts, from which we borrowed several protocol items.

The RAND Model of Arts Participation, the product of a seminal analysis of patterns of arts participation funded by the Wallace Funds,[4] was also quite helpful in setting the conceptual stage for this study. The centerpiece of the RAND study is a new behavioral model that defines distinct stages of an individual's decision to participate in an arts experience — and the complex factors affecting each stage.[5] The RAND model acknowledges that consumers bring a lifetime of experiences, attitudes and preconceptions to the decision process revolving around arts attendance. The study illustrates how arts organizations can do a better job of developing targeted strategies that recognize a range of predispositions and experiences.

While the RAND study posits a general, comprehensive model for how people come to participate in arts activities, our study focuses exclusively on classical music, recognizing that consumers have complex and often very different relationships and sophistication levels with the various art forms and genres of music.

The RAND model embraces the global viewpoint of cultural health and cultural possibilities for all. Marketing managers at orchestras, meanwhile, concern themselves with (and are rewarded for) selling the most tickets at the least cost per ticket in a sales environment where the product is essentially fixed (the artistic vision of a music director, usually) and hasn't fundamentally changed in decades. These two value systems — the "community cultural health" value system that advocates for increasing cultural participation and the "butts in seats" marketing value system — are often at odds with each other. Our study attempts to understand, if not reconcile, these two value systems in the context of orchestras and their potential consumers by examining in detail the structural tensions and constant trade-offs between sales and long-term audience development.

....

[4] *Knight Foundation contributed to the Wallace research by adding several of its orchestra grantees to the sample of arts organizations studied by RAND.*

....

[5] A New Framework for Building Participation in the Arts, *by Kevin F. McCarthy, Kimberly Jinnett, RAND Corporation, 2001*

The RAND model also goes a step further in suggesting that the experiences that people have attending arts programs continually shape their attitudes about the activity, which in turn shapes their behavior patterns (i.e., a circular model). In other words, customer satisfaction matters, and the experiences that people have at arts programs affect their interest in returning. Our protocols build on these important ideas by investigating customer satisfaction, values and benefits, perceptions of quality and loyalty.

Our work on this study was also informed by experiences and perspective gained over 10 years of observing, interviewing and surveying audiences and visitors for hundreds of cultural organizations across the United States, many of whom contributed indirectly to this study.

Summary of Methodologies & Data Resources

Further to the research goals and objectives, the following research methods were undertaken. A more detailed discussion of research methods may be found in the Appendix.

National Classical Music Consumer Segmentation Study (March 2001)

The initiative began with a multi-method study to create and refine the public survey protocols and to build a national model of classical music consumers.

- Four focus groups were conducted in November 2000 with orchestra ticket buyers and prospects in Charlotte and St. Paul. The overall purpose of the focus group research was to test protocol for the national telephone survey and to probe specific behaviors, attitudes and opinions related to classical music participation. The Summary Report from the design phase focus groups may be found in the Appendix.

- In February 2001 the national public telephone survey protocol was tested in Charlotte and St. Paul. A total of 700 interviews were conducted across the two markets. Results from the pre-test were analyzed, and the protocol was refined. Ipsos Reid completed the fieldwork.

- Following the pre-test, a total of 2,200 telephone interviews with U.S. adults (age 18 and older) were conducted in March 2001 using random-digit dialing.[6] The margin of error for the subset of 1,295 respondents who qualified as "potential classical consumers" is +/- 3 percentage points at the 95 percent level of confidence.

---

[6] *Respondents were screened on a series of eight questions relating to their recent history of attending seven types of arts programs, and on their preference levels for attending classical music concerts and other types of live performances. At the conclusion of the screener, respondents were divided into two pools: those who were considered to be potential classical music consumers, and those who were not. Qualified respondents (59 percent nationally) were administered a lengthy protocol with detailed questions about classical music, as well as a series of demographic questions. Respondents who did not qualify (41 percent) were administered the demographic questions only.*

- Based on data from the national study, a statistical model of potential classical consumers was constructed using cluster analysis. The model classifies respondents into 10 segments of potential classical consumers, based on their connections to the art form. SDR Consulting of Atlanta, GA assisted in the statistical analysis and model development.

Customer Data File Analyses for each Orchestra (2000 - 2001)

To assist in the definition of market areas for each orchestra, and to provide each orchestra with a detailed analysis of their current ticket buyers, Audience Insight prepared a Data File Analysis Report for each orchestra and an aggregate analysis for the 15 orchestras combined. Each orchestra was provided with a copy of the aggregate report along with a specific report on their own data file.

15 Market Area Public Telephone Surveys (August 2001 - March 2002)

Approximately 750 telephone interviews were completed in each of 15 markets between August 2001 and March 2002. In sum, a total of 11,318 interviews were completed. The protocols were nearly identical to the national survey protocol with the addition of series of questions about respondents' connections to the local orchestra. Also, each orchestra was allowed a small number of discretionary questions. The geography to be sampled in each market was determined through an analysis of the orchestra's actual customer records (see table, next page) and was defined as the contiguous area from which the orchestra draws approximately 85 percent its ticket buyers. The sampling methods were identical in each market. The margins of error for the local surveys were +/- 4 percentage points, at the 95 percent confidence level.

Based on data from the 15 local phone surveys, another statistical model of potential classical consumers was constructed using cluster analysis. This model classifies respondents into eight segments of potential classical consumers based on their connections to the specific local orchestra. SDR Consulting of Atlanta, GA assisted in the statistical analysis and model development.

Postal Surveys of Each Orchestra's Subscribers and Single-Ticket Buyers (August 2001 - Feb. 2002)

A total of 1,500 questionnaires were mailed to a random sample of each orchestra's subscribers (750) and single-ticket buyers (750). The mailings occurred on a rolling basis between August 2001 and February 2002. Prior to each waive of survey mailings, advance-notice postcards were mailed to all respondents, inviting their participation in the survey effort. Several weeks after the first mailing, a second survey package was mailed to everyone who had not yet responded. The overall response rate was 45 percent, and ranged from 35 percent to 60 percent for the individual orchestras. In sum, a total of 10,098 valid

responses were received, including 5,553 from current subscribers, 1,657 from former subscribers who are current single-ticket buyers and 2,888 from single-ticket buyers who are not former subscribers.

GEOGRAPHY DEFINITIONS: 15 PUBLIC TELEPHONE SURVEYS OF ORCHESTRA MARKETS		
Orchestra	**Market Area Definition**	**Approx. 2001 Adult Population (18+)**
Brooklyn Philharmonic Orchestra	Borough of Brooklyn (Kings County, NY)	1.8 million
Charlotte Symphony Orchestra	Area within a 25-mile radius of the Blumenthal Performing Arts Center	1.0 million
Colorado Symphony Association	Area within a 30-mile radius of downtown Denver	1.8 million
Detroit Symphony Orchestra Hall	Area within a 30-mile radius of Orchestra Hall	2.9 million
Fort Wayne Philharmonic Orchestra	Area within a 30-mile radius of downtown Fort Wayne	390,000
Kansas City Symphony	Area within a 30-mile radius of downtown Kansas City	1.2 million
Long Beach Symphony Association	An irregular area encompassed by 25 ZIP codes in and around Long Beach, CA (includes portions of southern LA County and northwestern Orange County)	657,000
Louisiana Philharmonic Orchestra	Area within a 35-mile radius of downtown New Orleans	938,000
New World Symphony	Miami-Dade County, Florida	1.7 million
Oregon Symphony Association	Area within a 30-mile radius of downtown Portland	1.3 million
Philadelphia Orchestra	Area within a 30-mile radius of the Kimmel Center	3.9 million
Saint Louis Symphony Orchestra	Area within a 30-mile radius of Powell Symphony Hall	1.7 million
Saint Paul Chamber Orchestra	Area within a 25-mile radius of Ordway Center (includes much of the Minneapolis area)	1.9 million
Symphony Society of San Antonio	Area within a 30-mile radius of downtown San Antonio	1.1 million
Wichita Symphony Society	Area within a 20-mile radius of downtown Wichita	355,000

Final Segmentation Model Development (April - July 2002)

Following the completion of all data collection, a third and final prospect model was developed for use in defining and characterizing the prospect universe for each orchestra in it's own market.

A final series of four focus group discussions was held in July 2002 in suburban Detroit to build out the profile of several of the key orchestra prospect segments. Focus group participants were pre-qualified through a postal survey and classified into the various prospect segments for subsequent recruitment by telephone. We wish to thank Julie Stapf and her colleagues at the Detroit Symphony Orchestra for their cooperation and assistance with these focus groups.

Data Resources and Archived Data Files

Figure 3 provides a thumbnail overview of the study's quantitative data resources and protocol design. Appendix Table N details the numbers of completed interviews and surveys for the various data collection efforts in each market.

FIGURE 3: QUANTITATIVE DATA COLLECTION SUMMARY	# of Respondents	Screener (eight core questions)	Connections to the Art Form	Connections to the Specific Orchestra	Consumer Behaviors	Values and Benefits	Demographics
Phone Survey of U.S. Adults (March 2001)	2,200	X					X
Sub-set of Potential Classical Consumers (59%)	1,295	X	X		X		X
Phone Surveys of Adults in 15 Orchestra Markets	11,318	X					X
Sub-set of Potential Classical Consumers (52%)	5,905	X	X	X	X		X
Subscriber Postal Surveys (15 markets)	5,553	X	X	X	X	X	X
STB Postal Surveys (15 markets)	4,545	X	X	X	X	X	X

In funding this study, the Knight Foundation sought to create an information resource for the entire orchestra field, in addition to the 15 participating orchestras. The data sets are large and hold a great deal of potential value to the orchestra field and the arts industry in general.

To encourage and facilitate further analysis, the three quantitative data files have been archived in electronic format (as SPSS data files) at the University of North Carolina's Odum Institute for Research in Social Science:

1. Public telephone survey of U.S. adults (N=2,200)

2. Rolled up data file from 15 market area public telephone surveys (N=11,318)

3. Rolled up data file from ticket buyer postal surveys (N=10,098)

The files may be accessed through the Odum's electronic catalog at: www.irss.unc.edu.

TOWARD A NEW MODEL OF
Classical Music Consumers

One of the goals of this study was to develop a new conceptual framework or "market model" for classical music consumers. Market segmentation has evolved into an essential planning strategy for marketers in almost every business sector. Segmentation is the process of sub-dividing markets into groups of potential customers with similar needs or characteristics who are likely to exhibit similar purchase behavior.[7]

While arts managers have an intuitive sense of who is in the audience — sometimes supported by audience research data — it is a far more complex proposition to gain a sense of who is not in the audience, or who might be in the audience, and what marketing approaches and products are most likely to stimulate them to purchase.

Historically, marketers in the nonprofit performing arts fields have relied heavily on direct marketing (i.e., direct mail and telemarketing) for generating sales. Customers are easily grouped into categories based on transaction history: subscribers, lapsed subscribers, mini-series buyers, single-ticket buyers (STB), inactive STB, and requests (i.e., people who have requested information but not purchased). Some of the largest arts groups, including orchestras, prospect for potential buyers on a methodical basis, often using mailing lists obtained from other arts groups and commercially-available response lists (e.g., L.L. Bean catalog buyers, Architectural Digest subscribers). Prospects, however, are seldom segmented into multiple typologies for targeting.

Market segmentation, as a planning tool, is a relatively new idea in the U.S. arts industry, although several general market models have been of some use to arts marketers in the past. Demographics, the family lifecycle model, psychographics (e.g., VALS — Values and Lifestyle Segmentation) and geo-demographics (e.g., MicroVision, Prizm) have been helpful to some extent as conceptual aids in developing marketing strategies. In the mid-1980s, VALS made a big splash in the arts industry, and numerous arts groups administered the VALS survey to their audiences in order to discover which of the 10 VALS typologies were present in the audience.

More recently, several orchestras and arts organizations in other fields have done innovative work with copy and images targeted toward psychographic "archetypes."[8] A groundbreaking study commissioned by the Heinz Endowments in 1998

---

[7] *Market Segmentation by Art Weinstein (1994, McGraw-Hill)*

[8] *Detroit Symphony Orchestra, Archetypes Study conducted by Dave Bostwick of DaimlerChrysler*

examined the personal values (i.e., emotional feelings, psychological factors, etc.) that individuals associate with arts attendance.[9]

A great deal of cultural policy research has been conducted over the years to measure arts participation levels and identify the characteristics associated with arts attendance. Several excellent monographs on classical music participation have been published by the National Endowment for the Arts, based on data from the Surveys of Public Participation in the Arts (SPPA). The SPPA studies provide detailed statistics on classical music participation in the U.S., but they were not conducted for marketing purposes, and the data are of limited use to marketers.

A comprehensive new behavioral model of cultural participation emerged in a recent study commissioned by the Wallace Funds and conducted by RAND, the nonprofit research institute and policy think tank. The study explores why people participate in arts and cultural activities generally (not specific to one discipline, such as classical music), and what institutions can do to encourage participation.[10] The RAND model of cultural participation set a useful conceptual stage for this study in that it recognizes the range of attitudes, perceptions and background factors that may incline or disincline a person to participate in the arts.

Classical Music: Prospects and Market Potential

Consumers have a unique relationship with classical music as an art form, distinct from other art forms. Some people have diverse cultural interests while others choose to focus exclusively on one art form.[11] Even among the most culturally active consumers, knowledge and experience levels vary significantly across the art forms. Thus, a new "market model" or segmentation scheme, in order to be useful to orchestra managers, must be specific to the product category of classical music.

According to 1997 SPPA data (a random sample of more than 12,000 adults conducted by telephone), approximately 15.6 percent of U.S. adults (age 18 and older) attended a live classical music concert in the past year. This figure varies

---

[9] *Zaltman, Gerald, et al,* Understanding Thoughts and Feelings About the Arts, *an application of the Zaltman metaphor elicitation technique for The Heinz Endowments, Mind of the Market Laboratory, Harvard Business School, August 1998.*

[10] A New Framework for Building Participation in the Arts, *by Kevin F. McCarthy, Kimberly Jinnett, RAND Corporation, 2001. Also see www.wallacefunds.org.*

[11] *Researchers have observed a trend towards diversification of tastes among culturally active adults. See* Changing Highbrow Taste: From Snob to Omnivore, *by Richard Peterson and Roger Kern,* American Sociological Review, *1996 Vol. 61 (October)*

substantially by market (e.g., 13 percent for Los Angeles, 24 percent for Boston).[12] Contrast these figures with actual attendance figures. For example, a total of about 370,000 tickets were sold to orchestra concerts during the 1998-99 season in Boston (classical and pops).[13] In 1999, the adult population of the Boston-Worcester-Lawrence MSA was approximately 4.5.million adults.[14] If the average frequency of attendance per year is three times (a low estimate, based on NEA data), then only about 3 percent of Boston area adults actually attended an orchestra concert that season.[15] This is a far cry from the 24 percent figure for live classical music participation in Boston.

What factors might account for the apparent gap between actual attendance at orchestra concerts and self-reported participation in live classical music concerts? This is a key area of investigation for our study.

Other figures are even more telling. According to results from a 1998 random sample survey of adults in the Charlotte 35-mile market area, 28 percent of adults had ever attended a concert by the Charlotte Symphony Orchestra. In a market of 1.1 million adults, this would suggest that approximately 300,000 adults have some experience with the Charlotte Symphony Orchestra. Only a fraction of these consumers, of course, are active buyers.[16] Even if one discounts the 28 percent figure substantially, the fact remains that a large number of adults in Charlotte have some relationship with the CSO institution but do not currently attend.

As lifestyles change and the subscription commitment slowly loses relevance, more consumers are making more frequent purchase decisions based on limited choices often constrained by top of mind awareness and previous experience. Moreover, research suggests that many consumers simply don't like to make decisions about

---

[12] Summary Report, Survey of Public Participation in the Arts, *by Jack Faucett Associates, Inc., Research Division Report #39, National Endowment for the Arts, 1998. For information about NEA publications, see the http://arts.endow.gov on the web.*

[13] *American Symphony Orchestra League survey of classical music activity in 1998-99*

[14] *Claritas and AMS/Audience Insight LLC*

[15] *Among those who claimed to have attended a live classical music concert in the past 12 months, the average frequency of attendance was 3.8 for Boston and 3.6 for Los Angeles (source: NEA 1997 SPPA data).*

[16] *The Charlotte Symphony offers a popular series of free outdoor programs in the summertime each year that attracts tens of thousands of area residents.*

[17] *In a general population survey of 400 adults in a northern California city, 37 percent of respondents said that they were more likely to "initiate an outing to a live performance," while 54 percent said that they were more likely to "accept someone else's invitation." (Source: AMS/Audience Insight LLC, March 2000)*

arts programs. Rather, they prefer to accept a friend's invitation or to join a small group without getting involved in the purchase decision.[17] If the average ticket order, industrywide, is approximately 2.5 tickets, then it stands to reason that over half of the individuals seated at any given live performance did not acquire their own ticket. Furthermore, some fraction of these "non-buyer attendees" played a passive or nominal role in the purchase decision process.[18] If so, then some portion of the audience, theoretically, may be defined as a unique class of prospects who have attended at least one concert, but who are unknown to the institution. Over the years, this suggests the accumulation of a highly qualified prospect base.

These and other observations lead us to two important hypotheses about prospects:

1. There are many adults who have various connections to the classical music art form (and other art forms, secondarily) but who do not regularly attend live orchestra concerts; and

2. In any given market there are many adults who have previous experience attending live classical concerts and who have some historical relationship with the local orchestra but who are not active buyers.

The primary goal of this segmentation analysis is to build a new conceptual framework for marketing to prospects. In the process, we will also develop segments of active buyers. Necessarily, there will be some set of characteristics that defines prospects. Consequently, a large portion of the adult market will be outside of the prospect base and not of primary concern to this study.

This study assumes that consumers come to the purchase decision process with a pre-existing set of attitudes and values surrounding arts attendance generally, and classical music concerts, specifically. We recognize that changing these accumulated attitudes and values is not a likely outcome of the marketing effort. As a result, this study focuses on consumer behavior variables (e.g., purchase decision factors) and other variables that are actionable from a marketing standpoint (i.e., packaging, pricing, marketing messages, etc.). Although a great deal can be done to re-contextualize the product and draw out its relevance to a wider potential audience, the core product is assumed to be essentially fixed.

At the policy level, segmentation analysis has value in portraying the constituency for a particular product or idea. From a marketing standpoint, the value of segmentation analysis depends on the orchestra field's ability to conceive and implement marketing strategies based on the research. While the primary purpose of this study was to develop a segmentation tool and deliver valuable market research data to the participating orchestras, it is hoped that the research results will lead to

---

[18] *When queried about their role in the purchase decision process, 43 percent of respondents to a recent audience survey indicated that "I am the primary decision-maker" while 56 percent indicated that "I participate in a joint decision process." (source: AMS/Audience Insight LLC, 1999 audience survey for a large arts organization in New Jersey)*

the design, testing, implementation and evaluation of new approaches to marketing classical music concerts.

Segmentation Strategy

A successful segmentation model is intuitive, elegant in its simplicity and useful in a range of marketing settings. As noted earlier, the study follows two lines of analysis in order to address the central hypothesis: 1) relationship with the art form (classical music), and 2) relationship with the institution (i.e., a specific orchestra).

Our segmentation strategy first required an understanding of the relationships that consumers have with the classical music art form, including attendance at live concerts. These and other factors were investigated: knowledge of the art form and desire to learn more; history of attendance at live concerts; preference levels for types of classical music (e.g., chamber music, choral works, recitals, orchestral works); use of classical music recordings and classical music radio; openness to attending live concerts independent of other factors; and whether classical music attendance is valued by a person's social reference group.

Using data from the national public telephone survey, cluster analysis was employed to create a 10-segment consumer model based on relationship with the art form.

The second major dimension of the segmentation model revolved around consumers' relationships with a specific orchestra. Have they ever attended or considered attending? Have they purchased, or repeatedly purchased? If they are a current or former buyer, what types of concerts did they purchase? When was the most recent attendance? Do they have friends or family who attend? Did they ever have an unsatisfactory experience? What are their attitudes about future attendance? Using data from the 15 local market public telephone surveys, cluster analysis was employed to create an eight-segment consumer model based on relationship with the local orchestra.

By contrasting consumers' relationships with the art form vs. their relationships with a specific orchestra, we gain a sense of the different types of prospects for local orchestras and gain support for the central hypothesis.

The two primary dimensions of analysis were merged into a final prospect model, and results were applied to each orchestra's market and audiences. Once the model was created, other variables were correlated with each segment to build a multi-dimensional profile, including demographics and lifestyle variables, purchase decision factors, attitudes about subscribing and many other variables.[19]

[19] *To assist with the segmentation analysis, Audience Insight retained the services of SDR Consulting of Atlanta, GA. SDR has conducted hundreds of segmentation studies in numerous industry sectors. The firm develops segmentation schemes based on attitudes, psychographics, needs, benefits and wants, and behaviors, as well as dynamic multi-stage segmentation incorporating multiple bases. For more information, see www.sdrnet.com*

DEFINING A POOL OF POTENTIAL
Classical Music Consumers

How does one begin to whittle down the prospect base for orchestras from the pool of all adults in a community? This was one of the primary challenges we faced in designing the study. A decade of research tells us that only small percentages of adults in a given community regularly attend orchestra concerts. But how many adults have <u>ever</u> attended a concert by their local orchestra? We must know about them. And what percentage of adults might have a meaningful relationship with the art form, independent of their concert attendance? We need to know about them, too.

From the outset, we realized that it would not be practical (or a good use of resources) to administer lengthy protocols about classical music to people who really aren't the least bit interested in it. On the other hand, it was our job to cast the net as widely as possible and find prospects for local orchestras in all corners of the cultural space.

In order to gain a broad sense of the arts activities of all adults interviewed, the telephone survey began with a series of 10 questions (the "initial screener"), as follows:

- Overall level of interest in arts activities (Appendix Table 1A)

- Role that arts activities play in the respondent's life (Appendix Table 1B)

- Preference ratings for seven types of arts activities (e.g., visiting art museums and galleries, attending classical music concerts) (Appendix Table 1C)

- Attendance at seven types of arts activities, past 12 months (i.e., arts participations rates); for these questions we replicated protocol from the NEA's Survey of Public Participation in the Arts (SPPA) (Appendix Table 1D)

- Number of live arts event attended, past 12 months (Appendix Table 1E)

- Number of classical music concerts attended, past 12 months (Appendix Table 1E)

- Description of last classical music concert attended (open ended)

- Whether or not respondent has ever volunteered for an arts or cultural organization (Appendix Table 1F)

- Whether or not respondent would like to attend live performances of music, dance or theater more often that (Appendix Table 1G); also an SPPA question

- Whether or not respondent would accept a free ticket to a classical concert by a symphony orchestra from a friend or family member who invited them to go (Appendix Table 1H)

The full text of the initial screener may be found in the protocol section of the Appendix.

Our solution to the "whittling down" challenge was imperfect but necessary. Based on their responses to a subset of these questions, respondents either qualified for a lengthier interview or did not. Those who qualified were administered the full arsenal of questions about classical music and their local orchestra. Those who did not qualify received an abbreviated interview.

We tested several potential screening solutions with the pre-test data and arrived at the following solution. "Potential Classical Consumers" were defined as...

- anyone who reported attending at least one of six types of live performing arts events in the past year (classical music, opera, ballet, jazz, stage plays, musical theater) at least once, or

- anyone who gave a neutral or positive preference rating to "attending classical music concerts" (five or higher on a scale of zero to 10);

Then, we <u>eliminated</u> anyone from the pool of potential classical consumers who responded negatively to the following question: "If a friend or family member had free tickets to a classical music concert by a symphony orchestra and invited you to join them, would you like to go?" This was our litmus test for a potential classical consumer. (Across the 15 markets, nearly a third of adults said "No.")

The classification algorithm was built in to the telephone interviewer's computer program such that respondents were immediately classified into one pool or the other, and the interview continued. Disqualified respondents were asked a series of demographic questions and were thanked for their cooperation. Qualified respondents were asked several sets of additional questions, including:

- questions about their consumer behaviors related to arts attendance

- questions about their connections to classical music

- questions about their connections to a specific local orchestra (local surveys only)

Screener Results

This screener qualified 59 percent of adults nationally and disqualified the remaining 41 percent. Across the 15 local market telephone surveys, the percentages of adults who qualified for an extended interview ranged from a low of 46 percent (Fort Wayne, IN) to a high of 63 percent (St. Paul, MN). The 15-market combined average was 52%. Appendix Table N presents complete results for all of the markets, including both weighted and unweighted data.[20]

....

[20] *To help correct for bias from non-response, mathematical weights were applied to the telephone survey final data sets, including the national survey and 15 local market surveys, to align the results with several key demographic figures for all adults in the applicable geography.*

This is a wide cut of all adults, but we wanted to include as many people as possible in the analyses that would spring forth from the lengthier data set. In fact, those who qualified are demographically similar to those who did not qualify, save for higher education levels and slightly lower incomes.

The large base of potential classical consumers serves as the population of interest to this study. Who are these people? A word of caution is in order here. "Potential classical consumers" should not be mistaken for orchestra ticket-buying prospects.[21] Rather, think of them as culturally active adults with some interest in classical music, however modest.

A comparative analysis of those who qualified vs. those who did not qualify for the extended interview suggests that only a very small number people in the "unqualified" group of respondents have positive indicators of arts attendance. By and large, we got who we wanted and saved the costs of interviewing approximately 40 percent of adults.

Just to reiterate, we did not ask all the questions of all respondents, so on most questions we cannot generalize about all adults without making assumptions about people who were not interviewed. In the few places in this report where estimates are made for all adults, we are explicit about these assumptions.

Demographics of Classical Music Consumer Groups

This study yielded a comprehensive demographic picture of five groups of classical music consumers:

1. **Potential Classical Consumers** — those who passed the initial screener described above (public telephone survey data)

2. **NOT Potential Classical Consumers** — those who did not pass the initial screener described above (public telephone survey data)

3. **Current Subscribers** to the 15 orchestras (ticket buyer postal survey data)

4. **Former Subscribers** to the 15 orchestras, who are current single-ticket buyers (ticket buyer postal survey data)

5. **Single-Ticket Buyers** of the 15 orchestras who have never subscribed (ticket buyer postal survey data)

....

[21] *Our understanding of the term "prospect" evolved over the course of the study into something quite specific to each local orchestra. We use the term "prospects" to refer to the subset of potential classical consumers in each market who have actually attended a concert by the Magic of Music orchestra at some point in their lives or whose interest in classical music is strong enough that the orchestra must consider them to be potential ticket buyers.*

Classical Music Consumer Segmentation Study
Final Report

Complete results may be found in Appendix Tables 5A through 5M, as follows:

Occupation Data

Additionally, participating orchestras asked for occupation data on their ticket buyers, in order to have a clearer sense of the range and frequency of different vocational affinities in the audience.

Almost 6,000 ticket buyers responded to an open-ended question about their occupation (i.e., "What is your occupation?"). Responses were coded by Audience Insight. Figures do not include retirees (40 percent of subscribers, 29 percent of former subscribers, and 21 percent of single-ticket buyers).

The overarching theme of the occupation data is human services (i.e., teaching, healing). In total, 41 percent of ticket buyers (who are not retired) work in human services.

- The most common occupation in the audience is teaching (20 percent, includes all types of professional instructors and academics)

- The next most common occupation is medical (10 percent), plus another 4 percent registered nurses.

Other human services occupations include:

- 4 percent homemakers

- 3 percent social workers, counselors and clergy

Among professional/technical occupations:

- 9 percent business/administration

- 8 percent engineering & computers

- 5 percent law

- 3 percent accounting

About 5 percent are artists (main occupation) of one sort or another (includes writers, architects).

Out of the 6,000 responses, there were only a handful of blue-collar occupations.

Unactualized Affinity — The Other Half of the Glass

Detailed results for all the telephone survey screener questions may be found in the Appendix tables noted above. Of particular interest here are the parallel sets of questions for each of the seven arts activities, one set of questions for preferences (rating for like-dislike doing the activities) and another for actual attendance in the past year. The purpose of these questions was to compare attitudes (i.e., affinity or predisposition for the activity) vs. actual behaviors, to see how they relate.

Affinity does not always translate into current participation.

Across all 15 markets, half of adults, on average, expressed a negative preference for attending classical music concerts (scores ranging from zero to four), and half expressed a neutral or positive rating for attending classical concerts (scores ranging from five to 10). At the low end, 22 percent absolutely dislike classical concerts (a score of zero). At the high end, 9 percent absolutely like going to classical concerts (a score of 10).

Although more people dislike going to classical concerts than like going, almost a quarter of adults expressed a moderate or "above-average" preference level for attending classical concerts (scores ranging from six to eight)

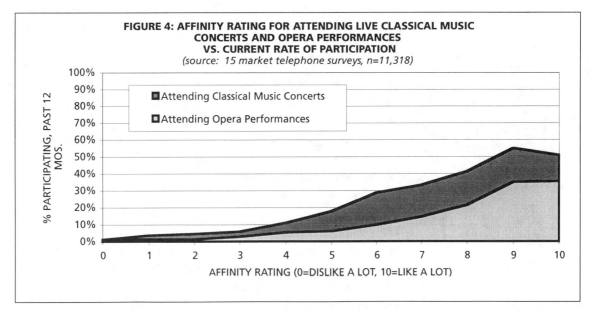

FIGURE 4: AFFINITY RATING FOR ATTENDING LIVE CLASSICAL MUSIC CONCERTS AND OPERA PERFORMANCES VS. CURRENT RATE OF PARTICIPATION
(source: 15 market telephone surveys, n=11,318)

As illustrated in Figure 4, affinity does not always translate into current participation. Of those respondents who indicated the strongest preference for

attending classical music concerts (a score of nine or 10), about half reported attending at least one classical concert in the past year, and about half did not. In other words, roughly half of those who enjoy classical concerts the most did not act on their affinity over the year preceding the survey. For comparative purposes, figures for opera are also illustrated. Over 60 percent of the people who gave a preference rating of nine or 10 for attending opera performances did not attend in the past year.

Look closely at the participation rates for people who expressed very strong affinities for attending classical music concerts, and notice that the people who rated their affinity a 10 reported slightly <u>lower</u> participation rates than those who rated their affinity a nine. Does this mean that participation might be inversely related to affinity at the very high end? It seems counterintuitive, but then again these might be the types of classical devotees who've heard all of Mahler's symphonies several times and don't need to hear them all again.

At the other end of the affinity scale, we see that there are current-year participators who are not terribly interested in the activity. About a quarter of current-year classical music concert attendees expressed a feeling of ambivalence or worse about the activity — <u>and</u> <u>they</u> <u>are</u> <u>still</u> <u>going</u>. Why? A later section of the report discusses the values and benefits that people seek from the classical concert experience, including some that have little to do with what's happening onstage.

Were respondents to the telephone surveys exaggerating their affinity for classical music, or is their affinity truly unrequited? If we are to take respondents at their word, we have a first glimpse of the substantial disconnect between preference and behavior, for whatever reasons. Depending on how you look at it, this gap between preference and behavior may be characterized as "unfulfilled desire," "unactualized interest," or even "latent demand."

For 20 years, researchers have been using arts participation rates as the primary indicators of the constituencies for these activities. Now, we are beginning to see the half of the glass that is not full — the percentages of adults who express a strong interest in doing the activities but who are not current participants. Anything we can do to better understand why their demand is latent will be helpful to marketers and to the arts industry as a whole.

We may not assume, of course, that all of the people with high interest in classical concerts but no recent attendance are ready to buy tickets to concerts offered by their local orchestra. Some of these people may not have access to classical concerts and may experience other barriers to attendance. The fact remains, however, that half of the people who most love classical music are not attending live concerts with any regularity, if at all.

Who are these people, and why are they staying at home?

HOW CONSUMERS RELATE TO
Classical Music

The study's first major area of investigation was the range of relationships that consumers have with classical music — the art form. A line of questioning was developed to explore a broad range of behaviors, attitudes and preferences related specifically to classical music in its many forms. The goal was to understand how consumers fit classical music into their lives in as much complexity as possible.

A series of approximately 20 questions was administered to respondents to the national telephone survey conducted in 2000. This set of questions was repeated in each of the 15 local market telephone surveys and again in the postal surveys of orchestra ticket buyers. In all, about 17,500 potential and current classical music consumers provided information about their connections to the art form. Recall that only respondents who passed the initial screener were administered these questions. So, remember that the data reported in this section reflect responses from potential classical music consumers, not all adults.[22]

Overall, consumers have highly personal, complex and multi-dimensional relationships with classical music. For some people — those most involved with the art form — classical music plays out like a sound track to their lives.

This section describes the many different connections that consumers have with classical music.

Types of Classical Music Concerts Attended

Orchestra concerts are just one of many different types of classical music concerts that consumers enjoy. Attendance at seven different types of classical music concerts was measured, both lifetime attendance (ever attended) and attendance in the past 12 months. The seven types of classical music concerts appear in Figure 5, along with summary figures from the national survey.

---

[22] *"Potential classical music consumers" are respondents who either reported some recent arts attendance, or who reported a neutral or positive preference for attending classical music concerts. All of them would accept a free ticket to a classical concert from a friend or family member.*

Figure 5. Attendance at Different Types of Classical Music Concerts	Percent Ever Attended*	Attended Past 12 Mos.*
Classical concert by a symphony orchestra	53.0%	22.3%
Special holiday performance of classical music	53.0%	22.3%
Classical concert by a choir or vocal ensemble	51.8%	23.2%
Pops concert by a symphony orchestra	47.9%	11.6%
Classical music recital by a singer or instrumentalist	45.8%	17.1%
Performance of classical music by a concert band or symphonic band	45.0%	16.3%
Classical concert geared for children or families	42.6%	18.4%
Chamber music concert	36.8%	12.5%

Source: National Survey of Classical Music Consumers, 2000
Notes: 1) Figures are reported for the subset of 59 percent of respondents classified as potential classical music consumers. 2) Figures do not reflect frequency of attendance at each type of concert.

....

Overall, results suggest that at least 31 percent of American adults have ever attended a classical concert by a symphony orchestra.

....

Appendix Table 3A presents complete figures for the percentage of respondents who have ever attended different types of classical music concerts, and Table 3B presents similar figures for the past 12 months. These categories are not all mutually exclusive (e.g., "special holiday performances of classical music" may involve several other categories) but are different enough to warrant investigation.

Among the large base of potential classical consumers, more than half have ever attended a classical concert by a symphony orchestra (at any point in their lives). Nationally, the figure is 53 percent, compared to 65 percent, on average, across the 15 markets with Magic of Music orchestras. The difference may relate to a higher level of availability of symphonic concerts in the 15 orchestra markets, compared to the country as a whole.

Overall, results suggest that at least 31 percent of American adults have <u>ever</u> attended a classical concert by a symphony orchestra (i.e., 53 percent of the 59 percent of adults who were classified as potential classical consumers). This is a conservative figure, as it assumes that none of the respondents who were not classified as potential classical consumers (41 percent nationally) have ever attended a classical concert.

As many potential classical consumers have ever attended a special holiday performance of classical music (e.g., The *Messiah, Nutcracker* — 53 percent) or a classical music recital by a singer or instrumentalist (52 percent) as have ever attended a classical concert by a choral or vocal ensemble (53 percent). In other words, lifetime rates of exposure to other types of classical concerts are just as high. About as many people are exposed to classical music through vocal concerts as through orchestra concerts.

With respect to recent attendance (i.e., attendance in the year preceding the survey), 58 percent of potential classical consumers reported attending at least one type of live classical concert, and 22 percent reported attending three or more different types of live classical concerts over the past year (see Figure 6).

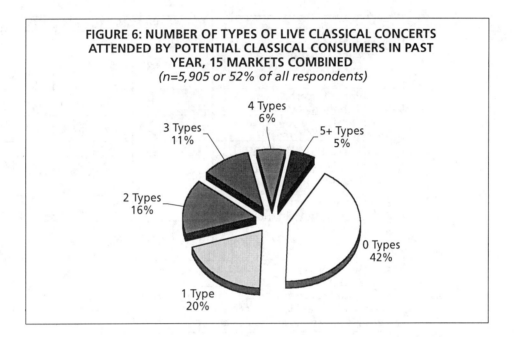

FIGURE 6: NUMBER OF TYPES OF LIVE CLASSICAL CONCERTS ATTENDED BY POTENTIAL CLASSICAL CONSUMERS IN PAST YEAR, 15 MARKETS COMBINED
(n=5,905 or 52% of all respondents)

4 Types
6%

5+ Types
5%

3 Types
11%

2 Types
16%

0 Types
42%

1 Type
20%

As noted above, 65 percent of potential classical consumers in the 15 markets, on average, reported having <u>ever</u> attended a live classical concert by a symphony orchestra. Of these people, 43 percent (or 27 percent of all potential classical consumers across the 15 markets) said that they had attended a classical concert by a symphony orchestra <u>within the past year</u>. Of these people, 17 percent <u>only attended</u> a classical concert by a symphony orchestra in the past year. In other words, 83 percent of those who reported current-year attendance at a classical concert by a symphony orchestra also attended at least one other type of live classical music concert, and almost 60 percent attended two or more other types.

Figure 7 reports rates of crossover attendance (past year) between seven different types of classical music. This information is helpful in understanding the overlap between audiences for different types of classical concerts. Key observations include:

- Pops concert attendees are most likely to also attend classical orchestra concerts (73 percent) and least likely to also attend chamber music concerts (51 percent).

- In contrast, classical orchestra concert attendees are least likely, on a percentage basis, to also attend pops concerts (43 percent), and most likely to also attend classical concerts by choirs or vocal ensembles (61 percent).

- Chamber music concertgoers are very likely to cross over to other types of classical music, except for pops concerts.

• Attendees of classical concerts geared for children and families are most likely to also attend special holiday concerts (71 percent) and classical concerts by choirs or vocal ensembles (also 71 percent), and least likely to attend pops concerts (40 percent).

FIGURE 7: CURRENT YEAR ATTENDANCE: CROSS-OVER BETWEEN SUB-GENRES		% Who Also Attended.... (in Past Year)						
		Pops	Classical	Chamber	Recital	Choral	Holiday	Family
Reference Group (Attended at least once in Past Year...)	Pops Concert by a Symphony Orchestra		73%	51%	61%	67%	64%	57%
	Classical Concert by a Symphony Orchestra	43%		50%	57%	61%	58%	53%
	Chamber Music Concert	41%	72%		74%	69%	62%	61%
	Classical Music Recital by a Singer or Instrumentalist	40%	66%	60%		73%	63%	62%
	Classical Concert by a Choir or Vocal Ensemble	38%	59%	47%	59%		65%	60%
	Special Holiday Performance of Classical Music	42%	62%	50%	55%	70%		69%
	Classical Concert Geared for Children or Families	40%	56%	49%	57%	71%	71%	

How to read this table: Find the reference group in the left-hand column, and read across to find what percentage of that group also attended the other types of concerts (past year). Source: 15 market surveys combined

Overall, results illustrate the diversity of live classical experiences that Americans fit into their lives. Classical concerts by symphony orchestras are an important source of live classical product, but they are not the only source. Just over half of potential classical consumers who reported any classical music attendance in the past year did not attend a classical concert by a symphony orchestra, but attended one or more other types of classical concerts that may or may not have involved an orchestra.

Venues Used for Live Classical Concerts

Consumers experience live classical music concerts in a range of formal and informal venues. Among the large base of potential classical consumers, 35 percent reported attending a classical music concert (of any type) in a concert hall, theater or opera house over the past year. Additionally, 31 percent reported using a school auditorium or gymnasium for a classical concert, 25 percent reported using a church or synagogue, 22 percent reported using an outdoor amphitheatre, and 5 percent reported using private residences for classical concerts. Appendix Table 3C presents rates of usage of five different types of venues over the past year. It is important to note that these figures do not account for frequency of use of each type of venue, just the incidence of use over the past year.

As might be expected, results suggest that formal concert venues are a common setting for experiencing live classical concerts, but not the only setting. A majority

A majority of active classical attendees (69 percent), in fact, used a mix of two or more types of venues over the past year.

of active classical attendees (69 percent), in fact, used two or more types of venues over the past year.

In addition to the many different types of classical concerts discussed above, here we gain a sense of the different settings used for live classical concerts. What does it mean to orchestras that 31 percent of active classical attendees did not visit a concert hall, theater or opera house over the past year?

Venue usage for classical concerts was also investigated in the postal survey of each orchestra's subscribers and single-ticket buyers. Among current subscribers, almost all used a formal concert venue over the past year, as would be expected. But 44 percent also used places of worship as venues for classical concerts, 37 percent used outdoor amphitheaters, and 18 percent used school auditoriums or gymnasiums. These are average figures for the 15 orchestras, and there are some interesting differences across the 15 markets — most notably in the use of outdoor amphitheaters. Half of Charlotte Symphony Orchestra ticket buyers used an outdoor venue in the past year (the CSO has a popular free summertime concert series), compared to about 15 percent of San Antonio Symphony ticket buyers.

....

Nearly 10 percent of orchestra ticket buyers are also experiencing live classical concerts in private homes.

....

From the consumer's perspective, houses of worship are key places where classical music "happens" — where people grow an interest in the art form. Four in 10 orchestra buyers also hear concerts in houses of worship (some orchestras, like the Saint Paul Chamber Orchestra, regularly perform in churches, so we would expect this to be reflected in their figures, and it is). If such a great deal of classical music activity happens in houses of worship, then it should not be a stretch to think of houses of worship as important, even critical venues for long-term audience development for orchestras.

It might surprise some to learn that nearly 10 percent of orchestra ticket buyers are also experiencing live classical concerts in private homes. One might guess that recitals by children and adults may account for some of this activity, but this may also point to what others have observed as an increase in chamber music activity in private homes.[23] In the future, private homes may be an increasingly important venue for audience development.

Consumption of Classical Music via Electronic Media

Any comprehensive analysis of how consumers relate to classical music must account for consumption of "non-live" classical music products, including classical radio, classical recordings, classical music programs on television or VCR, and the

---

[23] *"Home is where the musical heart is. And a growing number of people are keeping homes in mind as places to hear great recitals. The idea of holding concerts in private residences is flourishing across the country." Article by Benjamin Ivry, June 7, 2002, the Christian Science Monitor.*

small but growing consumption of classical music via the Internet. Consumption of classical music via digital cable television and satellite broadcast systems was not measured but is a growing trend.[24]

Our strategy for investigating "non-live" consumption first involved asking respondents if they "ever..."

>...listen to classical music on the radio

>...listen to classical music on records, tapes or CDs

>...listen to classical music through an Internet web site

>...watch classical music programs on television or VCR

Those who responded affirmatively to any of the above were then asked how often they do each of these things. Those who reported any consumption of classical radio or recordings were asked <u>where</u> they consume — in a car, at home, or at the office. All potential classical consumers were also asked if they have ever made a donation to a nonprofit radio station that plays classical music.

With respect to recordings, respondents were asked to estimate how many classical music records, tapes and CDs they own and how many they purchased in the past 12 months. Again, it is important to remember that all of these questions were asked of the large base of potential classical consumers (59 percent of adults nationally, and between 46 percent and 63 percent across the 15 markets with Magic of Music orchestras), and not of all adults. All of these questions were also asked of orchestra ticket buyers on the postal surveys.

Overall, results clearly indicate that the dominant mode of consumption of the art form is radio and, secondarily, recordings. Appendix Tables 3L presents results for the lifetime incidence of consumption of classical music via electronic media. Among the large base of potential classical consumers (national telephone survey data), fully 72 percent report having ever listened to classical radio, 66 percent say that they've ever listened to classical recordings, 64 percent say that they've ever watched a classical music program on television or VCR, while just 5 percent have ever listened to classical music via the Internet.

As might be expected, lifetime rates of consumption via the four types of electronic media are substantially higher for all types of ticket buyers. Of particular interest are the figures for lifetime consumption of classical music via the Internet. On

[24] *For an timely analysis of current and future demand for classical music via satellite transmission, see Lynne Margolis's July 5, 2002 article in the Christian Science Monitor entitled* Will Americans Pay To Turn On The Radio? *This article may be accessed from the www.csmonitor.com web site. Also, OPERA America published a three-part series on opera broadcasting in its OPERA America Newsline. The second part of the series, published in June 2002, discusses satellite broadcasting.*

average, about 10 percent of ticket buyers say that they have ever listened to classical music via an Internet web site. Compared to subscribers, single-ticket buyers reported slightly higher rates of consumption via this medium, which is probably a reflection of their younger age. There are some interesting variations across markets. In New Orleans, 19 percent of Louisiana Philharmonic Orchestra single-ticket buyers reported having ever listened to classical music via the Internet, a figure that is nearly matched by the New World Symphony in Miami Beach. At the other end of the spectrum, just five percent of Wichita Symphony Orchestra single-ticket buyers have ever listened online.

Frequency of Consumption via Electronic Media

With respect to frequency of consumption, national telephone survey data suggest that 28 percent of the large base of potential classical consumers listen to classical music on the radio either daily or several times per week, while 22 percent listen to classical recordings either daily or several times per week. Figure 9 summarizes results from the national survey.

Figure 9. Frequency of Consumption of Classical Music via Electronic Media Among Potential Classical Consumers	"Daily"	"Several Times per Week"	"Several Times per Month"
Listen to classical music on the radio	9.1%	19.4%	26.5%
Listen to classical music on records, tapes or CDs	5.0%	16.9%	24.3%
Listen to classical music through a web site	0.2%	1.1%	1.9%
Watch classical music programs on TV or VCR	1.0%	4.6%	19.2%
Source: National telephone survey of classical music consumers, 2000 *Notes: Figures are reported for the subset of 59 percent of respondents classified as potential classical music consumers.*			

Respondents who said that they listen "daily" or "several times a week" to "classical music on the radio" may be referring to any number of radio stations that play any classical music, religious music, ethnic or folk music or other formats that may be considered by the respondent to be "classical." In other words, we allowed respondents to self-define "classical music on the radio." Our figures refer to the whole of respondents' classical radio consumption, not just one station. For a variety of reasons, we would expect these figures to be higher than Arbitron ratings for specific radio stations that offer a classical format based on a traditional definition of "classical music."

An in-depth discussion of "what is classical music" is beyond the purview of this report. Other data from this study and other studies clearly suggest a "definition gap" between consumers and providers of classical product, both live and electronic. In July 2002, Joshua Kosman and Michael Dougan, staff writers for the *San*

Francisco Chronicle, authored a series of six articles about classical radio and recordings, in which they remarked, "One thing these stories make clear is that popular interest in all forms of classical music is as lively as it ever was. What have changed are the corporate and financial structures that deliver music to the public."[25]

In light of the decline of classical radio in many U.S. cities, perhaps this "definition gap" is one of the problems that classical radio shares with orchestras. Consumers have moved beyond the narrow definition of the art form that some orchestras and classical radio stations use to define themselves.

Ticket Buyer Data on Radio Consumption

On average, four in 10 subscribers to the 15 Magic of Music orchestras listen to classical radio "daily," and another two in 10 listen "several times per week." Across the 15 markets, average figures for "daily" classical radio listening are 41 percent for current subscribers, 38 percent for former subscribers, and 27 percent for single-ticket buyers. Two thirds of subscribers and former subscribers, and half of single-ticket buyers are basically classical radio junkies.

Frequency figures vary substantially across the 15 markets. In St. Paul, home of Minnesota Public Radio, 57 percent of Saint Paul Chamber Orchestra subscribers listen to classical radio "daily." In Detroit, where WQRS went off the air four years ago and classical radio choices are very limited, 29 percent of Detroit Symphony Orchestra subscribers listen to classical radio "daily." (Audience survey data from the DSO indicates that many of them are tuning in to CBC 89.9, a Canadian station based in Windsor, Ontario).[26]

The close relationship between classical radio and live concert attendees is reinforced by the observation that two-thirds of orchestra subscribers and half of single-ticket buyers have ever made donations to a classical radio station. The figures vary substantially across the 15 markets (see Appendix Table 30).

....

[25] Classical Music: Tuning Up for the 21st Centruy — The Lost Chord; There are more fans than ever, but classical music on radio and recordings is harder to find, *by Joshua Kosman and Michael Dougan, San Francisco Chronicle, July 15-16, 2002. See www.SFGate.com archives.*

....

[26] *Detroit and Miami, two of the markets that were examined in this study, top the list of the Top 20 cities without a classical radio station (source: Arbitron Market Survey, based on 2000 Census counts.). Philadelphia, also one of our 15 study sites, is the sixth largest U.S. market and does not have a commercial classical ratio station, although WWFM, a classical radio network operated by Mercer County Community College in Trenton, New Jersey can be heard in the Philadelphia area. Also, WHYY, Philadelphia's nonprofit public broadcasting corporation, broadcasts selected performances of the Philadelphia Orchestra and the Opera Company of Philadelphia as part of its Philadelphia Performs! Program and carries NPR's syndicated SymphonyCast programs on Sunday nights.*

On the other side of the coin, data from the audience surveys suggest that a third of orchestra subscribers and half of single-ticket buyers are <u>infrequent</u> classical radio listeners. So the relationship between radio consumption and live attendance is close but by no means a perfect correlation.

What orchestras can understand from this is that large percentages of their ticket buyers are listening to classical radio on a regular basis. They want classical music in their lives much more often than when they go to live concerts, so they are supplementing their diet of live concerts with radio listening (and recordings — see below). This reinforces the notion that classical radio complements — rather than supplants — live attendance.[27]

Consumption of Classical Recordings

In addition to listening to classical radio, consumers also experience the art form by listening to classical recordings (i.e., records, tapes and CDs). To investigate the extent of consumption of classical recordings, respondents were asked to estimate the number of classical recordings that they own and to indicate how frequently they listen to classical recordings. Appendix Table 3P presents results for the average number of recordings owned and bought in the past year by survey respondents.[28] Key observations include:

- Nationally, 72 percent of the large base of potential classical consumers indicated that they own at least one classical recording. (The average figure for the 15 markets is 75 percent.)

- Nationally, the average potential classical consumer owns 16 classical recordings. (The average figure for the 15 markets is 22, with a high of 32 for Philadelphia and Miami and a low of 14 for Wichita.)

- Nationally, of those who own at least one classical recording, the average number of recordings owned was 21. (The average figure for the 15 markets is 30.)

- Nationally, 39 percent of the large base of potential classical consumers said that they purchased at least one classical recording in the past year. (The average figure for the 15 markets is 35 percent.)

- Nationally, the average potential classical consumer purchased two classical recordings in the past year. (The average figure for the 15 markets is also two.)

The overall picture that emerges is that upwards of a third of Americans own at least one classical recording, and roughly 15 percent of Americans own more than 10 classical recordings.

---

[27] *For a substantial analysis of the audience for classical music that corroborates some of the key themes of this study, read* Whither the Audience for Classical Music? *by Douglas Dempster, Harmony: Forum of the Symphony Orchestra Institute, Number 11, October 2000 (www.soi.org).*

[28] *For the purposes of analysis, a very small number of observations were classified as outliers. Respondents who reported owning more than 1,500 recordings were not counted for this analysis. Similarly, respondents who reported purchasing more than 100 recordings in the past year were not counted.*

The overall picture that emerges is that nearly a third of Americans own at least one classical recording (i.e., a recording that they consider to be "classical'), and roughly 15 percent of Americans own more than 10 classical recordings. These figures represent their lifetime accumulation of classical recordings, including records, tapes and CDs.

Results from the ticket buyer surveys paint a very different picture. Over 95 percent of the 15 orchestras' ticket buyers own at least one classical recording. The average subscriber owns 105 classical recordings, the average former subscriber owns 98 classical recordings, and the average single-ticket buyer owns 63 classical recordings. These figures are skewed by the fact that a few individuals reported owning large libraries or recordings.[29] Median figures are much lower:

50 classical recordings owned for subscribers; 30 for former subscribers; and 20 for single-ticket buyers.

With respect to the purchase of new recordings in the past year, the average subscriber bought eight classical recordings (15 orchestras combined), the average former subscriber bought seven classical recordings, and the average single-ticket buyer bought six classical recordings. Across the 15 orchestras, Brooklyn Philharmonic ticket buyers (all types) reported the highest average number of recordings purchased in the past 12 months.

To summarize, a quarter to a third of current and former subscribers have extensive libraries of classical music recordings (100 or more) sitting on the shelf at home. Focus group data suggest that some people with large libraries of classical recordings only listen to a few of their favorite recordings, over and over, demonstrating a clear affinity for certain artists and recordings. Combine this observation with the fact that roughly half of all ticket buyer groups listen to classical recordings at least several times per week (Tables 3M1 and 3M2) and we see the important role that classical recordings play in helping concertgoers develop and evolve their relationship with the art form (and for specific artists and repertoire).

In addition to radio, listening to classical recordings is another way that consumers grow and sustain an interest in classical music. In this light, classical recordings might be considered as under-leveraged marketing assets; they have only one owner and most get played infrequently, if at all. Their value can only be realized when they are played. While the owner may have realized most of the value from a classical recording through repeated listenings, other people might find a great deal of additional value in the same recording, if they would buy it — or perhaps even just borrow it for a while.

The automobile is the most common setting for experiencing the art form, followed closely by the home.

....

[29] *Respondents who reported owning more than 1,500 recordings were not counted in this analysis. See the methodology section in the report appendix for more information about valid responses and outliers.*

Classical recordings represent an important frontier for audience development, if orchestras can figure out a way to unlock the hidden value of these recordings and get them off the shelves where they are gathering dust. As of late 2002, several orchestras are considering starting CD exchange programs for their subscribers.

Settings for Listening to Classical Radio & Recordings

Data from the national survey suggest that the automobile is the most common setting for experiencing the art form, followed closely by the home. Half of respondents in the large base of potential classical consumers listen to classical radio and recordings in their autos, while 46 percent listen at home. Appendix Table 3N presents results for the percentage of respondents who listen to classical radio or recordings at home, in a car or at work.

In each of the 15 markets, the incidence of listening at home exceeds the incidence of listening in a car, except in Charlotte, where the two rates are equal at 60 percent. For at-home listening, the figures range from 74 percent in Denver to 60 percent for Charlotte. For in-auto listening, the figures range from 63 percent in St. Paul, San Antonio and Kansas City to 39 percent in Brooklyn (where many more people may use other modes of transportation).[30]

As might be expected, the large majority of orchestra ticket buyers (roughly 80 percent to 90 percent) reported listening to classical radio or recordings at home. Figures for in-auto listening are just slightly lower. Roughly a quarter of orchestra ticket buyers say that they listen to classical radio or recordings at work.

Given the frequency figures discussed in the previous section, the role of these venues — the home and the auto — figures prominently in how consumers experience classical music. Focus group data reveal the range of listening experiences that people have in these different settings. In autos, some listen to classical music on their way to work to set a positive tone for the day. For some, the selection of music is an afterthought — background music, more or less — while others curate the listening experience carefully. At home, some rotate through their CD collections, while others withdraw into the peace of classical music at difficult or stressful times. One woman described how she turns to classical music after putting the children to bed, at the last moments in her day when she finally gets a chance to do "something for me." In all settings, people use classical music to calm themselves, like a balm.

However different, who is to say that the at-home or in-auto listening experience is any more or less valid, any more or less meaningful or worthwhile than the listening experience in a concert hall? Regardless, the data suggest that homes and autos —

---

[30] *We did not attempt to reconcile these figures with the actual supply of classical radio programming in each of the 15 orchestra markets, although such an analysis might be revealing.*

more so than concert halls — are the primary places where consumers grow and sustain a love for the art form, and therefore these are important venues for long-term audience development. How can orchestras get into people's cars and homes, where classical music is a vital part of the rich fabric of their lives?

Some Final Thoughts on Electronic Media

If classical music consumers' primary mode of consumption is radio and recordings, and if a large majority of orchestra buyers listen to classical radio and recordings between concerts, then an orchestra's involvement in classical radio and recordings is implied not just as a peripheral outreach activity, but as a mission-critical audience development challenge and opportunity.

Data from the Detroit focus groups (July 2002) point to the important role of classical radio as a channel of information about upcoming concerts. For some, classical radio is a substitute for consumption of live concerts. Although focus group data cannot be generalized, those who spoke of classical radio as a substitute for live concerts were more likely to have only a modest interest in the art form. They have other barriers to attendance. For the more sophisticated listeners, consumption via electronic media seems to enhance their interest in live concerts. *"I cannot duplicate the experience of a live concert in my living room,"* said one.

In markets where "classical radio" is turned off (e.g., Detroit, Miami-Dade), it is not difficult to understand that the prospect base for live classical concerts may wither — perhaps slowly, perhaps not so slowly. Absent the dominant mode of consumption in other markets, consumers in these markets may look to other modes of consumption to fill the void, or they may not. A great deal more information is needed to understand how these larger patterns of consumption change over time. Regardless, a cold look at the data begs the question of why orchestras don't own or operate classical radio stations.

If radio and recordings are the dominant ways that consumers develop and sustain a love for the art form, is there really any question about whether orchestras need to be active in the electronic market space?

Attitudes About Classical Music

In the preceding discussion we learned about attendance behaviors in some detail. The complexity and richness of consumers' connections to classical music, however, are also reflected in their knowledge level and self-perceptions as classical music listeners. In this section, we turn our attention to attitudes — how consumers <u>feel</u> about classical music, and their relationship with it — independent of their actual attendance patterns. Of course the two are related, but only by untangling the relationship between attitudes and behaviors (and social context, as will be discussed later) can we begin to understand how concert attendance fits in (or doesn't, as our hypothesis sets forth) to their larger relationship with the art form.

....

As self-reported, we see a wide diversity of knowledge levels in the base of potential classical consumers.

....

For this line of investigation, respondents were asked several questions about their knowledge level about classical music (self-perceived), their interest in learning more about classical music, their preference for classical music vis-à-vis other art forms, whether or not they have a favorite classical music composer or composition, and whether they consider themselves to be a critical listener, a casual listener, or an uninterested listener of classical music (self-defined).

Altogether, these variables paint a picture of a far-reaching continuum of sophistication about the art form, both in the audience and in the larger base of potential classical consumers.

Level of Knowledge

Among the large base of potential classical consumers, few consider themselves to be "very knowledgeable" about classical music, although many more consider themselves to be "somewhat knowledgeable." According to data from the national telephone survey, just 6 percent say that they are "very knowledgeable," while 44 percent consider themselves to be "somewhat knowledgeable." The remaining half say that they are "not very knowledgeable" about classical music. Average figures from the 15 local general population telephone surveys are quite similar, and there is little variation across markets. Appendix Table 3D presents results for this question.

As self-reported, we see a wide diversity of knowledge levels in the base of potential classical consumers, with only a few (6 percent) suggesting that they have a substantial command of the art form. As might be expected, the story is quite different for ticket buyers. Figure 10 presents average figures for the 15 orchestras. Nearly a quarter of subscribers say that they are "very knowledgeable" about classical music, but a majority (60 percent) consider themselves to be "somewhat knowledgeable." Single-ticket buyers, on average, think of themselves as being somewhat less knowledgeable, on average, that subscribers and former subscribers.

Across the 15 orchestras, we see a wide range of self-reported knowledge levels. Brooklyn Philharmonic subscribers are most knowledgeable — 36 percent consider themselves to be "very knowledgeable" — which may relate to the BPO's programmatic focus on contemporary music, or may reflect generally higher levels of knowledge among New York concertgoers, or other factors. Contrast this to Fort Wayne Philharmonic subscribers, 15 percent of whom consider themselves to be "very knowledgeable" and Long Beach Symphony Orchestra subscribers, for whom the figure is 17 percent.

FIGURE 10. LEVEL OF KNOWLEDGE ABOUT CLASSICAL MUSIC (SELF-REPORTED) AMONG ORCHESTRA TICKET BUYERS	Sub-scribers	Former Sub-scribers	Single-Ticket Buyers
"Very Knowledgeable"	23%	21%	17%
"Somewhat Knowledgeable"	60%	61%	56%
"Not Very Knowledgeable"	16%	19%	27%
Source: Postal surveys of 15 orchestras' subscribers and single-ticket buyers, 2001-2002			

In thinking about the self-reported knowledge levels of ticket buyers, bear in mind that 74 percent of them, on average, have ever played a musical instrument or performed vocal music (see Appendix Table B3).

Among single-ticket buyers (including former subscribers), we see higher levels of knowledge for several orchestras: the Brooklyn Philharmonic; the New World Symphony in Miami Beach (a professional training orchestra); and the Saint Paul Chamber Orchestra. These three orchestras share something important in common — they all operate in markets with other major orchestras. Given the availability of other orchestra product in these markets, it may not be surprising that single-ticket buyers for these orchestras are more knowledgeable than their counterparts in other cities with one major orchestra.

The level of knowledge in one audience base (Brooklyn) is twice that of another audience base (Fort Wayne). These audiences clearly have different abilities or "skill sets" when it comes to negotiating the concert experiences offered by the two orchestras. But the basic structure of the concert experiences offered by these two orchestras is remarkably similar.

Desire to Learn More About Classical Music

Most classical consumers, and almost all orchestra ticket buyers, are interested in learning more about the art form, at some level. Among the large base of potential classical consumers, 13 percent are "very interested" in learning more about classical music, and 53 percent are "somewhat interested." Average figures for the 15 local markets are similar, although there are some significant variations across markets. Appendix Table 3E presents results for this question.

Among subscribers and single-ticket buyers, there are strong indications of an appetite for more knowledge about the art form. On average, 38 percent of subscribers say that they are "very interested" in learning more, and the figures are almost as strong for former subscribers (34 percent) and single-ticket buyers (30 percent).

Do these statistics point to a deep vein of intellectual gregariousness in the audience? If so, why aren't pre-concert lectures filled to capacity? Why don't more

....

Among the large base of potential classical consumers, 13 percent are "very interested" in learning more about classical music.

....

people arrive at concerts earlier in order to thoroughly read the program notes? Of course, many people do avail themselves of these educational opportunities. But the data suggest that many more people would be interested in learning more about classical music if more attractive and interactive educational mediums can be found.

Further analysis reveals that people who are already "very knowledgeable" about classical music are most likely to be "very interested" in learning more. Across all ticket buyers, 67 percent of those who consider themselves to be "very knowledgeable" about classical music are "very interested" in learning more, compared to 31 percent of those who are "somewhat knowledgeable" and 12 percent of those who are "not very knowledgeable."

The data suggest that intellectually oriented education programs such as pre-concert lectures and detailed program notes are most likely to appeal to people who are <u>already</u> knowledgeable about classical music. For these people, orchestras provide a high level of service. A majority of ticket buyers, however, have only a moderate level of knowledge and a moderate interest in learning more. How can <u>their</u> appetite for more knowledge be satisfied?

Adding interpretive aspects to the concert experience itself would seem to be implied as an education strategy for the majority of moderately knowledgeable audience members. Some orchestras are experimenting successfully with interpretive components, including several of the Knight Foundation-funded Magic of Music orchestras. In discussing results with the 15 orchestras, a number of possibilities were raised, including the idea of offering a somewhat altered "interpretation-rich" concert experience on one night of the week, for those who would enjoy the less formal format. The risk of offending those who do not want added interpretation can be managed by explaining to people about the different formats in various marketing materials in order to help them select a preferred format.

Within the audience base for each of the 15 orchestras, roughly a third to a half of subscribers are self-described "critical listeners."

Type of Listener (Self-Perceptions)

Answer this question for yourself: Do you consider yourself to be a critical listener, a casual listener or an uninterested listener of classical music? Early on in the study, statistical analysis suggested that this was a pivotal question in defining consumers' overall relationship with the art form. Appendix Table 3H presents results for this question.

Within the audience base for each of the 15 orchestras, roughly a third to a half of subscribers are self-described "critical listeners." The figures range from 58 percent for the Brooklyn Philharmonic to 26 percent for the Fort Wayne Philharmonic. The rest are "casual listeners." On average, 28 percent of single-ticket buyers are "critical listeners," with similar variation across orchestras.

Among the large base of potential classical consumers in the national sample, 10 percent identified themselves as "critical listeners" and fully 78 percent identified themselves as "casual listeners" — a staggering figure by any measure. Upon reflection, there may be some acquiescent responding going on here — some people may have answered "casual listener" for fear of sounding culturally incompetent to the interviewer.[31] Regardless, even if the actual figure for "casual listeners" is substantially lower, the number of Americans who experience classical music on a casual basis is still quite large.

The classical music "definition gap" discussed earlier certainly helps to explain the large percentage of "casual listeners." Consider the many ways that consumers experience classical music outside of traditional settings:

- In the cinema, classical music is an integral part of countless film scores. Numerous recordings of film scores and compilations of selections from different film scores are released each year. Erich Kunzel and the Cincinnati Pops Orchestra have released several successful film music CD compilations on the Telarc label, including the May 2000 release Mega Movies, which includes selections from *The Mask of Zorro, The Prince of Egypt, Air Force One* and *The Mummy* (see www.telarc.com).

- On television, classical music is heard as the sound track to advertisements for everything from mortgages to laxatives. Some Olympic skaters perform to classical music, watched by very large television audiences (remember Jayne Torville and Christopher Dean's perfect performance to Ravel's Bolero?)

- Many people consider musical theater performances of such works as *Phantom of the Opera* and *Les Miserable* as classical music experiences.

- With online orders of its Turbo Tax software, Intuit distributes a free CD compilation called "Relaxing with the Classics" (under license agreement with BMG) — music to calm your nerves by, evidently, while doing your taxes.

- Britain's "Opera Babes," two attractive young women who were discovered busking in London's Covent Garden piazza, had a top selling album in 2002. Their rendition of "Un Bel Di" from Puccini's Madama Butterfly (accompanied by the Kodo drummers) is a theme song for British channel ITV's coverage of the World Cup soccer match.

- In 1999, a techno remix of The Flower Duet from Lakmé, an 1883 opera by Leo Delibes, was released — a worldwide hit in the underground dance scene.

- To the horror of some and the glee of others, some cellular telephones can be programmed to ring to the tune of Beethoven's *Für Elise* or another snippet of classical melody.

---

[31] *The protocol was specifically designed to avoid this phenomenon. Unfortunately, we cannot quantify this form of bias on this question or any other question in the survey.*

In September 2002, the Boston Lyric Opera presented two free outdoor performances of the opera *Carmen* on the Boston Common, fully staged. Leading up to the event, publicity reached a fervor. The company expected 8,000 people on each night. Instead, an estimated 50,000 people showed up on the first night and 60,000 turned up on the second night (the low end of estimates provided by the Boston Park Service). Surveys conducted on-site indicate that two-thirds of attendees were under age 35.

The point here is that classical music, in some way shape or form, is all around us. Popular culture has so thoroughly appropriated classical music that is has nearly disappeared for its ubiquity.

Is it really a wonder that a third or even a half of Americans might have a casual relationship with classical music? This does not mean, of course, that they are ready to buy an orchestra ticket. But it is an undeniable fact, corroborated here by several data points, that the relationships with the art form, however defined, are there — that the seeds of affinity for classical music are widely sewn.

Favorite Composers and Compositions

Nationally, 43 percent of the large base of potential classical consumers said they have a favorite classical music composer, and 24 percent indicated they have a favorite classical music composition. Twenty percent have both. Similar figures were observed across the 15 markets. Appendix Table 3I presents these results.

In an effort to verify these preferences, a follow-up question in the national survey asked those respondents who said that they have a favorite composer or composition to actually name one. This top-of-mind exercise produced some predictable results — and suggests that most consumers know what "classical music" is, in a conventional sense. Among those who could name a favorite composer, Beethoven topped the list (119 mention, 23 percent) followed closely by Mozart (115 mentions, 23 percent). They were followed by Bach (74 mentions, 15 percent), Tchaikovsky (45 mentions, 9 percent) and Chopin (23 mentions, 4 percent). A multitude of other composers made the list, with only a few mentions.

Among those who could name a favorite composition, results were somewhat less predictable and more diverse, with four Beethoven compositions in the lead: *Symphony No. 5* (25 mentions, 10 percent), *Symphony No. 9* (12 mentions, 5 percent), *Moonlight Sonata* (11 mentions, 5 percent) and *Für Elise* (9 mentions, 4 percent). Other pieces mentioned with any regularity were Handel's *The Messiah*, Bach's *Brandenburg Concertos*, Vivaldi's *The Four Seasons*, Tchaikovsky's *Nutcracker Suite* and *Pachelbel's Canon*.[32]

....

[32] *Of the 43 percent of potential classical consumers who indicated a favorite composer, 9 percent could not name one. Of the 24 percent of potential classical consumers who indicated a favorite composition, 22 percent could not name one. This question was not asked of orchestra ticket buyers.*

The overall indication is that potential classical consumers, broadly defined, are about twice as likely to identify with composers as they are to identify with specific compositions. If one were to presume that serious classical listeners should at least be able to name a favorite composer <u>and</u> composition, the data would suggest that approximately 12 percent of Americans fit this bill.

On an annual basis, most major orchestras serve somewhere in the neighborhood of 2 percent to 3 percent of adults in their markets.

Preferences for Classical Music Vis-à-vis Other Art Forms

Another line of questioning asked respondents to indicate whether their preference for classical music (self-defined) is greater than, less than or equal to their preference for six other art forms: jazz, stage plays, musical theater, opera, ballet and popular music. Appendix Table 3G presents these results. Among the large base of potential classical consumers:

- About as many prefer jazz over classical music as prefer classical music over jazz.

- Stage plays and musical theater are preferred over classical music by 62 percent and 60 percent, respectively.

- Classical music is much preferred over opera (78 percent) and ballet (69 percent).

- While 63 percent prefer popular music over classical music, 24 percent prefer classical music over popular music — another indication of a broad constituency for the art form. (The balance, 13 percent, prefer them equally.)

Ticket buyers, as one might assume, as more likely to prefer classical music over other art forms, but not always. Results vary substantially across markets. Generally, single-ticket buyers appear to have broader tastes, while subscribers tend to prefer classical music over other art forms more strongly. While just 11 percent of subscribers prefer popular music over classical music, the figure rises to 26 percent for single-ticket buyers. Roughly a third of single-ticket buyers prefer musical theater over classical music

Some Final Thoughts on Attitudes About Classical Music

What does it mean to an orchestra that roughly a third of the audience is more sophisticated about the art form, and that roughly two-thirds of the audience is less sophisticated about the art form? The data are clear as day — their audiences have said it themselves.

If anything, we've learned that knowledge is not a prerequisite for enjoyment. Latin pop artist Marc Anthony was quoted in a recent news story as saying, *"I believe my greatest advantage is that I don't know the music theoretically, I just feel it."* The same might be said by a majority of orchestra ticket buyers. Less sophisticated listeners have sublime experiences at concerts, and they love to talk about them in focus

....

Less sophisticated consumers of classical music, especially, thirst for a more interesting concert experience.

....

groups. Are their experiences any more or less valid, meaningful or worthwhile because they have little or no theoretical knowledge backing them up?

Both the quantitative data presented here and qualitative data from focus groups suggest that less sophisticated consumers of classical music, especially, thirst for a more interesting concert experience. They want help understanding the music and its context because they believe it will make them better listeners and increase their enjoyment level. If orchestra concerts are like any other entertainment product, increased enjoyment should translate into increased attendance.

Why are orchestras reluctant to sate this desire for more meaning? In discussions about this research, orchestra musicians expressed fear that "dumbing down" the concert experience will somehow compromise the artistic integrity of the institution and demean their own artistic accomplishments. But we are not talking about compromising quality here, quite the contrary — consumers are asking for more context and more meaning. No one is suggesting that the quality standard be abandoned.

Who, then, are orchestras playing for? Musicians and music directors — who, quite naturally, care deeply about maintaining professional standards, along with orchestra administrators? Or, do orchestras play for a public that exists in a rapidly evolving cultural space — consumers with a wide range of interests and sophistication levels? [33]

The data suggest an opportunity for orchestras to accommodate — even indulge — the varying abilities of their audiences to negotiate the concert experience. This begins to frame two fundamental and related questions arising from the study:

- What can orchestras do to recognize and accommodate the range of sophistication levels in their audience?

- What can orchestras do to help their less sophisticated listeners — a majority in the audience — gain a little more knowledge and, by implication, a more satisfying concert experience?

Listening to focus group after focus group talk about their desire for more context as part of the basic concert experience, it may not be an exaggeration to suggest that growth in audience has a great deal to do with answering these questions. Most orchestra managers agree — embracing the next two or three percent of adults in their market is probably not going to happen through more and better marketing. Rather, audience growth is more likely to happen through an evolution of the concert experience itself, much like opera has embraced a new audience through use of supertitles, and museums have embraced a new public through interpretive listening devices.

....

[33] *"Wouldn't orchestras sell more tickets if they cared more deeply about what the audience thought, knew more about it, and spoke more actively with the audience about why difficult music appears on the schedule?" – Greg Sandow,* The Beginning of a Beautiful Friendship – Orchestras, Meet Your Audience, *Symphony, July-August 2002, published by the American Symphony Orchestra League*

Segmentation Model: Art Form Relationship

The first of three consumer segmentation models developed in this study classifies potential classical consumers into one of 10 unique groups based on a composite picture of their relationship with the art form of classical music. Over 30 separate variables went into the cluster analysis, representing both behaviors and attitudes. For more information about the cluster analysis, see the methodology section in the report appendix.

This analysis was conducted on data from the national survey. Of the 2,200 respondents to the national survey, 1,286 (or 59 percent) were classified as potential classical consumers. (An earlier section in this report describes this qualification process.) These 1,286 cases form the data set that was used in the cluster analysis.

Figure 11 summarizes results of the cluster analysis. The 10 segments are ordered by their overall consumption levels and sophistication about classical music.

FIGURE 11. CONSUMER SEGMENTATION MODEL: RELATIONSHIP WITH THE ART FORM OF CLASSICAL MUSIC	Percent of Potential Classical Consumers[1]	Percent of U.S. Adults[2]
1. Educated Classical Audience	6.5%	3.8%
2. Classical Ghosts (Low-Yield Sophisticates)	8.9%	5.2%
3. Aspiring Classical Enthusiasts	5.8%	3.4%
4. Casual Listeners	9.2%	5.4%
5. Classical Lite	10.7%	6.2%
6. Out-of-Reach	13.2%	7.7%
7. "Blue Moon"	10.8%	6.3%
8. Family Occasion	7.6%	4.4%
9. Disinclined	11.5%	6.7%
10. Least Interested	15.8%	9.2%
NOT INTERVIEWED/FAILED SCREENER		41.2%

Source: National Survey of Classical Music Consumers, 2000
1) Potential Classical Consumers are the subset of 59 percent of respondents who qualified for an extended interview. 2) Assumes that none of the respondents who failed the initial screener have any relationship with the art form.

Later in the study, this segmentation model was used to classify respondents to the 15 local telephone surveys into these 10 segments (see Appendix Table S1-A). For example, Portland has nearly three times the percentage of "Educated Classical Audience" consumers as Detroit (14 percent vs. 5 percent, respectively). Similarly, Miami-Dade has nearly four times the percentage of "Aspiring Classical Enthusiasts" (11 percent vs. 3 percent, respectively), and Charlotte has twice the percentage of "Family Occasion" consumers compared to St. Paul (10 percent vs. 5 percent, respectively).

Also, the segmentation model was later applied to the ticket-buyer data in order to see where orchestra ticket buyers fit in to the art form segmentation model. Figure

12 summarizes results for ticket buyers. Bear in mind that these figures represent ticket buyers from the 15 orchestras whose names were in the orchestras' customer data files and who responded to the postal surveys. In other words, non-buyers (i.e., people who attended with ticket buyers) and walk-up ticket buyers whose names are not in the customer data files are not reflected in these figures. Detailed results for subscribers, former subscribers and single-ticket buyers may be found in Appendix Tables S1-B through S1-D.

FIGURE 12: PERCENT OF TICKET BUYERS IN EACH ART FORM SEGMENT	Current Subscribers (n=5,325)	Former Subscribers (n=1,594)	Single-Ticket Buyers (n=2,721)
1. Educated Classical Audience	59%	49%	36%
2. Classical Ghosts (Low-Yield Sophisticates)	19%	21%	21%
3. Aspiring Classical Enthusiasts	2%	3%	3%
4. Casual Listeners	12%	13%	16%
5. Classical Lite	3%	5%	8%
6. Out-of-Reach	1%	2%	3%
7. Blue Moon	1%	2%	4%
8. Family Occasion	2%	2%	5%
9. Disinclined	1%	2%	4%
10. Least Interested	1%	1%	2%
Source: postal surveys of 15 orchestras' ticket buyers			
Note: The Art Form Segmentation Model derived from a cluster analysis of national telephone survey data was applied to the ticket buyer data to produce these results.			

Segment Descriptions

Over the following pages, each of the 10 segments is described in terms of its arts participation profile, patterns of classical music consumption, demographics, and consumer behaviors related to arts attendance. To assist with interpretation, several terms used to describe the segments are provided here.

Help with Terminology

- "Core Performing Arts Disciplines" – stage plays, musical theatre such as Broadway shows, jazz concerts, classical music, opera and ballet

- "Arts Participation Rates" – rates of attendance at live performances over the past 12 months

- "Social Context" – degree to which the respondent has friends or family who attend classical music concerts

- "Initiators" – people who agree at above-average rates with the statement "I am the kind of person who likes to organize outings to cultural events for my friends.

- "Responders" – people who agree at above-average rates with the statement "I'm much more likely to attend cultural outings if someone else invites me.

- "Subscribers" – people who indicated an above-average level of inclination to subscribe to performing arts programs (of any kind)

- "Consumption Level" – an aggregate measure of all types of classical music consumption (all behavioral, not attitudinal), including live concerts, as well as consumption of classical radio and recordings

- "Sophistication Level" – an aggregate measure of sophistication about classical music (strictly attitudinal, not behavioral), including knowledge of the art form, desire to learn more, etc.

Segment 1: Educated Classical Audience
6.5 Percent of Potential Classical Consumers, 3.8 Percent of U.S. Adults

Summary: These are the most sophisticated classical music consumers with a well-established history of consuming all types of classical product. They prefer classical music to all other disciplines, except opera. They are most inclined of all segments to subscribe, and actively organize cultural activities for their friends.

Arts Participation Profile

- Very high arts participation generally, with an emphasis on classical music, opera and ballet

- Prefer classical music to all other core arts disciplines

Classical Consumption Profile

- High consumption levels of all types of live classical product

- Most knowledgeable about classical music of all segments

- Very high consumption of classical music radio and recordings

- Very high social context within family, also friends to a lesser extent

- Most likely of all segments to have a favorite composer and composition

- They're subscribers and organizers, but less likely to be Responders

- Have attended in different venues, but strongest for concert hall

- Most likely of all segments to subscribe

Demographics

- High percentage male (53 percent)

- Oldest median age of any segment — median age of 46

- 20 percent are retired

- 38 percent urban (second highest)

- 86 percent white

- 48 percent report household income over $75,000 (highest of any segment)

Consumer Behaviors

- Very acquisitive — most are always looking for information about cultural activities

- The specific works to be performed and likelihood of a high quality performance are the most important decision factors for this segment

- They would go more often with some price and convenience inducements (i.e., cost and last-minute tickets)

Segment 2: Classical Ghosts (Low Yield Sophisticates)
8.9 Percent of Potential Classical Consumers, 5.2 Percent of U.S. Adults

Summary: These are choosy, sophisticated classical music consumers, with lower frequency of attendance at live concerts than one would expect. They are similar to high-end consumers in terms of attitudes, but not behaviors. If they're not going to live concerts, they're at home or in their cars listening to classical music.

Arts Participation Profile

- Above-average participation rates for all core arts disciplines, with much higher than average participation in classical music (57 percent)

- Frequency of classical music attendance is average

- Below average preference for musical theatre

Classical Consumption Profile

- This segment has the second highest overall consumption levels of classical music — the like classical music over all other types of art forms (highest of any segment)

- They have above-average pops and classical attendance but are average for other forms of live classical concerts

- Relative to others, they consider themselves to be quite knowledgeable about classical music and have above-average interest in learning more

- They are the least interested of all segments in hearing more familiar music, which suggests that they might be interested in more challenging repertoire

- They have substantial libraries of classical music records and CDs at home and have moderately high consumption of new recordings

- They have strong social context, both friends and family but not as strong as the "Educated Classical Audience" segment

- Average inclination to subscribe; most likely to use traditional concert venues and private residences

Demographics

- High percentage male (53 percent); 87 percent white, 61 percent married

- Only 12 percent are retired, income is moderate to high; second highest education levels of any segment (47 percent with college degree and above)

- Somewhat older, most likely of any segment to be married without children

Consumer Behaviors

- Content is very important (i.e., "specific work to be performed"); many other inducements don't matter

- Not very acquisitive — many don't look for information about cultural activities; below average for Initiators and Responders

Segment 3: Aspiring Classical Enthusiasts
5.8 Percent of Potential Classical Consumers; 3.4 Percent of U.S. Adults

Summary: This segment of consumers is curious about classical music. They are an eclectic mix of urban singles (both young and old) and couples with children who actively consume classical music via radio and television. On a percentage basis, this segment has the largest representation of non-whites, including 24 percent Hispanics and 15 percent African-Americans. They use alternative venues for classical concerts and tend to consume other types of live classical product besides orchestra concerts. They're always looking for cultural activities to do, and aspire to a higher level of involvement with classical music.

Arts Participation Profile

- Higher than average rates of participation in most arts activities, twice the average rates for traditional disciplines

- Very high preference for opera and ballet ("experience seekers"), but only average actual participation

Classical Consumption Profile

- Slightly above-average consumption of live classical music concerts but more likely to consume non-orchestra product; very high consumption of family concerts

- They are moderately knowledgeable about classical music and very much want to learn more

- They have relatively low social context — they don't have the reference group yet for classical music

- They are favorably inclined to subscribe, and most likely of all segments to use non-traditional venues for classical music

- Very high radio and TV consumption; moderate ownership of recordings; high consumption of new recordings

Demographics

- Younger segment, but skewed at the high end (median age is 39, but mean is 43); 52 percent have children in the household (2nd highest of any segment); 60 percent are single, divorced or widowed (highest of all segs.)

- 50 percent urban (highest of any segment); only 53 percent are white; 24 percent Hispanic; 15 percent black

Consumer Behaviors

- They are most likely of all segments to be both Initiators and Responders

- Transportation is a key issue for this segment (highest of all groups on the inducement "if someone else did the driving"), as well as children at home

- They need to be convinced to go and identify numerous decision factors of high importance, including convenience of parking, safety concerns, etc.

Segment 4: Casual Listeners
9.2 Percent of Potential Classical Consumers, 5.4 Percent of U.S. Adults

Summary: These consumers are not very sophisticated about classical music but consume a lot of different types of live classical product as well as lots of other types of arts programs. First and foremost they love Broadway musicals, but their interests do transfer to the traditional arts disciplines.

Arts Participation Profile

- High participation rates for all core arts disciplines, including classical music

- Strongly prefer stage plays and musical theatre over classical music

- Highest participation rates of all segments for stage plays (80 percent) and musical theatre (67 percent)

Classical Consumption Profile

- This is a low-involvement, high consumption classical music prospect segment.

- They have average sophistication levels but above-average consumption of classical products; some are subscribers

- They are not very knowledgeable about classical music, nor do they want to learn more; they are self-described "casual" listeners.

- Moderate consumption of classical music radio and recordings

- They might be considered "Samplers" — high consumption of live classical product, especially special holiday concerts

- They have very high social context; friends are critical

- They attend classical music at a variety of venues, not just the concert hall (they use non-traditional venues)

Demographics

- Median age of 45 (somewhat older); 77 percent white

- Average marital status, employment status, and presence of children in the home; slightly above average on education and income

Consumer Behaviors

- They're likely to be looking for arts and cultural activities to do on a regular basis, and are organizers of cultural outings

- They are likely to select programs based on the artists and specific pieces to be performed; although they desire more familiar music

- Likely to respond to social inducements (ability to go out for dinner), and some convenience inducements (i.e., if tickets can be exchanged)

- They are most likely of all segments to prefer weeknight concert times (27 percent)

Segment 5: Classical Lite
10.7 Percent of Potential Classical Consumers, 6.2 Percent of U.S. Adults

Summary: Consumers in this segment enjoy stage plays and musicals but are not too interested in opera, ballet or classical music. They consider themselves to be relatively knowledgeable about classical music, but are not eager to learn more. They might be convinced to buy more live classical product "if the conductors talked to the audience more." They hold some promise as special-event attenders (e.g., special holiday concerts).

Arts Participation Profile

- Above-average participation for museums, stage plays, musical theatre and jazz

- Lower than average participation for opera, ballet and classical music

- Prefer most other disciplines to classical music, but prefer classical music to opera and ballet

Classical Consumption Profile

- They have average to below-average consumption of all types of live classical music concerts except special holiday performances

- Their social context for classical music is above average, but this does not translate into active classical attendance

- They consider themselves moderately knowledgeable about classical music and have moderately high identification of favorite composers but less so for favorite compositions

- They are not very interested in learning more about classical music

- They have an above average home library of classical music recordings but have below average consumption of new recordings

- Average consumption of classical radio

- Average inclination to subscribe

- Average use of traditional and non-traditional venues

Demographics

- Younger than average (median age of 41); 81 percent white

- Slightly higher than average income and education levels

- Somewhat below average for presence of children

Consumer Behaviors

- They are actively looking for cultural activities to do

- Price and convenience are not the barriers keeping these people away from more classical music

- They like buying tickets online

Segment 6: Out-of-Reach
13.2 Percent of Potential Classical Consumers, 7.7 Percent of U.S. Adults

Summary: Although they like classical music, many of these consumers live in rural areas and do not have access to live professional classical product. They consider themselves to be relatively sophisticated about classical music and attend classical concerts at schools and churches at average rates. They have above-average consumption of classical music recordings. They do not like other art forms.

Arts Participation Profile

- Very low levels of interest in all art forms, except classical music

- Strongly prefer classical music to all other art forms (highest of all segments)

- Arts participation rates are very low — lowest for all core arts disciplines; clearly there is an issue with product availability in their area

Classical Consumption Profile

- They have above-average consumption of classical radio and recordings

- Very low consumption of live classical product

- They have a relatively high sophistication score but a negative overall consumption score.

- They use school and church venues for classical music consumption but are less likely to use traditional venues.

Demographics

- 29 percent rural (highest of all segments), and least urban of all (only 25 percent)

- Older than average (median age of 45)

- 22 percent are retired (highest of any segment)

- 40 percent have children in the household

- Lower than average income and education levels

Consumer Behaviors

- Highest of all segments for preferring weekend afternoons for concert times

- Purchase decision factors are average, except for a somewhat higher value placed on safety concerns and if someone else invited them to go

- Driving is an issue, as many would be more likely to go if someone else did the driving

- Besides the transportation issue, the most salient inducements for this segment relate to more convenient concert times and shorter concerts

Segment 7: Blue Moon
10.8 Percent of Potential Classical Consumers, 6.3 Percent of U.S. Adults

Summary: These are marginal to non-productive classical music consumers who prefer popular entertainment. They go to stage plays at average rates, but consume live classical product at a low rate — "once in a blue moon." The large majority are married couples with children, but they do not participate as families in classical music activities.

Arts Participation Profile

- Average participation in stage plays and musicals but low participation rates for classical music, opera and ballet

- Prefer jazz, stage plays, musical theatre and popular music to classical music

Classical Consumption Profile

- Below average live attendance at all types of live classical concerts

- Average use of schools and outdoor venues for classical music concerts but below average use of traditional venues

- Below average social context for attending classical music

- They are below average in terms of knowledge of the art form and desire to learn more

- Below average consumption of classical radio and recordings

- Not interested in hearing conductors talk to the audience more often (lowest score of all segments)

- Purchase decision factors relate less to the product and more to cost, logistics and social circumstances

Demographics

- 75 percent are married, and 64 percent have children in the household

- Younger than average (median age of 41); 77 percent white

- More likely to be female (66 percent); average to below average incomes and education

Consumer Behaviors

- These people are Responders; 93 percent agreed that they would go to cultural outings more often if someone else invited them

- They are very unlikely to be Initiators

- More likely to have a shorter planning horizon (50 percent plan 10 days or less ahead of time)

- They are most likely to respond to price incentives and last minute deals.

- They strongly prefer weekend nights for concert times (highest of all segments)

Segment 8: Family Occasion
7.6 Percent of Potential Classical Consumers, 4.4 Percent of U.S. Adults

Summary: The youngest of all segments, these are unsophisticated classical music consumers with a very narrow but keen interest in special holiday concerts and family programs. It takes a special occasion to get them out. Otherwise, they are more likely to attend musicals, plays and jazz concerts.

Arts Participation Profile

- Above-average rates of participation in stage plays, musical theatre, jazz and museums but average participation in classical music

- Below average participation in opera but very high participation in ballet, which may relate to children in the household

Classical Consumption Profile

- They are very likely to attend special holiday concerts and are the highest segment for attendance at classical concerts geared for children or families

- They have above-average likelihood of attending choral concerts and recitals but below average likelihood of attending classical and pops concerts by orchestras

- They are more likely than average to use church and school venues and have below average likelihood of using traditional concert venues

- They're not knowledgeable about classical music and are not interested in learning more

- They have below average consumption levels of classical radio and recordings

- They would be more likely to attend live orchestra concerts more often if concerts weren't as long and if orchestras played more familiar pieces

Demographics

- Youngest segment of all (median age is 37); 68 percent white, 22 percent black (second highest of any segment)

- 80 percent are married, and 59 percent have children in the household (highest of any segment);

- Average education but above-average income levels; 66 percent work full-time (highest of all segments)

Consumer Behaviors

- They like to initiate cultural activities for their friends but are not very inclined to subscribe to anything

- In terms of concert times, they prefer weeknights and weekend afternoons

- Important decision factors include whether or not it's an activity for the whole family, whether or not they have a special occasion to celebrate, and whether or not their spouse or partner wants to attend

Segment 9: Disinclined
11.5 Percent of Potential Classical Consumers, 6.7 Percent of U.S. Adults

Summary: These consumers have low interest levels in classical music, and are relatively disconnected with the art form in all respects. They aspire to attend opera and ballet, however, and have average rates of participation in these traditional disciplines.

Arts Participation Profile

- Below average rates of participation in all core disciplines, except average participation in ballet

- Lowest of all segments for classical music participation

- They strongly prefer ballet to classical music

Classical Consumption Profile

- They have low social context for attending classical music concerts

- They have very low consumption levels of classical radio and recordings

- They are unlikely to attend any types of live classical concerts

- They're not at all knowledgeable about classical music, are not interested in learning more and are most likely of all segments to describe themselves as "uninterested listeners"

- They have average likelihood of using school venues but are well below average for all other types of venues for classical music

- The only inducements that might attract them to classical music concerts are if someone else did the driving and if concerts weren't as long

Demographics

- 72 percent female (highest of any segment)

- Average age (median age is 41)

- 47 percent are single, divorced or widowed

- Average education and income levels

- 60 percent white, 25 percent black (highest of any segment)

Consumer Behaviors

- They are Responders and like to plan their cultural activities well ahead of time

- They are least likely to have purchased ticket online

- Important decision factors include availability of transportation, whether or not they have a special occasion to celebrate, and if a friend invites them to go

Segment 10: Least Interested
15.8 Percent of Potential Classical Consumers, 9.2 Percent of U.S. Adults

Summary: These consumers don't like attending any of the core disciplines very much, especially classical music. At best, they could be described as very reluctant Responders. The product is not a relevant purchase decision factor for them, although they might respond to someone else's invitation. It's probably best not to think of them as potential classical consumers at all.

Arts Participation Profile

- Rates of participation in all core disciplines are far below average; the highest level of participation is with stage plays, which is still 15 percent below average

- Very low rates of participation in the traditional arts disciplines

Classical Consumption Profile

- They have the lowest consumption levels of all segments for classical radio and recordings

- They are very unlikely to attend any types of live classical concerts

- They have very low social context for attending classical music concerts

- They're not at all knowledgeable about classical music and are least interested of all segments in learning more

- They are lowest of all segments in use of all types of venues for classical music

- The only inducements that might attract them to classical music related to social opportunities and abbreviated concerts

Demographics

- 27 percent are live in rural areas

- 50 percent are single, divorced or widowed

- Younger than average (median age is 39)

- Somewhat less likely than average to have children in the household

- Below average incomes; over half have only a high school education

- 73 percent are white

Consumer Behaviors

- They are unlikely to be looking for information about cultural activities

- The product is not an important decision factor; whether or not someone else invites them to go is the most important decision factor

- They are extremely disinclined to subscribe

HOW CONSUMERS RELATE TO
Their Local Orchestras

The study's second major area of investigation was to explore the range of relationships that consumers have with their specific local orchestras. In each of 15 markets, potential classical music consumers were polled about their connections to a specific local orchestra. A total of 750 adults were sampled in each market using a random-digit-dialing telephone survey methodology. Each of the 15 protocols was virtually identical to the protocol used for the national survey, with the addition of a group of questions about the specific local orchestra. The sampling methodologies were replicated in each market, so results would be comparable.

Questions about respondents' connections to their local orchestras covered awareness and history of attending (frequency and recency of attendance), types of programs attended, ticket purchase history, social context for attending, loyalty, perceptions of quality, incidence of unsatisfactory experiences, attitudes about contemporary music, and overall level of interest in future attendance.

As the study was designed, these questions were asked only of the large base of respondents who passed the initial screener and qualified for an extended interview. We refer to this subset of respondents throughout this report as "potential classical consumers" (i.e., 59 percent of respondents in the national survey, and between 46 percent in Fort Wayne and 63 percent in St. Paul) of respondents to the 15 local surveys.

The Market "Footprints" of 15 Orchestras

Of course, consumers can only comment on their local orchestra if they know there is one. On average, 12 percent of the large base of potential classical consumers reported that they were previously unaware of the specific orchestra being investigated, although the figures vary widely across the 15 markets. For example, 41 percent of potential classical consumers in Brooklyn were unaware of the Brooklyn Philharmonic Orchestra, 33 percent of potential classical consumers in Miami-Dade County were unaware of the New World Symphony, and 23 percent of potential classical consumers in the Long Beach area were unaware of the Long Beach Symphony Orchestra. Each of these three orchestras operates in markets with other, larger orchestras. Awareness levels of orchestras in the other markets are much higher.

For respondents who had ever heard of the specific local orchestra being investigated, a series of questions probed their history of attendance. Appendix Table 4C presents results for all 15 orchestras. Responses are used to classify respondents into one of five mutually exclusive groups based on their history with the orchestra. Average results for the 15 orchestras appear in Figure 13.

The percentage of potential classical consumers who've <u>ever</u> attended a concert by a specific orchestra (i.e., ever attended or ever subscribed) may be taken as an indication of that orchestra's "footprint" in its marketplace — the cumulative percentage of potential classical consumers who've had some trial experience with the orchestra.

FIGURE 13. HISTORY OF ATTENDANCE AT A SPECIFIC LOCAL ORCHESTRA (Source: 15 Local Market Telephone Surveys)	Potential Classical Consumers[1]
Ever subscribed	6%
Ever attended, but not subscribed	37%
Aware, considered attending but never have	25%
Aware, never considered attending	18%
Unaware	13%

Source: 15 local telephone surveys, 2001 – 2002
[1] Figures are reported for the subset of respondents classified as potential classical consumers in each market. Figures vary substantially across markets.

Many factors help to account for these figures, including the number of concerts offered, the number of years that the orchestra has been in business, the recent population churn in the community, and the overall size and quality of the market itself. As might be expected, the "footprint" figures vary from a low of 14 percent for the Brooklyn Philharmonic to a high of 64 percent for the Saint Louis Symphony Orchestra. Survey results suggest that, on average, the 15 orchestras have a cumulative market "footprint" of 43 percent of the large base of potential classical consumers.

Year after year, tens of thousands of consumers — hundreds of thousands in some markets — hear live concerts played by their local orchestras. If one were to add up the total number of adults in a given area who've ever been to a concert by their local orchestra, the numbers would be very large. Is it surprising to learn that an institution like the Philadelphia Orchestra has imprinted on nearly a million consumers in its market? Not really, if you consider the cumulative flow of audiences in and out of its venues, year after year.

By no means, however, should these figures be taken as an orchestra's "report card" on community service. What the "footprint" figures do suggest is that different orchestras face very different market situations. Some orchestras, such as the Saint Louis Symphony and the Fort Wayne Philharmonic (both the dominant orchestras in their markets) have already "touched" a majority of potential classical consumers in their areas. While this does not mean that these orchestras have exhausted their respective prospect bases, it does suggest that a primary marketing thrust for these orchestras should be to re-engage the alumni base — the cumulative body of former audience members who already know them. Other orchestras — those with smaller

On average, the 15 orchestras have a cumulative market "footprint" of 43 percent of the large base of potential classical consumers.

"footprints" like the Brooklyn Philharmonic and the New World Symphony —
clearly face a different challenge. For them, building awareness and stimulating trial
experiences are indicated as important marketing strategies.

Recency of Attendance

Respondents who said that they've ever been to a concert by the local orchestra (43
percent of potential classical consumers, on average) were asked how recently they
had attended, to the best of their recollection. Six potential answers were provided:
within the past year; about one to two years ago; about two to three years ago;
about four to five years ago; about six to 10 years ago; and 10 or more years ago.
These are semantic units of time subject to respondents' perceptions of elapsed
time.[34] Appendix Table 4G presents results for all 15 markets.

Thirty-eight percent of respondents with any history of attendance at concerts by a
specific local orchestra reported that their most recent attendance was "within the
past year," while 62 percent estimated that their most recent attendance was some
time prior to a year ago. A quarter of respondents with any history of attendance
estimated that they haven't been to a concert in four or more years.[35]

Further analysis was conducted to see if there are differences in attitudes about future
attendance across respondents in different recency cohorts. Indeed, attitudes about
future attendance change as recency of attendance grows more distant (see Figure
14). While 44 percent of respondents who've attended a concert by their local
orchestra within the past year are "very interested" in attending again, the figure
declines precipitously to 28 percent for those who are one to two years away from
their most recent attendance, and falls to 16 percent for those who are two to three
years away from their most recent attendance. In other words, people's enthusiasm
about attending wanes as the experience of their last concert grows more distant.

This reinforces the critical importance of retention efforts, not just for new
subscribers but for all attendees. With each passing season, the data suggest, the job
of re-engaging orchestra alumni gets harder and harder.

It also suggests that orchestras that cannot accommodate demand from their alumni
base (because concerts are sold out or substantially sold on subscription) have a
strategic issue in the diminishing probability of ever getting them back — when
(or if) they need them later.

....

[34] *Research conducted by the National Endowment for the Arts in 1980s suggests a "telescoping
effect" in time estimate data related to arts participation. In other words, respondents compress time
and report behaviors somewhat more recently than they may have actually occurred. Thus, responses
to this question are subject to an additional source of bias.*

....

[35] *These figures reflect any attendance at concerts by the local orchestra, free or ticketed, and would
include those who had actually bought tickets and those who had not.*

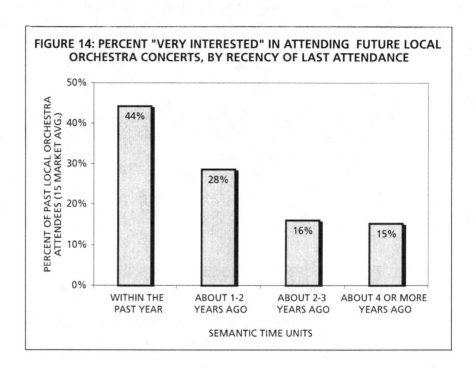

FIGURE 14: PERCENT "VERY INTERESTED" IN ATTENDING FUTURE LOCAL ORCHESTRA CONCERTS, BY RECENCY OF LAST ATTENDANCE

Frequency of Attendance

The study produced a large amount of data on respondents' frequency of attendance at all live performing arts events, frequency of attendance at classical music concerts, and frequency of attendance at concerts by a specific local orchestra. Frequency of attendance data may be found in the following Appendix Tables:

- Appendix Table 1E presents average figures for overall frequency of attendance at all live performances over the past year. Since this question appeared in the initial screener, results are available for all respondents and can be generalized to the adult population in the 15 communities. Table 1E also includes average frequency figures for classical concert attendance over the past year. For general population telephone surveys, these figures relate to the subset of respondents who reported any classical music attendance in the past year. Similar figures from the ticket buyer surveys are included in this table, for context.

- Appendix Table 4H presents average figures for frequency of attendance at local orchestra concerts.

- Appendix Table F is a combined analysis of frequency figures from the ticket buyer surveys, including figures for classical music attendance as a percentage of all live performance attendance and figures for specific orchestra attendance as a percentage of all classical music attendance.

Frequency of attendance data are revealing on several levels of analysis, notwithstanding some special limitations.[36] Nationally, the average adult attended four live performing arts events over the 12-month period preceding the survey. There is little variation in this figure across the 15 markets surveyed.

Earlier, it was observed that 17 percent of respondents to the national survey reported attending at least one classical music concert in the past 12 months.[37] Of the 17 percent who reported any classical music attendance over the past year, the average frequency of classical music attendance was three times. Appendix Tables 1D and 1E present these results for each of the 15 markets.

Among ticket buyers, there are some interesting variations in frequency of attendance. The average Brooklyn Philharmonic subscriber attended 31 arts performances over the preceding year, while the average Charlotte Symphony subscriber attended 15 arts performances. Given the large number of performance offerings in the New York City area, this is hardly surprising. What it does suggest, however, is that these two orchestras play very different roles in the lives of their subscribers.

On average, orchestra subscribers in the 15 cities report that classical music accounts for 58 percent of their total "diet" of performing arts activities. For former subscribers, the figure is 48 percent, and for single-ticket buyers the figure is 41 percent. It may be inferred that single-ticket buyers are more interested than subscribers in doing other types of cultural activities, especially in light of the earlier discussion about preferences for classical music vs. other art forms. A diversity of interest in other types of arts programs, the data suggest, is one of the underlying reasons why single-ticket buyers don't subscribe.

....

On average, orchestra subscribers in the 15 cities report that classical music accounts for 58 percent of their total "diet" of performing arts activities.

....

[36] *Asking survey respondents to recall their frequency of attendance at categories or specific types of arts programs is problematic in several respects. First, estimates of frequency are necessarily tied to a specific time period – usually a year. Some respondents have difficulty remembering what they did last week, much less a year ago. Furthermore, data from this study and other studies suggest that as frequency increases, respondents are more likely to make estimates. A close examination of frequency data suggests that people seem more able to actually remember something that they did just once or twice or three times in the past year, but as the number of times increases, they are less likely to be able to count the times in their heads quickly during a telephone interview, or while filling out a written questionnaire. So, they make estimates. Estimates tend to be based on calendar units (12 times = once a month; 52 times = once a week), or units of 5 and 10. For example, while some people will estimate that they did a certain activity 20 times in the past year, few will say that they did it 21 times or 19 times. This is an inherent limitation of recall-based frequency data. From a methodological standpoint, a preferable approach would be to ask consumers to log their activities in a diary for a period of time, and then submit their diaries for analysis by researchers, much like Arbitron measures radio listening.*

[37] *This compares to a figure of 16 percent of adults from the National Endowment for the Arts' 1997 Survey of Public Participation in the Arts (SPPA). The questions were worded identically.*

Within the realm of classical music, individual orchestras account for the lion's share of their ticket buyers' concert-going activity, but not all of it. On average, subscribers to the 15 orchestras say that concerts by that orchestra accounted for 77 percent of all classical concerts they attended in the past year. Former subscribers and single-ticket buyers reported lower figures of 57 percent and 58 percent, respectively.

In cities like Charlotte and Fort Wayne, the CSO and FWP supply upwards of 80 percent of all of the live classical concerts that their ticket buyers attend in a given year. Other orchestras figure differently in their ticket buyers' overall diet of classical concerts. The Saint Paul Chamber Orchestra, for example, accounts for 53 percent of its subscribers' concert-going activity and 41 percent of its single-ticket buyers' concert-going activity. The Minnesota Orchestra and other classical ensembles in the Twin Cities area offer a range of classical programs, and the SPCO's single-ticket buyers appear to be availing themselves of this choice of offerings. Similarly, the New World Symphony accounts for 63 percent of its subscribers' concert-going activity but just 37 percent of its single-ticket buyers' activity. At the low end of the range, the Brooklyn Philharmonic accounts for 31 percent of its subscribers concert-going activity and just 16 percent of its single-ticket buyers' concert-going activity. Both Miami and New York are markets with numerous other classical offerings.

While orchestras generally use similar marketing strategies and tactics — relying heavily on subscription marketing as the primary means of selling tickets — classical ticket buyers in these cities experience orchestras quite differently. Single-ticket buyers to the Brooklyn Philharmonic could not look more different than single-ticket buyers to the Fort Wayne Philharmonic, in terms of sophistication, experience level and frequency of attendance at classical music concerts and other arts programs. Should these two orchestras use different marketing tactics to attract audiences?

Frequency of attendance data suggest that orchestras in different cities face entirely different marketing situations and competitive landscapes and might respond with different strategies for attracting audiences.

Drive Time to the Venue

Respondents to the ticket buyer survey in 10 of the 15 markets were asked to estimate their average drive time to the specific venue where the orchestra in question usually performs.[38] Detailed results are presented in Appendix Table 4B, and a summary is illustrated in Figure 15.

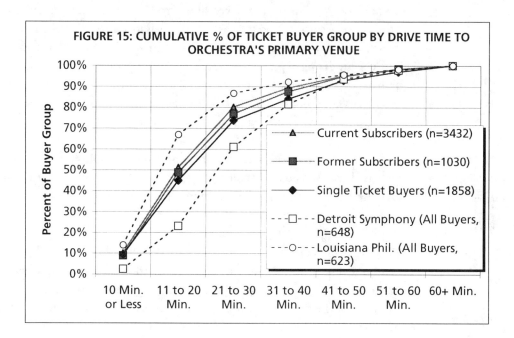

FIGURE 15: CUMULATIVE % OF TICKET BUYER GROUP BY DRIVE TIME TO ORCHESTRA'S PRIMARY VENUE

The 10 orchestras, on average, draw approximately 75 percent to 80 percent of their buyers from within a 30-minute drive time, and about 95 percent of all buyers drive 50 minutes or less.[39]

Among the 10 orchestras, average drive time varies substantially. At the near end of the spectrum, the Louisiana Philharmonic's ticket buyers live closest to the orchestra's primary venue, the Orpheum Theater — almost 70 percent live within a 20-minute travel time. Contrast this to the Detroit Symphony, which draws only 25 percent of its ticket buyers from within 20 minutes of Orchestra Hall. The other orchestras fall somewhere in between.

> *The 10 orchestras, on average, draw approximately 75 percent to 80 percent of all buyers from within a 30-minute drive time.*

---

[38] *The ticket buyer surveys were mailed in three cycles of five orchestras each. The drive time question was asked on the ticket buyer surveys for the ten orchestras in survey cycles 1 and 2, but not cycle 3 (see methodology section in the appendix for survey cycle assignments).*

---

[39] *Note that these figures do not account for frequency of attendance, just the percentage of each buyer group.*

Results of the customer data file analyses conducted for each of the 15 orchestras corroborate these findings and point to a relationship between frequency of attendance and the customer's proximity to the venue.

The key observation here is the sharply declining rate of draw outside of the 30-minute drive-time sphere. Most orchestras perform in downtown venues. Over the past decades, suburban sprawl has slowly moved the center of gravity of the prospect base for some orchestras further away from the venue. In some markets, growth in suburban areas has dramatically changed the landscape of the market for cultural programs (e.g., Detroit, St. Louis). Results of the study suggest that orchestras and other arts groups who use downtown venues will have increased difficulty attracting customers who live around the periphery of their geographical sphere of influence, holding everything else constant.[40]

As competing pressures make leisure time more valuable than ever, consumers place increased emphasis on convenience, and they demand more and more intense experiences.[41] These trends are not going in the right direction for some orchestras, especially those serving large urban areas.

This discussion should not be taken as a recommendation for orchestras to abandon or stop investing in downtown venues. But it does suggest that special programming and marketing efforts might be necessary to attract customers who live outside the primary venue's sphere of geographical influence, or that a certain number of programs be offered in strategically-located secondary venues each year. Several orchestras (Saint Paul Chamber Orchestra, Charlotte Symphony Orchestra) have adopted or are experimenting with a strategy of venue diversification as a means of serving constituencies in different areas of their market.

Ticket Buyer Status

At any given ticketed performance of music, dance or theater, a majority of those in the audience did not personally buy a ticket. Someone else bought it for them. The average number of tickets per order, industrywide, is somewhere around 2.5. Of the people who did not actually buy their ticket, a portion of them did not engage in any part of the purchase decision process at all. They accepted an invitation from a friend or family member.

On average, 60 percent of respondents who had any attendance history with their local orchestra said that they had actually purchased a ticket.

---

[40] *The exception to this trend is blockbuster attractions, for which consumers will travel much longer distances.*

[41] *For an interesting economic analysis of the negative effect of the rising opportunity cost of time on demand for orchestra concerts, see* An Exploration of the Beckerian Theory of Time Costs: Symphony Concert Demand, *by Robert B. Ekelund, Jr. and Shawn Ritenour, American Journal of Economics and Sociology, Vol. 58, No. 4 (October 1999). According to the authors, "A rising cost of time, due to increases in the average real wage rate, has had a significant negative effect on symphony orchestra concert demand." This supports the idea that as the perceived cost of leisure time increases, people will choose less time-intensive means to enjoy classical music (e.g., radio and recordings).*

We've come to think of these people as "passive attendees" — a different class of orchestra consumers in that they have some product exposure but no purchase activity. They've experienced the product but didn't buy it. Of course many of these folks are spouses and partners of ticket buyers, but some are not. In many cases, the organization has no idea who they are and no record of how to reach them again — except, possibly, through the person who took them before.

From a research standpoint, "passive attendees" are easy to find — they're in the audience on the night of the concert. But once they go home, they're difficult (and expensive) to find. They cannot be found by mailing surveys to ticket buyers.

Realizing that this study was an opportunity to find them, a question was included in the public telephone surveys to identify those who had ever attended a concert by their local orchestra but who had never purchased a ticket. Appendix Table 4M presents results for this variable.

On average, 60 percent of respondents who had any attendance history with their local orchestra said that they had actually purchased a ticket at some point in their lives. The remaining 40 percent had not or could not remember.[42]

While all this seems intuitive, the simple fact that four in 10 people who make up an orchestra's cumulative constituency are "passive attendees" and have no experience buying tickets points to a vast "shadow" audience, at least from a marketing perspective. At 40 percent of the audience, this is a critical user group for orchestras to consider, however invisible they may be. Their ticket is worth no more or less than the ticket held by the "host" person sitting next them who made the transaction on their behalf.

If orchestras could capture only another 10 percent to 20 percent of the adults in their market who are "very interested" in attending their concerts, the average orchestra's audience would approximately double in size.

Detailed analysis of this group is outside the purview of this report but is one of many worthwhile questions for secondary research. Preliminary analysis suggests that their connections to the art form are substantially weaker than their ticket-buying counterparts — but they still go.

The prevalence of "passive attendees" in an orchestra's constituency, now quantified at approximately 40 percent, corroborates one of the major themes of this study — the important role of social context in driving arts attendance.

[42] *There is not much variation across the 15 orchestras. The exception is the Charlotte Symphony (46 percent), whose free outdoor programs in the summertime attract large crowds who don't need to buy tickets, and this seems to be reflected in their data for this variable.*

Attitudes About Future Attendance

All protocols included a question about the respondent's attitudes about future attendance at concerts by the specific local orchestra. Appendix Table 4P presents detailed results.

The wording of this question was somewhat different on the public surveys and the ticket-buyer surveys. On the public surveys, potential classical consumers were asked "Which of the following statements best describes your current attitude about attending concerts by the [specific local orchestra]?

- "I'm not at all interested in attending a concert"

- "I'm open to attending a concert, but it's not a high priority"

- "I'm very interested in attending a concert"

On average, 22 percent of the large base of potential classical consumers indicated that they are "very interested" in attending a concerts by their specific local orchestra in the future. If one assumes that respondents who did not pass the initial screener have no interest in attending, then the "very interested" figure for all adults across the 15 markets would be 11 percent. If orchestras could capture only another 10 percent to 20 percent of the adults in their market who are "very interested" in attending their concerts, the average orchestra's audience would approximately double in size. Of course a positive attitude about attendance does not always translate into ticket purchase behavior, but it does suggest that the consumer is pre-disposed to the product (or at least the art form).

The vast majority of potential classical consumers — 71 percent on average — are "open to attending, but it's not a high priority," and only 8 percent, on average, said they were "not at all interested." Some level of bias from socially acceptable responses may be present here; respondents may have exaggerated their interest in attending concerts by the local orchestra in order to appear more sophisticated to the interviewer. Even if the responses to this question are substantially biased, we still observe a vast population of moderately or modestly interested prospective customers for orchestras.

On the postal survey of ticket buyers, respondents were asked to respond to the following question: "In the future, do you anticipate attending [specific local orchestra] concerts <u>less often</u>, <u>about as often as I do now</u>, or <u>more often</u>?"

Subscribers, as a lot, seem to have found their desired level of involvement — only 10 percent anticipate attending more often in the future, while 88 percent say that there will be no change in their future attendance levels. Only 2 percent of subscribers say that they plan to attend less frequently. This observation appears to be inconsistent with actual subscriber renewal rates, which range from 50 percent to 80 percent for most orchestras.[43] It is possible that subscribers who did not plan to renew were less likely to complete the survey than those who planned to renew.

[43] *Results from numerous other studies conducted by Audience Insight indicate that roughly half of subscribers lapse for reasons beyond the organizations' direct control (e.g., death of a spouse).*

Former subscribers and single-ticket buyers are less likely to be happy with their present attendance levels; three in 10 anticipate increased attendance in the future.[44] For one reason or another, their actual attendance levels (i.e., behaviors) are not consistent with their attitudes, suggesting a healthy amount of latent demand among infrequent orchestra attendees.

Later in the report, we will see that the large majority of single-ticket buyers are not inclined to subscribe. How can orchestras activate the latent demand for additional product among infrequent attendees, if subscription is not a relevant choice?

Social Context

The powerful role of social context in driving arts attendance is a major theme of this study. In this section, we'll examine several different indicators of social context.[45]

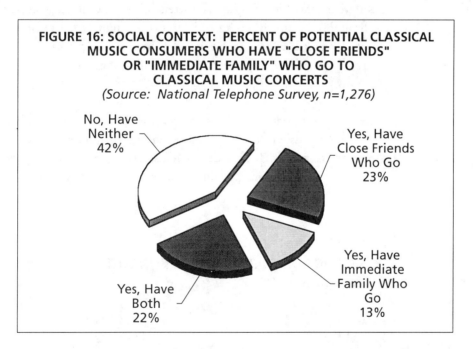

FIGURE 16: SOCIAL CONTEXT: PERCENT OF POTENTIAL CLASSICAL MUSIC CONSUMERS WHO HAVE "CLOSE FRIENDS" OR "IMMEDIATE FAMILY" WHO GO TO CLASSICAL MUSIC CONCERTS
(Source: National Telephone Survey, n=1,276)

- No, Have Neither 42%
- Yes, Have Close Friends Who Go 23%
- Yes, Have Immediate Family Who Go 13%
- Yes, Have Both 22%

In the section of protocol devoted to the art form relationship, potential classical consumers were asked if they have close friends who go to classical music concerts and if anyone in their immediate family goes to classical music concerts. In the section of protocol devoted to the local orchestra relationship, potential classical consumers were asked if they have friends or family members who attend concerts by the specific local orchestra. Thus, social context data are available at both the art form and orchestra-specific levels.

------

[44] *Since the ticket-buyer surveys were completed in written format in the privacy of respondents' homes and no interviewer was involved, the bias from socially acceptable responses should be less of a factor.*

[45] *We are indebted to John Bare of the Knight Foundation for his encouragement and guidance on this line of questioning.*

Nationally, 45 percent of the large base of potential classical consumers have close friends who attend classical concerts, while 35 percent have immediate family members who attend classical concerts. Figure 16 illustrates social context for attending classical music concerts for the large base of potential classical consumers, based on data from the national telephone survey.

On average, figures across the 15 markets are slightly higher for social context. Appendix Table 3F presents results for this social context variable. With respect to orchestra ticket buyers, a large majority have close friends or immediate family who attend classical concerts, as might be expected, although there are some interesting patterns.

As the level of involvement (i.e., frequency of attendance at the orchestra's concerts) decreases, so does social context. Across the 15 orchestras, an average of 85 percent of subscribers have close friends who attend classical concerts, compared to 81 percent of former subscribers and 75 percent of single-ticket buyers. Similarly, 69 percent of subscribers have immediate family members who attend classical concerts, compared to 66 percent of former subscribers and 59 percent of single-ticket buyers.

Note the disparity between the figures for friends and family members. More ticket buyers have friends who attend classical concerts than have immediate family members who attend. This is true regardless of marital status, and it is especially true, as one might imagine, for single, divorced and widowed ticket buyers (see Figure 17).

FIGURE 17:

SOCIAL CONTEXT FOR CLASSICAL CONCERTS
BY MARITAL STATUS

Marital Status	Close Friends*	Immediate Family*
Married	79%	73%
Partnered, Not Married	89%	67%
Single, Never Married	83%	45%
Divorced or Separated	82%	50%
Widowed	91%	52%

* Percent with "close friends" or "immediate family" who go to classical concerts (source: combined data from public telephone surveys of potential classical consumers in 15 cities)

Although the concert experience is deeply personal, it is also a highly social activity for most ticket buyers, in the sense that they identify with a social group that goes to classical concerts.

Personal vs. Communal Experience

Following up a theme of another study, ticket buyers were asked if classical music concerts are primarily a personal experience or primarily a communal experience.[46] Of course, the concert experience is both personal and communal, but we forced respondents to choose in order to better understand this fundamental duality and to see if there are groups of classical consumers who value one over the other.

On average, 88 percent responded that classical concerts are primarily a personal experience, and 12 percent said they are primarily a communal experience. Younger buyers were slightly more likely to respond that classical concerts are primarily a communal experience (16 percent for respondents ages 18-34 vs. 10 percent for respondents ages 75+). Results did not vary by gender or by subscriber status.

As the level of sophistication about the art form increases, so does the perception that classical music is primarily a personal experience. Among those who consider themselves to be "very knowledgeable" about the art form, 93 percent say that classical music concerts are primarily a personal experience, compared to 80 percent for those who consider themselves to be "not very knowledgeable" about the art form. Both of these percentages are high. Nevertheless, we must consider an important implication — that classical consumers at the lower end of the sophistication spectrum rely more on the social aspect of the concert experience. This corroborates a variety of other data related to social context, and it reinforces the notion that creating social context is a viable audience development strategy. People with less background on classical music — those who may be unfamiliar with the classical music vocabulary and who are less able to make decisions about concerts based on product attributes (i.e., artists, composers and repertoire) — are more likely to attend in the comfort of a safe and supportive social envelope.

Focus group data suggest that some married couples experience a healthy amount divergence in terms of musical tastes — especially when it comes to classical music. In these situations, one partner likes classical music and would like to go to concerts more often, while the other partner is strongly disinclined. We have seen both men and women in either role. The net effect, usually, is that they don't go; the potential demand represented by the positively-inclined partner remains latent. We have come to regard this phenomenon of "taste dissonance" as a major barrier to attendance, although a great deal more research is needed to understand the nuances.

In a "taste dissonant" couple, latent demand can be activated when the positively-inclined partner develops a friendship network with shared values around classical music attendance. The same is true for single people who move to a new area and

---

[46] *In 2000 – 2001, the American Symphony Orchestra League conducted an extensive study of the motivations for classical music attendance. Results are not available to the general public or to orchestras that did not buy in to the study.*

have difficulty making friends who enjoy going to classical concerts. This study sparked a great deal of discussion about how orchestras (and other arts groups, by extension) might activate some of this latent demand by doing a better job of facilitating attendance by small social groups.

Initiators and Responders

Respondents to all surveys, including the general population telephone surveys and the ticket-buyer surveys, were asked about their mode of planning for cultural outings. Two independent questions allowed respondents to self-identify as:

- **Initiators:** respondents who 'agreed a lot' with the statement *"I'm the kind of person who likes to organize cultural outings for my friends."* Nationally, 18 percent of the large base of potential classical consumers 'agreed a lot' with this statement, while the remaining 82% agreed less strongly (for the purposes of analysis, they are not considered to be Initiators).

- **Responders:** respondents who 'agreed a lot' with the statement *"I'm much more likely to attend cultural outings if someone else invites me."* Nationally, 56 percent of the large base of potential classical consumers 'agreed a lot' with this statement, while the remaining 44% agreeing less strongly (for the purposes of analysis, they are not considered to be Responders).

Results are summarized in the charts that follow. Detailed figures for all 15 markets may be found in Appendix Tables 2A-2 and 2A-3. Please note that Initiators and Responders are not mutually exclusive groups; people may identify as neither or both.

In the discussions with board and staff members of the 15 orchestras that followed the study, these simple statistics seem to have resonated as much as anything in the study. Perhaps this is because the data confirm something that we all know intuitively — that when it comes to planning cultural outings, some people are instinctive organizers while other people tend to be more passive in their planning mode. They wait for an invitation. Most everyone can think of people who fit both typologies.

Initiators

Who are "Initiators?" An analysis of the characteristics of Initiators suggests that they are culturally active, culturally knowledgeable people who are actively scanning the media for cultural activities to do:

- Initiators are more likely to be "extremely interested" in arts activities (24 percent vs. 8 percent of those who are not Initiators)

- Initiators are more likely to say that arts activities play a "major role" in their lives (58 percent vs. 23 percent of those who are not Initiators)

- On average, Initiators attended significantly more performing arts events over the 12 months preceding the study (7.9 vs. 4.1 for those who are not Initiators)

- Initiators are much more likely than those who are not Initiators to "always be looking for cultural activities to do" (58 percent vs. 16 percent, respectively)

- Initiators are more likely to be knowledgeable about classical music and are more likely to be "very interested" in learning more about classical music (26 percent vs. 9 percent those who are not Initiators)

- Initiators are twice as likely as those who are not Initiators to be "very interested" in attending concerts by the specific local orchestra (33 percent vs. 15 percent, respectively)

- In terms of demographics, Initiators are more likely than those who are not Initiators to be single (36 percent vs. 22 percent), more likely to be younger (avg. age is 42 compared to 48), slightly more likely to be female (60 percent vs. 53 percent), and are more likely to be African-American (25 percent vs. 10 percent) or Hispanic (17 percent vs. 9 percent)

Initiators are no more or less likely to be found in an orchestra's audience as they are in the large base of potential classical consumers, and this trait does not vary by subscriber status. As indicated in Figure 18, single-ticket buyers are just as likely as subscribers to be Initiators.

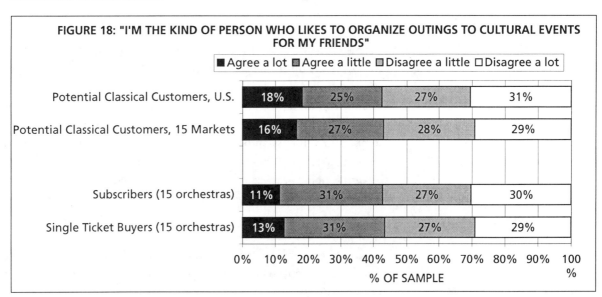

FIGURE 18: "I'M THE KIND OF PERSON WHO LIKES TO ORGANIZE OUTINGS TO CULTURAL EVENTS FOR MY FRIENDS"

	Agree a lot	Agree a little	Disagree a little	Disagree a lot
Potential Classical Customers, U.S.	18%	25%	27%	31%
Potential Classical Customers, 15 Markets	16%	27%	28%	29%
Subscribers (15 orchestras)	11%	31%	27%	30%
Single Ticket Buyers (15 orchestras)	13%	31%	27%	29%

% OF SAMPLE

In July 2002, a final series of focus group discussions was held in Detroit, in cooperation with the Detroit Symphony Orchestra. Among the four discussion groups was one group of Initiators. To qualify for the discussion, each of the participants had self-identified as an Initiator in a pre-recruitment survey.

A more complex and subtle picture of Initiators emerged from this discussion group. Initiators are psychologically wired to "get it together" when it comes to cultural events. Some Initiators do the organizing because no one else is around to do it — *"If I don't do it, it won't happen."* In some cases, they are single adults or are in a relationship where the other partner does not share the same cultural interests.

Their initiating behavior creates the social context for attendance that is otherwise absent in their lives.

There are other, more subtle reasons that drive Initiators to do their thing. In the focus group discussions, several participants suggested that initiating cultural outings satisfies a deep need to nurture and enrich the lives of their friends and family. For these people, the process of working through the logistics of planning a cultural outing (identifying activities, contacting people, getting the tickets, etc.) is meaningful because it satisfies an emotional need to nurture. [47]

The types of groups that Initiators get together include:

- Groups of co-workers (particularly when the Initiator is new to the area)

- College alumni groups (went to school together, trying to sustain friendships)

- Church friendship groups (shared religious values)

- Small family groups (e.g., daughters with widowed mothers and their friends — the Initiator wants to "be a good son or daughter")

- Friendship groups that are not connected by an external institution like church, employer or family (e.g., girlfriends)

In some cases the group's membership is more or less fixed or static, while in other cases membership in the group is quite fluid — people come and go.

When it comes to selecting events to attend, decision processes range from carefully negotiated consensus scenarios — whereby the Initiator engages each of the group members in a discussion of the choices (which is made much easier through e-mail, one participant noted) — to unilateral decisions (*"we're going, would you like to come with us?"*). Some of these processes happen far in advance of the event (particularly when a group is deciding whether or not to subscribe together), while some happen at the very last minute.

In some cases, the Initiator provides background information about the cultural event to each group member prior to the event. One model that comes to mind is

....

[47] *The concept of "Initiators" and "Responders" has interesting parallels to several of the themes developed in Malcolm Gladwell's 2001 book,* The Tipping Point. *Gladwell devotes a chapter to "The Law of the Few," in which he describes several types of people who control "word of mouth epidemics," including "Mavens" and "Connectors." Mavens are people whom "...we rely on to connect us to other people," and whom "...we rely on to connect us with new information. There are people specialists, and there are information specialists." {page 59} Connectors "...are the kinds of people who know everyone." {page 38} "They are people whom all of us can reach in only a few steps..." {page 48} Also, see* Emotional Contagion, *by Elaine Hatfield and John Cacioppo (1994), in which the authors discuss how humans naturally "...imitate each other's emotions as a way of expressing support and caring and, even more basically, as a way of communicating with each other." One might infer from these authors that Initiators and Responders fulfill basic human psychological, emotional and social needs – as well as cultural roles.*

the book club. In recent years, book clubs have become quite fashionable. In light of the study's findings with respect to social context and planning modes, it is not difficult to understand why.

Can arts groups appropriate the book club paradigm and create new opportunities for small social groups to get involved in cultural activities (e.g., concert clubs, opera clubs)? Results from this study indicate that a new marketing model that leverages social context in its many shapes and forms would be very productive in driving increased attendance and in helping cultural consumers have more meaningful experiences with the art.

Responders

At home, waiting for a telephone call from their favorite Initiator, is a vast population of Responders. Over half of the large base of potential classical consumers (56%) self-identified as Responders — people who acknowledge that they usually need an external social stimulus to cause them to engage in cultural activities (see Figure 19). By any measure, they are a large and potentially powerful constituency for orchestras — if their interest in classical music can be converted into attendance.

In terms of their attitudes about future attendance at local orchestra concerts, 21 percent of Responders are "very interested in attending a concert" compared to 33 percent of Initiators. Recall, however, that there are three times as many Responders as Initiators in the large base of potential classical consumers. On average, Responders are 18 percent more likely than Initiators to be "open to attending, but it's not a high priority."

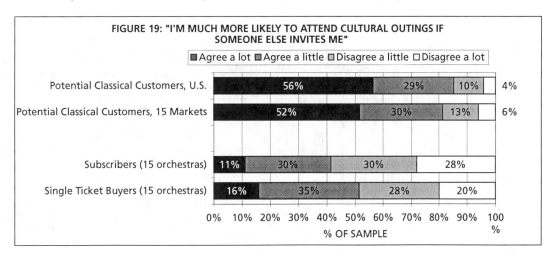

FIGURE 19: "I'M MUCH MORE LIKELY TO ATTEND CULTURAL OUTINGS IF SOMEONE ELSE INVITES ME"

Agree a lot ■ Agree a little ■ Disagree a little □ Disagree a lot

	Agree a lot	Agree a little	Disagree a little	Disagree a lot
Potential Classical Customers, U.S.	56%	29%	10%	4%
Potential Classical Customers, 15 Markets	52%	30%	13%	6%
Subscribers (15 orchestras)	11%	30%	30%	28%
Single Ticket Buyers (15 orchestras)	16%	35%	28%	20%

% OF SAMPLE

Unlike Initiators, Responders are far less likely to be found in an orchestra's audience, as one might imagine. But we must be careful here in generalizing about Responders in the ticket buyer samples because surveys were mailed to ticket buyers — people who've already demonstrated some initiative. Intuitively, we would expect fewer of them to be Responders.

An earlier discussion of telephone survey data pointed to a substantial contingent of non-buyers or "passive attendees" in each orchestra's market (i.e., 40% of all potential classical consumers who've ever attended a concert by the orchestra, on average). These "passive attendees" are 20 percent more likely than their counterparts who have purchased tickets to be Responders (55 percent vs. 45 percent, respectively).

Arts organizations expend their marketing resources trying to convert both Initiators and Responders into active buyers through direct mail acquisition efforts and media advertising.[48] The findings of this study suggest that a more productive approach to activating the demand embodied in Responders would be to market to them indirectly through Initiators, since they normally require a social stimulus.

Here we may have unearthed one of the reasons why telemarketing for cultural events still works. In the telemarketing situation, the caller steps into a surrogate Initiator role and extends an invitation to the Responder on the other end of the line. Even the slightest suggestion of social context — in the form of an invitation from a knowledgeable but hardly objective sales representative — is enough to unlock demand.

Initiators and Responders are not mutually exclusive typologies, although there are some clear inter-relationships. The table below illustrates how the two typologies overlap. While 53 percent of Initiators are also Responders, only 17 percent of Responders are Initiators. What this may suggest, quite simply, is that most Initiators are also happy to be invited out to cultural outings by others. But Responders, as a class of cultural consumers, are unlikely to take on the organizer role.

FIGURE 20. INITIATORS AND RESPONDERS: SUMMARY MATRIX	RESPONDERS: "I'm much more likely to attend cultural outings if someone else invites me."				
	Agree a lot	Agree a little	Disagree a little	Disagree a lot	**TOTAL INITIATORS**
INITIATORS: "I'm the kind of person who likes to organize cultural outings for my friends." — Agree a lot	9%	4%	3%	1%	**16%**
Agree a little	14%	8%	3%	1%	**27%**
Disagree a little	14%	9%	4%	1%	**28%**
Disagree a lot	15%	9%	3%	3%	**29%**
TOTAL RESPONDERS	**52%**	**30%**	**13%**	**6%**	**100%**

Source: 15 public telephone surveys combined (n=5,826 potential classical consumers)

---

[48] *"The entire arts industry is fixated with encouraging conservative, non-attenders to become adventurous frequent attenders. Why?"* – Richard Hadley, Only Connect: A New Blueprint for Audience Development, *Arts Professional (UK), June 2002*

Length of Residence

Analysis of respondents' self-reported length of residence shows a clear relationship with local orchestra attendance. Appendix Table 4A presents length of residence data from both the 15 public telephone surveys and the ticket buyer surveys.

Generally, orchestra ticket buyers are long-time residents. Only 6 percent of orchestra subscribers across the 15 markets have lived in the area for less than 5 years, compared to 16 percent of single-ticket buyers. In total, 88 percent of subscribers have lived in their city for 10 years or more, compared to 73 percent of single-ticket buyers.

Drawing on public survey data from the 15 markets, Figure 21 illustrates how three related indicators of local orchestra involvement increase markedly with length of residence:

- Percent aware of local orchestra by length of residence — begins at 60 percent in the first year of residence and grows steadily

- Percent with close friends or immediate family who attend concerts by the local orchestra — rises from below 30 percent in the first year of residence to 50 percent in the fourth year or residence

- Percent who've ever attended a local orchestra concert as an adult — begins at an average rate of 10 percent for the first year of residence, and more than doubles in three years

Is a customer someone who buys tickets, or is a customer someone who enjoys the concert?

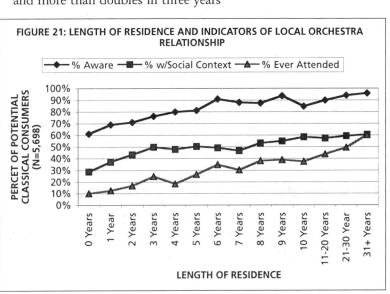

FIGURE 21: LENGTH OF RESIDENCE AND INDICATORS OF LOCAL ORCHESTRA RELATIONSHIP

One clear implication is that it takes people several years after moving to a new area to develop the social context for attending and to get involved with their local orchestra. Corporate marketing programs that offer new employees and their families low-risk trial experiences with cultural programs in their new environs are implied as a long-term audience development strategy, whether undertaken by individual arts groups or collaboratively by groups of organizations.

Both social context and attendance rates continue to rise with length of residence, although other factors are undoubtedly working in the background (age, occupational status, wealth, etc.). Nevertheless, the data suggest that, on average, it takes 30 years for people to reach equilibrium between social context and actual attendance.

Some Final Thoughts About Social Context

Aside from the relatively few people who come alone to concerts, the concert experience happens in a social context. Different people like different amounts of social activity before, during and after concerts. For some people, the social context opportunity itself is what triggers consent to attend. An attractive social context, from a consumer behavior perspective, lubricates the purchase decision process. Those who go alone require none or have overcome their need for it. For some, the social trappings around the concert experience (i.e., cocktail parties, receptions, intermission socializing, dinner afterwards, etc.) are unnecessary and even superfluous. They drive to the venue, sit down for the concert and then drive home — and are satisfied with the experience.

If one begins to look at the larger group of potential classical consumers who are not attending their local orchestra, or those who are attending infrequently, it must be acknowledged that for many, if not most, a relationship with the orchestra is contingent on an external social stimulus — an invitation.

All of this raises an urgent question for orchestras: What defines the customer? Is a customer someone who buys tickets? Or is a customer someone who enjoys the concert? The difference is important.

If the prospective customer is someone would enjoy a concert but won't initiate a purchase process without an invitation, then a fundamental realignment of marketing strategy is implied: a shift toward strategies that create and facilitate attendance in small social groups.

Other Results — Local Orchestra Relationship

A variety of additional questions were fielded pertaining to respondents' feelings about their local orchestra. These questions were included mostly for the benefit of the individual orchestras. A brief summary of these orchestra-specific variables follows.

Unsatisfactory Experiences (Appendix Table 4K)

Respondents to the ticket buyer surveys were asked if they'd ever had an unsatisfactory experience at a concert by their local orchestra. On average, 24 percent of subscribers said that they had. The figures were 19 percent for former subscribers and just 7 percent for single-ticket buyers. A follow-up, open-ended question invited respondents to describe the unsatisfactory experience: "If so, what was unsatisfactory about the experience?" Verbatim responses were provided to each

> *Customer satisfaction matters, and subscribers have long memories. The outpouring of responses suggests that orchestras would benefit from creating a regular feedback loop with their audience.*

orchestra. Generally, the types of unsatisfactory experiences related to (in no particular order):

- Parking problems

- HVAC problems in the hall (too hot/cold)

- Excessive sound levels at pops concerts with amplified sound

- Poor acoustics and distracting ambient noise

- Ticketing problems (e.g., "someone was in my seat"), unsympathetic customer service

- Poor quality of performance by a guest artist, conductor or orchestra

- Dislike selection of music (e.g., too much contemporary music), uninteresting programs

- Problems with the concert etiquette of other patrons (late arrivers, coughing, noisy neighbors, etc.)

- Uncomfortable seats, not enough leg room

In some cases, respondents wrote about experiences that happened five to 10 years ago. Remember that these are responses from current, mostly loyal customers — not from unhappy former customers. What seems remarkable is that subscribers (and to a much lesser extent single-ticket buyers) care enough to remember unsatisfactory concert experiences from 10 years ago.

Customer satisfaction matters, and subscribers have long memories. The outpouring of responses to this question suggests that orchestra audiences (subscribers, at least) have a lot to say, and that orchestras would benefit from creating a regular feedback loop with their audience. This is not to suggest that artistic decisions should be driven by customer feedback, or that orchestras can or should attempt to respond to every customer gripe. But, if strengthening the customer relationship truly matters, the findings suggest that orchestras can do a better job of listening to their audiences.

Loyalty (Appendix Tables 4L-1 through 4L-4)

Customer loyalty was a theme of discussion during Knight Foundation's 2001 Magic of Music retreat in St. Paul, a gathering of key board and staff members of the 15 Magic of Music orchestras. The keynote speaker for that session was Fred Reicheld, CEO of Bain & Company and author of *The Loyalty Effect*. At the time, the ticket-buyer survey protocols for this study were still being designed. To pursue the subject, we decided to include a question on loyalty.[49] The question asked respondents to indicate their level of agreement with four different statements

....

[49] *We wish to acknowledge Mr. Reicheld's support and guidance with this protocol area.*

relating to loyalty, in this order:

1. The [local orchestra] really cares about building a relationship with me.

2. I feel a strong connection with the musicians of the [local orchestra].

3. I have confidence in the [local orchestra] organization.

4. I believe that the [local orchestra] deserves my loyalty.

The last statement was designed to measure overall loyalty, while the first three statements were designed to assess loyalty in specific dimensions that are not necessarily related. The first statement addresses the customer's acknowledgement of the marketing relationship; the second statement goes to the customer's feeling of connectedness with the musicians of the orchestra; and the third statement pertains to the customer's level of confidence in the orchestra organization.

Overall feelings of loyalty are approximately twice as strong for subscribers as they are for single-ticket buyers. Across the 15 orchestras, 71 percent of subscribers "agree a lot" that the orchestra deserves their loyalty, but the figure dips to 42 percent for former subscribers and 35 percent for single-ticket buyers (never subscribed). Figures for all four indicators of loyalty vary across the 15 orchestras. Overall, ticket buyers of the Louisiana Philharmonic Orchestra and the New World Symphony reported the highest loyalty figures.

Orchestras invest a great deal of effort in creating and sustaining relationships with subscribers. The loyalty figures suggest that the 15 orchestras have been more or less successful in this endeavor, whether the feelings of loyalty derive from frequency of exposure to the product or from the orchestras' efforts at nurturing the customer relationship (or both).

The story with single-ticket buyers is very different and suggests a need for further analysis and dialogue in the orchestra field about how to build loyalty among non-subscribers, especially those who are frequent attendees.

Quality of Playing (Appendix Table 40)

Respondents to the ticket-buyer surveys were asked to rate the quality of their local orchestra's playing on a scale of 0 (poor quality) to 10 (excellent quality). On average, subscribers rated their local orchestra's quality of playing at 9.2, compared to 8.9 for former subscribers and 8.8 for single-ticket buyers. [50]

....

Overall feelings of loyalty are approximately twice as strong for subscribers as they are for single ticket buyers.

....

---

[50] *In his April 29, 2001 essay* What's New in Classical Music? Not Much, *Anthony Tommasini of The New York Times wrote: "The classical music field has long encouraged superficial talk about which American orchestras constitute the Big Five. Which has the richest string sound? The most powerful brasses? The most incisive ensemble? Such talk just compounds the problem. How orchestras play matters. But what they play, and why, matters more. The overall quality of American orchestras is high."*

Looking at subscribers across the 15 markets, average quality ratings ranged from a high of 9.6 (Philadelphia Orchestra, Saint Louis Symphony, Saint Paul Chamber Orchestra) to 8.4 (Kansas City). The New World Symphony, a professional training orchestra, received one of the highest quality ratings (9.4). This raises the question of whether the energy of the young players of the New World Symphony translates into perceptions of high quality as well as higher feelings of loyalty among its audiences.

On average, there was little difference between the quality ratings of "critical listeners" (9.0) and "casual listeners," (9.1), although in several markets "casual listeners" rated quality somewhat higher than "critical listeners" (e.g., Charlotte, Long Beach, Portland). Going into the study, we had hypothesized that the more sophisticated classical consumers would rate quality lower, because of their presumed ability to discern quality. This hypothesis was not corroborated by the data. If anything, the data seem to suggest that critical listeners are not any more likely than casual listeners to discern quality.

Quality ratings are inherently subjective and may be influenced by a host of factors that do not necessarily relate to the actual quality of playing, such as media coverage, acoustics and other qualities of the venue, and the orchestra's reputation in the community — what people are told to think.

Feelings About Contemporary Classical Music (Appendix Table 4N)

Respondents were asked if their attendance would increase, decrease or stay the same if the orchestra played "more classical music compositions by contemporary composers." About two-thirds of ticket buyers said there would be no change in their frequency of attendance. On average, 29 percent of subscribers said their attendance would decrease, while 6 percent said their attendance would increase. Single-ticket buyers seemed somewhat more interested in hearing more contemporary music — while 23 percent said their attendance would decrease, 14 percent said their attendance would increase. Ironically, single-ticket buyers — not subscribers — have larger appetites for contemporary classical music.

Segmentation Model: Local Orchestra Relationship

The second of three consumer segmentation models developed in this study classifies potential classical consumers into one of eight unique groups based on their lifetime relationship with a specific local orchestra. The critical determinants of the orchestra relationship are:

- Whether or not trial has occurred (i.e., "ever" attended as an adult)

- How recent was the last concert attendance

- Frequency of attendance, past year

- Ever subscribed

- Ticket-buyer status (ever personally bought tickets)

- If social context exists (i.e., if friends or family members attend that orchestra)

- Attitude about future attendance (level of interest in future attendance)

Seven variables were used in the cluster analysis. For more information, consult the methodology section in the report appendix. Figure 23 summarizes results, which are detailed for all 15 orchestras in Appendix Tables S2-A through S2-D.

FIGURE 23. CONSUMER SEGMENTATION MODEL: LOCAL ORCHESTRA RELATIONSHIP (15 MARKET WEIGHTED AVERAGE)	Percent of Potential Classical Consumers[1]	Percent of Adults[2]
Group 1: Captured Active Audience		
1. High Involvement Subscribers	3.3%	1.6%
2. Involved Single-Ticket Buyers	5.3%	2.6%
Group 2: Alumni		
3. Low Frequency & Former Subscribers	3.5%	1.7%
4. Very Interested, Low Frequency STBs & Ghosts	9.7%	4.8%
5. Low Involvement STBs & Ghosts	23.5%	11.7%
Group 3: Non Users		
6: Non-Users With Social Context	15.1%	7.5%
7: Non-Users Without Social Context	29.3%	14.6%
8: Unaware of Local Orchestra	10.4%	5.2%
NOT INTERVIEWED/FAILED SCREENER		50.1%

Source: 15 Local Market Public Telephone Surveys of Classical Music Consumers, 2001 – 2002
1) Potential Classical Consumers are the subset of respondents who qualified for an extended interview. 2) Assumes that none of the respondents who failed the initial screener have any relationship with the orchestra

This analysis was conducted on the rolled up data file from the 15 local market public telephone surveys. Only respondents who passed the initial screener (i.e., potential classical consumers) were administered the protocol section that serves as the basis for this analysis. A total of 5,646 cases were used in the cluster analysis. Short descriptions of each segment follow.

Segment 1: High-Involvement Subscribers

The segment with the strongest connection with the local Magic of Music orchestra is comprised of current subscribers and those who had subscribed previously and remain active as single-ticket buyers. On average, these individuals attend just over 7.4 of the orchestra's concerts annually (twice the frequency of the next highest segment). This group has the oldest age distribution of any segment — an average age of 60 years.

Segment 2: Involved Single-ticket buyers:

Current, active single-ticket buyers had the next strongest connection with the local Magic of Music orchestra. None are subscribers or former subscribers. Average frequency of attendance at the Magic of Music Orchestra is 3.4 concerts annually. This segment is significantly younger than subscribers — averaging 47 years.

Segment 3: Low-Frequency & Former Subscribers

This segment is populated by former subscribers, 70 percent of whom are not active attendees. In fact, 21 percent have been inactive for four or more years. Among the 30 percent who did attend in the past year, average frequency is 1.3 times. A small number are current subscribers, but have a low frequency of attendance. Average age is 56 years.

Segment 4: Very Interested, Low-Frequency STBs & Ghosts:

Only one in five of these individuals attended their local Magic of Music orchestra in the past year (with an average frequency of 1.1 times), and 44 percent attended within the past two years. This segment is younger — averaging 45 years. What distinguishes these people is that they all say they are "very interested" in attending concerts by their local Magic of Music orchestra. While three-quarters of them have ever attended as an adult, only 61 percent of those people have purchased a ticket. The remaining 39 percent are "passive attendees" — they may have attended a free concert or came as the guest of a ticket buyer.

Segment 5: Low-Involvement STBs & Ghosts:

While all of the individuals in this segment have attended a concert by their local Magic of Music orchestra at some point in their adult lives, nearly half are "passive attendees" — they've never personally purchased a ticket. About one-quarter of the people in this segment are active attendees. Among those who are active, they attended an average of just one concert in the past year. None of these people are "very interested" in attending their local orchestra, but all of them are "open to attending" to some degree. Average age is 47 years.

Segment 6: Non-Users With Social Context:

No one in this segment currently attends their local Magic of Music orchestra, and only 10 percent ever have as an adult. This segment is distinguished by a high social context of family and friends who attend the local Magic of Music orchestra, and almost all of them say that they are "open to attending." Nevertheless, they do not. This segment is young — averaging 43 years, has lived in the area for a shorter period of time than average, and has a longer average drive time to the venue.

Segment 7: Non-Users Without Social Context:

There are no current attendees of the local Magic of Music orchestra in this segment, and only 5 percent have ever attended. This segment has no social context (family or friends) for attending the local Magic of Music orchestra. Twelve percent of them, however, are "very interested" in doing so. This segment is among the youngest — averaging 43 years. Of all the segments, they have resided in the area for the shortest period of time, and have a longer average drive time to the venue.

Segment 8: Unaware of Local Orchestra:

Respondents who were not aware of the local orchestra were not classified into a segment. Generally, this is a small group of people, but it varies substantially from market to market. On average, 14 percent of this group is "very interested" in attending a concert by the local orchestra. Average age is 36 years.

THE PROSPECT UNIVERSE FOR
15 Orchestras

The overall goal of this study was to gain a sense of the prospect base for 15 separate orchestras. Our central hypothesis, illustrated in Figure 2, was that there are many adults with connections to classical music who do not regularly attend concerts by their local orchestra.

In the previous two sections, we explored the two dimensions of analysis in detail and defined clusters of consumers for each dimension: Relationship with the Art Form (10 segments of potential classical consumers); and Relationship with the Local Orchestra (8 segments of potential classical consumers). Here, we bring the two dimensions together in order to shed light on our hypothesis.

FIGURE 2: Central Hypothesis

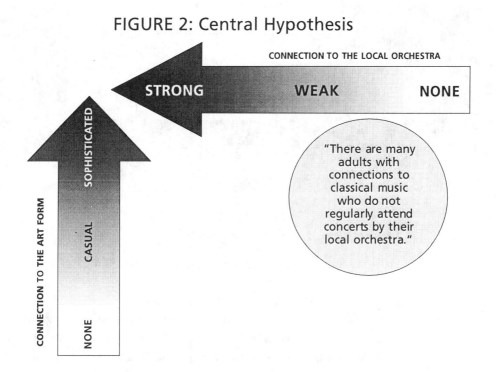

Essentially, we sub-divided the two dimensional conceptual space in Figure 2 into an 80-cell matrix — 10 segments along the vertical axis (Art Form Relationship) by 8 segments across the horizontal axis (Local Orchestra Relationship).

Classical Music Consumer Segmentation Study
Final Report

We arrived at the final prospect model by grouping the 80 cells into nine categories of orchestra prospects, based on an analysis of the cross-tabulation of the two consumer models. Figure 24 illustrates how the 80 cells of potential classical consumers were grouped into nine categories of orchestra prospects (and a large pool of non-prospects).

FIGURE 24: PROSPECT MATRIX		DIMENSION 2: RELATIONSHIP WITH THE LOCAL ORCHESTRA							
		1. High Involvement Subscribers	2. Involved Single Ticket Buyers	3. Low Freq. & Former Subscribers	4. Very Interested, Low Freq. STB & Ghosts	5. Low Involvement STB & Ghosts	6. Non-Users with Social Context	7. Non-Users, Low Interest in Local Orch.	8. Unaware of Local Orchestra
DIMENSION 1: RELATIONSHIP WITH THE ART FORM	1. Educated Classical Audience	Sophisticated Active Audience		Sophisticated Low-Frequency Alumni			Uninitiated Prospects with Social Context	Uninitiated Prospects without Social Context	
	2. Classical Ghosts	Casually-Involved Active Audience		Interested STB & Ghosts					
	3. Emerging Classical Audience								
	4. Casual Listeners								
	5. Classical Lite	Anomalies		Low-Interest Dabblers					Unaware
	6. Out-of-Reach								
	7. Blue Moon			Special Occasion Only			Uninitiated Suspects		
	8. Family Occasion								
	9. Disinclined								
	10. Least Interested					Non-Prospects			
		CAPTURED PROSPECTS		LOW FREQUENCY "ALUMNI"			NO TRIAL EXPERIENCE		

The Prospect Matrix

There are three overall categories of prospects in the final model:

1. **Captured Prospects** – Since the model is comprehensive, it includes active buyers. Captured Prospects are all current subscribers or single-ticket buyers who attended more than once in the past year. They are sub-divided into two segments based on their relative sophistication level with the art form.

2. **Low-Frequency Alumni** – A second category of orchestra prospects was established for consumers who have been to a concert by the specific local orchestra at some point in their adult lives but who are not currently attending or are attending infrequently. We define them as prospects because they've had a trial experience, regardless of how long ago. Prospects in this category range from former long-term subscribers to the most dispassionate single-ticket buyers. There are four segments of Low Frequency Alumni, based on their overall connection to the art form.

3. **Uninitiated Prospects** – A third category of prospects was established for consumers with no trial experience with the specific local orchestra. Their connections to the art form are strong enough, however, to suggest that they should be considered prospects for orchestra concerts. None of these consumers have ever been to a concert by the local orchestra included in the study,[51] although some of them have friends and family who go. There are three segments of Uninitiated Prospects.

Figure 25 summarizes average figures for the three types of prospects for the 15 orchestras combined.

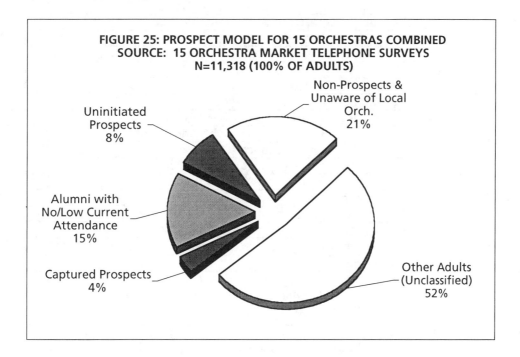

FIGURE 25: PROSPECT MODEL FOR 15 ORCHESTRAS COMBINED
SOURCE: 15 ORCHESTRA MARKET TELEPHONE SURVEYS
N=11,318 (100% OF ADULTS)

- Non-Prospects & Unaware of Local Orch. 21%
- Uninitiated Prospects 8%
- Alumni with No/Low Current Attendance 15%
- Captured Prospects 4%
- Other Adults (Unclassified) 52%

Many respondents who qualified as potential classical consumers (i.e., they passed the initial screener) responded to the questions about the art form and their local orchestra and did not qualify as orchestra prospects. Either they had little or no relationship with the art form or they expressed no desire to attend a concert by the local orchestra, or both. Respondents who were unaware of the specific local orchestra could not answer questions about the orchestra and also were ruled out of the prospect pool.

In order to extrapolate the orchestra prospect model to the adult populations in each of the 15 cities, we make the conservative assumption that none of the people who failed the initial screener are prospects for their local orchestra (i.e., they are unclassified). Average figures for the nine segments of local orchestra prospects appear in Figure 26, as well as figures for all other respondents including those who were

---

[51] *It is possible that they have attended concerts by another orchestra in their community.*

aware of the local orchestra but did not qualify as prospects, those who were unaware of the local orchestra (and hence unclassified), those whose answers were anomalous (unclassified), and those who did not pass the initial screener (unclassified). Detailed segment descriptions may be found at the end of this section.

FIGURE 26. PROSPECT MODEL FOR LOCAL ORCHESTRAS (15 MARKET WEIGHTED AVERAGE)	Percent of Adults[1]
Group 1: Captured Prospects	
1. Sophisticated Active Audience	1.7%
2. Casually Involved Active Audience	2.0%
Group 2: Low/No Involvement Alumni	
3. Sophisticated Low-Frequency Alumni	1.7%
4. Interested Single-Ticket Buyers and Ghosts	4.4%
5. Low-Interest Dabblers	4.8%
6. Special Occasion Only	4.6%
Group 3: Uninitiated Prospects	
7: Uninitiated Prospects without Social Context	2.4%
8: Uninitiated Prospects with Social Context	1.7%
9: Uninitiated Suspects	3.7%
Total Orchestra Prospect Universe	**27.0%**
Non-Prospects & Unclassified	
Qualified Non-Prospects (Aware of Local Orchestra)	14.0%
Unaware of Local Orchestra (Disqualified)	6.5%
Anomalies & Outliers (Disqualified)	0.9%
Unclassified (Failed Initial Screener or Incomplete Data)	51.6%
All Adults	100.0%

Source: 15 Random Sample Public Telephone Surveys,2001-2002
(1) Assumes that none of the respondents who failed the initial screener are orchestra prospects.

Across the 15 orchestras, there are nearly four times as many Low-Frequency Alumni (15 percent) as Captured Prospects (4 percent) and twice as many Uninitiated Prospects (8 percent).

On average, the percentage of "Sophisticated Low-Frequency Alumni" equals the percentage of "Sophisticated Active Audience" (1.7 percent each). We are speaking now of the most sophisticated classical music lovers, and the results point to *again as many* sophisticated alumni who do not attend their local orchestra regularly as who do attend regularly.

Below the top tier of non-attending sophisticates, the percentages of low frequency alumni get larger: Low-Frequency Single-Ticket Buyers and Ghosts (4.4 percent), Low-Interest Dabblers (4.8 percent) and Special Occasion Only (4.6 percent). Moreover, another 7.8 percent of adults in these 15 markets (Uninitiated Prospects) have connections with the art form but have no history of attendance at the local orchestra included in the study.

Overall, the findings tend to support the central hypothesis of the study. There are many adults with connections to classical music who do not regularly attend concerts by their local orchestra.

There are substantial differences, however, across the 15 markets. Appendix Table S3-A details the prospect universe for each of the 15 orchestras. A summary appears in Figure 27.

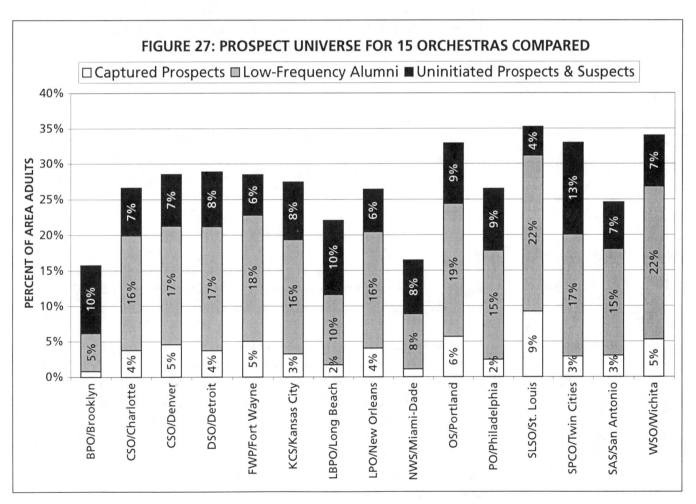

FIGURE 27: PROSPECT UNIVERSE FOR 15 ORCHESTRAS COMPARED

□ Captured Prospects ▨ Low-Frequency Alumni ■ Uninitiated Prospects & Suspects

Orchestras with the largest prospect universes include the Saint Louis Symphony Orchestra (35 percent of adults), the Wichita Symphony Orchestra (34 percent), the Saint Paul Chamber Orchestra (33 percent) and the Oregon Symphony (32 percent). But there are major differences in the types of prospects for these orchestras. For

example, the Saint Paul Chamber Orchestra has by far the largest group of Uninitiated Prospects (13 percent), compared to just 4 percent for the Saint Louis Symphony Orchestra. In other words, the Saint Paul Chamber Orchestra has three times as many classical lovers in its market with no previous experience attending the Saint Paul Chamber Orchestra.

As noted earlier, the Saint Paul Chamber Orchestra shares it market with another major orchestra — the Minnesota Orchestra. The presence of a large, sophisticated pool of prospects for the Saint Paul Chamber Orchestra undoubtedly relates to the long and illustrious history of the Minnesota Orchestra. Still, the data suggest a deep vein of market potential for the Saint Paul Chamber Orchestra, if it can offer programs of interest to its prospect base.

In contrast, the Saint Louis Symphony Orchestra has already reached the vast majority of its prospect universe, and it serves the largest share of Captured Prospects of any of the 15 orchestras (9 percent). The Saint Louis Symphony Orchestra's potential for future audience expansion appears to lie in its ability to re-engage its large base of Low-Frequency Alumni (22 percent).

Aside from the Saint Paul Chamber Orchestra, the three other orchestras that operate in markets with other major orchestras have the smallest prospect universes. The Brooklyn Philharmonic and the New World Symphony both have prospect universes of 16 percent of adults in their markets (Brooklyn and Miami-Dade County, respectively). The Long Beach Symphony Orchestra claims a 22 percent prospect universe in its market, a custom geography of ZIP codes in southern Los Angeles County and northwestern Orange County. For all three of these orchestras, Uninitiated Prospects equal or outnumber Low Frequency Alumni. Not unexpectedly, the Brooklyn Philharmonic has twice as many prospects with no trial experience as alumni. Gaining a larger share of the potential audience base for these orchestras means creating marketing and programmatic "points of entry" for the large base of already-sophisticated classical consumers in their markets.

Other orchestras share similar prospect universes in the range of 25 percent to 30 percent of adults. By any standard, these are very large numbers, and by no means do we mean to suggest that all of these people — or even the majority of them — are ready to buy tickets to a local orchestra concert. By definition, however, they have already been to a concert by the orchestra (i.e., alumni), or their interest in classical music is substantial enough to warrant their inclusion in the prospect base.

Even if one considers only the most sophisticated prospects, the overall picture that emerges is of a high-quality prospect base of approximately two to three times the active audience base.

....

Even if one considers only the most sophisticated prospects, the overall picture that emerges is of a high quality prospect base of approximately two to three times the active audience base.

....

Orchestra Prospect Model — Segment Descriptions

One-page descriptions for each segment appear over the following pages. Appendix Table S3-B compares each segment along key attitudinal and behavioral variables.

Throughout the segment descriptions that follow, use of the term "local orchestra" refers to the specific Magic of Music participating orchestra.

Group 1: Captured Active Audience
Segment 1: Sophisticated Active Audience

(15 Market Weighted Average: 1.7 Percent of Adults)

Summary: These are sophisticated lovers of classical music who have a deep relationship with the specific local orchestra. These individuals report very high arts participation generally, with an emphasis on classical music. While they are likely to satisfy their hunger for classical music in multiple ways (including radio and recordings), they are frequently seen in the local orchestra's concert hall. The segment includes current subscribers and high frequency single-ticket buyers. They are most inclined of all segments to subscribe.

Classical Consumption Profile

- Very high classical music participation generally

- High consumption levels of all types of live classical product

- Very high consumption of classical music radio and recordings

- Most knowledgeable about classical music of all segments

- Self described "critical listeners" of classical music

Relationship with Their Local Orchestra

- Are all currently attending their local orchestra (within past year)

- Highest average frequency of attending local orchestra

- Very high social context (family and friends) for attending local orchestra

- They are active in the decision to attend — most have personally purchased tickets

- They live closest to the orchestra's venue of any segment

Demographics

- Highest percentage female (58 percent)

- Oldest average age of any segment — 52 years (tie with segment 2)

- 31 percent are retired (highest of any segment)

- 87 percent white

- 30 percent report household incomes over $75,000; 72 percent report a college degree or post-graduate studies

Consumer Behaviors

- Very acquisitive — most are always looking for information about cultural activities

- They are active beyond attendance — more than half have volunteered for an arts or cultural organization, nearly three-quarters have made a donation to a nonprofit classical music radio station

Group 1: Captured Active Audience
Segment 2: Casually Involved Active Audience

(15 Market Weighted Average: 2.0 Percent of Adults)

Summary: These individuals also have a strong relationship with their local Magic of Music orchestra. However, this relationship does not appear to be as motivated by a profound appreciation of the art form. This segment is only moderately knowledgeable about classical music — they are more likely to be "casual listeners." While this segment also experiences classical music in a variety of ways — radio, recordings and live performances — their focus is less intense. The segment includes both current subscribers and higher frequency single-ticket buyers. These individuals indicate some inclination to subscribe.

Classical Consumption Profile

• Higher than average classical music participation generally

• Consume a variety of live classical product

• High ownership of recordings but only moderate consumption of new recordings

• They are moderately knowledgeable about classical music and only somewhat interested in learning more

• Are self described "casual listeners" of classical music

Relationship with Their Local Orchestra

• Are all currently attending their local orchestra (within past year)

• Moderate to high average frequency of attending local orchestra

• Very high social context (family and friends) for attending local orchestra

• Nearly three-quarters participate in a joint decision to attend or let someone else decide; however most have personally purchased tickets

• They live nearby the performance venue

Demographics

• 50 percent are married or partnered

• Oldest average age of any segment — 52 years (tie with segment 1)

• Are long-time residents of the area — average 34 years

• 85 percent white

• 39 percent report household incomes over $75,000; 55 percent report a college degree or post-graduate studies

Consumer Behaviors

• They are Responders — most would be more likely to attend cultural outings if someone else invited them

Group 2: Low/No Involvement Alumni
Segment 3: Sophisticated Low-Frequency Alumni

(15 Market Weighted Average: 1.7 Percent of Adults)

Summary: These individuals are also very sophisticated consumers of classical music. But they are significantly less likely to get their classical music fix through their local Magic of Music orchestra. These individuals report the second highest classical music participation generally but average only a single concert by their Magic of Music orchestra annually. Although these individuals experience classical music in multiple forms — radio, recordings and live performances — and multiple locales — home, work, concert hall and other venues — they are not frequently seen in the local Magic of Music orchestra's concert hall. Distance from the concert venue may be a barrier to attendance for these individuals — they report significantly longer drive time than their more active counterparts. The segment includes some former subscribers and low freq. single-ticket buyers.

Classical Consumption Profile

- High classical music participation generally and high consumption levels of all types of live classical product

- High consumption of classical music radio and recordings

- Highly knowledgeable about classical music and are interested in learning more; more than one-third consider themselves "critical listeners" of classical music

Relationship with Their Local Orchestra

- Most have social context (family and friends) for attending local orchestra

- 34 percent attended their local orchestra over the past year at an average rate of 1.2 times

- Three-quarters have personally purchased tickets, and one in five have subscribed in the past

- They live further away from the venue — average drive time 25 minutes

Demographics

- Highest percentage married or partnered (63 percent); average age — 50 years; 85 percent white

- 38 percent report household incomes over $75,000; 73 percent report a college degree or post-graduate studies — highest of any segment

Consumer Behaviors

- They are frequent attendees of other arts programs (12.4 times in past year)

- More than half have volunteered for an arts or cultural organization, and 70 percent have made a donation to a nonprofit classical music radio station

- Very acquisitive — most are always looking for information about cultural activities

Group 2: Low/No Involvement Alumni
Segment 4: Interested Single-Ticket Buyers and Ghosts

(15 Market Weighted Average: 4.4 Percent of Adults)

Summary: These individuals are only moderately sophisticated consumers of classical music. However, they are interested in learning more. They only have a limited relationship with their local Magic of Music orchestra. Compared to the other top segments, fewer of them have family and friends who attend concerts by the local Magic of Music orchestra. This segment is the most racially diverse of the top four segments. While the segment includes some former subscribers along with low frequency single-ticket buyers, they have a below average inclination to subscribe.

Classical Consumption Profile

- Low annual frequency of attending any classical music concert — two times on average

- Low to moderate social context for attending classical music concerts

- Likely to have a favorite classical composer and to a lesser extent a favorite classical composition

- Somewhat knowledgeable about classical music but are interested in learning more

- While most consider themselves as "casual listeners," 20 percent are self-defined "critical listeners" of classical music

Relationship with Their Local Orchestra

- Slightly below average social context (family and friends) for attending local orchestra

- 26 percent are currently attending their local orchestra (within past year) at an annual frequency of 1.1 times

- 59 percent have personally purchased tickets; 11 percent have subscribed in the past

- 40 percent are "very interested" in attending concerts in the future

Demographics

- 51 percent married or partnered; average age — 46 years

- 14 percent African-American; 13 percent Hispanic ethnicity

- 33 percent report household incomes over $75,000; 50 percent report a college degree or post-graduate

Consumer Behaviors

- Most desire to attend live performing arts events more often

- 79 percent would be much more likely to attend cultural outings if someone else invited them

Group 2: Low/No Involvement Alumni
Segment 5: Low-Interest Dabblers

(15 Market Weighted Average: 4.8 Percent of Adults)

Summary: These individuals are less sophisticated consumers of classical music, and they are not particularly interested in learning more about the art form. Their relationship with the local Magic of Music orchestra is limited. Less than one-third attended over the past year. Among those who did attend, frequency averaged once annually. These people are interested in attending live performing arts events more often, and nearly one-third are very interested in attending concerts in the future. They are not inclined to subscribe.

Classical Consumption Profile

- Low annual frequency of attending any classical music concert — two times on average

- Low to moderate social context for attending classical music concerts

- Less knowledgeable about classical music and less interested in learning more

- Most consider themselves as "casual listeners" of classical music

- Much lower ownership of recordings than top segments and very low consumption of new recordings

Relationship with Their Local Orchestra

- Average social context (family and friends) for attending local orchestra

- 26 percent are currently attending their local orchestra (within past year) at an annual frequency of 1.2 times

- 56 percent have personally purchased tickets; 10 percent have subscribed in the past

- 28 percent are very interested in attending concerts

Demographics

- 56 percent married or partnered

- Average age — 47 years

- 79 percent white

- 38 percent report household incomes over $75,000; 46 percent report a college degree or post-graduate studies

Consumer Behaviors

- 81 percent would be much more likely to attend cultural outings if someone else invited them

- Nearly one-third have volunteered for an arts or cultural organization, and nearly one-quarter have made a donation to a nonprofit classical music radio station

Group 2: Low/No Involvement Alumni
Segment 6: Special Occasion Only

(15 Market Weighted Average: 4.6 Percent of Adults)

Summary: Consumers in this segment could be accurately described as "unsophisticated" consumers of classical music. More than half of these people describe themselves as being "not very knowledgeable" about classical music. Their interest in learning more about classical music is substantially less than most other segments. Their relationship with the local orchestra may be best defined as sporadic. Less than one-quarter attended over the past year, averaging only one performance. One-third are classified as "Family Occasion" classical consumers in the art form model. Their attendance revolves around family programs, special holiday concerts and other special occasions.

Classical Consumption Profile

- Low annual frequency of attending any classical music concert — one to two, times on average

- Very low social context for attending classical music concerts

- Less knowledgeable about classical music and less interested in learning more; most consider themselves as "casual listeners" of classical music

- Own few classical recordings and have purchased few new recordings

Relationship with Their Local Orchestra

- Below average social context (family and friends) for attending local orchestra

- 19 percent are currently attending their local orchestra (within past year) at an annual frequency of 1.2 times

- Less than half have personally purchased tickets; only 3 percent have subscribed in the past

- 22 percent are very interested in attending concerts in the future, but they live further away from the venue — average drive time is 25 minutes

Demographics

- 60 percent married or partnered; average age — 47 years; 79 percent white, 13 percent African-American

- They have lived in the area longer than any other segment — 34 years on average

- 38 percent report household incomes over $75,000; 47 percent report a college degree or post-graduate

Consumer Behaviors

- 83 percent would be much more likely to attend cultural outings if someone else invited them; 19 percent let someone else make the decision to attend live performances

Group 3: Non-Users
Segment 7: Uninitiated Prospects without Social Context
(15 Market Weighted Average: 2.4 Percent of Adults)

Summary: These individuals are relatively sophisticated about classical music but have no history of attendance with the local Magic of Music orchestra. The probability of a future relationship with the local Magic of Music orchestra, however, is diminished by a total lack of social context for attending (i.e., none reported having family or friends who attend the local orchestra). Most are interested in attending live performing arts events in general, and more than one-quarter are very interested in attending local orchestra concerts in the future. This segment is racially diverse. These individuals are also younger, have a shorter length of residence, and a longer drive time to the local performance venue.

Classical Consumption Profile

- Moderate annual frequency of attending any classical music concert — three times, on average

- Moderate social context for attending classical music concerts (generally), and moderate ownership and recent purchases of classical music recordings

- Somewhat knowledgeable about classical music with significant interest in learning more

- While most consider themselves as "casual listeners" of classical music, 25 percent are self-defined "critical listeners"

Relationship with Their Local Orchestra

- No social context (family and friends) for attending local orchestra

- None are currently attending their local orchestra (with past year), and none have personally purchased tickets

- 27 percent are very interested in attending concerts; most of the others are open to attending (69 percent);

Demographics

- 44 percent married or partnered; average age — 44 years

- 65 percent white, 17 percent African-American; 11 percent Hispanic ethnicity

- 28 percent report household incomes over $75,000; 50 percent report a college degree or post-graduate studies

Consumer Behaviors

- 78 percent would be much more likely to attend cultural outings if someone else invited them

- Nearly one-third have volunteered for an arts or cultural organization in the past, and approximately one-quarter have ever made a donation to a nonprofit classical music radio station

Group 3: Non-Users
Segment 8: Uninitiated Prospects with Social Context
(15 Market Weighted Average: 1.7 Percent of Adults)

Summary: These people are moderately sophisticated about classical music but have no history of attendance with the local Magic of Music orchestra. This segment is distinguished by the fact that most have friends or family who attend their local Magic of Music orchestra. Most are interested in attending live performing arts events more often. Attending the local orchestra, however, is not a high priority for most. Several factors may be behind this lack of interest. These individuals are younger, have a lower length of residence, and a longer drive time to the local performance venue.

Classical Consumption Profile

- Moderate annual frequency of attending any classical music concert — three times on average

- High social context for attending classical music concerts

- Somewhat knowledgeable about classical music, with some interest in learning more

- While most consider themselves as "casual listeners" of classical music, 17 percent are self-defined "critical listeners"

- Low ownership of recordings very low consumption of new recordings

Relationship with Their Local Orchestra

- None are currently attending their local Magic of Music orchestra (with past year), and none have personally purchased tickets

- Among those who have had past exposure none was as recent as six years ago

- Universal social context (family and friends) for attending local Magic of Music orchestra

- Most are open to attending but it not a high priority (97 percent); Only 1 percent report being very interested in attending concerts

Demographics

- 51 percent married or partnered; average age — 45 years

- 75 percent white

- 35 percent report household incomes over $75,000; 40 percent report a college degree or post-graduate studies

Consumer Behaviors

- 79 percent would be much more likely to attend cultural outings if someone else invited them

- 25 percent let someone else make the decision to attend live performances — highest of any segment

Group 3: Non-Users
Segment 9: Uninitiated Suspects

(15 Market Weighted Average: 3.6 Percent of Adults)

Summary: None of these individuals have ever attended a concert by their local Magic of Music orchestra. They have only a moderate level of involvement in the art form — enough so that they should be considered prospects but at the lower end of the spectrum within the group of people who connect with classical music.

CONSUMER BEHAVIORS
Related to Arts Attendance

In addition to the protocol areas discussed earlier, respondents to the public telephone surveys who passed the initial screener and qualified for an extended interview were also asked a series of questions pertaining to their consumer behaviors, especially the purchase decision process. These questions were replicated on the ticket buyer postal surveys, and results from both the ticket buyer and general population samples are discussed in this section.

Questions were designed to investigate:

- Acquisitiveness of information about cultural programs and print and radio sources for orchestra ticket buyers (market-specific, see Appendix Table 2A-1 for results)

- Respondent's typical role in the purchase decision process (Appendix Table 2B)

- Typical purchase decision timeframe (Appendix Table 2C)

- Previous use of the Internet for purchasing tickets to live performances and attitude about future use (Appendix Table 2F)

- Inclination to subscribe to performing arts programs, generally (Appendix Table 2G)

For the precise wording of these questions, consult the protocol section of the Report Appendix. A related series of questions about values and benefits is discussed in the next section of the Report.

Results begin to uncover the complex dynamics surrounding the classical consumer's purchase decision process and should be of some practical use to arts marketers working in all performing arts disciplines. While a comprehensive analysis of these variables is not possible in the context of this report, a few key observations follow.

Information Acquisitiveness (Appendix Table 2A-1)

Respondents were asked their level of agreement with the statement *"I'm always looking for information about cultural activities to do."* Results for this question will help arts marketers gain a better sense of who is on the receiving end of their advertising, promotions, calendar listings, etc.

Age does not seem to be a factor, although gender is; 52 percent of females "agree a lot" with this statement, compared to 43 percent of males. Another way of looking at this: females are 21 percent more likely than males to agree that they are highly acquisitive of information about cultural activities.

Marital status also appears to be related to acquisitiveness in that married respondents were significantly less likely to "agree a lot" (45 percent) that they are highly acquisitive of cultural information. This compares to single or never married (53 percent), divorced or separated (59 percent), widowed (52 percent), and partnered but not married (64 percent), the most acquisitive of all marital status groups. This does not seem to have much to do with presence of children in the household. Overall, people who live outside of marriage are much more likely to be actively looking for information about cultural events.

Similarly, non-whites (60 percent) agree more often than whites (48 percent) that they are always looking for information about cultural activities to do.

Ticket buyers, as one might think, are much more likely to be highly acquisitive of information about cultural activities, and results are not markedly different across subscribers, former subscribers and single-ticket buyers. Results do vary significantly, however, across markets. For example, the Brooklyn Philharmonic's ticket buyers and the New World Symphony's ticket buyers are twice as likely as other orchestras' ticket buyers to "agree a lot" that they're always looking for information about cultural activities. Perhaps this observation relates to the overall media climate in the New York and Miami markets, but it may also point to differences in the specific constituencies of these two orchestras, as compared to the others. In any case, results suggest that some orchestras have to work harder to reach potential ticket buyers than others do.

Respondent's Typical Role in the Decision Process (Appendix Table 2B)

How do decisions get made about attending live performances, and who makes them? A simple question reveals some interesting patterns. Respondents were asked to identify their typical role in the process of deciding whether or not to attend live performances. [Note that this question was not asked on the national survey.] There were three possible responses:

- I am the primary decision-maker

- I participate in a joint decision process

- Someone else usually decides and I go along

Across the 15 markets, 25 percent of potential classical consumers report that they are the "primary decision maker" when it comes to live performances, while 56 percent say that they typically engage in a joint decision process with one or more other people. Another 20 percent say that someone else usually decides for them (here we see another indication of the "passive audience" for arts events).

Ticket buyers, as one might expect, are more likely to be the primary decision makers (i.e., surveys were mailed to people whose names were in the orchestras' databases), although over half of ticket buyers, on average, report that they typically make joint decisions with at least one other person.

Most culturally active adults negotiate their concert-going activities with other people. For these consumers, a social dynamic is embedded in the purchase decision process.

While roles in the decision process have much to do with marital status, to some extent the results are counterintuitive. Sixty-five percent of married respondents, on average, reported that they typically make joint decisions, but 34 percent do not. Conversely, 71 percent of single/never married respondents say that they make unilateral decisions, but 28 percent do not (i.e., they make joint decisions). Widowed respondents are even more likely to make joint decisions (37 percent).

The important observation here is that most culturally active adults negotiate their concert-going activities with other people. For these consumers, a social dynamic is embedded in the purchase decision process. One implication is that arts groups can increase the likelihood of favorable decisions by adding "relationship enhancement" value to the activity (see next section), or by highlighting the implicit "relationship enhancement" value in the activity.

Purchase Decision Timeframe (Appendix Table 2C)

Respondents were asked how far in advance, typically, they plan leisure activities like going out to live performances. Nationally, 52 percent of the large base of potential classical consumers typically plan 10 days or less in advance of an activity, while 23 percent like to plan several weeks in advance, and 26 percent like to plan a month or more ahead of time.

Planning horizon is a key factor that distinguishes subscribers and single-ticket buyers, but not entirely. Only half of subscribers to the 15 orchestras say that they typically plan their leisure activities a month or more ahead of time. One might infer from this that orchestras have trained their subscribers to break their typical mode of planning, since subscription often involves planning eight to 12 months in advance of the concerts. It may also suggest that people use very different planning horizons for different types of activities. Liberal exchange policies are undoubtedly of help here.

Single-ticket buyers, in contrast, are much less likely to plan far in advance and generally prefer a little more spontaneous planning horizon. Thirty-six percent of single-ticket buyers typically plan their leisure activities within 10 days of the event, and another 37 percent typically plan several weeks beforehand. Another 28 percent of single-ticket buyers like to plan a month or more ahead of time.

There are some interesting relationships between demographic characteristics and planning horizon, but there is no obvious pattern. With respect to age, the youngest adults (18-34) are significantly more likely than older adults to have short planning horizons. Only 18 percent of young adults (18-34) typically plan a month or more ahead of time, and 27 percent typically plan several days to a week in advance.

Compared to full-time workers, retirees are somewhat more likely to plan in advance, and married and widowed respondents are significantly more likely to

report longer planning horizons, as compared to singles and divorced or separated respondents.

More research is needed to understand how people's planning horizons change and what lifestyle factors and psychological traits influence how and when people plan their arts activities.

Use of the Internet for Purchasing Tickets (Appendix Table 2F)

Across the 15 markets, 25 percent of the large base of potential classical consumers report having ever purchased tickets on the Internet to any live performance. The figures range from a low of 12 percent (Fort Wayne) to a high of 38 percent (Denver). Figures appear to be higher for the west coast cities (Portland, 34 percent, Long Beach, 31 percent) and lower for some mid-western cities (St. Louis, 21 percent, Wichita, 17 percent).

A number of factors may influence these figures, including the supply of live events (particularly large popular music concerts), the extent to which area promoters and producers have made online ticketing available, digital infrastructure and socioeconomic factors as well. The average age of respondents who answered affirmatively to this question is 39, while the average age of those who responded negatively is 47. Figure 28 illustrates results for this question by age cohort. Here we observe that respondents in the 35 to 44 age bracket are three times as likely to have ever purchased tickets online than respondents in the 65 to 74 age bracket.

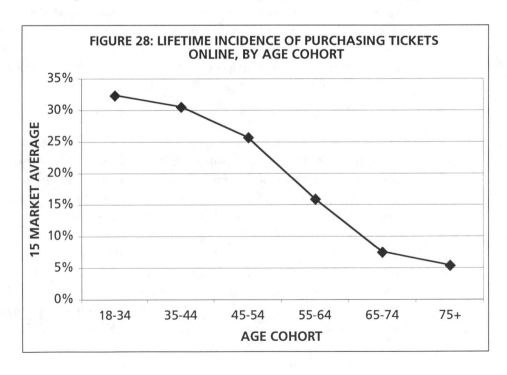

FIGURE 28: LIFETIME INCIDENCE OF PURCHASING TICKETS ONLINE, BY AGE COHORT

For those respondents who answered "No" to this question, a follow-up question was administered regarding likelihood of future online purchase. Among those who have not yet purchased a ticket online, an average of 10 percent say that they're "very likely" to purchase online in the future (average age is 41), and another 29 percent say that they're "somewhat likely" to buy online (average age is 42). A majority of these people, however (61 percent), say that they're "not very likely" to purchase online in the future (average age is 50).

Across the 15 orchestras, single-ticket buyers are substantially more likely than subscribers to have ever purchased tickets online (38 percent vs. 25 percent, respectively). Results for ticket buyers vary quite a bit from orchestra to orchestra, from a low of 21 percent for Fort Wayne Philharmonic single-ticket buyers and 22 percent of Wichita Symphony Orchestra single-ticket buyers to a high of 54 percent of Brooklyn Philharmonic single-ticket buyers and 51 percent of Louisiana single-ticket buyers.

Orchestras were also provided with data on what percentage of their ticket buyers have ever visited the orchestra's web site, and what percentage have ever purchased tickets via the web site (and if not, their likelihood of doing so in the future).

Inclination to Subscribe (Appendix Table 2G)

Of the large base of potential classical consumers, 8 percent are highly inclined to subscribe to performing arts programs (i.e., scores of nine or 10 on a scale ranging from zero, "not at all inclined", to 10, "extremely inclined"), and another 11 percent are moderately inclined (i.e., scores of seven or eight). The large majority of potential classical consumers (i.e., culturally active adults) are neutral about subscribing (30 percent) or disinclined (51 percent). Figure 29 illustrates comparable figures for ticket buyers and potential classical consumers.

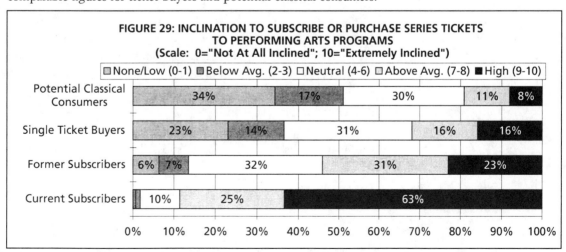

FIGURE 29: INCLINATION TO SUBSCRIBE OR PURCHASE SERIES TICKETS TO PERFORMING ARTS PROGRAMS
(Scale: 0="Not At All Inclined"; 10="Extremely Inclined")

□None/Low (0-1) ▨Below Avg. (2-3) □Neutral (4-6) □Above Avg. (7-8) ■High (9-10)

	None/Low (0-1)	Below Avg. (2-3)	Neutral (4-6)	Above Avg. (7-8)	High (9-10)
Potential Classical Consumers	34%	17%	30%	11%	8%
Single Ticket Buyers	23%	14%	31%	16%	16%
Former Subscribers	6%	7%	32%	31%	23%
Current Subscribers		10%	25%	63%	

Classical Music Consumer Segmentation Study
Final Report

Compared to the large base of potential classical consumers, larger percentages of all types of orchestra ticket buyers are inclined to subscribe, as one might expect, and it is interesting to compare figures for current subscribers, former subscribers that are now attending on a single-ticket basis, and single-ticket buyers who've never subscribed to the local orchestra. Over half of former subscribers, it should be noted, are positively inclined to subscribe, although they have opted out of the subscription commitment. In comparison, just 16 percent of single-ticket buyers are highly inclined to subscribe, and again as many are moderately inclined. Two-thirds of single-ticket buyers are neutral or negatively inclined, despite the fact that orchestras invest a great deal of resources trying to convert these customers into subscribers.

Within the base of single-ticket buyers, younger people are substantially less inclined to subscribe. The average rating of inclination to subscribe for single-ticket buyers in the 18-44 age cohort is 4.2 compared to 5.4 for those in the 65-74 cohort and 6.8 for those age 75 and older.

Who subscribes? A comparison of the demographics of subscribers vs. single-ticket buyers highlights substantial differences. About half of subscribers across the 15 markets are 65 or older, and 17 percent are 75 or older (see Appendix Table 5E). Comparatively, half as many single-ticket buyers are 65 or older. Just 15 percent of subscribers across the 15 markets are under age 45, compared to 32 percent of single-ticket buyers.

Subscribers are almost twice as likely as single-ticket buyers to be retired (45 percent vs. 24 percent, respectively) and are significantly more likely than single-ticket buyers to have incomes above $150,000 (26 percent vs. 16 percent, respectively). Moreover, subscribers are half as likely as single-ticket buyers to have children in the household (12 percent vs. 23 percent, respectively).

Notwithstanding its advantages, subscription marketing acts as a filter on an orchestra's constituency that runs counter to the goal of attracting younger audiences.[52] Moreover, the lion's share of prospects for these orchestras — including many of those who are highly knowledgeable about classical music — are disinclined to subscribe.

Consider ratings for inclination to subscribe across the top three prospect segments for orchestras:

- Segment #1: Sophisticated Active Audience (average rating = 5.9)

....

[52] *"Common sense suggests that the current younger generation won't turn to classical music when they're older, because they take popular culture so seriously. So orchestras have begun to search for younger listeners, and it's fair to ask if they know how to do that." – Greg Sandow,* Music: False Notes – Dire Warnings About the Health Of American Orchestras Appear More Provocative Than True, *Wall Street Journal, Feb. 5, 2002.*

- Segment #3: Sophisticated Low-Frequency STB and Ghosts (average rating = 4.4 - 25 percent lower than segment #1)

- Segment #7: Uninitiated Prospects without Social Context (average rating = 3.8 - 36 percent lower than segment #1)

Recall that the scale for this question was zero ("not at all inclined") to 10 ("extremely inclined").

While 26 percent of consumers in the Sophisticated Active Audience segment are highly inclined to subscribe (ratings of nine or 10), just 17 percent of Sophisticated Low-Frequency STB and Ghosts report the highest inclination ratings, and just 8 percent of Uninitiated Prospects without Social Context. Again, these are the prospect segments that are most sophisticated about the art form.

Many consumers enjoy subscribing, and there are many good reasons why orchestras focus their marketing efforts on subscription. Nevertheless, results from the study suggest that reliance on subscription marketing is impeding the orchestras' ability to serve large cohorts of potential classical music consumers who are disinclined to subscribe for one reason or another.

One implication is that orchestras could benefit from creating alternate involvement opportunities (e.g., frequent buyer clubs, attendance in small social groups) that reward loyalty but do not require advance commitment. This was a focus of discussions with each of the 15 orchestras during the technical assistance phase.

VALUES AND BENEFITS
Associated with Classical Music

The final area of investigation of this study relates to benefits or "derived values" from listening to classical music and from attending live classical music concerts. This analysis is limited to ticket buyer data.

Benefits are the sum of product advantages or satisfactions that meet a customer's needs or wants. Benefit segmentation probes users' buying motives and is linked directly to the marketing discipline of consumer behavior.[53] Orchestras can use results of this analysis to craft more resonant marketing messages and — more importantly — to gain a clearer understanding of the range of reasons why people listen to classical music and why they attend orchestra concerts.

A great deal of qualitative research relating to benefits and values has been conducted with respect to arts attendance generally. Some of this research was discussed in the earlier section entitled "Toward a New Model of Classical Music Consumers." Until recently, however, few resources have been devoted to exploring the values, benefits and utility that consumers derive from listening to classical music and from attending live classical concerts.[54]

FIGURE 30:

Extrinsic	Occasion value
	Social interaction/social reference value
	Ritual/ambience value
	Relationship enhancement value
Intrinsic	Artistic/educational value
	Healing/therapeutic value
	Spiritual/self-enrichment value

The analysis plan for this line of investigation began with the design phase focus groups, during which respondents were asked to respond to a series of questions about why they attend orchestra concerts. A copy of the Summary Report from the design phase focus groups may be found in the Report Appendix. Based on data from these focus groups, seven "value clusters" were defined for further investigation on the ticket buyer surveys. The seven value clusters, illustrated in Figure 30, are

---

[53] Market Segmentation *by Art Weinstein (1994, McGraw-Hill).*

---

[54] *During the period of this study, the American Symphony Orchestra League conducted substantial research on audience motivations. Results are proprietary to the ASOL member orchestras that contributed financially to that study, so it has not been possible to reconcile the findings of this study with the findings of the ASOL study, although such a dialogue could be beneficial to the orchestra field.*

divided into two categories: intrinsic values that can be derived from listening to classical music in any setting and extrinsic values that are particular to the live concert experience and do not relate specifically to the music.

It is important to recognize that the value clusters are not mutually exclusive and that there are at least several aspects to each cluster. In other words, they are not perfectly distinct from each other and may overlap in many combinations. Focus group data suggest that they are different enough, however, to consider individually.

To test each of these value clusters, a series of 26 statements was crafted and tested in the Charlotte Symphony ticket-buyer survey. Based on an analysis of responses to these statements, the list of 26 statements was narrowed down to 14, which were included in each of the other 14 orchestra's ticket-buyer surveys. Following is a key to the statements used to evaluate each value cluster.

Seven Value Clusters and 14 Statements

Respondents to the ticket-buyer postal surveys were asked to indicate their level of agreement with each of the following statements using a scale of zero ("Strongly Disagree") to 10 ("Strongly Agree"). Each statement expresses a somewhat different aspect of the value cluster. Mean values for all respondents to the ticket-buyer surveys are in parentheses following each statement. Complete results may be found in Appendix Tables B1-A (subscribers), B1-B (former subscribers) and B1-C (single-ticket buyers).

Therapeutic/healing value

1. "Classical music is an important healing force in my life." (5.7)

2. "Listening to classical music helps me make it through difficult times." (6.4)

Artistic/educational value

3. "Hearing specific artists and repertoire is what I value most about the concert experience." (6.8)

4. "I carefully read program notes and enjoy the educational aspect of a classical music concert." (7.6)

Spiritual/self-enrichment value

5. "Classical music connects me with a higher power." (5.0)

6. "Attending classical concerts is an important way that I nourish my soul." (5.9)

Occasion value

7. "I go to classical concerts to celebrate birthdays, anniversaries and other special occasions." (3.1)

8. "I am very likely to take visiting friends and family to classical concerts." (5.2)

Relationship enhancement value

9. "Going to classical music concerts is a great way to strengthen personal relationships." (4.6)

10. "I nurture people that I care about by taking them to classical music concerts." (4.3)

Social interaction/social reference value

11. "I wish that there were more opportunities to socialize at concerts." (3.6)

12. "For me, going out to dinner beforehand is an essential part of the concert experience." (3.6)

Ritual/ambience value

13. "People should dress up and look sharp when they go to classical music "concerts. (6.4)

14. "The ambience and architectural setting is an important part of the concert experience for me." (6.7)

Results for these rating questions help to paint a picture of how these different value statements resonate with ticket buyers, as independent statements. But further information is needed to understand how consumers prioritize the seven value clusters. Hence, a separate ranking question was included in five of the orchestras' postal surveys (cycle 3 mailing) to assess the relative importance of each value cluster. The question was worded as follows:

> *People value different things about the concert experience. Following are seven types of benefits and values that some people associate with attending live classical concerts. Read all seven items, then rank them in order of their value to you. (Write in a number next to each line, with "1" indicating your highest value, and "7" indicating your lowest value, etc.)*

Complete results for each of the five orchestras may be found in Appendix Table B2. Figure 31 compares average rankings for the seven value clusters based on all responses.

FIGURE 31.
VALUE CLUSTER RANKINGS
(source: five orchestra ticket buyer surveys, n=3,054)

Avg. Rank (1-7)

2.0	Artistic or educational value (intrinsic)
2.9	Spiritual or self-enrichment value (intrinsic)
4.3	Therapeutic or healing value (intrinsic)
4.4	Value of the ambience/architectural setting (extrinsic)
4.5	Social/community interaction value (extrinsic)
4.6	An opportunity to enhance your personal relationships (extrinsic)
5.5	An opportunity to celebrate special occasions (extrinsic)

General observations:

• Current ticket buyers value the intrinsic benefits associated with listening to classical music (e.g., healing value) much more than the extrinsic benefits (e.g., occasion value). This helps to explain why radio and recordings are the dominant modes of consumption of classical music.

• "Artistic or educational value' was ranked as the number one value by 57 percent of ticket buyers. Put another way, 43 percent of ticket buyers value other things more than the *prima face* artistic or educational value.

• A quarter of the ticket buyers who responded to this question ranked "spiritual or self-enrichment value" as the number one value among the seven listed, and 56 percent ranked it first or second.

• Many current ticket buyers value the ritualistic aspect of the concert experience — the formality, ambience and architectural setting. In fact, results suggest that most ticket buyers would value "ambience enhancements."[55]

• For several of the value clusters, results were distributed almost evenly, suggesting that different people in the audience value different things about classical music and the concert experience. For example, approximately the same percentage of ticket buyers ranked "value of the ambience/architectural setting" as the second highest value as ranked it seventh (last). A similar pattern was observed for "social/community interaction value."

---

[55] *For an excellent discussion of the visual aspects of the classical concert experience from the perspective of a musician, see violinist David Lasserson's article* Are Concerts Killing Music? *in* The Guardian, *July 19, 2002, which may be accessed from the www.guardian.co.uk web site. Also, award-winning sound editor Walter Murch offers extraordinary insight on the relationship between sight and sound in his essay* Stretching Sound To Help the Mind See, *The New York* Times, *October 1, 2000. (www.nytimes.com)*

FIGURE 1: LAYERS OF VALUE AROUND CLASSICAL MUSIC AND THE CONCERT EXPERIENCE

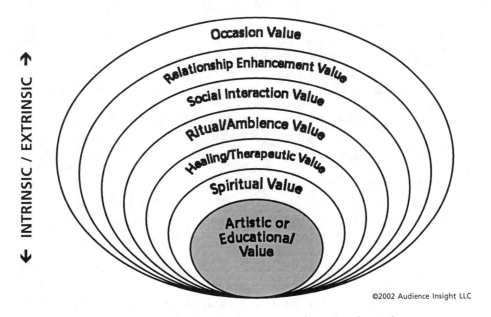

©2002 Audience Insight LLC

Figure 1 illustrates the seven layers of value surrounding the classical concert experience, in order of their overall importance to current ticket buyers. Altogether, the qualitative and quantitative data suggest that each classical consumer seeks a unique set of values around the live concert experience, some of which may be intrinsic and some of which may be extrinsic to the musical performance. In other words, each current ticket buyer places different weights on each value cluster.

All values contribute to the core "artistic or educational value" of the concert experience, which is valued differently by each ticket buyer. Any value or combination of values may be important enough to trigger purchase or consent to attend.

Focus group data indicates that some people will not attend classical concerts on their own, but will attend if a friend invites them to go with a small group in which they'll feel comfortable. For these consumers, "social reference value" is of paramount importance and triggers consent to attend. The same consumer may have strongly positive beliefs about the worthiness of going to classical concerts, but this alone is not sufficient to trigger attendance.

Another consumer might construct a much more complex and nuanced set of values around the concert setting (e.g., a church) and highly value both the spiritual aspect of the concert (i.e., a transformation opportunity) and the art itself (e.g., a sacred choral work).

It is important here not to confuse purchase decision factors (i.e., ticket price, concert time, exchange policy, guest artists and specific repertoire to be performed, etc.) with values surrounding the classical concert experience. Purchase decision factors are variables in the marketing mix that can be controlled by the orchestra, more or less. Values are deeply held beliefs and feelings about classical music and classical concerts that each current ticket buyer brings to the attendance decision.

How Values Vary Across Different Groups of Classical Consumers

A great deal of further analysis is necessary to understand more about what these data tell us and how orchestra's can put this information to work. A cursory analysis reveals that:

- Younger ticket buyers are more likely to value the extrinsic benefits of the concert experience (e.g., ambience value, occasion value, social interaction value), while older ticket buyers with more experience are more likely to value the intrinsic benefits (e.g., artistic value, spiritual value).

- The youngest ticket buyers (age 18-34) are as likely as the oldest ticket buyers (age 75 and older) to value the formality of the concert experience. Middle-aged ticket buyers (age 45-54) are the least likely to value formality.

- Hispanic ticket buyers are more likely than non-Hispanics to value formality.

- Ticket buyers with the lowest educational attainment (high school graduate or less) are more likely than those with graduate school educations to value the formality of the concert experience.

- Women are more likely than men to value the "relationship enhancement" aspect of classical concerts, as well as younger buyers ages 35-44.

- Women are quite a bit more likely than men to appreciate the "spiritual/self-enrichment value" of classical music.

- Asians and Hispanics are much more likely than whites to value the "relationship enhancement" and "social/community interaction" aspects of classical concerts, and they are also more likely to appreciate the "spiritual value."

- As educational attainment rises, so does appreciation for the "artistic or educational" aspects of classical music.

This line of questioning was limited to the ticket buyer surveys, so it is only possible to generalize about ticket buyers' values, and not prospects'. Inferences can be made, however, by comparing data for "critical listeners" (10% of the large base of potential classical consumers) and "casual listeners" (78%). Figure 32 lists average rankings of the seven value clusters for the two types of listeners.

FIGURE 32.
VALUE CLUSTER RANKINGS: CRITICAL VS. CASUAL LISTENERS

(source: five orchestra ticket buyer surveys, n=3,054)

	Avg. Rank (1-7)	
	Critical Listeners	Casual Listeners
Artistic or educational value	1.9	2.0
Spiritual or self-enrichment value	2.6	3.2
Therapeutic or healing value	4.1	4.6
Value of the ambience/architectural setting	4.6	4.3
Social/community interaction value	4.7	4.4
An opportunity to enhance your personal relationships	4.8	4.5
An opportunity to celebrate special occasions	5.4	5.1

Both groups place the greatest value on the artistic and educational aspect of the concert experience. Critical listeners, however, are more in tune with the spiritual and therapeutic values surrounding the artistic experience, while casual listeners are more likely to value what's not happening on stage — the ambience and architectural setting, as well as each of extrinsic value clusters.

Closing Note

The narrative portion of this report now draws to a close. The Classical Music Consumer Segmentation Study covered a wide range of topics, some general and some specific to classical music. We hope that the report stimulates interest in further analysis. All of the data files, protocols and results are publicly available. Electronic copies of the report are available through the Knight Foundation's web site at www.knightfdn.org. For more information about obtaining the data files, see the methodology section in the report appendix.

For technical information about the study or for information about obtaining additional copies of the report, email Audience Insight at info@audienceinsight.com, or call 203-256-1616.

REPORT
Appendix

RESEARCH GOALS
& Objectives

Purpose

The overall purpose of this study is to advance the participating orchestra's knowledge of their audiences and markets and to develop a conceptual model that will assist the orchestras in understanding prospects and in capturing additional market potential.

General Goals

- To provide orchestras with high-quality market research data on their audiences and market areas, as general marketing support

- To better understand the potential for increased attendance in each of the 15 markets

- To apply some of the theoretical constructs of consumer behavior to the marketing of classical music concerts

- To develop a general conceptual framework or "market model" for classical music consumers for use in developing more effective marketing strategies, with a focus on defining and profiling different types of prospects

- To stimulate the participating orchestras to design and test new marketing strategies based on the research results

Specific Objectives (RQ = Research Question)

Objective 1

To segment the aggregated customer bases of 15 orchestras by product usage: product category (i.e., classical, pops, holiday, etc.) type of ticket, tenure, dollar amount and other usage variables

RQ: What defines "heavy use?"

RQ: When do active buyers become inactive? After one season? Two seasons?

RQ: How can STB best be sub-divided by product usage?

Objective 2

To build a multi-dimensional profile of the aggregated customer databases of 15 orchestras using appended data sources, for use by all study participants

RQ: What are the geodemographic profiles of orchestra buyers in 15 markets?

RQ: How do other appended variables (e.g., wealth rating, length of residence) compare to the base population of the aggregated 15 markets?

RQ: What other appended variables might be useful to orchestras?

RQ: What is the relationship between distance and draw? What products are "long-distance" ticket buyers more likely to buy? At what distance or drive time from the venue should orchestras stop trying to acquire new ticket buyers?

RQ: Can orchestras develop a general predictive model for direct mail response, using in-house and appended data?

Objective 3

To develop a theoretical model for the different ways in which consumers relate to classical music

RQ: Aside from attendance at live concerts, how else do people experience classical music?

RQ: What levels of knowledge about the art form are associated with attendance at live concerts?

RQ: To what extent do preference levels for different types of classical music vary (i.e, chamber music, orchestral music, vocal recitals, choral works, etc.)?

RQ: What critical behaviors or attitudes distinguish prospects from buyers, and prospects from non-prospects?

RQ: How can consumers be grouped according to their relationship with the art form?

RQ: What percentage of adults can be called "classical music consumers?"

Objective 4

To develop a theoretical model for the range of relationships that consumers have with individual orchestras

RQ: Across the 15 markets, what are the ranges of awareness levels, incidence rates for trial (i.e., "ever attended") and repeat purchase, recent purchase, and key attitudes and opinions about orchestras?

RQ: What proportion of "classical music consumers" have a pre-existing relationship with their home area orchestra, and what proportion of "classical music consumers" have no relationship with their home area orchestra?

RQ: What "barriers" or personal characteristics are associated with "classical music consumers" who do not attend concerts offered by their home area orchestra?

RQ: What proportion of "classical music consumers" are (and are not) open to live concert attendance under any circumstances?

RQ: What are the attitudes about subscribing across the prospect base?

RQ: How can consumers be grouped according to their relationship a specific orchestra?

Objective 5

To understand "classical music consumers" in terms of the benefits they seek and the values they derive from attending live classical music concerts

RQ: What benefits do classical music consumers seek from the live concert experience? What psychological, social and emotional values do they derive from the experience?

RQ: Are these benefits hierarchical in any way, or mutually exclusive, or correlated with each other?

Objective 6

To develop a simple and intuitive segmentation model for classical music consumers (active buyers, prospects, suspects, all others) that orchestra managers will find useful in designing marketing campaigns

RQ: What dimensions of the model are most helpful in conceptualizing prospects? Buyers?

RQ: What factors are most closely associated with "prime prospects?"

RQ: How many segments should be defined?

RQ: Can we hypothesize how people move through the model?

Objective 7

To build profiles for each segment using a number of relevant dimensions such as demographics, other leisure activities, etc.

RQ: What are the demographic profiles of each segment?

RQ: What other factors and personal characteristics can be cross-referenced with the different segments in order to make them most useful?

RQ: What other types of leisure activities are associated with each segment?

Objective 8

To develop a better understanding of the purchase decision process for different types of "classical music consumers"

RQ: What purchase decision factors are most valued by each segment?

RQ: How and when do they typically buy?

RQ: How much information do they want before deciding?

RQ: Where do they get their information?

RQ: What are the roles people play in the purchase decision process (e.g., initiator, passive agreement, right of refusal, etc.)?

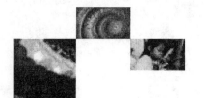

METHODOLOGY

National Classical Music Consumer Segmentation Study (March 2001)

The initiative began with a multi-method study to create and refine the public survey protocols and to build a national model of classical music consumers.

- A series of four focus groups were conducted in November 2000 with orchestra ticket buyers and prospects (non-buyers) in Charlotte and St. Paul. The overall purpose of the focus group research was to test protocol for the national telephone survey and to probe specific behaviors, attitudes and opinions related to classical music participation. The Summary Report from these focus groups may be found in the next section of the Appendix.

- In February 2001 the national public telephone survey protocol was tested in Charlotte and St. Paul. A total of 700 interviews were conducted across the two markets. Results from the pre-test were analyzed, and the protocol was refined. Ipsos Reid completed the fieldwork.

- Following the pre-test, a total of 2,200 telephone interviews with U.S. adults (age 18+) were conducted in March 2001 using a random digit dialing sampling method.[56] The margin of error for the total sample is +/- 2 percentage points at the 95 percent level of confidence. For the subset of 1,295 respondents who qualified as "potential classical consumers," the margin of error is +/- 3 percentage points at the 95 percent level of confidence.

- Based on data from the national study, a statistical model of potential classical consumers was constructed using cluster analysis. The model classifies respondents into 10 segments of potential classical consumers based on their connections to the art form. SDR Consulting of Atlanta assisted in the statistical analysis and model development.

Customer Data File Analyses for each Orchestra (2000 - 2001)

To assist in the definition of market areas for each orchestra, and to provide each orchestra with a detailed analysis of their current ticket buyers, Audience Insight prepared a Data File Analysis Report for each orchestra and an aggregate analysis for the 15 orchestras combined. Each orchestra was provided with a copy of the aggregate report along with a specific report on their own data file. The following analyses were provided for subscribers and single-ticket buyers:

- Market area definition analysis, including distance vs. draw analysis

- Market penetration analysis

- MicroVision analysis, including cross-profile correlations with consumers of other products and services

- Market quality analysis based on MicroVision

Also, each orchestra was provided with a comprehensive package of current demographic data on their custom-defined market geography.

15 Market Area Public Telephone Surveys (August 2001 - March 2002)

Approximately 750 telephone interviews were completed in each of 15 markets between August 2001 and March 2002. The geography to be sampled in each market was determined through an analysis of the orchestra's actual customer records (see table on the following page) and was defined as the area from which the orchestra draws approximately 85 percent its ticket buyers.

In sum, a total of 11,318 interviews were completed. The protocols were nearly identical to the national survey protocol, with the addition of series of questions about respondents' connections to the local orchestra. Also, each orchestra was allowed a small number of discretionary questions. The sampling methods were identical in each market (i.e., random-digit dialing).

Based on data from the 15 local phone surveys, another statistical model of potential classical consumers was constructed using cluster analysis. This model classifies respondents into eight segments of potential classical consumers based on their connections to the specific local orchestra. SDR Consulting of Atlanta assisted in the statistical analysis and model development.

Final Report Appendix

GEOGRAPHY DEFINITIONS: 15 PUBLIC TELEPHONE SURVEYS OF ORCHESTRA MARKETS		
Orchestra	**Market Area Definition**	**Approx. 2001 Adult Population (18+)**
Brooklyn Philharmonic Orchestra	Borough of Brooklyn (Kings County, NY)	1.8 million
Charlotte Symphony Orchestra	Area within a 25-mile radius of the Blumenthal Performing Arts Center	1.0 million
Colorado Symphony Association	Area within a 30-mile radius of downtown Denver	1.8 million
Detroit Symphony Orchestra Hall	Area within a 30-mile radius of Orchestra Hall	2.9 million
Fort Wayne Philharmonic Orchestra	Area within a 30-mile radius of downtown Fort Wayne	390,000
Kansas City Symphony	Area within a 30-mile radius of downtown Kansas City	1.2 million
Long Beach Symphony Association	An irregular area encompassed by 25 ZIP codes in and around Long Beach, CA (includes portions of southern LA County and northwestern Orange County)	657,000
Louisiana Philharmonic Orchestra	Area within a 35-mile radius of downtown New Orleans	938,000
New World Symphony	Miami-Dade County, Florida	1.7 million
Oregon Symphony Association	Area within a 30-mile radius of downtown Portland	1.3 million
Philadelphia Orchestra	Area within a 30-mile radius of the Kimmel Center	3.9 million
Saint Louis Symphony Orchestra	Area within a 30-mile radius of Powell Symphony Hall	1.7 million
Saint Paul Chamber Orchestra	Area within a 25-mile radius of Ordway Center (includes much of the Minneapolis area)	1.9 million
Symphony Society of San Antonio	Area within a 30-mile radius of downtown San Antonio	1.1 million
Wichita Symphony Society	Area within a 20-mile radius of downtown Wichita	355,000

*source: Claritas and Audience Insight LLC

Specific date ranges for telephone interviews in each of the 15 markets are as follows:

Orchestra Market	Dates of Phone Interviews
Brooklyn	Nov. - Dec. 2001 (delayed because of 9/11)
Charlotte	Jul. - Aug. 2001 (test site)
Denver	Feb. 2002
Detroit	Jan. - Feb. 2002
Fort Wayne	Sept. 2001
Kansas City	Feb. 2002
Long Beach	Jan. - Feb. 2002
New Orleans	Oct. - Nov. 2001
Miami-Dade	Jan. 2002
Portland	Feb. - Mar. 2002
Philadelphia	Feb. - Mar. 2002
Saint Louis	Sept. 2001
Saint Paul	Sept. 2001
San Antonio	Oct. 2001
Wichita	Sept. 2001

Postal Surveys of Each Orchestra's Subscribers and Single-Ticket Buyers (August 2001 - Feb. 2002)

A total of 1,500 machine-readable questionnaires (an eight-page booklet) were mailed to a random sample of each orchestra's subscribers (750) and single-ticket buyers (750). The mailings occurred in three cycles between August 2001 and February 2002. Each orchestra was assigned to one of the three survey cycles, as follows:

- Cycle 1: Brooklyn Philharmonic Orchestra, Charlotte Symphony Orchestra, Fort Wayne Philharmonic, Saint Louis Symphony Orchestra, Saint Paul Chamber Orchestra

- Cycle 2: Detroit Symphony Orchestra Hall, Kansas City Symphony, Louisiana Philharmonic, San Antonio Symphony, Wichita Symphony Orchestra

- Cycle 3: New World Symphony, Colorado Symphony Orchestra, Long Beach Symphony Orchestra, Oregon Symphony, Philadelphia Orchestra

Prior to each cycle of survey mailings, advance notice postcards were mailed to all respondents, inviting their participation in the survey effort. Several weeks after the first mailing, a second survey package was mailed to everyone who had not yet responded.

The overall response rate was 45 percent, and ranged from 35 percent to 60 percent for the individual orchestras. A Table of Cooperation Rates appears below. In sum, a total of 10,098 valid responses were received, including 5,553 from current

subscribers, 1,657 from former subscribers who are current single-ticket buyers, and 2,888 from single-ticket buyers who are not former subscribers.

In order to improve the quality of the data, every form that was returned was edited by hand to correct markings that were either too light or incomplete and to erase stray marks on the forms that would cause scanning errors. Verbatim answers to open-ended questions were also entered at this time.

Final Segmentation Model Development (April - July 2002)

Following the completion of all data collection, a third and final prospect model was developed for use in defining and characterizing the prospect universe for each orchestra in it's own market.

A final series of four focus group discussions was held in July 2002 in suburban Detroit to build out the profile of several of the key orchestra prospect segments. Focus group participants were pre-qualified through a postal survey and classified into the various prospect segments for subsequent recruitment by telephone. We wish to thank Julie Stapf and her colleagues at the Detroit Symphony Orchestra for their cooperation and assistance with these focus groups.

Response Rates

Cooperation rates for the general population telephone surveys are illustrated in Appendix Table N2. Rates averaged 38 percent across the 15 markets. The rate was 35 percent for the national survey. The formula for calculating cooperation rates was as follows:

$$\frac{\text{Total Willing to Participate (Completes + Midway Terminations + Call Back Mid-Interview)}}{\text{Total Willing to Participate + Refuse to Participate}}$$

Response rates for the 15 postal surveys are reported in Figure 33. Identical procedures were followed for each orchestra.

RESPONSE RATE ANALYSIS: TICKET BUYER POSTAL SURVEYS						
ORCHESTRA	Current Subscribers		Single-Ticket Buyers		Total Responses (1500 Mailed)	
	# In	%	# In	%	# In	%
Colorado Symphony	541	72%	360	48%	901	60%
Philadelphia Orchestra	452	60%	250	33%	702	47%
Wichita Symphony	418	56%	362	48%	780	52%
Saint Paul Chamber Orchestra	418	56%	361	48%	779	52%
Charlotte Symphony	418	56%	268	36%	686	46%
Fort Wayne Philharmonic	385	51%	375	50%	760	51%
Saint Louis Symphony	377	50%	275	37%	652	43%
Louisiana Philharmonic	371	49%	301	40%	672	45%
New World Symphony	362	48%	307	41%	669	45%
Long Beach Symphony	354	47%	253	34%	607	40%
Detroit Symphony	344	46%	329	44%	673	45%
San Antonio Symphony	342	46%	224	30%	566	38%
Kansas City Symphony	295	39%	315	42%	610	41%
Oregon Symphony	242	32%	277	37%	519	35%
Brooklyn Philharmonic	234	31%	288	38%	522	35%
15 SURVEYS COMBINED	**5,553**	**49%**	**4,545**	**40%**	**10,098**	**45%**

Weighting

To help correct for bias from non-response, mathematical weights were applied to the telephone survey final data sets (national and 15 local) to align the results with several key demographic figures for all adults in the applicable geography: age, race, income, education, and gender

The data were weighted using the strata weighting method. Strata weighting was selected to reduce the effects of interaction between variables. Thirty-two different strata were created using dichotomized variables: Age (55 and over/54 and under), Education (High School or less/Some college or more), Income (Less than $75,000/$75,000 or more), Race (white/all others), and Gender (Male/Female). For each possible combination, the percentages of the five variables were multiplied together to form the population incidence. Dividing the population incidence by the sample incidence produced the initial weight for each respective stratum. Additional weighting was conducted to account for missing data. Each market averaged about 175 cases with missing weights after the initial procedure because these respondents did not answer all of the demographic questions and therefore were not included in the initial strata weighting. The final weight variable brought all demographic variables to within 1 to 1.5 percentage points of the population incidence.

Appendix Table N presents both weighted and unweighted data for the numbers of potential classical consumers in each sampled geography. Generally, the weighting procedure had the effect of lowering most indicators of arts participation. The table below illustrates the weighting effects on several key variables from the Detroit area general population telephone survey:

	Unweighted	Weighted
Attended any classical music concert/past year	19.5%	14.7%
Would accept a free ticket to an orchestra concert	58.9%	54.7%
Qualified as "Potential Classical Consumer"	56.1%	49.5%
"Very Knowledgeable" about Classical Music*	6.2%	5.6%
Has a favorite classical music composer*	43.4%	42.3%
Critical listeners (self-defined)*	9.5%	10.3%
Ever listens to classical music on the radio*	64.2%	60.7%

sub-set of "Potential Classical Consumers"

Outliers

To reduce the effect of extreme observations on the calculation of mean values for some numeric variables, limits were set for acceptable answers. Valid responses were defined as follows:

VARIABLE	Valid Responses
Number of live performing arts events attended, past 12 months (Appendix Table 1E)	0-125
Number of classical music concerts attended, past 12 months (Appendix Table 1E)	0-125
Number on classical music recordings owned (Appendix Table 3P)	0-1500
Number on classical music recordings purchased, past 12 months (Appendix Table 3P)	0-100
Number of concerts by local orchestra attended, past 12 months (Appendix Table 4H)	0-30

Cluster Analysis

The two segmentation solutions (Dimension #1 and Dimension #2) were developed using the K-means cluster technique. K-means clustering is a nonhierarchical method that creates clusters of cases with maximum internal similarity while maximizing their differences from all other clusters. The method is suited for large data files. The procedure requires the researcher to select a target number of clusters. A single case is then assigned to each cluster so that the points are mutually farthest apart. Cases are then assigned to the cluster with the minimum distance between its mean and the cluster's centroid. The centroid's position is recalculated every time a case is added until all the cases are grouped into the final required number of clusters.

Creating each of the two segmentation schemes was an iterative process that involved reviewing and refining the model many times until the product was both

intuitive and statistically stable. In some cases, variables were recoded to reduce the number of variables and simplify the model. After the final models were approved, algorithms were created (i.e., SPSS syntax) for use in classifying each case into one of the segments.

A Note About Bias

In the current telemarketing environment, it is increasingly difficult and prohibitively expensive to reach every household that is randomly dialed. Our experience is that people with an interest in the survey subject matter tend to complete culturally-oriented surveys, despite the researcher's best efforts to complete the interview with eligible respondents selected at random. For example, people with higher education levels tend to complete general population surveys related to arts and cultural activities. As described above, generally accepted weighting techniques were used to reduce bias from self-selection. Ultimately, an unknown amount of bias from non-response remains in the data.

Other sources of bias must be recognized, including the acquiescent response phenomenon, in which respondents provide answers that they think the interviewer wants to hear. While the protocol was carefully designed to provide respondents with unbiased response choices, we cannot guarantee that respondents provided completely accurate answers. For example, in the national survey, respondents were asked if they have a favorite classical music composer and composition. Of the 43 percent of potential classical consumers who indicated that they have a favorite composer, 9 percent could not name one. Of the 24 percent of potential classical consumers who indicated that they have a favorite composition, 22 percent could not name one. We cannot know if these respondents provided acquiescent responses or whether they could not spontaneously identify their favorite composer or composition.

Another source of bias in the data relates to estimates of frequency of doing certain activities and is discussed in a footnote on page 72. Other research suggests that some respondents are likely to "telescope" their activity (i.e., compress time, such that they might count an activity that happened 14 months ago in an estimate of activity over the previous 12 months).

Data Resources and Archived Data Files

Figure 3 provides a thumbnail overview of the study's quantitative data resources and protocol design. Appendix Table N details the numbers of completed interviews and surveys for the various data collection efforts in each market.

In funding this study, Knight Foundation sought to create an information resource for the entire orchestra field, in addition to the 15 participating orchestras. The data sets are large and hold a great deal of potential value to the orchestra field and the arts industry in general.

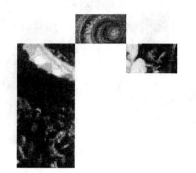

FIGURE 3: QUANTITATIVE DATA COLLECTION SUMMARY	# of Respondents	PROTOCOL SUBJECT AREAS					
		Screener (eight core questions)	Connections to the Art Form	Connections to the Specific Orchestra	Consumer Behaviors	Values and Benefits	Demographics
Phone Survey of U.S. Adults (March 2001)	2,200	X					X
Sub-set of Potential Classical Consumers (59%)	1,295	X	X		X		X
Phone Surveys of Adults in 15 Orchestra Markets	11,318	X					X
Sub-set of Potential Classical Consumers (52%)	5,905	X	X	X	X		X
Subscriber Postal Surveys (15 markets)	5,553	X	X	X	X	X	X
STB Postal Surveys (15 markets)	4,545	X	X	X	X	X	X

To encourage and facilitate further analysis, the three quantitative data files have been archived in electronic format (as SPSS data files) at the University of North Carolina's Odum Institute for Research in Social Science (IRSS):

1. Public telephone survey of U.S. adults (N=2,200)

2. Rolled up data file from 15 market area public telephone surveys (N=11,318)

3. Rolled up data file from ticket buyer postal surveys (N=10,098)

The files may be accessed through the Odum's electronic catalog at: www.irss.unc.edu.

For technical information about the study or for information about obtaining additional copies of the report, email Audience Insight at info@audienceinsight.com, or call 203-256-1616.

PROTOCOL:
National Telephone Survey

Section 1: Screener

[INTRODUCTION] Hello, my name is _____, and I'm calling for the Knight Foundation with a short survey about leisure activities in your area. This is a bona fide survey and does not involve sales or fund-raising of any kind. May I speak with someone over 18 years of age? [REPEAT INTRODUCTION, IF NECESSARY.] The survey takes about 10 to 15 minutes, and I can assure you that your answers will remain confidential. May I ask you some questions? Thank you!

1A. Arts activities may include attending live performances of music, dance or theatre, visiting museums and galleries, listening to recordings at home, or creating art yourself such as painting or singing in a chorus. Would you say that you are.... [READ ITEMS, DO NOT ROTATE] in arts activities? [ACCEPT ONE RESPONSE ONLY]

Extremely interested

Very interested
Somewhat interested
Not very interested
Not at all interested
DK/Refused [DO NOT READ]

1B. Would you say that arts activities play a major role, minor role, or no role at all in your life? [ACCEPT ONE RESPONSE ONLY]

Major role
Minor role
No role at all
DK/Refused [DO NOT READ]

1C. Now I'd like to ask how much you like or dislike a few different kinds of cultural activities. Use a scale of 0 to 10, with 0 meaning that you <u>dislike</u> it <u>a lot</u>, and 10 meaning that you <u>like it a lot</u>. OK?

The [first/next] activity is... [READ ITEM, DO NOT ROTATE ORDER. ACCEPT ONE RESPONSE FOR EACH]. In general, how much do you like or dislike [REPEAT ITEM]? [REVIEW SCALE IF NECESSARY] [NOTE: If respondent refers to particular experience, say: "We're interested in your overall feeling towards [ITEM]. IN GENERAL, how much do you like or dislike [ITEM]?

[RECORD RESPONSE 0-10]

ITEM LIST
visiting art museums or galleries
attending jazz concerts
attending stage plays
attending musical theatre performances such as Broadway shows
attending opera performances
attending ballet performances
attending classical music concerts

1D. Did YOU visit an art museum or gallery during the last 12 months?

Yes
No

DK/Ref

1E. With the exception of elementary, middle, or high school performances, did YOU [READ ITEM, DO NOT ROTATE, ACCEPT RESPONSE FOR EACH] during the last 12 months?

ITEM LIST
attend a jazz concert
attend a stage play
attend a musical theatre performance such as Broadway show
attend an opera performance
attend a ballet performance
attend a classical music concert

RESPONSE LIST
Yes
No
DK/Ref.

[IF 'attend a classical music concert = YES IN Q1E, ASK Q1F AND Q1G. OTHERS SKIP TO Q1H]

1F. About how many classical music concerts did you attend during the last 12 months?

[RECORD NUMBER — DO NOT ACCEPT A RANGE]
DK/Refused

1G. Now, think about the last time you attended a classical music concert of any kind. What was the name of the performance or the performers? [RECORD VERBATIM. DO NOT CODE. IF ANSWER IS NOT CLEAR, PROBE. POSSIBLE PROBES: What type of concert was that? What type of ensemble was that? (e.g., symphony orchestra, church choir concert, school band performance)]

1H. In total, about how many times did you attend live performing arts events of any kind over the last 12 months? [A ROUGH ESTIMATE IS OK.]

[RECORD NUMBER]
DK/Refused

1I. Have you ever volunteered for a nonprofit arts or cultural organization?

Yes
No
DK/Refused

1J. Would YOU like to attend live performances of music, dance or theater more often than you do now?

Yes
No
DK/Refused
[IF NO IN Q1J, ASK Q1K. OTHERS SKIP TO Q1L]
1K. Why not? [RECORD VERBATIM RESPONSE. DO NOT CODE.]

1L. If a friend or family member had FREE TICKETS to a classical music concert by a symphony orchestra and invited you to join them, would you like to go? [NOTE: IF RESPONDENT SAYS COULDN'T BECAUSE 'NO TIME' OR 'NO TRANSPORTATION', SAY: If that wasn't a barrier, would you like to go?]

Yes
Maybe/it depends
No
DK/Refused [DO NOT READ]

[IF ANSWER IS YES IN Q1L SKIP TO Q2A]

1M. What would keep you from going? [RECORD VERBATIM ANSWER, POST-CODE] PROBE: Any other reasons?

CONTINUE WITH Q2A IF ANY OF THE FOLLOWING RULES APPLY (THESE RULES INCLUDE ANY PEOPLE WITH A POSITVE PREFERENCE FOR CLASSICAL MUSIC OR WHO CURRENTLY PARTICIPATE IN STAGE PLAYS, MUSICAL THEATER, OPERA, BALLET, OR CLASSICAL MUSIC):

IF Q1C7>=5 (ANY PREFERENCE RATING FOR CLASSICAL MUSIC ABOVE 5), OR
Q1E2=1 (CURRENT STAGE PLAY PARTICIPATOR), OR
Q1E3=1 (CURRENT MUSICAL THEATER PARTICIPATOR), OR
Q1E4=1 (CURRENT OPERA PARTICIPATOR), OR
Q1E5=1 (CURRENT BALLET PARTICIPATOR), OR
Q1E6=1 (CURRENT CLASSICAL MUSIC PARTICIPATOR)

SKIP TO Q4A (DEMOGRAPHICS) FOR ALL OTHER RESPONDENTS OR IF OF THE FOLLOWING RULE APPLIES:

Q1L=3 (NO, WOULD NOT ACCEPT INVITATION)

[NOTE: THIS RESULTED IN AN ABBREVIATED INTERVIEW FOR ABOUT 40% OF THE TOTAL SAMPLE]

Section 2: Consumer Characteristics and Purchase Decision Factors

[ROTATE Q2A-F WITH Q2G, SO THAT 50% OF THE SAMPLE GETS EACH QESTION SET.] [SPLIT SAMPLE IN HALF RANDOMLY. TYPE 1 CONTINUES. TYPE 2 SKIPS TO INTRO TO Q2G]

2A. We're interested in how you decide to attend cultural programs. For each statement that I read, tell me if you agree a lot, agree a little, disagree a little, or disagree a lot. The [first/next] is... [READ ITEMS. DO NOT ROTATE. ACCEPT RESPONSE FOR EACH]

I'm always looking for information about cultural activities to do.
I'm the kind of person who likes to organize outings to cultural events for my friends.
I'm much more likely to attend cultural outings if someone else invites me.

Agree a lot
Agree a little
Disagree a little
Disagree a lot
DK/Refused [DO NOT READ]

2B. Typically, how far in advance do you plan leisure activities like going out to live performances? Do you typically plan... [READ ITEMS. DO NOT ROTATE. ONE RESPONSE ONLY]

The day of the event
Several days to a week beforehand
A week to 10 days beforehand
Several weeks beforehand
A month or more beforehand
DK/Refused [DO NOT READ]

2C. What is your... [READ ITEM. DO NOT ROTATE] of buying tickets to a live show of any kind? Is it ...[READ RESPONSE LIST]? . [EACH RESPONSE ITEM CAN ONLY BE GIVEN ONCE. SHOW REDUCED RESPONSE LIST ONLY WITH EACH ITEM.] [IF RESPONDENT SAYS DK, PROBE ONCE. IF STILL DK, MOVE ON TO Q2D.] [AUTOMARK 4TH MOST PREFERRED.]

ITEM LIST
most preferred method
second most preferred
third most preferred
fourth most preferred

RESPONSE LIST
By Mail
By Phone
On the web
In Person at the box office

2D. Have you EVER purchased tickets on the Internet for a live performance?

YES
NO
DK/Refused [DO NOT READ]

2E. Generally, how inclined are you to subscribe to or purchase series tickets to performing arts programs? Use a scale of 0 to 10, with 0 meaning <u>not</u> <u>at</u> <u>all</u> <u>inclined</u>, and 10 meaning <u>extremely</u> <u>inclined</u>.

[RECORD RESPONSE 0-10]
DK/Refused [DO NOT READ]

2F. Would you say that week nights, weekend nights, or weekend afternoons are the most convenient times for you to attend live performances? [ONE RESPONSE ONLY]

Week nights
Weekend nights
Weekend afternoons
DK/Refused [DO NOT READ]

[ALL WHO ANSWERED THIS SECTION - Q2A TO Q2F - SKIP TO INTRO TO Q3A]

Now I'd like to ask about the factors you consider when deciding whether or not to attend live performances.

2G. How important are each of the following factors to your decision to attend <u>any</u> <u>type</u> <u>of</u> <u>live</u> <u>performance</u>? Use a scale of 0 to 10, with 0 meaning <u>not</u> <u>at</u> <u>all</u> <u>influential</u>, and 10 meaning <u>extremely</u> <u>influential</u>. OK? The [first/next] factor is.... [READ ITEM, ROTATE ITEMS, REPEAT SCALE AS NECESSARY]

[RECORD RESPONSE 0-10 FOR EACH ITEM]

ITEM LIST
knowing if you can get good seats
being able to buy tickets at the last minute
the day and time of the performance
transportation arrangements
convenience of parking
safety concerns
whether or not your spouse or partner wants to go
if it's an activity for the whole family
if a friend invites you to go with them
if you can go out for dinner or drinks beforehand or afterwards
whether or not you have a special occasion to celebrate
the specific works to be performed
the likelihood of a high quality performance
the guest artists or featured performers
the cost of tickets
if tickets can be exchanged

Section 3: Relationship with the Classical Music Art Form

SCRIPT INSTRUCTIONS: Q3A, 3B, 3C ARE TO BE ASKED IN LOOP. IE. GO THROUGH SEQUENCE FOR FIRST ITEM AS MUCH AS APPLIES, THEN RETURN TO Q3A TO BEGIN SEQUENCE FOR NEXT ITEM.

Now I'm going to ask about your attendance at different types of concerts. Please answer "YES" or "NO."

3A. As an adult, have you EVER attended a... [READ FIRST ITEM, DO NOT ROTATE, ONLY READ EXAMPLES IF RESPONDENT ASKS OR SEEMS CONFUSED]?

YES
NO
DK/Refused [DO NOT READ]

[IF "NO/DK" TO Q3A, ASK Q3A FOR THE NEXT ITEM]
[IF "NO/DK" TO ALL ITEMS, SKIP TO Q3E]

3B. Was this within the past 12 months?

Yes
No
DK/Refused [DO NOT READ]

[IF "NO/DK" IN 3B, SKIP TO NEXT ITEM, ASK Q3A]
[IF "NO/DK" TO ALL ITEMS IN 3B, SKIP TO Q3E]

3C. Did YOU attend MORE THAN ONE of these concerts in the past 12 months?

Yes
No
DK/Refused [DO NOT READ]

[IF "YES" IN 3C, SKIP TO NEXT ITEM, ASK Q3A]
[IF "NO" IN3C, SKIP TO NEXT ITEM, ASK Q3A]

ITEM LIST FOR Q3A, 3B, 3C
pops concert by a symphony orchestra
classical concert by a symphony orchestra
chamber music concert (example: string quartet, piano trio, small chamber orchestra)
classical music recital by a singer or instrumentalist (example: piano recital, violin recital)
classical concert by a choir or vocal ensemble
performance of classical music by a concert band or symphonic band
a special holiday performance of classical music (example: Handel's Messiah, Tchaikovsky's Nutcracker)
a classical music concert geared for children or families

3D. Now think about where you've attended classical music concerts over the past year. Did you attend a live classical concert at a... [READ ITEM, ROTATE ORDER. ACCEPT RESPONSE FOR EACH] over the past year? How about a [NEXT ITEM]?

ITEM LIST
church or synagogue
school auditorium or gymnasium
concert hall, theatre or opera house
outdoor amphitheater
private residence

RESPONSE LIST
Yes
No
DK/Refused [DO NOT READ]

3E. How knowledgeable are you about classical music? Would you describe yourself as being very knowledgeable, somewhat knowledgeable or not very knowledgeable? [ACCEPT ONE RESPONSE]

Very Knowledgeable
Somewhat Knowledgeable
Not Very Knowledgeable
DK/Refused [DO NOT READ]

3F. How interested are you in <u>learning</u> <u>more</u> about classical music? Are you very interested, somewhat interested or not very interested? [ACCEPT ONE RESPONSE ONLY]

Very interested
Somewhat interested
Not very interested
DK/Refused [DO NOT READ]

3G. Do you have any close friends who go to classical music concerts?

Yes
No
DK/Refused [DO NOT READ]

3H. Does anyone in your immediate family go to classical music concerts?

Yes
No
DK/Refused [DO NOT READ]

3IA. We'd like to know how your interest in classical music relates to other art forms. Do you prefer... [READ ITEM, ROTATE ITEMS. ACCEPT RESPONSE FOR EACH] to classical music?

ITEM LIST
jazz
stage plays
musical theatre such as Broadway shows
opera
ballet
popular music like rock, rap, blues, or soul

RESPONSE LIST [DO NOT READ]
Yes
Equally
No
DK/Ref.

3IB. Would you describe yourself as a <u>critical</u> <u>listener</u>, a <u>casual</u> <u>listener</u>, or an <u>uninterested</u> <u>listener</u> of classical music?

Critical listener
Casual listener
Uninterested listener
DK/Refused [DO NOT READ]

3J. Do you have one or more favorite classical music composers?

Yes
No
DK/Refused [DO NOT READ]

[IF "NO" IN 3J, SKIP TO Q3L]

3K. Who is your favorite composer? [RECORD VERBATIM ANSWER. POST CODE. ACCEPT ONE RESPONSE ONLY]

[ALAPHA ORDER ANSWERS FROM THE PRE-TEST:]

Bach, Beethoven, Berlioz, Bernstein, Brahms, Britten, Chopin, Copland, Debussy, Dvorak, Gershwin, Glass, Grieg, Handel, Haydn, Janacek, Joplin (Scott), Liszt, Mahler, Mendelssohn, Mozart, Mussorgsky, Puccini, Rachmaninov, Ravel, Respighi, Rodrigo, Saint-Saens, Scarlotti, Schubert, Schumann, Shostakovitch, Sibelius, Strauss, Stravinsky, Tchaikovsky, Vaughan-Williams, Vivaldi, Wagner, Williams (John)

3L. Do you have a favorite classical music composition?

Yes
No
DK/Refused [DO NOT READ]

[IF "NO/DK" IN 3L, SKIP TO Q3N]

3M. Can you name one of your favorite pieces? [RECORD VERBATIM ANSWER. POST CODE. ACCEPT ONE RESPONSE ONLY]

[ALAPHA ORDER ANSWERS FROM THE PRE-TEST:]

1812 Overture (Rossini), Adagio for Strings (Barber), Appalachian Spring (Copland), Ave Maria (Schubert), Bolero (Ravel), Brandenburg Concertos (Bach), Cannon in D (Pachelbel)
Carmina Burana (Orff), Cavalleria Rusticana (Mascagni), Claire De Lune (Debussy), Don Giovanni (Mozart), Eine Kleine Nachtmusik (Mozart), Flight of the Bumblebee (Rimsky-Korsakov), Four Seasons (Vivaldi), Fur Elise (Mozart), March from Aida (Verdi), Messiah (Handel), Moonlight Sonata (Beethoven), New World Symphony (Dvorak), Nutcracker Suite (Tchaikovsky), Peter and the Wolf (Prokofiev), Piano Concerto n.1 (Tchaikovsky), Pictures at an Exhibition (Mussorgsky), Requiem (Mozart), Rhapsody in Blue (Gershwin), Ride of the Valkeries (Wagner), Rite of Spring (Stravinsky), Symphony #5 (Beethoven), Symphony #9 (Beethoven), Tales of Hoffman (Offenbach), Toccata and Fugue in D minor (Bach), Water Music (Handel), William Tell Overture (Rossini)

3N. How likely would you be to attend <u>symphony</u> <u>orchestra</u> concerts <u>more</u> <u>often</u> <u>than</u> <u>you</u> <u>do</u> <u>now</u> if... [READ ITEM, ROTATE ORDER]? Use a scale of 0 to 10, with 0 meaning <u>not</u> <u>any</u> <u>more</u> <u>likely</u>, and 10 meaning <u>much more likely</u>. [What about if...?]

[RECORD RESPONSE 0-10]

ITEM LIST
more people invited you to go with them
tickets were less expensive
there was more opportunity to socialize
orchestras played more familiar music
you could get half price tickets on the day of the concert
someone else did the driving
the concerts weren't so long

tickets were always available at the last minute
the quality of performances was higher
concerts were at more convenient times for you
getting tickets online was fast and easy
you could always exchange your tickets
conductors talked to the audience more

SCRIPT INSTRUCTION: Q3O AND Q3P ARE TO BE ASKED IN A LOOP; ASK Q3O AND THEN Q3P (IF APPLICABLE) FOR EACH ITEM BEFORE GOING ON TO NEXT ITEM AT Q3O.

3O. Do you ever [READ ITEM, DO NOT ROTATE. ACCEPT RESPONSE FOR EACH]?

listen to classical music on the radio
listen to classical music on records, tapes or CDs
listen to classical music through an internet web site
watch classical music programs on television or VCR

RESPONSE LIST
Yes
No
DK/Refused [DO NOT READ]

[IF "YES" IN 3O, ASK Q3P FOR ITEM]
[IF "NO/DK" IN 3O, SKIP TO NEXT ITEM ON LIST AND ASK Q3O]

3P. About how often do you... [READ ITEM, DO NOT ROTATE] On average, would you say you do this [READ RESPONSES]?

ITEM LIST
listen to classical music on the radio
listen to classical music on records, tapes or CDs
listen to classical music through an internet web site
watch classical music programs on television or VCR

RESPONSE LIST
Daily
Several times a week
Several times a month
Several times a year
DK/Refused [DO NOT READ]

[IF DO NOT LISTEN TO RADIO, OR CASSETTES/TAPES/CDS IN Q3O, SKIP TO Q3R]

3Q. Do you listen to classical music radio or recordings ... [READ LIST, DO NOT ROTATE. ACCEPT RESPONSE FOR EACH]

ITEM LIST
at home
in a car
at work

RESPONSE LIST
Yes
No
DK/Ref.

3R. Have you ever made a donation to a nonprofit radio station that plays classical music?

Yes
No

DK/Refused [DO NOT READ]

3S. Approximately how many classical music records, tapes and CDs do you own?

[RECORD NUMBER — DO NOT ACCEPT A RANGE; ASK FOR BEST GUESS IF NECESSARY]
DK/Refused [DO NOT READ]

3T. Over the past 12 months about how many classical music records, tapes and CDs have you purchased?

[RECORD NUMBER — DO NOT ACCEPT A RANGE; ASK FOR BEST GUESS IF NECESSARY]
DK/Refused [DO NOT READ]

Section 4: Demographics

We're almost through. Just a few more questions.

4A. What is your living situation? Are you: [READ LIST] [ONE RESPONSE ONLY]

Married or partnered
Single/never married
Divorced or separated
Widowed
DK/Refused [DO NOT READ]

4B. Altogether, how many people live in your household, including yourself, and all other adults as well as children?

One/self only
More than one [RECORD NUMBER]
DK/Refused [DO NOT READ]

[IF ANSWER IS "ONE/SELF ONLY" IN 4B, SKIP TO Q4E]

4C. Are there any children in your household?

Yes
No
DK/Refused

[IF "NO/DK" IN 4C, SKIP TO Q4E]

4D. How many are children ages [READ ITEM]?

[RECORD NUMBER IN EACH AGE RANGE. STOP ASKING IF TOTAL NUMBER IN Q4D EQUALS RESPONSE IN Q4B MINUS 1.]

ITEM LIST
6 or under
7 to 12
13 to 17
Older than 17

4E. What is the last level of school you completed? Did you...? [READ LIST]

Attend Grade School Only
Attend High School but not complete it
Complete High School
Attend Some College
Get a College Degree
Attend some Post College
DK/Refused [DO NOT READ]

4F. In what year were you born?

Year Born [WRITE IN YEAR OF BIRTH. RECORD 4 DIGITS]
DK/Refused [DO NOT READ]

4G. What is your employment status? Are you currently: [READ, DO NOT ROTATE]

Working full-time for pay
Working part-time for pay
Retired
A homemaker
Unemployed but looking for work
In school full-time
Refused [DO NOT READ]

[IF MARRIED/PARTNERED IN Q4A, ASK Q4H. OTHERS SKIP TO Q4I)
4H. What is your spouse's employment status? [READ LIST IF NECESSARY]

Working full-time for pay
Working part-time for pay
Retired
A homemaker
Unemployed but looking for work
In school full-time
Refused [DO NOT READ]

4IA. Are you ... ... [READ LIST. ENTER SINGLE RESPONSE.]

White
Black
Asian
Other [SPECIFY]
Refused [DO NOT READ]

4IB. Are you of Hispanic ethnicity?

Yes
No
Refused [DO NOT READ]

4J. Is your total family income before taxes: [READ LIST]

Less than $75,000
$75,000 or more
Refused [DO NOT READ]

[IF '$75,000 OR MORE' IN 4J, SKIP TO 4L]
[IF "REFUSED" IN 4J, SKIP TO Q4M]

4K. Is your total family income before taxes: [READ LIST]

Under $35,000
From $35,000 to just under $50,000
From $50,000 to $75,000
DK/Refused [DO NOT READ]

[IF ASKED Q4I, SKIP TO Q4M]

4L. Is your total family income before taxes: [READ]

From $75,000 to just under $100,000
From $100,000 to just under $125,000
From $125,000 to just under $150,000
From $150,000 to just under $175,000
From $175,000 to just under $200,000
$200,000 or more
DK/Refused [DO NOT READ]

4M. What is your home ZIP Code?

4N. [GENDER — BY OBSERVATION ONLY]

Male
Female
DK

That's everything. You've been extremely helpful. On behalf of the Knight Foundation, thanks so much for your cooperation.

PROTOCOL:
Local Market Telephone Surveys (e.g., Philadelphia)

Section 1: Screener

[INTRODUCTION] Hello, my name is _____, and I'm calling for the Knight Foundation with a short survey about leisure activities in your area. This is a bona fide survey and does not involve sales or fund-raising of any kind. May I speak with someone over 18 years of age? [REPEAT INTRODUCTION, IF NECESSARY.] The survey takes about 10 to 15 minutes, and I can assure you that your answers will remain confidential. May I ask you some questions? Thank you!

1A.   Arts activities may include attending live performances of music, dance or theatre, visiting museums and galleries, listening to recordings at home, or creating art yourself such as painting or singing in a chorus. **Would you say that you are**.... [READ ITEMS, DO NOT ROTATE] in arts activities?

Extremely interested	1
Very interested	2
Somewhat interested	3
Not very interested	4
Not at all interested	5
[VOLUNTEERED] DK/Refused	99

1B.   Would you say **that arts activities play a** <u>major role, minor role,</u> **or** <u>no role at all</u> in your life?

Major role	1
Minor role	2
No role at all	3
[VOLUNTEERED] DK/Refused	99

Now I'd like to ask how much you like or dislike a few different kinds of cultural activities. Use a scale of 0 to 10, with 0 meaning that you <u>dislike it</u> <u>a</u> <u>lot</u>, and 10 meaning that you <u>like it a lot</u>. OK?

1C.   The first [next] activity is... [READ ITEM, DO NOT ROTATE ORDER]. In general, how much do you like or dislike ...? [REPEAT ITEM. REVIEW SCALE IF NECESSARY.] [NOTE: THIS QUESTION DOES NOT REFER TO MOST RECENT EXPERIENCE AT A SPECIFIC SHOW.]

0-10 SCORE:
1C1.   visiting art museums or galleries . . . . _____
1C2.   attending jazz concerts. . . . . _____
1C3.   attending non-musical stage plays . . . . _____
1C4.   attending musical theatre performances such as Broadway shows. . . . . . . _____
1C5.   attending opera performances . . . . _____
1C6.   attending ballet performances . . . . _____
1C7.   attending classical music concerts . . . . _____

1D.   Did YOU... during the last 12 months?

	YES	NO	DK/Ref.
1D1. visit an art museum or gallery	1	 2	 99

With the exception of elementary, middle, or high school performances, did YOU... [READ ITEM, DO NOT ROTATE] during the last 12 months?

	YES	NO	DK/Ref.
1D2. attend a jazz concert	1	. . 2	 99
1D3. attend a non-musical stage play	1	. . . 2	 99
1D4. attend a musical theatre performance such as Broadway show	1	. . . 2	 99
1D5. attend an opera performance	1	. . . 2	 99
1D6. attend a ballet performance	1	. . . 2	 99
1D7. attend a classical music concert	1	. . . 2	 99

1D8.   [IF Q1D7="YES"] About how many classical music concerts did you attend during the last 12 months?

                                            Number . . . . ._____

        [VOLUNTEERED]   DK/Refused 9999

1D9.   [IF Q1D7="YES"] Now think about the last time you attended a classical music concert of any kind. What was the name of the performance or the performers? [RECORD VERBATIM. DO NOT CODE. IF ANSWER IS NOT CLEAR, PROBE.] What type of concert was that? [PROBE FOR TYPE OF ENSEMBLE (e.g., symphony orchestra, church choir concert, school band performance)]

1E.   In total, about how many times did you attend live performing arts events of any kind over the last 12 months? [A ROUGH ESTIMATE IS OK.]

                                            Number . . . . ._____

        [VOLUNTEERED]   DK/Refused 9999

1F.   Have you ever volunteered for a nonprofit arts or cultural organization?

                                            YES 1
                                            NO 2
                                            DK/Refused 99

1G.   Would YOU like to attend live performances of music, dance or theater <u>more often</u> than you do now?

                                              YES 1
                                            NO 2
        [VOLUNTEERED]   DK/Refused 9

1H.   If a friend or family member had FREE TICKETS to a <u>classical music concert by a symphony orchestra</u> and invited you to join them, would you like to go? [ASSUMING THAT RESPONDENT IS AVAILABLE AND TRANSPORTATION IS NOT A BARRIER]

                                            YES 1
                                            MAYBE/IT DEPENDS 2
                                            NO 3
        [VOLUNTEERED]   DK/Refused 99

CONTINUE WITH Q2A IF ANY OF THE FOLLOWING RULES APPLY (THESE RULES INCLUDE ANY PEOPLE WITH A POSITVE PREFERENCE FOR CLASSICAL MUSIC OR WHO CURRENTLY PARTICIPATE IN STAGE PLAYS, MUSICAL THEATER, OPERA, BALLET, OR CLASSICAL MUSIC):

IF Q1C7>=5 (ANY PREFERENCE RATING FOR CLASSICAL MUSIC ABOVE 5), OR
IF Q1D3=1 (CURRENT STAGE PLAY PARTICIPATOR), OR
IF Q1D4=1 (CURRENT MUSICAL THEATER PARTICIPATOR), OR
IF Q1D5=1 (CURRENT OPERA PARTICIPATOR), OR
IF Q1D6=1 (CURRENT BALLET PARTICIPATOR), OR
IF Q1D7=1 (CURRENT CLASSICAL MUSIC PARTICIPATOR)

SKIP TO Q5A (DEMOGRAPHICS) FOR ALL OTHER RESPONDENTS OR IF OF THE
FOLLOWING RULE APPLIES:

Q1H=3 (NO, WOULD NOT ACCEPT INVITATION)

[NOTE: THIS SHOULD RESULT IN AN ABBREVIATED INTERVIEW FOR ABOUT 40% OF THE
TOTAL SAMPLE]

Section 2: Consumer Characteristics and Purchase Decision Factors

2A.   We're interested in how you decide to attend cultural programs. For each
statement that I read, tell me if you agree a lot, agree a little, disagree a little,
or disagree a lot. [READ ITEMS. DO NOT ROTATE.]

1. I'm always looking for information about cultural activities to do.
2. I'm the kind of person who likes to organize outings to cultural events
   for my friends.
3. I'm much more likely to attend cultural outings if someone else invites me.

	Agree a lot 1
	gree a little 2
	Disagree a little 3
	Disagree a lot 4
[VOLUNTEERED]	DK/Refused 99

2B.   Which of the following best describes your role in the process of deciding
whether or not to attend live performances? [READ ITEM, DO NOT ROTATE]

	I am the primary decision-maker 1
	Someone else usually decides and I go along .2
	I participate in a joint decision process 3
[VOLUNTEERED]	DK/Refused 99

2C.   Typically, how far in advance do you plan leisure activities like going out to live
performances? [READ ITEMS. DO NOT ROTATE.]

	The day of the event 1
	Several days to a week beforehand 2
	A week to 10 days beforehand 3
	Several weeks beforehand 4
	A month or more beforehand 5
[VOLUNTEERED]	DK/Refused 99

2D.   I'm going to read a list of radio stations in the Philadelphia area. For each, tell
me whether you listen <u>regularly</u>, <u>occasionally</u>, or <u>never</u>. [READ ITEM, ROTATE
ORDER]

	READ REGULARLY	OCCASIONALLY	NEVER	DK/Ref.
1. KYW Newsradio 1060	1	2	3	99
2. WRTI 90.1	1	2	3	99
3. WHYY - 91FM	1	2	3	99
4. WWFM The Classical Network	1	2	3	99
5. WXPN 88.5	1	2	3	99
6. Smooth Jazz WJJZ 106.1	1	2	3	99

2E.   I'm going to read a list of publications in the Philadelphia area. For each, tell me whether you read **regularly**, <u>occasionally</u>, or <u>never</u>. [READ ITEM, ROTATE ORDER]

	READ REGULARLY	OCCASIONALLY	NEVER	DK/Ref.
A. *Philadelphia Inquirer*	1	2	3	99
B. *Philadelphia Daily News*	1	2	3	99
C. *Philadelphia Weekly*	1	2	3	99
D. *Jewish Exponent*	1	2	3	99
E. *Courier Post*	1	2	3	99
F. *Philadelphia Tribune*	1	2	3	99

2F1.   Have you EVER purchased tickets on the Internet to any live performance?

	YES	1
	NO	2
[VOLUNTEERED]	DK/Refused	99

2F2.   [IF "NO" TO Q2F1] How likely are you to purchase tickets online in the future? Are you <u>very likely</u>, <u>somewhat likely</u>, or <u>not very likely</u>?

	Very likely	1
	Somewhat likely	2
	Not very likely	3
[VOLUNTEERED]	DK/Refused	99

2G.   Generally, how inclined are you to subscribe or purchase series tickets to performing arts programs? Use a scale of 0 to 10, with 0 meaning <u>not at all inclined</u>, and 10 meaning <u>extremely inclined</u>.

0-10 SCORE:

	Inclination rating (0-10)	_____
[VOLUNTEERED]	DK/Refused	99

Section 3: Relationship with the Classical Music Art Form

Now I'm going to ask about your attendance at different types of concerts. Please answer "YES" or "NO."

3A.   As an adult, have you EVER attended a... [READ FIRST ITEM, DO NOT ROTATE, ONLY GIVE EXAMPLES IF RESPONDENT ASKS OR SEEMS CONFUSED]?

	YES	1
[SKIP TO NEXT ITEM, ASK Q3A]	NO	2
[VOLUNTEERED]	DK/Refused	99

IF "NO" TO ALL ITEMS, SKIP TO Q3D]
3B.   Was this within the past 12 months?

[SKIP TO NEXT ITEM, ASK Q3A]	YES	1
[SKIP TO NEXT ITEM, ASK Q3A]	NO	2
[VOLUNTEERED]	sDK/Refused	99

[IF "NO" TO ALL ITEMS, SKIP TO Q3D]
   1.   pops concert by a symphony orchestra
   2.   classical concert by a symphony orchestra
   3.   chamber music concert (e.g., string quartet, piano trio, small chamber orchestra)
   4.   classical music recital by a singer or instrumentalist (e.g., piano recital, violin recital)
   5.   classical concert by a choir or vocal ensemble

6.   a special holiday performance of classical music (e.g., Handel's Messiah, Tchaikovsky's Nutcracker)

7.   a classical music concert geared for children or families

3C.   Now think about where you've attended classical music concerts over the past year. Did you attend a live classical concert at a... [READ ITEM, ROTATE ORDER] over the past year? How about a....? [SKIP TO NEXT ITEM]

YES 1
NO 2
[VOLUNTEERED]   DK/Refused 99

1.   church or synagogue
2.   school auditorium or gymnasium
3.   concert hall, theatre or opera house
4.   outdoor amphitheater
5.   private residence

3D.   How knowledgeable are you about classical music? Would you describe yourself as being... [READ ITEMS, DO NOT ROTATE]?

Very Knowledgeable 1
Somewhat Knowledgeable 2
Not Very Knowledgeable 3
[VOLUNTEERED]   DK/Refused 99

3E.   How interested are you in <u>learning</u> <u>more</u> about classical music? Are you... [READ ITEMS, DO NOT ROTATE]

Very interested 1
Somewhat interested 2
Not very interested 3
DK/Refused 99

3F1.   Do you have any close friends who go to classical music concerts?

YES 1
NO 2
[VOLUNTEERED]   DK/Refused 99

3F2.   Does anyone in your immediate family go to classical music concerts?

YES 1
NO 2
[VOLUNTEERED]   DK/Refused 99

3G.   We'd like to know how your interest in classical music relates to other art forms. Do you prefer... [READ ITEM, ROTATE ITEMS] to classical music?

	YES	(do not read) EQUALLY	NO	DK/Ref.
1. jazz	1	2	3	99
2. non-musical stage plays	1	2	3	99
3. musical theatre such as Broadway shows	1	2	3	99
4. opera	1	2	3	99
5. ballet	1	2	3	99
6. popular music (for example, rock, rap, blues, or soul)	1	2	3	99

3H.   Would you describe yourself as a critical listener, a casual listener, or an uninterested listener of classical music?

Critical listener 1
Casual listener 2
Uninterested listener 3
[VOLUNTEERED]   DK/Refused 99

3I.   Do you have one or more favorite classical music composers?

YES 1
NO 2
[VOLUNTEERED]   DK/Refused 99

3J.   Do you have a favorite classical music composition?

YES 1
NO 2
[VOLUNTEERED]   DK/Refused 99

3K.   How likely would you be to attend <u>symphony</u> <u>orchestra</u> concerts <u>more</u> <u>often</u> <u>than</u> <u>you</u> <u>do</u> <u>now</u> if... [READ ITEM, ROTATE ORDER]? Use a scale of 0 to 10, with 0 meaning <u>not</u> <u>any</u> <u>more</u> <u>likely</u>, and 10 meaning <u>much</u> <u>more</u> <u>likely</u>.

SCORE (0-10)
1.   more people invited you to go with them . . . . _____
2.   tickets were less expensive . . . . _____
3.   there was more opportunity to socialize . . . . _____
4.   orchestras played more familiar music . . . . _____
5.   you could get half price tickets on the day of the concert . . . . _____
6.   someone else did the driving . . . . _____
7.   the concerts weren't so long . . . . _____
8.   tickets were always available at the last minute . . . . _____
9.   the quality of performances was higher . . . . _____
10.   getting tickets online was fast and easy . . . . _____
11.   conductors talked to the audience more . . . . _____

[SKIP TO NEXT ITEM, REPEAT Q]

3L.   Do you ever _____ [READ ITEM, DO NOT ROTATE]?

1.   listen to classical music on the radio?
2   listen to classical music on records, tapes or CDs?
3.   listen to classical music through an internet web site?
4.   watch classical music programs on television or VCR?

[ASK Q3M FOR ITEM]   YES 1
[SKIP TO NEXT ITEM ON LIST]   NO 2
[VOLUNTEERED, SKIP TO
NEXT ITEM ON LIST]   DK/Refused 99

3M.   About how often do you... [READ ITEM, DO NOT ROTATE] On average, would you say you do this [READ RESPONSES]?
1.   listen to classical music on the radio?
2.   listen to classical music on records, tapes or CDs?
3.   listen to classical music through an internet web site?
4.   watch classical music programs on television or VCR?
Daily 1
Several times a week 2
Several times a month 3
Several times a year 4
[VOLUNTEERED]   DK/Refused 99

[SKIP TO Q3O IF Q3L1="NO" AND Q3L2="NO"]

3N.   Do you listen to classical music radio or recordings ... [READ LIST, DO NOT
        ROTATE]

	YES	NO	DK/Ref.
A. at home?	1	2	99
B. in a car?	1	2	99
C. at work?	1	2	99

3O.   Have you ever made a donation to a nonprofit radio station that plays classical
        music?

	YES	1
	NO	2
[VOLUNTEERED]	DK/Refused	99

3P.   Approximately how many <u>classical</u> <u>music</u> records, tapes and CDs do you own?

	Est. Number	_____
[VOLUNTEERED]	DK/Refused	9999

3Q.   Over the past 12 months about how many classical music records, tapes and
        CDs have you purchased?

	Est. Number	_____
[VOLUNTEERED]	DK/Refused	9999

Section 4: Relationship with the Philadelphia Orchestra

Now just a few questions about your experience in the Philadelphia area.

4A.   For how many years have you lived in the Philadelphia area?

[use "0" for less than 1 year]	# of Years	_____
[VOLUNTEERED]	DK/Refused	99

4C.   Have you heard of the Philadelphia Orchestra?

	YES	1
[SKIP TO Q4O2]	NO	2
[VOLUNTEERED]	DK/Refused	99

4D.   Do any of your friends or family members attend concerts by the Philadelphia
        Orchestra?

	YES	1
	NO	2
[VOLUNTEERED]	DK/Refused	99

4E.   As an adult, have you ever attended a concert by the Philadelphia Orchestra?

[SKIP TO Q4G]	YES	1
[ASK Q4F]	NO	2
[VOLUNTEERED]	DK/Refused	99

4F.   [IF Q4E="NO"] Have you ever considered attending a concert by the
        Philadelphia Orchestra?

[SKIP TO Q4O2]	YES	1
[SKIP TO Q4O2]	NO	2
[VOLUNTEERED]	DK/Refused	99

4G.   As best you can remember, when was the last time that you attended a concert by the Philadelphia Orchestra? [READ EACH ITEM]

Within the past year	1
About 1 to 2 years ago	2
About 2 to 3 years ago	3
About 4 to 5 years ago	4
About 6 to 10 years ago	5
More than 10 years ago	6
[VOLUNTEERED] DK/Can't Remember	99

4H.   [IF Q4G=1] How many concerts by the Philadelphia Orchestra did you attend in the past year? [A ROUGH ESTIMATE IS OK]

Number . . . . ._____

[VOLUNTEERED]   DK/Refused 9999

4I.   As an adult, have you EVER subscribed to any series of concerts offered by the Philadelphia Orchestra?

YES 1
NO 2
[VOLUNTEERED]   DK/Refused 99

4J.   What types of Philadelphia Orchestra concerts have you (ever) attended? Have you attended... [READ EACH, RECORD ANSWER]

1. Classical Concerts 1
2. Pops Concerts 1
3. Family Concerts 1
4. Outdoor Concerts at the Mann Center 1
5. Holiday Concerts 1
6. Access Concerts 1
7. Chamber Concerts 1
8. Neighborhood Concerts 1

4K.   Have you ever had an unsatisfactory experience attending a Philadelphia Orchestra concert?

YES 1
[SKIP TO Q4M]   NO 2
[VOLUNTEERED]   DK/Refused 99

4L.   Can you tell me what was unsatisfactory about the experience? [RECORD VERBATIM ANSWER, DO NOT CODE]

4M.   Have you, personally, ever bought tickets for a Philadelphia Orchestra concert?

YES 1
NO 2
[VOLUNTEERED]   DK/Refused 99

4N.   If the Philadelphia Orchestra played more works by contemporary classical composers, would you attend concerts <u>less often, about as often as you do now,</u> or <u>more often</u>?

Less Often 1
About As Often As I Do Now 2
More Often 3
[VOLUNTEERED]   DK/Refused 99

4O.   Overall, how would you rate the quality of the Philadelphia Orchestra's playing? Use a scale of 0 to 10, with 0 meaning poor quality, and 10 meaning excellent quality.

                                            Quality Rating . . . . ____
             [VOLUNTEERED]   DK/Refused 99

4O2.   Are you aware that a new performing arts center, called the Kimmel Center for the Performing Arts, opened in downtown Philadelphia in December?

                                            YES 1
                                            NO 2
             [VOLUNTEERED]   DK/Refused 99

4B.   Assuming normal driving conditions, how many minutes would it take you to drive from your home to the **Kimmel Center for the Performing Arts in Center City**? Do not include the time it takes to park. (NOTE: The Kimmel Center is located at the corner of Broad and Spruce Streets.)

                                            # of Minutes . . . . ._____
             [VOLUNTEERED]   DK/Refused 99

4O3.   [IF Q4O2="YES"] Who do you think owns and operates the Kimmel Center for the Performing Arts? [READ EACH ITEM]
                                            The City of Philadelphia 1
                                            The Philadelphia Orchestra 2
                                            The Academy of Music 3
                                            The Regional Performing Arts Center, Inc.
                                            Authority 4
                                            A Private Management Company 5
             [VOLUNTEERED]   DK/Refused 99

4P.   Which of the following statements best describes your current attitude about attending concerts by the Philadelphia Orchestra? [READ EACH AND RECORD ANSWER]

                                            I'm <u>not</u> <u>at</u> <u>all</u> <u>interested</u> in attending a concert 1
                                            I'm <u>open</u> <u>to</u> <u>attending</u> a concert, but it's not a high priority 2
                                            I'm <u>very</u> <u>interested</u> in attending a concert 3

Section 5: Demographics

We're almost through. Just a few more questions.

5A.   What is your living situation? Are you: [READ]

                                            Married (or partnered) 1
                                            Single/never married .2
                                            Divorced or separated 3
                                            Widowed 4
             [VOLUNTEERED]   DK/Refused 99

5B.   Altogether, how many people live in your household, including yourself, and all other adults as well as children? [READ]

                         [SKIP TO Q5D]   One/self only 1
           [WRITE IN NUMBER, ASK Q5C1]   If more than one: . . . . ____
                         [VOLUNTEERED]   DK/Refused 0

5C1.   Are there any children in your household?

                                    YES 1
              [SKIP TO Q5D]   NO 2
[VOLUNTEERED, SKIP TO Q5D]   DK/Refused 99

5C2.   How many are children ages_____?

              [WRITE IN NUMBER]   6 or under: . . . . ._____
                                   7 to 12 . . . . ._____
                                   13 to 17 . . . . ._____
                                   Older than 17 . . . . ._____

5D.   What is the last level of school you completed? Did you...?[READ]

                                   Attend Grade School only 6
                                   Attend High School but not complete it 5
                                   Complete High School 4
                                   Attend Some College 3
                                   Get a College Degree 2
                                   Attend some Post College 1
              [VOLUNTEERED]   DK/Refused 99

5E.   In what year were you born? [RECORD ANSWER]

       [WRITE IN YEAR OF BIRTH]   Year Born . . . . ._____
              [VOLUNTEERED]   DK/Refused 99

5F1.   What is your employment status? Are you currently: [READ, DO NOT ROTATE]

                                   Working full-time for pay 1
                                   Working part-time for pay 2
                                   Retired 3
                                   A homemaker 4
                                   Unemployed but looking for work 5
                                   In school full-time 6
              [VOLUNTEERED]   Refused 99
5F2.   [IF Q5A="MARRIED"] What is your spouse's employment status? [READ IF
        NECESSARY]

                                   Working full-time for pay 1
                                   Working part-time for pay 2
                                   Retired 3
                                   A homemaker 4
                                   Unemployed but looking for work 5
                                   In school full-time 6
              [VOLUNTEERED]   Refused 99

5G.   Are you? [READ]

                                   White 1
                                   Black 2
                                   Asian 3
                                   Other 4
              [VOLUNTEERED]   DK/Refused 9

5H.   Are you of Hispanic ethnicity?

Yes 1
No 2
[VOLUNTEERED]   DK/Refused 9

5I.   Is your total family income before taxes: [READ]

[ASK Q5J]   Less than $75,000 1
[ASK Q5K]   More than $75,000 2
[SKIP TO Q5L]   Refused 99

5J.   [IF LESS THAN $75,000] Is your total family income: [READ]

Under $35,000 1
Between $35,000 and $49,999 2
Between $50,000 and $75,000 3
[VOLUNTEERED]   DK/Refused 99

5K.   [IF MORE THAN $75,000] Is your total family income: [READ]

Between $75,000 and $99,999 4
Between $100,000 and $124,999 5
Between $125,000 and $149,999 6
Between $150,000 and $174,999 7
Between $175,000 and $199,999 8
$200,000 or more 9
[VOLUNTEERED]   DK/Refused 99

5L.   What is your home ZIP Code?

5M.   [GENDER — BY OBSERVATION ONLY]

Male 1
Female 2
DK/Refused 0

That's everything. You've been extremely helpful. On behalf of the Knight Foundation, thanks so much for your cooperation.

PROTOCOL:

Ticket-Buyer Surveys (e.g., Detroit Symphony Orchestra)

Note: These questionnaires were designed as machine-readable forms and printed by National Computer Systems. The following protocol does not look like the actual forms.

SURVEY INSTRUCTIONS

Your cooperation with this survey will be of great assistance to the Detroit Symphony. Your answers will remain confidential. The survey should be completed by the addressee (preferably) or by another person in the same household who is involved in the decision to purchase tickets. A postage-paid reply envelope is provided.

BEGIN HERE

First, we'd like to hear your opinions about different kinds of cultural activities:

A1. Arts activities may include attending live performances of music, dance or theatre, visiting museums and galleries, listening to recordings at home, or creating art yourself such as painting or singing in a chorus. How interested would you say you are in arts activities? *(mark one)*

 ☐ Extremely interested ☐ Somewhat interested ☐ Not very interested
 ☐ Very interested ☐ Not at all interested

A2. Would you say that arts activities play a <u>major role</u>, a <u>minor role</u>, or <u>no role at all</u> in your life?

 ☐ Major Role ☐ Minor Role ☐ No Role at All

A3. How much do you like or dislike the following cultural activities? Use a scale of 0 to 10, with 0 meaning that you <u>dislike it a lot</u>, and 10 meaning that you <u>like it a lot</u>. *(mark a number for each)*

 Visiting art museums or galleries
 Attending jazz concerts
 Attending non-musical stage plays
 Attending musical theatre performances such as Broadway shows
 Attending opera performances
 Attending ballet performances
 Attending classical music concerts

A4. With the exception of elementary, middle, or high school performances or exhibits, did <u>YOU</u> do any of the following cultural activities <u>during the last 12 months</u>? *(mark all that apply)*

 Visit art museums or galleries
 Attend jazz concerts
 Attend stage plays
 Attend musical theatre performances such as Broadway shows
 Attend ballet performances
 Attend opera performances
 Attend classical music concerts

A5. In total, about how many times did you attend <u>live performing arts events</u> of any kind over the last 12 months? *(a rough estimate is OK)*

A6.   Have you ever volunteered for a nonprofit arts or cultural organization?
☐ YES ☐ NO

A7.   Would you like to attend live performances of music, dance or theater
<u>more often</u> than you do now?
☐ YES ☐ NO

Now, a few questions about how you go about selecting cultural activities to do.

B1.   Indicate which newspapers and magazines you read <u>regularly</u>. *(mark all that apply)*

B2.   Indicate which radio stations you listen to <u>regularly</u>. *mark all that apply)*

B3.   Indicate your level of agreement with each of the following statements. *(mark one for each)*

I'm always looking for information about cultural activities to do.
I'm the kind of person who likes to organize outings to cultural events for my friends
I'm much more likely to attend cultural outings if someone else invites me.

Response Set: Agree A Lot, Agree A Little, Disagree A Little, Disagree A Lot

B4.   Which of the following best describes your role in the process of deciding
whether or not to attend live performances? *(mark one)*

I am the primary decision-maker
I participate in a joint decision process
Someone else usually decides and I go along

B5.   Typically, how far in advance do you plan leisure activities like going out to live
performances? *(mark one)*

The day of the event
Several days to a week beforehand
A week to 10 days beforehand
Several weeks beforehand/
A month or more beforehand

B6.   How do you prefer to buy tickets — <u>by mail</u>, <u>by telephone</u>, <u>on the web</u>, or <u>in
person</u> **at the box office**? Below, please rank your preference for each method
of buying tickets. (mark one for each)

	BY MAIL	BY PHONE	ON THE WEB	IN PERSON
A. Most preferred method	☐	☐	☐	☐
B. Second most preferred method	☐	☐	☐	☐
C. Third most preferred method	☐	☐	☐	☐
D. Fourth most preferred method	☐	☐	☐	☐

B7.   Generally, how inclined are you to subscribe or purchase series tickets to
performing arts programs? Use the scale provided below. (mark a number)

NOT AT ALL <u>INCLINED</u>				NEITHER INCLINED <u>NOR DISINCLINED</u>				EXTREMELY <u>INCLINED</u>		
0	1	2	3	4	5	6	7	8	9	10

B8.   Do you have Internet access....   ☐ At home   ☐ At work   ☐ Both
☐ Neither

B9.   Over the past 6 months did you purchase <u>anything</u> on the Internet? ☐ YES ☐ NO

B10.   Have you <u>ever</u> purchased tickets on the Internet to any live performance? ☐ YES ☐ NO

B11.   Have you <u>ever</u> visited our web site (www.detroitsymphony.org)? ☐ YES ☐ NO

B12.   Have you <u>ever</u> purchased tickets through our website? ☐ YES ☐ NO

B13.   If "no," <u>would you</u> purchase tickets through our website? ☐ YES ☐ Maybe ☐ NO

B14.   If "no," why not? _____

B15.   Which of the following times are most convenient for you to attend live performances? *(mark all that apply)*

    ☐ Week nights ☐ Weekday mornings ☐ Weekend nights
    ☐ Weekend afternoons

B16.   How influential are each of the following factors on your decision to attend *any type of live performance*? Use the scale provided. *(mark a number for each)*

    Scale: 0=NOT AT ALL INFLUENTIAL; 10= EXTREMELY INFLUENTIAL

    Knowing if you can get good seats
    Being able to buy tickets at the last minute
    The day and time of the performance
    Transportation arrangements
    Convenience of parking
    Safety concerns
    Whether or not your spouse or partner wants to go
    If it's an activity for the whole family
    If a friend invites you to go with him/her
    If you can go out for dinner or drinks before or after
    Whether or not you have a special occasion to celebrate
    The specific works to be performed
    The likelihood of a high quality performance
    The guest artists or featured performers
    The cost of tickets
    If tickets can be exchanged

Now we'd like to ask about your relationship with classical music, the art form.

C1.   About how many classical music concerts did you attend during the last 12 months?

C2.   For each of the following types of concerts, indicate whether you have <u>never attended, attended sometime as an adult, attended in the past 12 months,</u> or <u>attended more than once in the past 12 months.</u>

    Pops concert by a symphony orchestra
    Classical concert by a symphony orchestra
    Chamber music concert
    Classical music recital by a singer or instrumentalist
    Classical concert by a choir or vocal ensemble
    Performance by a concert band or symphonic band
    A special holiday performance of classical music
    Classical concert geared for children or families

C3.   Over the past 12 months, did you attend a live classical concert at a... *(mark all that apply)*

Church or synagogue
School auditorium or gymnasium
Concert hall, theatre or opera house
Private residence

C4.   How knowledgeable are you about classical music? Would you describe yourself as being... *(mark one)*

Very knowledgeable
Somewhat knowledgeable
Not very knowledgeable

C5.   How interested are you in <u>learning</u> more about classical music? *(mark one)*

Very interested
Somewhat interested
Not very interested

C6.   Would you describe yourself as a <u>critical</u> <u>listener</u>, <u>a</u> <u>casual</u> <u>listener</u>, or <u>an</u> <u>uninterested</u> <u>listener</u> of classical music? *(mark one)*

A critical listener
A casual listener
An uninterested listener

C7.   Do you have any close friends who go to classical music concerts?   ☐ YES   ☐ NO

C8.   Does anyone in your immediate family go to classical music concerts? ☐ YES   ☐ NO

C9.   We'd like to know how your interest in classical music relates to other art forms. *(mark one for each)*

	YES	NO	PREFER EQUALLY
Do you prefer jazz to classical music?	☐	☐	☐
Do you prefer stage plays to classical music?	☐	☐	☐
Do you prefer Broadway shows to classical music?	☐	☐	☐
Do you prefer opera to classical music?	☐	☐	☐
Do you prefer ballet to classical music?	☐	☐	☐
Do you prefer popular music to classical music?	☐	☐	☐

(*for example, rock, country, rap, or soul)

C10.   About how often do you listen to classical music... *(mark one for each)*

	NEVER	SEVERAL TIMES A YEAR	SEVERAL TIMES A MONTH	SEVERAL TIMES A WEEK	DAILY
...on the radio?	☐	☐	☐	☐	☐
...records, tapes or CDs?	☐	☐	☐	☐	☐
...through an internet website?	☐	☐	☐	☐	☐
...on television or VCR/DVD?	☐	☐	☐	☐	☐

C11.   Do you listen to classical music radio or recordings... *(mark all that apply)*
         ☐ At home   ☐ In a car   ☐ At work

C12.   Have you ever made a donation to a nonprofit radio station that play classical music? ☐ YES   ☐ NO

C13.   Approximately how many <u>classical</u> <u>music</u> records, tapes and CDs do you own?

C14.   Over the past 12 months about how many <u>classical</u> <u>music</u> records, tapes and CDs have you purchased?

Now, please tell us about your experiences with the Detroit Symphony:

D1.   Assuming normal driving conditions, how many minutes does it take you to drive from your home to Orchestra Hall? (Do not include the time it takes to park.)

[Box with write-in number AND circles to darken, 3 columns]

D2.   What types of Detroit Symphony concerts have you attended? *(mark all that apply)*

Classical Concerts
Pops Concerts
Family Concerts
Outdoor Concerts
Holiday Concerts
Jazz Concerts

D3.   How many concerts by the Detroit Symphony did you attend in the <u>past</u> <u>year</u>?

D4.   For about how many years have you been attending concerts by the Detroit Symphony?

D5.   Are you currently a Detroit Symphony subscriber?   ☐ YES   ☐ NO

D6.   If so, for how many years have you subscribed to the Detroit Symphony?

D7.   <u>If</u> <u>you're</u> <u>not</u> <u>a</u> <u>current</u> <u>subscriber</u>, have you EVER subscribed to the Detroit Symphony?   ☐ YES ☐ NO

D8.   Have you ever had an unsatisfactory experience attending a Detroit Symphony concert?   ☐ YES ☐ NO

D9.   If so, what was unsatisfactory about the experience?

D10.   Overall, how would you rate the quality of the Detroit Symphony's playing? Use a scale of 0 to 10, with 0 meaning <u>poor</u> <u>quality</u>, and 10 meaning <u>excellent</u> <u>quality</u>. *(mark a number)*

<u>POOR QUALITY</u>   <u>EXCELLENT</u> <u>QUALITY</u>

0   1   2   3   4   5   6   7   8   9   10

D11.   Indicate your level of agreement with each of the following statements. *(mark one for each)*

The Detroit Symphony really cares about building a relationship with me.
I feel a strong connection with the musicians of the Detroit Symphony.
I have confidence in the Detroit Symphony organization.
I believe that the Detroit Symphony deserves my loyalty.

Response Set: Agree A Lot, Agree A Little, Disagree A Little, Disagree A Lot

D12.   In the future, do you anticipate attending Detroit Symphony concerts... ? *(mark one)*
☐ Less often   ☐ About as often as I do now   ☐ More often

D13.   If the Detroit Symphony played more works by contemporary classical composers, would you attend DSO concerts... ? *(mark one)*
☐ Less often   ☐ About as often as I do now   ☐ More often

D14.   Using the scale provided, indicate your level of agreement with each of the following statements. (darken one oval underneath each statement)

Scale: 0=STRONGLY DISAGREE; 10= STRONGLY AGREE
A.   For me, going out to dinner beforehand is an essential part of the concert experience.
B.   People should dress up and look sharp when they go to classical music concerts.
C.   Listening to classical music helps me make it through difficult times.
D.   I carefully read program notes and enjoy the educational aspect of a classical music concert.
E.   I am very likely to take visiting friends and family to classical concerts.
F.   I nurture people that I care about by taking them to classical music concerts.
G.   Classical music connects me with a higher power.
H.   The ambience and architectural setting is an important part of the concert experience for me.
I.   Hearing specific artists and repertoire is what I value most about the concert experience.
J.   Classical music is an important healing force in my life.
K.   I go to classical concerts to celebrate birthdays, anniversaries and other special occasions.
L.   Going to classical music concerts is a great way to strengthen personal relationships.
M.   Attending classical concerts is an important way that I nourish my soul.
N.   I wish that there were more opportunities to socialize at concerts.

D15.   Which statement best describes how you feel about classical music concerts? *(mark one)*

☐ Classical music concerts are primarily a personal experience for me.
☐ Classical music concerts are primarily a communal experience for me.

The following questions are for statistical purposes only. Your answers are confidential.
E1.   Your gender?   ☐ Female   ☐ Male

E2.   What is your age?
☐ 18 - 34   ☐ 55 - 64
☐ 35 - 44   ☐ 65 - 74
☐ 45 - 54   ☐ 75 and over

E3.   For how many years have you lived in the Detroit area? (use "0" for less than one year) # of Years:_____

E4.   Your marital status?
☐ Married
☐ Partnered/Not Married
☐ Single/Never Married
☐ Divorced or Separated
☐ Widowed

E5.   Are you of Hispanic ethnicity?   ☐ Yes   ☐ No

E6. What is your racial/ethnic background? *(mark one)*
☐ Asian
☐ Black/African American
☐ White/Anglo
☐ Other:_____

E7. How many people live in your household in each of the following age groups, including yourself? *(write in a # for each)*
_____ # of children age 5 and under
_____ # of children ages 6 to 12
_____ # of teens ages 13 to 17
_____ # of adults (ages 18+)

E8. What is the last level of school you completed? *(mark one)*

☐ Attended Grade School only
☐ Attended High School but did not complete it
☐ Completed High School
☐ Attended Some College
☐ Received a College Degree
☐ Post College Course Work

E9. Please indicate your employment status, as well as your spouse's, if applicable.

	YOUR	
YOU	SPOUSE	
☐	☐	Working full-time (for pay)
☐	☐	Working part-time (for pay)
☐	☐	Self-employed
☐	☐	In school full-time
☐	☐	Not employed, but looking
☐	☐	Fulltime Family Caregiver
☐	☐	Retired

E10. Your annual household income?
(include employment and other sources of income for all members of your household.)

☐ Under $35,000
☐ $35,000 - $49,999
☐ $50,000 - $74,999
☐ $75,000 - $99,999
☐ $100,000 - $124,999
☐ $125,000 - $149,999
☐ $150,000 - $174,999
☐ $175,000 - $199,999
☐ $200,000 or more

Thank you! Please return your completed survey in the postage-paid reply envelope provided, or mail to Audience Insight, P.O. Box 423, Southport, CT 06490-0423.

SUMMARY REPORT
Design Phase Focus Groups

Magic of Music Research Initiative

Commissioned by the John S. and James L. Knight Foundation and 15 American orchestras:

Brooklyn Philharmonic Orchestra
Charlotte Symphony Orchestra
Colorado Symphony Association
Detroit Symphony Orchestra Hall
Fort Wayne Philharmonic Orchestra
Kansas City Symphony
Long Beach Symphony Association
Louisiana Philharmonic Orchestra
New World Symphony
Oregon Symphony Association
Philadelphia Orchestra Association
Saint Louis Symphony Orchestra
Saint Paul Chamber Orchestra
Symphony Society of San Antonio
Wichita Symphony Society

November 2000

RESEARCH GOALS &
Methodology

A series of four focus groups were conducted in November 2000 to aid in the design of a national study of classical music consumers, funded by the John S. and James L. Knight Foundation. The overall purpose of this research was to test protocol for a national telephone survey to be fielded in early 2001 and to probe specific behaviors, attitudes and opinions related to two dimensions of classical music participation:

1. Relationship with the art form of classical music

2. Values, attitudes and inducements to increase frequency

Two discussion groups were held on Nov. 29 in Charlotte where the Charlotte Symphony AOrchestra (CSO) and North Carolina Blumenthal Performing Arts Center (NCBPAC) provided lists for recruitment. On the following evening, two more discussion groups were held in the Twin Cities, where the St. Paul Chamber Orchestra (SPCO) provided lists for recruitment.

Recruitment parameters were as follows:

Charlotte Group 1: CSO subscribers (current season/any series, recruitment list provided by CSO)

Charlotte Group 2: CSO Prospects (no recent CSO attendance, recruitment list provided by NCBPAC)

St Paul Group 3: SPCO Single-ticket Buyers (current season, recruitment list provided by SPCO)

St. Paul Group 4: SPCO Prospects (no recent SPCO attendance, recruitment list provided by SPCO)

Handouts were prepared for each group, representing sections of telephone survey protocol adapted for written completion. Each group completed different sections of protocol, organized by topic, after which discussions were held on that topic. A consolidated moderator's topic guide is attached.

The focus of the two Charlotte discussions was participants' relationship with the art form of classical music. The focus points of the St. Paul discussions were values ascribed to the live performance experience and inducements to increase classical music attendance. In addition to qualitative data from these discussions, responses to the written questions were tabulated and analyzed.

Discussion Summary

Classical Music vs. Other Art Forms

Respondents expressed a wide range of attitudes, beliefs and opinions about classical music in relation to other art forms (i.e., dance, theatre, opera). For most respondents, the relationship with classical music occurs in the context of participation in many different art forms, both popular and traditional. Only several respondents reported an exclusive affinity for classical music above all other types of live arts programs. In discussing their purchase decision patterns, some respondents described choosing between classical music concerts, plays, musicals, jazz concerts and even rock concerts.

> *"I am finding on any given night there are three things I could possibly do or would very much like to do... I like to pick and choose... There's so much going on."*

Substantial discussion revolved around what distinguishes the classical music experience from other types of performances and what attributes other performances have that classical music doesn't. Respondents expressed varying levels of preference for classical music in relation to other art forms.

> *"{we're} very interested in the arts. We have subscriptions to the Broadway Lights {series} and also the symphony pops. We attend the opera and the classical series based on who's performing. We go to lots of concerts at Blockbuster {Pavilion} because we like to sit outside on the grass."*

> *"I have a classical music subscription, but I go to just as many rock concerts."*

One of the distinguishing attributes of classical music concerts is the setting (i.e., concert hall or performing arts center). Many respondents described the setting as an aspect of the experience that adds value, not just architecturally and acoustically, but in terms of the associated values that respondents infer from the setting. This is described in terms of a sense of dignity, formality and even pageantry and grandeur (esp. for opera). For some, this is a major positive factor. For others, it is oppressive and a disincentive.

> *"When we go to classical concerts, its just special... You dress up a little nicer than you do for anything else... It's just a mood when you walk through those generally beautiful buildings where orchestras play."*

A number of respondents cited the visual experience offered by other art forms — dance, stage plays, musicals and film — as a satisfying aspect of the live arts experience that is lacking in classical music. Some strongly negative comments were offered as to the dreariness of the visual experience during classical music concerts, both on stage and in the audience.

"I see guys like me sleeping."

"Most of the musicians look like they're at a funeral... Part of it's not their fault, though. They're stuck back 100 years as far as relating to the audience."

"It's funny, though, there's more of that {interaction between musicians and the audience} at children's concerts, and there's also more of a visual element. And they could take some of that and put it in their other concerts.

With respect to other types of musical concerts, respondents seemed to attach a greater social value to popular concerts where "you can have a conversation with someone" and a more "introspective, deeply personal" value to the classical music, especially via recordings.

"When I'm feeling kind of low, I listen to classical music [recordings]*."*

An extensive discussion of the values that respondents derive from the classical music experience follows in the next section of this report.

Classical Music vs. Other Music

A major theme of all four groups was the <u>diversity of musical tastes</u> present within both the audience and prospect groups. While one or two participants in each group expressed a strong affinity for classical music (above all other types of music), the majority of participants, even in the subscriber and single-ticket buyer groups, cited numerous other types of music — including rock, jazz, R&B and even country music — that they consume. By and large, all participants could be described as "music lovers" with varying degrees of affinity for classical music. A love for music, generally, was common across all respondents. <u>Some respondents came to classical music via other types of music</u>.

"I listen to some classical music, not a great deal. I'm an avid music listener. I just love music, period."

A somewhat wider diversity of musical tastes was observed among prospects, suggesting that orchestras with access to audiences for other types of live concerts may cultivate a prospect base for classical and classical pops product.

"I can enjoy many kinds of different music. I've had experiences at classical music concerts where you just wait for the last note to die away so you can jump up and yell 'yea' and clap your hands off. It's the same thing with jazz, blues or folk concerts."

Some respondents in the prospect groups had their last live classical music experience at a free outdoor concert. For others, their last live classical music

experience was part of another music experience, such as a pop concert (Jose Feliciano or Roberta Flack) at school or at church. In these cases classical music was part of the experience but not the focal point.

Respondents experience classical music as part of a spectrum of musical influences that is highly personal. Generally, they do not experience classical music to the exclusion of other music genres. This suggests the symbiotic relationships between orchestras and other music presenters in their communities. Another implication is that orchestras that present other types of musical performances may create demand for classical programming in the long run.

Relationship with the Art Form vs. Relationship with the Local Orchestra

Respondents experience classical music in many ways. Their relationship with the classical music art form is much larger than their relationship with the local orchestra. All discussion participants integrate classical music into their lives via a mix of home audio, radio, television, film, the web, in all sorts of settings, including home, work, car, and in all sorts of venues including schools, churches and traditional concert halls. While respondents in the two prospect groups attend local orchestra concerts infrequently, they continue to experience the art form in other ways.

In fact, both prospect groups contained individuals with very close relationships with the art form of classical music but distant relationships with their local orchestra.

Consumption levels were high for classical music radio. The local classical music radio station is pre-programmed on almost everyone's car radio. For some respondents, the radio was their first recalled exposure to classical music.

> *"I started my interest in {classical} music when I was 14 years old listening to the Metropolitan Opera on radio."*

Several respondents are regular watchers of *Great Performances* on PBS, and one gentleman reported listing to classical music radio via the Internet.

If one assumes that consumption of live concerts increases as familiarity with the art form grows, and if affinity for classical music transfers across media and venues, then it can be reasoned that orchestras may cultivate audiences for live concerts by facilitating consumption of all types of classical music, both live and recorded, in all types of settings.

These discussions also seem to support the theory that the relationship between orchestras and their local classical radio stations can be strategic in terms of cultivating an educated audience for live concerts and increasing frequency of attendance in the long term. Several respondents who could be termed "good listeners" got that way by listening to classical music radio.

Knowledge Level

A wide range of self-perceptions was observed with respect to knowledge of the art form. Some respondents in the subscriber group described themselves as being <u>blissfully</u> <u>ignorant</u> about classical music, while some respondents in the prospect groups (i.e., infrequent attenders) were <u>self-described</u> <u>aficionados</u>. Everyone in the subscriber group agreed that you don't need to be knowledgeable about classical music in order to enjoy it, although they were aware that there are some extremely knowledgeable people in the audience.

> *"...I think some of the CSO classical series people are very high caliber... They know those scores... They know more than I do." {moderator: But you said that you don't have to be knowledgeable to enjoy it?} "No because it's the way it makes you feel that's important — what it does to you, that's important."*

The data seem to support the hypothesis that the local prospect base for each orchestra, in addition to the audience base, varies significantly with respect to knowledge of the art form, adding a layer of complexity to the acquisition task.

Knowledge vs. Enjoyment

Respondents with modest levels of knowledge about the art form seemed to describe the live concert experience in more rapturous terms as a sort of raw pleasure, whereas the more critical listeners were more difficult to please and tended to buy specific programs or guest artists, or to retreat to their favorite recordings at home. One might infer, paradoxically, that the most satisfied audience members (and perhaps the best prospects) are not necessarily those with the highest level of knowledge about classical music. Certainly, this would be something to test in the future. One respondent theorized an inverse relationship between knowledge and enjoyment:

> *"Sometimes I think that people who know too much don't enjoy things because they're look for the mistakes and they're honing in on that so hard that they don't relax and enjoy what's going on."*

Several respondents, looking back at their own experiences, generalized that it must be a widely held misconception that you have to understand classical music in order to enjoy it. Several described what might be termed "threshold experiences" where they overcame misconceptions and realized that they were not out of place at a classical music concert.

Respondents reported gaining knowledge about classical music from family members, through music lessons as children and music appreciation courses in college, through repeat exposure to classical music radio, and through repeat attendance at concerts. While some respondents seemed "wired for classical music" at a very young age, others "graduated" into classical music as adults. Several respondents recalled with some amusement how strongly they <u>disliked</u> classical

music (and especially opera) as children, but how they <u>gained</u> a <u>taste</u> <u>for</u> <u>classical</u> <u>music</u> as adults. Other respondents suggested that gaining a love for classical music is simply a rite of passage for some people, or a reward for endurance.

> *"I didn't enjoy {classical music} that much when I was growing up... As I got older, I kind of developed a taste for it, and now I play it all the time in the car when I'm driving around." {moderator: And how did that happen}? "Maturity."*

This reversal of tastes (from bitter medicine to a sweet balm) might be a marketing metaphor for the transformational experience that orchestra audiences seek.

What is Classical Music?

An exploratory line of questioning related to each respondent's definition of "classical music." Some respondents had very clear and narrow definitions of classical music and do not consider symphonic pops concerts to be classical music experiences, independent of their level of enjoyment. Other respondents, however, had a <u>considerably</u> <u>broader</u> <u>notion</u> <u>of</u> <u>the</u> <u>classical</u> <u>music</u> <u>experience</u>, including ballet (e.g., *The Nutcracker Suite*), opera, musical theatre (*Phantom of the Opera, Les Miserables*), and even film (*Fantasia, Amadeus, Out of Africa*). The conceptual territory between these narrow and broad definitions of the art form may be useful in defining different types of classical music prospects.

This led to a discussion about product equivalency — what other types of performances were considered interchangeable with classical music concerts? Some respondents had a clear sense of the uniqueness of the classical music concert while others suggested that going to a jazz concert or a Broadway musical was the equivalent of going to a classical music concert, in terms of value derived.

> *"They're equivalent {choices} for me. It would depend on the specifics then, and maybe what the {Charlotte} Observer said about them..."*

> *"It would depend on the company, for me. 'Cause if I was going with my Mom, I would go to something more classical, but if I was going with my husband, well he's not having that, so we would go to a jazz concert, or something like that."*

The marketing implications here are substantial, especially in terms of positioning the classical music concert product advantageously in relation to other types of arts programs.

Some respondents were unclear as to the distinction between "professional orchestra" and "community orchestra," although a few respondents were able to articulate that some musicians "earn their livelihood" playing in an orchestra, while others do not. Some respondents, even subscribers, expressed no preference for a professional orchestra over a semi-professional or community orchestra, although

they were confident that they could tell a good performance from a great performance.

Values and Inducements

Respondents articulated many different values associated with the live performance experience, generally, and the live classical music concert experience, specifically. A synthesis of the data suggests the following "value clusters":

- Occasion value

- Social value

- Ritual value

- Relationship value

- Therapeutic/Transformational value

- Artistic value

- Spiritual/Transcendence value

Many of these values are derived in combination with other values, to varying degrees. They do not appear to be mutually exclusive or strictly hierarchical. Each "value cluster" is described below.

Occasion Value

The most basic value is activity value, implicit to all respondents and explicitly articulated by some. Some respondents described going to concerts as a "worthwhile" thing to do; an activity that will make them feel good about themselves and proud of their community. Numerous respondents described special occasions such as birthdays, anniversaries and visits by out-of-town friends or family as stimuli for organizing concert tickets. When asked if attendance at a live concert was a "regular thing to do" or more of a "special occasion," respondents in the St. Paul prospect group unanimously agreed that it was a "special occasion."

> *"When you go to a {classical} music performance its kind of an occasion... It's more of a big deal. There's an extra dimension to it. This is more special than something like a movie."*

Part of this had to do with ticket price (i.e., the high risk-reward threshold), but also the need to plan ahead and the general perception that classical concerts are not the kind of thing that you do on a moment's notice. Further probing suggested that some of this perception might be due to lack of information about ticket availability.

One might infer from this that orchestras could stimulate attendance by positioning the live concert experience as an activity that validates and fulfills special occasions.

Social Value

The social value of attending classical music concerts was explored in some depth. Feelings were mixed. Most respondents recognized that they value the social context in which the concert experience happens, and some respondents go to elaborate lengths to draw out the social value of attending by constructing adjunct activities such as dinner beforehand and dessert afterwards, etc. Respondents described attending classical concerts in various configurations of friends and family, co-workers, church friends, clients and friends from other contexts.

> *Some respondents described classical music concerts as being more socially "introverted" than other types of concerts and were able to distinguish between social value as a primary motivation and social value as a byproduct of an artistic experience.*

A number of respondents, whether they placed a high social value on the concert going experience or not, described the music itself as a highly individual activity. Other respondents saw the act of listening to a classical music concert as a communal experience shared with others in the audience.

> *"A relationship develops between you and the other audience members. That's part of the experience."* (St. Paul Single-ticket Buyer)

Relationship Value

The live performance experience was discussed by some respondents in terms of its ability to maintain, enhance or transform a personal relationship. This interpersonal sense of product utility took several forms:

- Several respondents expressed how they use classical concerts as a way of maintaining and enhancing their relationship with their spouse or partner.

- One respondent suggested that attending a classical concert was a sort of litmus test for sizing up a new boyfriend.

- Other respondents discussed how they like to nurture and bond with their children by taking them to children's concerts.

- Another respondent buys subscription tickets and "chooses" a different friend for each performance, thereby allowing her to maintain friendships in a rather calculated way.

> *"It broadens your relationship. You can have a stimulating exchange of ideas and opinions."* (Charlotte subscriber)

Some respondents who are married (or partnered) described various stages of reconciliation with their spouse or partner over discordant values surrounding classical music. Some described going out to classical concerts without their spouse as a liberating experience, while others could not reconcile.

> *"We don't do everything together... It's not like if he doesn't want to go somewhere then I don't go [and vice versa]... We have our own outside circle of people who like to do different kinds of things."*

> *"He [my husband] gets first refusal... He enjoys that I enjoy it, and can go do it... He enjoys that he doesn't have to go!"*

> *"I have a friend who would go [to classical music concerts] but her husband doesn't care for that venue, and so they don't go, because he doesn't like to go and she's not comfortable asking someone else to go... She's one of those, you know, where her husband goes, she goes... So, she listens to [classical music] on the radio all the time and she's very knowledgeable about it, but they don't go."*

"Taste dissonance" as a barrier to attendance should be investigated further in the quantitative research.

Ritual Value

Some respondents discussed the classical music experience in terms of its ritual aspects, including getting dressed up, watching the musicians in their tuxedos, the ritualistic aspect of the musicians tuning up, the conductor's entrance, as well as the concert etiquette. Both the overall sense of pageantry and the ceremonial aspects of attending are major selling factors for some respondents.

> *"I like to get dressed up as a sign of respect for the performers. Certain things require a certain amount of formality to remind me where I am and that this is special."*

> *"There is a fundamental difference between watching or listening to a concert at home and going to a live performance. At the live performance you participate with the audience... There is the common act of applause... the anticipation of the beginning, being surrounded by others. That experience has reverberations long after the event is over."*

Most respondents, however, said that the formality and pageantry surrounding the classical music concert experience was a remnant of the past.

> *"You can't get a younger audience if it's going to be more formal... That's the beauty of the classical music experience — you can go in a tuxedo and you can go in jeans, and its OK."*

Therapeutic-Transformational Value

Some respondents use classical music as a private retreat; a "space" where they go to get away from their daily routine.

> *"It takes you out of your everyday life. I don't think about my problems."*

In various ways, respondents described using classical music to <u>define</u> <u>a</u> <u>space</u> <u>for</u> <u>themselves</u>, in autos, at work, at home and in the concert hall. Classical music is like a soundtrack to their lives. It follows them around almost everywhere. In this sense, classical music is valued as very personal, emotional space, even though the experience is communal. One respondent described how she creates a private space in her work environment by closing her office door and listening to classical music.

> *"I turn it on in my office... when there's something I need to work on... I can put it on and that really takes away all the other... I mean it helps me focus... There's no words in it, so I don't get distracted by the words..."*

The escape value of classical music was part of the concert experience as well. This was the case even for those individuals attending in groups.

> *"It's a social event in that I go with friends. But once the music starts I just loose myself in it and pay attention to what I'm listening to. It's pretty much a private thing."*

Several respondents identified music as a healing power in their lives and seek renewal through listening to music, especially classical music, both through live concerts and via recordings.

> *"How does it {classical music} affect your heartbeat? It's usually after I've taken a bath, or just have time to relax... that I'll listen to classical music."*

> *"I'd be more inclined to put it on after I've been out battling traffic or shopping — things I don't like to do."*

> *"It's a road rage reliever."*

> *"I use classical music to soothe my nerves when I get very upset...It's more of a mood-altering event."*

Artistic Value

While some respondents are oblivious to the program details, others seek out specific composers, pieces and guest artists. For these respondents, the concert experience is a more purposeful exercise in fulfilling an artistic desire. They may have a strong affinity for the art form but attend live concerts only when a specific

program piques their interest.

> *"For me it's the performer... that's the driving force."*

> *"There's a kind of interaction that occurs between a fine classical concert and the audience."*

Respondents cited their ability to connect with a performer they were familiar with.

> *"They* [the performers] *have a passion that you can really connect with. When you see a performer with such passion you can feel it. It enhances the whole experience."*

Spiritual-Transcendence Value

Some respondents articulated a spiritual aspect to their concert experience, both personally and collectively.

> *"It's more inward, rather than outward... 'To nourish my soul'... it's a spiritual question."*

> *"I get a feeling of exhaltation. I'm not relaxed exactly. The kinds of music I go to I'm 'purged of pity and terror' as they say. I'm moved in a different way than 'fun' or 'relaxation'."*

> *"Classical music floods me with a feeling of beauty and power."*

Some respondents — the "attentive listeners" — enjoy watching the musicians during concerts and listening for specific instruments and melodies. In stark contrast, others withdraw into a highly dynamic creative or meditative state. On a simplistic level, achieving this tantric-like state allows them to forget about their worries and, essentially, to suspend reality. On a more metaphysical level, it allows some respondents to visualize images they think the composer sought to evoke through the music, almost like self-induced hallucinations. So, for some respondents the concert experience is a highly visual experience that unlocks their imagination.

> *"I like to visualize what the artist {composer} was intending."*

Inducements

Respondents discussed a number of factors that would spur their increased attendance. Many of these involved the logistics of purchasing tickets and getting to and from the concert hall. There was considerable variability among respondents in their perceptions of the availability of single tickets.

Some respondents assumed that seats would only be available if they purchased a subscription or at the beginning of the season.

> *"We're pretty spur of the moment. It's the quickest, simplest entertainment for us. We decide on a Thursday what we are going to do on the weekend. We can't decide about two months from now."*

Others felt confident that they could purchase tickets for a performance a week or even the day before.

> *"Last minute tickets are really helpful. I've gone to lots this year because it was easy to drop by and pick them [tickets] up. I call the box office when I'm out in my car. I've got relatively good seats from those that were turned in."*

Several single-ticket buyers and prospects felt that the orchestras focused on subscribers to the exclusion of their needs.

> *"I got a mailing from the orchestra. I was trying to figure out how to buy a single ticket but everything was about 'pick three' or 'pick six.' I don't want three or six. I just want one."*

Asked if more familiar music would attract them to more concerts, respondents expressed mixed attitudes about the performance of new compositions or music that is not commonly programmed.

> *"Just because a piece has not been played in Charlotte before doesn't mean it has to be played here."*

Some respondents liked hearing unfamiliar pieces along with music that they had heard before. For the most part, however, respondents were under the general impression that they would enjoy a concert more if the program included at least one piece that made them feel comfortable, if it included something that they recognized.

> *"New works are a good experience, but I want a treat along with it — something I know and like."*

Some respondents found the very concept of getting an explicit "benefit" from going to a classical music concert as problematic. Clearly, however, they derive a range of values from the experience, both explicitly and implicitly. Underscoring these different values, and using the appropriate inducements, may be useful in converting different sub-groups of prospects into more frequent attenders.

Other Topics

E-mail marketing and ticket acquisition on the web was another topic given some airtime. Consistent with other research, there was a clear divide by age, with the younger respondents articulating a strong affinity for information acquisition via the web and a strong preference for e-mail marketing versus telemarketing. Convenience was cited as one reason why some respondents prefer the web for information and ticket acquisition.

"Convenience of time. I'm often using the computer after the kids go to bed."

Many respondents said that they would like to receive e-mails from orchestras with last-minute ticket availability information. It's only a fraction of the perceived invasion of privacy that telemarketing encumbers.

MAGIC OF MUSIC RESEARCH INITIATIVE

DESIGN PHASE FOCUS GROUPS

MODERATOR'S TOPIC GUIDES — CONSOLIDATED MASTER

- GROUPS 1 & 2: NOVEMBER 29, 2000 — CHARLOTTE, NC
- GROUPS 3 & 4: NOVEMBER 30, 2000 — ST. PAUL, MN

MODULE KEY

CSO Group 1 (subscribers): Parts 2A-C, 4A, 4B
CSO Group 2 (prospects): Warm-up, Parts 2A-C, 4A, 4C
SPCO Group 3 (STB): Parts 2A-C, 4A, 4B
SPCO Group 4 (prospects): Warm-up, Parts 3, 4A, 4B, 4C

[All participants should complete parts 1A, 1B, and 1C prior to the discussion. These data are not for discussion.]

Moderator's Introduction, Disclosures and Participant Self-Introductions

Warm-Up: Last Classical Music Experience

[CSO Group 2 & SPCO Group 4]

1. Please think about the last time that you attended a live concert of classical music of any kind, such as a recital or a symphony orchestra concert or a choral concert or anything else. Can you describe the circumstances for me? What concert was that? What venue was that? [write on board]

Probe: *Who did you go with?*
Probe: *Was it your decision to attend, or did someone else initiate the outing?*
Probe: *Who purchased the tickets?*

PART 2A — Relationship with the Art Form

[CSO Groups 1 & 2, SPCO Group 3]

Now, please turn to the next sheet in your handout, and complete part 2A.

1. Please indicate how often you have attended the following types of classical music concerts. Check one box for each item.

RESPONSE SET:

☐ Never Attended   ☐ Attended in Past 12 Months
☐ Ever Attended   ☐ Attended More Than Once in Past 12 Months

A. Classical concert by a professional symphony orchestra

B. Classical concert by a community symphony orchestra *(not professional)*

C. Symphonic pops concert by a professional orchestra

D. Symphonic pops concert by a community symphony orchestra *(not professional)*

E. Chamber music concert by professional musicians *(e.g., string quartet, piano trio, chamber orchestra)*

F. Recital by one or more professional instrumentalists *(e.g., piano recital, violin recital)*

G. Recital by one or more professional vocalists

H. Concert by a professional choir or vocal ensemble

I. Opera performance by a professional opera company

J. Student band concert

K. Student orchestra concert

L. Student choral concert

PROBE EACH TYPE
Were there any questions?

Has anyone been to all of the types listed?

Ask several respondents to explain their answers, and follow-up with questions about where, when, etc. Probe for sources of classical music programming besides the CSO/SPCO.
Is the distinction between professional and community orchestras clear?
How many people have been to community orchestra concerts but not professional concerts?
Probe the student categories — can we consolidate the categories?

PLEASE STOP. DO NOT TURN THE PAGE.

Now, please turn to the next sheet in your handout, and complete part 2B.

PART 2B — What is Classical Music?
[CSO Groups 1 & 2, SPCO Group 3]

Everyone has a different idea of exactly <u>what</u> <u>is</u> classical music. The next few questions relate to how YOU define classical music.

2.   For each item below, indicate whether you have ever attended, and if so,
      whether you would consider it to be a classical music experience.

A. The Nutcracker Suite
B. The musical Phantom of the Opera
C. The musical Les Miserables
D. A church choir concert
E. A big band concert
F. A film with a classical music sound track

PROBE EACH.
*What makes this a classical music experience, or why not? Can you think of other classical
music experiences, beside the obvious ones?*

3.   In relation to other cultural activities, would you say that going to a live
      classical music concert is roughly equivalent to...?

	YES	NO
Attending a rock concert	☐ YES	☐ NO
Attending a jazz or blues concert	☐ YES	☐ NO
Attending a Broadway show	☐ YES	☐ NO
Attending a ballet performance	☐ YES	☐ NO
Attending an opera performance	☐ YES	☐ NO

PROBE EACH.
Why is this similar to going to a classical music concert?
*Is going to a classical music concert unique or are there lots of alternatives that are pretty much
the same thing, from your point of view?*

4.   How knowledgeable are you about classical music? Would you describe
      yourself as being...?

Extremely Knowledgeable
Very Knowledgeable
Somewhat Knowledgeable
Not Very Knowledgeable
Not At All Knowledgeable

PROBE:
Where did you gain knowledge about classical music?
*Do you think other people in the audience are more or less knowledgeable about classical music,
compared with you?*
Do you need to be knowledgeable about classical music in order to enjoy concerts?
*If you are very knowledgeable about classical music, does this make it harder or easier to enjoy
concerts?*

PLEASE STOP. DO NOT TURN THE PAGE.

Now, please turn to the next sheet in your handout, and complete part 2C.

PART 2C — Consumption via Electronic Media
[CSO Groups 1 & 2, SPCO Group 3]

5. About how often do you listen to classical music on the radio? On average, would you say you do this:

> Daily
> Several times a week
> Several times a month
> Several times a year
> Never (or Almost Never

6. About how often do you listen to classical music on records, tapes or CDs? On average, would you say you do this:

> Daily
> Several times a week
> Several times a month
> Several times a year
> Never (or Almost Never)

7. About how often do you watch classical music programs on television or VCR? On average, would you say you do this:

> Daily
> Several times a week
> Several times a month
> Several times a year
> Never (or Almost Never)

8. Where you are likely to listen to classical music? Do you listen to classical music:

	YES	NO
at home	☐ YES	☐ NO
at work	☐ YES	☐ NO
in a car	☐ YES	☐ NO

9. Where else are you likely to listen to classical music?

10. Approximately how many classical music records, tapes and CDs do you own?

> Write in Number _____

11. Over the past 12 months about how many classical music records, tapes and CDs have you purchased?

Write in Number _____

PROBE RADIO & RECORDINGS:
How much exposure to classical music do you get outside of the concert hall?
Can you have a "serious" classical music experience listening to recordings?
Are you satisfied with the availability of classical music on the radio?
Does listening to radio or recordings increase your interest in going to live performances
Are there any other ways in which you experience classical music?

Overall, is your attendance at live classical music concerts a reflection of your interest in the art form of classical music, or would you say that your interest level in classical music is not reflected in your attendance at live concerts? If not, why not?

PLEASE STOP. DO NOT TURN THE PAGE.

Now, please turn to the next sheet in your handout, and complete Part 4A.

PART 3 — relationship with the Institution
[SPCO Group 4 Only]

1. For how many years have you lived in the Minneapolis-St. Paul area?
    (if less than 1 year, enter "0")   Write in number of Years   _____

6. Do any of your friends or family members attend concerts by the St. Paul Chamber Orchestra?

                    ☐ YES   ☐ NO

10.   As best you can remember, when was the last time that you attended a concert by the St. Paul Chamber Orchestra?
                    NEVER   ☐
                    Within the past 12 months
                    About 2 to 3 years ago
                    About 4 to 5 years ago
                    About 6 to 10 years ago
                    More than 10 years ago

PROBE: When you moved here, how long did it take you to attend a SPCO concert?
PROBE: What was your first SPCO experience?
PROBE: Are there any people who don't attend SPCO concerts, but their friends do?

11. Have you, personally, ever bought tickets for a St. Paul Chamber Orchestra concert, either by mail, by phone or in person at the box office?

□ YES   □ NO

PROBE: Are there SPCO attenders who don't buy their own tickets?
PROBE: Do you like buying tickets? Why or why not?
PROBE: Do you think it's easy to get tickets to SPCO concerts? Is this a disincentive to attending?

12A. Have you ever had an unsatisfactory experience attending a St. Paul Chamber Orchestra concert?

□ YES   □ NO

12B. What was unsatisfactory about the experience?

PROBE: If "YES," tell me about what went wrong. Does this affect your attitude about returning? How so?

Can you tell me who is the current music director of the St. Paul Chamber Orchestra?

[Test unaided and aided awareness.]

Which of the following statements best describes your current attitude about attending concerts by the St. Paul Chamber Orchestra?
     I'm very interested in attending a concert
     I'm open to attending a concert, but it's not a high priority
     Going to concerts is just not the kind of thing I like to do
     I'm not at all interested in attending a concert

PROBE: Take hand count for each answer. Why is the SPCO not a priority? If not interested, what would get you to go?

15. If a friend or family member had **FREE TICKETS** to a St. Paul Chamber Orchestra concert, and invited you to join them, would you go, assuming that you had time, and that transportation was not a problem?

□ YES   □ NO

PROBE: If not, why not? What would keep you from going?

{Moderator: try to distinguish between logistical factors, attitudinal factors, and experience factors}

- Afraid you won't like the music?
- Concerned that you won't fit in with the crowd?
- Had a bad experience once?
- If it depends on the program, what type of program(s) would keep you home?

PROBE: If yes, how heavy would they have to sell you on it? How important is the program to be performed?

16. If you attended a concert by the St. Paul Chamber Orchestra, do you imagine that you would:

>   Enjoy it a lot
>   Enjoy it a little
>   Not really enjoy it, or
>   Hate it

PROBE: Why?

PLEASE STOP. DO NOT TURN THE PAGE.

PART 4A — *Level of Interest in Classical Music*

[All Groups]

1. The next question relates to your level of interest in classical music in relation to other art forms like ballet, modern dance, stage plays or musical theatre. Would you say that your interest level in classical music is h<u>igher</u> <u>than,</u> <u>equal</u> <u>to</u> or <u>less</u> <u>than</u> your level of interest in other art forms?

Probe: Why is that? What is it that other art forms give you that classical music doesn't?

Probe: In your experience going out to live performances, would you say that you tend to concentrate your attention on one art form, or that you tend to go to lots of different types of programs?

Probe: As you get older, would you say that your tastes in the arts are expanding and diversifying, or narrowing and focusing more?

Now, please turn to the next sheet in your handout, and complete Part 4A.

1. Listed below are a number of reasons why some people go out to live performing arts programs. Please indicate how important each reason is to YOU, using a scale of zero to 10, with zero meaning not at all important, and 10 meaning extremely important.

IMPORTANCE
RATING (0-10)

To socialize with friends or family   _____
To relax and have fun   _____
To do something worthwhile   _____
To escape from my daily routine   _____
To spend time with my spouse or partner   _____
To see a specific performer   _____
To celebrate a special occasion like a birthday or anniversary _____
To nourish my soul   _____

PROBE: What social groups do you attend with? What are their relationships to you? (family, friends, co-workers, other) Does your spouse enjoy the same kinds of activities that you do? If not, what do you do about it?

PROBE: How does sharing the experience affect your relationships with these people?

PROBE: What prompts you to go out to live performances? Anything else? Why is this important to you?

PLEASE STOP. DO NOT TURN THE PAGE.

PART 4B — Benefits
[CSO Group 1 & SPCO Group 3]

2. For each statement below, indicate if you <u>strongly agree, somewhat agree, somewhat disagree</u> or <u>strongly disagree.</u>

The main benefit of concert-going is being inspired by the music.

The main benefit of attending concerts is to relax and spend quality time with friends or family.

I go to classical music concerts more for the music and less for the socializing.

Getting together with friends and family is an important part of the concert-going experience.

I prefer listening to classical music pieces that I'm familiar with.

I prefer hearing pieces that I've never heard before.

I like the whole pageantry of getting dressed up and going to dinner before concerts.

I wish that more people dressed casually for concerts.

PROBE EACH GROUP OF STATEMENTS: Was anything confusing? Probe for discordant answers to paired questions. Why do you feel so strongly about that?

PLEASE STOP. DO NOT TURN THE PAGE.

[Continue Exercise]

Getting tickets to symphony orchestra concerts is a hassle.

The performances I'd like to hear are probably sold out.

I would enjoy longer intermissions, if that created more time to catch up with friends.

I would like earlier starting times for nighttime concerts, so that I could get home earlier.

I enjoy reading program notes and learning about the music being performed.

I wish that conductors would speak to the audience more often.

I wish that audience members had better manners during concerts.

People should be allowed to applaud between movements of a symphony if they want to.

PROBE EACH GROUP OF STATEMENTS: Was anything confusing? Probe for discordant answers to paired questions. Why do you feel so strongly about that?

PLEASE STOP. DO NOT TURN THE PAGE.

[Continue Exercise]

I wish that I could attend live classical music concerts more often than I do now.

I'm satisfied with my current frequency of attendance at classical music concerts.

I like listening to classical music at home more than I like attending live concerts.

Attending live concerts is preferable to listening to classical music recordings at home.

I might leave early if I'm not enjoying the concert.

Even if I don't enjoy the concert, it's still a worthwhile activity.

PROBE EACH GROUP OF STATEMENTS: Was anything confusing? Probe for discordant answers to paired questions. Why do you feel so strongly about that?

PLEASE STOP. DO NOT TURN THE PAGE.

PART 4C — Decision Factors and Inducements

[CSO Group 2, SPCO Group 4]

3. The next question relates to what factors you consider when thinking about attending a live performance of any kind. Please rate each factor below, using a scale of one to five, with one meaning <u>not at all important,</u> and five meaning <u>extremely</u> <u>important</u> to your decision to attend. *(circle a number for each item)*

    The specific pieces being performed
    The date and time of the performance
    If good seats are still available
    Ticket price
    Ease of acquiring tickets
    Drive time to the venue
    If you can arrange transportation

4. If _____, would you be <u>much</u> <u>more</u> <u>likely,</u> <u>somewhat</u> <u>more</u> <u>likely,</u> or <u>not</u> <u>any</u> <u>more</u> <u>likely</u> to attend symphony orchestra concerts more often than you do now? *(check one for each item)*

    you could dress casually and feel more comfortable
    you had a friend who invited you to go
    tickets were less expensive
    intermissions were longer
    orchestras played more familiar music
    someone else drove you to and from the concert hall
    the concerts weren't so long
    you knew that tickets were available at the last minute
    concerts were at more convenient times
    getting tickets online was fast and easy
    you could always exchange your tickets
    there were more people like you in the audience
    conductors talked to the audience more

    END

SUMMARY REPORT
Prospect Focus Groups

Magic of Music Research Initiative

Commissioned by the John S. and James L. Knight Foundation and 15 American orchestras:

Brooklyn Philharmonic Orchestra
Charlotte Symphony Orchestra
Colorado Symphony Association
Detroit Symphony Orchestra Hall
Fort Wayne Philharmonic Orchestra
Kansas City Symphony
Long Beach Symphony Association
Louisiana Philharmonic Orchestra
New World Symphony
Oregon Symphony Association
Philadelphia Orchestra Association
Saint Louis Symphony Orchestra
Saint. Paul Chamber Orchestra
Symphony Society of San Antonio
Wichita Symphony Society

July 2002

Research Goals & Methodology

Four focus groups were conducted in July 2002 as a follow-up to the classical music prospect segmentation model developed through the Magic of Music research initiative. The overall purpose of this research was to explore, in-depth, the attitudes and behaviors of those prospect segments that currently do not attend the local orchestra, or who attend infrequently. Additionally, a group of self-described "Initiators" were interviewed to explore the special circumstances surrounding their organizing activities.

Potential discussion participants were pre-recruited through a postal survey that replicated key protocol elements from the ticket buyer mail survey conducted as part of the larger Magic of Music research initiative. Approximately 2,000 pre-recruitment surveys were mailed to a combination of inactive Detroit Symphony Orchestra single ticket buyers and randomly selected households in a five-mile radius around the focus group facility in Farmington Hill, Michigan. A total of 120 surveys were returned.

Based on their responses to the various survey questions, respondents were classified into one of the 10 prospect segments defined in the study. Eligible respondents, who had already indicated their availability for the focus groups, were then recruited by the focus facility, using a $75 cash incentive.

The focus group discussions were conducted at MORPACE International, Inc. of Farmington Hills, Michigan. Alan Brown and Andrew Fish of Audience Insight LLC moderated the discussions. The four groups were composed as follows:

Group 1: <u>Uninitiated Prospects and Special Occasion Only</u> — These individuals attend the Detroit Symphony infrequently or not at all. Uninitiated Prospects are relatively sophisticated about classical music but have never attended. Special Occasion Only Prospects are less sophisticated but have some history of attendance, however distant.

Group 2: <u>Sophisticated Low Frequency Single Ticket Buyers and Ghosts</u> — These individuals are sophisticated consumers of classical music who attend the Detroit Symphony Orchestra only infrequently.

Group 3: <u>Initiators</u> — These individuals all 'agreed a lot' with the statement: "I'm the kind of person who likes to organize cultural events for my friends." No further parameters were imposed on this group, in order to gain a sense of the full spectrum of Initiators, form devotees to casual listeners.

Group 4: <u>Low-Interest Dabblers</u> — These individuals are less sophisticated consumers of classical music. In addition, they are not particularly interested in learning more. Their history of attendance at the Detroit Symphony is very limited.

A consolidated moderator's topic guide is attached.

Key Themes and Observations

Generally, the focus groups reinforced and added qualitative dimension to the quantitative results of the study. Participants in the "Low-Interest Dabblers" group were, in fact, classical consumers with only moderate knowledge of the art form and interested in other cultural activities besides classical music. Participants in the "Special Occasion Only" were very infrequent DSO attendees but nevertheless interested in classical music at various levels.

Initiators were, of course, people who like to organize outings to cultural programs for their friends, but there were many different social contexts and meanings behind the initiating. Among the key observations:

- Social support for experiencing classical music is lacking for a substantial number of low-involvement prospects (e.g., taste dissonance, lack of friendship group with shared values around classical music) and is seen as a major barrier to increased consumption of live concerts.

- The loss of WQRS, Detroit's primary classical music station, is still a hot topic four years after the station changed format and is viewed as a significant problem for the Detroit Symphony Orchestra

- For most prospects, their actual attendance at Detroit Symphony Orchestra concerts is not a reflection of their overall level of interest in classical music.

- Many prospects are interested in broadening their avenues for experiencing classical music beyond radio, recordings and the concert hall. Low-involvement prospects expressed a clear desire for more meaning in the concert experience. They want help negotiating the concert experience in order to become better listeners.

- Initiators (organizers) are motivated by their interest in classical music but also by the social aspects of attending concerts and the deep, personal satisfaction that they derive from providing cultural experiences for their friends.

- Most initiators enjoy the process of organizing outings and are not very interested in having all of the logistics taken care of by some outside agent (such as an orchestra or a concierge service offered jointly by several arts organizations in a community). There is intrinsic value in the organizing work that give Initiators satisfaction. Discount offers and other price incentives would be of greatest value.

"Pop Quiz" on Classical Music — An Exercise

As an experiment in trying to develop an objective measure of knowledge about classical music, each participant in the Detroit focus groups was asked to complete the "Pop Quiz" on classical music that appears on the following page. The exercise generated quite a buzz among participants as they waited for the discussions to start, and several participants asked for the answers to the questions during the focus groups and afterwards.

Correct answers are in bold type.

1. How many symphonies did Beethoven compose?
   - ☐ five   ☐ **nine**   ☐ ten   ☐ three

2. The instrument that Chopin played, and for which he composed most of his music.
   - ☐ the violin   ☐ the cello   ☐ **the piano**   ☐ the organ

3. Which of the following string instruments is analogous to the tenor voice in a vocal quartet?
   - ☐ contrabass   ☐ violin   ☐ **cello**   ☐ viola

4. One of the higher wind instruments in the modern orchestra, yet of great antiquity, having a penetrating pastoral quality of tone.
   - ☐ clarinet   ☐ flute   ☐ trumpet   ☐ **oboe**

5. His sixth symphony is named "Pathétique."
   - ☐ Rachmaninoff   ☐ Saint-Saëns
   - ☐ Prokofiev   ☐ **Tchaikovsky**

6. An extended virtuosic section for the soloist usually near the end of a movement of a concerto.
   - ☐ trill   ☐ **cadenza**   ☐ encore   ☐ cadence

7. The fastest of the following four tempos.
   - ☐ adagio   ☐ largo   ☐ andante   ☐ **allegretto**

8. Which of the following is NOT a percussion instrument?
   - ☐ xylophone   ☐ **piccolo**   ☐ triangle   ☐ maraca

9. The name of the Italian composer who wrote a symphonic poem called The Fountains of Rome.
   - ☐ Verdi   ☐ **Respighi**   ☐ Puccini   ☐ Vivaldi

10. A conducting term, which indicates the part of the conducting pattern that identifies where the beat lies; the pulse at the bottom of the pattern.
    - ☐ baton   ☐ **ictus**   ☐ syncopation   ☐ upbeat

Results are based on a very limited number of cases and should be interpreted with caution. This was exploratory in nature. That said, the results indicate some discrepancy between respondents' subjective sophistication level about classical music (as measured by self-reported attitudinal survey data) and the objective measure of their classical music knowledge, based on the "Pop Quiz."

- The 10 participants classified as "Interested Single-Ticket Buyers and Ghosts" had the highest average quiz score: six out of a possible 10. Scores ranged from three to nine. There were also three "Sophisticated Low Frequency Alumni" prospects in this focus group. We would expect these individuals to score relatively highly, as they were classified in the prospect segment with the closest relationship to classical music. Instead, they scored three, four and six points on the quiz.

- "Low-Interest Dabblers" (a total of 13 participants) reported an average quiz score of five. Individual scores ranged from three to nine. We would expect them to have modest knowledge levels and to score lower that the first group, which they did.

- The "Special Occasion Only" segment (nine participants) also averaged a quiz score of five (individual scores ranged from two to eight). There were also three "Uninitiated Prospects" in this group. Two of them scored three points, and the other scored seven points.

As tenuous as it may seem, the "Pop Quiz" approach to measuring knowledge of classical music may be worth further experimentation and evaluation, with the goal of seeing if people's self-reported sophistication levels can be substantiated on a more objective basis. Much larger sample sizes would be necessary, and the quiz should be further tested and refined. Meanwhile, we'll have to rely on respondent's self-reported knowledge levels, gathered through survey questions.

Discussion Summary — Prospect Groups

Relationship with Classical Music

Participants in the three prospect groups talked about classical music in the context of a larger spectrum of musical experiences. Some participants have only a passing interest in classical music while others consider themselves classical music devotees. Regardless of their level of interest in classical music, participants view classical music in relation to the other musical forms that they consume. Overall, their responses to the "Relationship with Classical Music" questions were very consistent with our expectations for each prospect group.

A variety of reasons for listening to classical music were cited. For some, classical music provides a pleasant background for their day — a sort of wallpaper. For others, the connection is on a deeper level — as a means of preparing for (or coming down from) their stressful everyday lives. For others still, classical music is a transcendent experience.

> *"My alarm is set to classical music."* (Uninitiated Prospect)

> *"I listen for a reason. I listen to relax. I listen to prepare myself for the insanity at work."* (Low-Interest Dabbler)

> *"I was raised on classical music. My mother wanted Van Cliburn and she got me. I studied piano for all my childhood. When I turned 21, I rebelled and avoided classical music, because I was put off by all the years I put into it. When I get down on humanity, I listen to classical music. It's the other side; we have all this brilliant creativity; after 9/11 I turned on the classical station."* (Low-Interest Dabbler)

Several participants in each group reported that their classical music activity is limited for lack of social support group. This was the case regardless of sophistication level. Several respondents indicated that their spouses do not enjoy classical music, while they do.

The lack of a supportive social environment for listening to classical music impedes all modes of classical consumption. With respect to classical radio, several discussion participants reported that they constantly struggle with their children for control of the radio pre-set buttons in their car. The children reset the buttons to popular radio stations, and the respondents change it back to classical. With respect to consumption of recordings, several respondents said that they have to almost hide in their own homes in order to listen to classical music, when others in the family don't want to listen — literally and perhaps symbolically retreating into a personal space in order to have the classical listening experience.

> *"Classical music is a private part of my life, I do not share with the rest of my family."* (Special Occasion Only Prospect)

With respect to live attendance among "taste dissonant" couples, the net affect was non-attendance, as they felt a need to defer to their spouse's musical tastes.

Relationship with their Local Orchestra

Like their art form relationships, respondents discussed having a range of relationships with the Detroit Symphony Orchestra (DSO). Few respondents attended the DSO frequently. For some respondents, their limited exposure to the DSO reflected their limited interest in the art form of classical music. However, this was the exception rather than the rule. Most respondents are interested in classical music but do not express their interest by attending DSO concerts.

Respondents noted a variety of reasons why they do not attend DSO concerts more frequently — including lack of time, safety concerns about downtown Detroit, and the dearth of nearby amenities.

"Downtown Detroit is not safe. You can't leave early or hang around (after the concert) because you have to stay with the crowd." (Special Occasion Only Prospect)

The most evident reason for not attending DSO concerts, however, seemed to be competition from other arts and entertainment offerings. Respondents talked about prioritizing DSO concerts with the other arts and cultural activities they enjoy.

"The DSO competes with other forms of entertainment, Cirque du Soleil, jazz and R&B concerts, going to a museum; you have so many options. You try to weave it in, pick and choose." (Low Interest Dabbler)

The loss of Detroit's only classical music format radio station (and the change in format to all news-talk by WUOM, University of Michigan Ann Arbor's station) was seen as a major detriment to the Detroit Symphony Orchestra. Respondents said the lack of information about the DSO that used to be provided via the radio was a significant reason for their not attending concerts more frequently. Many respondents said they found out about upcoming DSO concerts via the radio. Radio was seen as the major means by which the DSO stayed on people's "radar maps." Several respondents felt that it was through radio that the "buzz" around concerts was created.

"The Detroit Symphony Orchestra should purchase a radio station like sports teams do." (Special Occasion Only Prospect)

Still, discussion participants value the live classical music experience provided by the Detroit Symphony Orchestra. Most expressed satisfaction with the DSO experience and a desire to attend more frequently.

"My sound system can't duplicate what goes on in the concert hall." (Sophisticated Low-Frequency Single-ticket Buyer)

Inducements to Attend the Detroit Symphony Orchestra More Often

An exercise was completed with each of the three prospect segment groups in order to measure the impact of a variety of factors that might influence their likelihood of attending Detroit Symphony Orchestra concerts more often in the future. A sheet of paper was distributed to each participant with a list of 14 inducements to attend. Each participant was then instructed to rank their "top five" choices. Results are presented in Appendix Table FG-1.

A reduction in ticket prices was the most frequently cited inducement to attending DSO concerts. Twenty-one out of thirty-two participants ranked "I would probably go to Detroit Symphony concerts more often if tickets were less expensive" among their top five inducements. Seven respondents ranked ticket price reductions as their top inducement.

Sixteen participants rated "I would probably go to Detroit Symphony concerts more if there was always a group of friends to go with" among their top five inducements, and 13 participants said they would probably go more if "a friend of mine invited me to go," suggesting the power of social context as an inducement to attend.

Discussion Summary — Initiator Group

Participants in the Initiator group, after introductions, slowly figured out that they all share something important in common — they all organize outings to a variety of arts and cultural activities, including classical music concerts.

Some Initiators are motivated by the social benefits gained through organizing. They enjoy the process of organizing events for their friends, family and themselves to attend, and some of these respondents value the social aspects of attending as a group over the specific event.

> *"It's a delight to organize." (Initiator)*

A majority of the Initiators organize outings because they enjoy arts and cultural activities and do not want to attend alone. These individuals exert influence over the selection of activities that their social group attends because they are willing to put the effort into organizing.

> *"I'm a planner. I enjoy doing it (planning) because I enjoy going to these places."*
> *(Initiator)*

> *"We're going to Stratford with another couple and we're doing all the organizing. If we didn't organize, they wouldn't go." (Initiator)*

Initiators are also motivated by their love of a particular art form (in some cases classical music) and a desire to share their passion with their family and friends.

> *"I want to bring others into it, share the joy." (Initiator)*

Initiators consider the other members of their party when organizing outings to classical music concerts. This is certainly also the case for organizing other types of outings, but respondents indicated this was of particular concern with classical music concerts. Several of the participants felt they needed to persuade their family or friends to go or prep them prior to the concert experience.

> *"When I go and bring friends, I worry if they will enjoy it... I play the music for them ahead of time so they will know when to clap." (Initiator)*

> *"My husband and his family are not culturally involved. So my avenue is through work (clients/staff). If I had a social context, I would go much more." (Initiator)*

Initiators — Stimulating Attendance in Small Social Groups

Cost was seen as a significant barrier to small group attendance. Initiators had to not only account for the cost of tickets to the event but also ancillary activities such as parking and dinner. Scheduling was also cited as a major factor in determining small group attendance. The larger groups increased the likelihood of scheduling conflicts. Some Initiators organized fluid groups of family and friends in which individual members drop in and out.

> *"Last time I just sent off an e-mail to several of my friends with a general invitation... A few took me up on it." (Initiator)*

Initiators offered a number of factors that would stimulate small group attendance — discounts for smaller groups; coupon books (so they could mix and match programs with group members); special packages (including parking and dinner at a local restaurant) to reduce the cost of "making a night of it"; and making incentives available to their entire group not just the organizer.

Generally, Initiators were not interested in a concierge service that would do the work of organizing for them. Initiators like to organize. For most, organizing is part of the fun (and meaning) of group outings. They might, however, use a concierge program as one of their tools for organizing group outings. The discounts and special offers provided by such a program would be of primary value. Most said that they would respond to a solicitation related to initiating attending in small social groups, but their decision to use a concierge-like service would depend on the offer.

Most Initiators expressed excitement about the idea of a concert club in which they would meet in small groups to discuss a particular piece (or program) of classical music. Such a club would resemble the traditional book club with the small group discussion followed by a trip to the symphony. Most were also interested in the opportunity to meet with a member of the orchestra through the concert club. One suggestion was for a music appreciation class linked to individual concerts. Respondents did not think a concert club would have to be limited to a group of friends but instead should be open to the public. It was suggested that several concert clubs could be organized for people with varying levels of knowledge about classical music — and that you could "graduate" to higher level groups.

MAGIC OF MUSIC RESEARCH INITIATIVE

PROSPECT SEGMENT FOCUS GROUPS

MODERATORS TOPIC GUIDES — CONSOLIDATED MASTER

- GROUP 1: UNINITIATED PROSPECTS & SPECIAL OCCASION ONLY; MONDAY, JULY 15 AT 6:00PM

- GROUP 2: SOPHISTICATED LOW FREQUENCY ALUMNI & INTERESTED STB & GHOSTS; MONDAY, JULY 15 AT 8:00PM

- GROUP 4: LOW INTEREST DABBLERS; TUESDAY, JULY 16 AT 8:00PM

Moderator Introduction, Disclosures and Participant Self-Introductions

Relationship with the Art Form

1. First, I'd like to ask each of you, what types of music do you like to listen to?

[NOTE: we're talking about attitudes here, not behaviors]

[write down responses on board, using a matrix: type of music by respondent]

Of all of these, what's your favorite kind of music? [circle response on matrix]

2. In relation to other types of music, how much do you like listening to classical music?

[IF NECESSARY: Now, just a word of caution: Just because we're talking mostly about classical music tonight, don't feel like you need to overstate your interest in classical music. As a matter of fact, your comments will be most valuable is you DO NOT exaggerate your interest in classical music.]

So, HONESTLY, how much do you like listening to classical music?

3. How about in relation to other art forms like dance, theater and the visual arts and crafts — how does your interest in classical music stack up?

4. How do you fit classical music into your life? Think about all the ways in which you experience classical music — all the places where you hear it and the many different types of classical music that you might listen to. How does classical music "happen" in your life?

Probe: *Where are you likely to listen to classical music? At home? In the car? At work?*

Probe: *Where do you go to hear live classical music concerts?*

Probe: *How about radio and recordings? TV?*

Radio & Recordings [GROUP 2 ONLY]

1. How important are classical radio and classical recordings to your overall enjoyment of the art form?

2. Can you have a "serious" classical music experience listening to classical music on the radio? How about recordings?

3. Are you satisfied with the availability of classical music on the radio in the Detroit area?

Probe: *If "No," Why not?*

4. Does listening to radio or recordings increase your interest in going to live classical music concerts, or is it a substitute for going to live concerts?

5. Do you think that the absence of a strong classical music radio station in Detroit is a problem for the Detroit Symphony? Why or why not?

Evolution of Tastes

1. How did you grow to enjoy classical music?

Probe: *When in your life did this happen?*

2. Would you say that you tend to concentrate your attention on one art form, or that you tend to go to lots of different types of programs?

3. As you get older, would you say that your tastes in the arts are expanding and diversifying, or narrowing and focusing more?

Probe: *Can you give me an example of how your tastes are changing?*

Knowledge vs. Enjoyment

1. How knowledgeable are you about classical music?

2. Do you need to be knowledgeable about classical music in order to enjoy concerts?

3. Do you think that you are more or less knowledgeable about classical music than the average concertgoer?

4. Do you think that people who are very knowledgeable and experienced with classical music have an easier time or a harder time enjoying concerts? Why?

sRelationship with the DSO

1A. [GROUP 1 ONLY] With a show of hands, how many of you have ever attended a concert by the Detroit Symphony Orchestra?

1B. [GROUP 1 ONLY] For those of you who have never been to a concert by the Detroit Symphony Orchestra, is your lack of attendance a reflection of your level of interest in attending, or are there other reasons why you've not made it to a concert?

Probe: *What are the reasons for not attending?*

Probe: *Realistically, what would it take to get you there?*

Probe: *If a friend or family member offered to take you to a DSO concert, would you go? How much convincing would it take?*

2. For those of you who HAVE attended at DSO concert at some point in your life, think about your most recent Detroit Symphony concert experience. Can you describe the circumstances for me, in terms of the who/what/when and where?

Probe: *When was that? Where was that?*

Probe: *Whom did you attend?*

Probe: *Was it your decision to go, or did someone else initiate the outing?*

Probe: *Who purchased the tickets?*

Probe: *Can you remember the program?*

3. Overall, is your attendance at Detroit Symphony concerts <u>a reflection of your interest</u> in the art form of classical music, or would you say that your interest level in classical music <u>is</u> <u>not reflected</u> in your attendance at DSO concerts?

Probe: *If not, why not?*

4. Do you think that the Detroit Symphony assumes that you have too much knowledge about classical music, or too little knowledge about classical music? Why?

Projective Exercise: Who is the DSO?

1. OK, now we're going to have some fun. If the Detroit Symphony were a person, what kind of person would it be? You can describe the person in terms of gender, age, race/ethnicity, income, occupation, hairstyle or anything at all. Use your imaginations! Please write down your answer on the sheet in front of you.

    [Probe responses, write results on board to accumulate a list]

2. What's the ideal relationship that you'd like with that person, if any? Can you describe in your own words what the relationship would be like?

Examples: a distant friendship, married for life, a cheap date

Probe: *Why do you feel that way?*

Inducements to Attend

[PASS OUT INDUCEMENTS RANKING SHEET — SEE NEXT PAGE]

1. On the sheet of paper in front of you is a list of a few things that might cause you to attend Detroit Symphony concerts more often than you do now. Read the list, and then rank the top three things that might cause you to increase your attendance at DSO concerts. Put a "1" next to your first choice, and so forth.

    If nothing would cause you to increase your DSO attendance, leave the sheet blank.

    DISCUSS RANKINGS

***PASS IN SHEETS

***GET PERMISSION TO RELEASE VIDEOTAPE

INDUCEMENTS RANKING SHEET

[WRITTEN EXERCISE]

THINGS THAT MIGHT CAUSE YOU TO ATTEND DETROIT SYMPHONY
CONCERTS MORE OFTEN THAN YOU DO NOW

Read the whole list, then rank the top five things that would be most likely to
cause you to attend DSO concerts more often.

Put a "1" next to your first choice
Put a "2" next to your second choice
Put a "3" next to your third choice
Put a "4" next to your fourth choice
Put a "5" next to your fifth choice

I WOULD PROBABLY GO TO DETROIT SYMPHONY CONCERTS MORE
OFTEN IF...

RANK:

_____ ...I could dress casually and feel more comfortable with that crowd
_____ ...a friend of mine invited me to go
_____ ...tickets were less expensive
_____ ...safety wasn't a concern
_____ ...there was always a group of friends to go with
_____ ...someone else did the organizing, and I could just show up
_____ ...the DSO played more of the kind of music that I like
_____ ...concerts weren't so long and I could get home earlier
_____ ...I knew that good seats were still available, without calling to ask
_____ ...I could buy tickets at the last minute
_____ ...the DSO played concerts at a venue closer to my home
_____ ...I knew that I could always exchange my tickets for another date, even if
          I'm not a subscriber
_____ ...each piece was given a short introduction from the stage

_____ ...the DSO did more things to make concerts more interesting to watch

Other:_____

MAGIC OF MUSIC RESEARCH INITIATIVE

PROSPECT SEGMENT FOCUS GROUPS

MODERATORS TOPIC GUIDES — CONSOLIDATED MASTER

- GROUP 3: INITIATORS; TUESDAY, JULY 16 AT 6:00PM

Recent Cultural Outing

To begin, I'd like you all to think about the last two or three times that you went out to an arts or cultural event with a group of friends or family members. On the sheet of paper in front of you, write down the last several arts events that you did, and a few key details about each event. [wait two minutes; distribute sheets in the waiting area, so some of this work can be done beforehand]

1. Now I'd like to take a few minutes to discuss some of your answers. [moving around the table, have each participant to talk through their most typical experience]

Probe: *What is the social context of the group? Family ties? Neighbors? Co-workers? Church friends? Book club members?*

Probe: *How far in advance was the event planned?*

Probe: *How did you contact people? By phone? By e-mail?*

Probe: *Is this typical of your experience?*

Probe: *What could have made the experience easier for you?*

Typical Planning Mode

2. Which is more typical for you — that you react to someone else's invitation to a cultural outing, or that you do the inviting and organizing?

Probe: *Do you share organizing duties with others (rotate organizing)?*

Probe: *How much does it vary?*

Probe: *Do others in your group expect you to be the organizer?*

Reasons for Initiating Cultural Experiences

3. To one degree or another, you all take on the "organizer" role when it comes to planning cultural outings for your family and/or friends. We're interested in learning why you do this, and how this role developed in each you. What motivates you to organize cultural outings?

Probe: *To make sure you have someone to attend with?*

Probe: *To share your enjoyment of the arts with others (i.e., a nurturing instinct)?*

Probe: *What's more important — the particular program or just being together as a group?*

Probe: *How important are the ancillary activities that go along with attending — dinner, drinks, etc...*

Probe: *Would these outing occur if you did not organize them?*

Selection of Group Activities

4. Are there particular types of arts and cultural activities that you do as a group, or does it vary?

Probe: *How do you decide if an event is going to be worthwhile?*

Probe: *Does it have to be something that the entire group will enjoy?*

Probe: *Do you always go with the same group of people?*

5. What factors are important in considering what cultural activities to do with your friends and family?

Probe: *If there is an opportunity to socialize?*

Probe: *How do you decide if an event is going to be worthwhile?*

Probe: *Whether the experience gives your group something to talk about afterwards?*

Probe: *Does the venue make a difference?*

6. How about classical music concerts? Is this a cultural activity that you would do with your group?

Probe: *What makes classical music concerts more or less appropriate as a "group" activity?*

Probe: *Are particular types of classical music concerts more appropriate than others?*

Probe: *What about the Symphony Orchestra concert — like the DSO?*

7. What's the hardest part of organizing a group cultural outing? What's the biggest pain the neck?

Stimulating Attendance in Small Social Groups

8. How could arts and cultural organizations do a better job of helping you organize cultural activities?

9. Let's say that one cultural organization or a group of cultural organizations wanted to help you bring small groups of friends and family to cultural events more often. What support services and incentives would be most likely to stimulate you to organize group outings more often?

Probe: *Is the cost of tickets really a major factor? What about knowing if you could get good seats?*

Probe: *What if you had a personal representative or "concierge" to help you with tickets, restaurant reservations, and other logistics?*

10. If you received a letter from a cultural organization asking if you'd like to participate in a special program designed to support and facilitate attendance in small social groups — something like a "cultural concierge" service — would you step forward and identify yourself as someone who'd take advantage of such a service?

Probe: *Why or why not?*

11. Would you be more interested in a "cultural concierge" service offered by a single organization, such as the Detroit Symphony, or by a consortium of cultural organizations such as the symphony, the opera, the museum, a theatre company, etc.?

Probe: *Why or why not?*

12. Would you want from a relationship with a personal representative or "cultural concierge?"

Probe: *Would you want to be reminded of upcoming activities that you like? By e-mail or leaving a telephone message? Would you be open to suggestions for group activities?*

***GET PERMISSION TO RELEASE VIDEOTAPE

TABLE OF TABLES

Classical Music Consumer Segmentation Study
Final Report Appendix

Other Tables

MAGIC OF MUSIC RESEARCH INITIATIVE: NUMBER OF CASES FOR ANALYSIS GROUPS

TABLE N

	NAT'L SURVEY	TOTAL OF 15 MARKET SURVEYS	BPO/Brooklyn	CSO/Charlotte	CSO/Denver	DSO/Detroit	FWP/Fort Wayne	KCS/Kansas City	LBSO/Long Beach	LPO/New Orleans	NWS/Miami (Dade)	OS/Portland	TPO/Philadelphia	SLSO/Saint Louis	SPCO/Saint Paul	SAS/San Antonio	WSO/Wichita
PHONE SURVEYS - ALL RESPONDENTS	2,200	11,318	751	751	755	753	757	759	753	764	751	760	755	750	754	755	751
UNWEIGHTED DATA																	
Potential Classical Consumers (Respondents Who Passed The Initial Screener)	1,439	6,592	440	413	421	433	388	413	457	429	516	469	408	464	519	369	453
% of All Respondents	65%	58%	59%	55%	56%	58%	51%	54%	61%	56%	69%	62%	54%	62%	69%	49%	60%
NOT Potential Classical Consumers (Respondents Who DID NOT Pass The Initial Screener)	761	4,726	311	338	334	320	369	346	296	335	235	291	347	286	235	386	298
% of All Respondents	35%	42%	41%	45%	44%	42%	49%	46%	39%	44%	31%	38%	46%	38%	31%	51%	40%
WEIGHTED DATA																	
Potential Classical Consumers (Respondents Who Passed The Initial Screener)	1,295	5,905	358	381	388	383	345	389	419	375	425	434	361	424	474	344	405
% of All Respondents	59%	52%	48%	51%	51%	51%	46%	51%	56%	49%	57%	57%	48%	57%	63%	46%	54%
NOT Potential Classical Consumers (Respondents Who DID NOT Pass The Initial Screener)	905	5,412	393	370	367	369	411	370	334	389	326	326	395	326	279	411	346
% of All Respondents	41%	48%	52%	49%	49%	49%	54%	49%	44%	51%	43%	43%	52%	43%	37%	54%	46%
Ticket Buyer Postal Surveys[1]																	
Current Subscribers		5,553	234	418	541	344	385	295	354	371	362	242	452	377	418	342	418
Former Subscribers (Current STB)		1,659	94	65	161	118	142	111	78	96	104	146	90	97	149	69	139
Single Ticket Buyers (Not Former Subscribers)		2,886	194	203	199	211	233	204	175	205	203	131	160	178	212	155	223
TOTAL SAMPLE SIZE		10,098	522	686	901	673	760	610	607	672	669	519	702	652	779	566	780

[1] For the Ticket Buyer Surveys, a total of 1500 were mailed for each orchestra - 750 to a random sample of subscribers, and 750 to a random sample of single ticket buyers (STB).
On the questionnaire, respondents self-identified their subscriber status, which enabled identification of former subscribers among single ticket buyers.

TELEPHONE SAMPLING
CALL DISTRIBUTION / COOPERATION RATES

TABLE N-2

		NAT'L SURVEY	TOTAL OF 15 MARKET SURVEYS	BPO/Brooklyn	CSO/Charlotte	CSO/Denver	DSO/Detroit	FWP/Fort Wayne	KCS/Kansas City	LBSO/Long Beach	LPO/New Orleans	NWS/Miami (Dade)	OS/Portland	TPO/Philadelphia	SLSO/Saint Louis	SPCO/Saint Paul	SAS/San Antonio	WSO/Wichita
NON-SAMPLE NUMBERS	No Answer - Answering Machines, hang-ups, dosconects, (up to 5 callbacks)	3,754	35,033	3,009	1,832	2,180	2,244	2,996	1,944	1,579	2,613	5,124	1,448	2,019	2,161	2,083	2,803	998
	Not In Service	17,218	43,997	2,302	3,786	3,780	2,556	1,882	3,176	2,521	2,127	6,741	2,724	2,499	2,143	2,919	3,001	1,840
HOUSEHOLDS WITH WILLING SURVEY PARTICIPANT	Terminated Interview	319	835	148	36	42	48	63	48	49	69	69	32	36	32	32	91	40
	Call Back	1,081	3,243	393	149	269	166	181	238	104	397	138	132	200	109	183	357	227
	Disqualified - Language Barrier gender, age, etc.	1,748	3,675	886	117	183	138	41	154	242	157	977	142	179	54	84	270	51
	Total Completed Interviews	2,201	11,319	751	751	755	753	757	759	753	764	751	760	755	750	754	755	751
Total Refusals		10,030	20,623	1,548	1,323	1,216	1,318	1,435	1,279	1,446	1,323	1,634	1,388	1,278	1,234	1,326	1,399	1,476
COOPERATION RATE		35%	38%	37%	38%	40%	38%	37%	39%	36%	39%	34%	36%	40%	39%	37%	38%	35%

TABLE 1A

OVERALL LEVEL OF INTEREST IN ARTS ACTIVITIES

Category	Interest Level	NAT'L SURVEY	AVERAGE OF 15 MARKET SURVEYS	BPO/Brooklyn	CSO/Charlotte	CSO/Denver	DSO/Detroit	FWP/Fort Wayne	KCS/Kansas City	LBSO/Long Beach	LPO/New Orleans	NWS/Miami (Dade)	OS/Portland	TPO/Philadelphia	SLSO/Saint Louis	SPCO/Saint Paul	SAS/San Antonio	WSO/Wichita
All Respondents (Public Telephone Surveys)	Extremely interested	7%	8%	11%	7%	9%	8%	4%	7%	8%	10%	11%	7%	8%	7%	10%	6%	5%
	Very interested	20%	20%	20%	18%	22%	18%	14%	18%	22%	18%	19%	23%	21%	23%	22%	19%	18%
	Somewhat interested	40%	39%	32%	40%	40%	36%	39%	41%	40%	38%	38%	43%	38%	41%	38%	38%	43%
	Not very interested	14%	16%	14%	16%	15%	18%	20%	18%	15%	17%	14%	15%	14%	14%	18%	17%	21%
	Not at all interested	19%	17%	23%	20%	14%	21%	23%	16%	16%	17%	18%	13%	18%	16%	12%	20%	14%
Current Subscribers	Extremely interested	N/A	43%	69%	40%	47%	40%	24%	38%	33%	48%	56%	38%	51%	39%	41%	41%	46%
	Very interested	N/A	45%	30%	47%	45%	43%	55%	50%	50%	44%	37%	47%	40%	50%	49%	46%	44%
	Somewhat interested	N/A	11%	1%	12%	8%	17%	19%	11%	17%	7%	7%	15%	8%	10%	9%	12%	10%
	Not very interested	N/A	1%	0%	1%	1%	0%	2%	1%	0%	1%	0%	0%	1%	1%	1%	0%	1%
	Not at all interested	N/A	0%	0%	1%	0%	0%	0%	0%	0%	0%	0%	0%	0%	1%	1%	0%	1%
Former Subscribers	Extremely interested	N/A	41%	72%	45%	43%	39%	35%	32%	33%	46%	52%	30%	43%	33%	40%	38%	35%
	Very interested	N/A	48%	27%	33%	48%	42%	49%	53%	48%	44%	44%	59%	46%	53%	50%	52%	52%
	Somewhat interested	N/A	12%	1%	17%	9%	19%	16%	14%	20%	10%	4%	11%	0%	13%	9%	10%	13%
	Not very interested	N/A	0%	0%	5%	0%	0%	1%	0%	0%	0%	0%	1%	0%	0%	0%	0%	0%
	Not at all interested	N/A	0%	0%	0%	0%	0%	0%	0%	0%	0%	0%	0%	0%	1%	1%	0%	0%
Single Ticket Buyers	Extremely interested	N/A	40%	76%	29%	42%	36%	25%	37%	36%	50%	60%	33%	47%	30%	37%	35%	26%
	Very interested	N/A	42%	22%	47%	43%	44%	43%	47%	45%	40%	35%	49%	40%	43%	47%	44%	47%
	Somewhat interested	N/A	17%	2%	24%	14%	19%	31%	15%	18%	10%	6%	17%	12%	26%	16%	20%	24%
	Not very interested	N/A	1%	0%	1%	2%	0%	0%	0%	1%	0%	0%	1%	1%	2%	1%	0%	2%
	Not at all interested	N/A	0%	0%	0%	0%	2%	0%	1%	0%	0%	0%	0%	0%	0%	0%	0%	0%

NOTES:

All figures from the national and local area telephone surveys are weighted. See the methodology section for details on weighting procedures.

Figures for subscribers, former subscribers, and single ticket buyers derive from the postal surveys of ticket buyers and are not weighted.

TABLE 1B

ROLE THAT ARTS ACTIVITIES PLAY IN RESPONDENT'S LIFE

		NAT'L SURVEY	AVERAGE OF 15 MARKET SURVEYS	BPO/Brooklyn	CSO/Charlotte	CSO/Denver	DSO/Detroit	FWP/Fort Wayne	KCS/Kansas City	LBSO/Long Beach	LPO/New Orleans	NWS/Miami (Dade)	OS/Portland	TPO/Philadelphia	SLSO/Saint Louis	SPCO/Saint Paul	SAS/San Antonio	WSO/Wichita
All Respondents (Public Telephone Surveys)	Major role	26%	24%	29%	21%	25%	20%	17%	19%	25%	26%	31%	26%	25%	25%	26%	21%	19%
	Minor role	51%	54%	42%	55%	54%	51%	56%	59%	53%	49%	48%	57%	56%	56%	62%	53%	59%
	No role at all	23%	23%	29%	25%	21%	29%	27%	22%	22%	25%	21%	18%	20%	20%	13%	27%	22%
Current Subscribers	Major role	N/A	70%	87%	66%	78%	61%	57%	64%	61%	77%	80%	62%	77%	70%	69%	63%	75%
	Minor role	N/A	30%	13%	34%	22%	39%	43%	35%	40%	23%	21%	38%	23%	30%	31%	37%	25%
	No role at all	N/A	0%	0%	0%	0%	0%	0%	1%	0%	0%	0%	0%	0%	1%	0%	0%	0%
Former Subscribers	Major role	N/A	65%	93%	65%	66%	59%	54%	59%	57%	60%	80%	56%	63%	63%	76%	61%	66%
	Minor role	N/A	35%	8%	35%	34%	40%	46%	41%	43%	40%	20%	43%	37%	36%	24%	39%	34%
	No role at all	N/A	0%	0%	0%	0%	2%	0%	0%	0%	0%	0%	0%	0%	1%	0%	0%	1%
Single Ticket Buyers	Major role	N/A	61%	94%	51%	66%	55%	43%	60%	59%	73%	78%	55%	66%	50%	65%	55%	50%
	Minor role	N/A	38%	6%	48%	34%	45%	56%	40%	40%	28%	22%	44%	34%	48%	35%	43%	49%
	No role at all	N/A	1%	0%	1%	0%	0%	1%	1%	1%	0%	1%	1%	0%	2%	0%	3%	2%

NOTES:

All figures from the national and local area telephone surveys are weighted. See the methodology section for details on weighting procedures.

Figures for subscribers, former subscribers, and single ticket buyers derive from the postal surveys of ticket buyers and are not weighted.

TABLE 1C

MEAN PREFERENCE RATINGS FOR ARTS ACTIVITIES (SCALE: 0=DISLIKE A LOT; 10=LIKE A LOT)

		NATL SURVEY	AVERAGE OF 15 MARKET SURVEYS	BPO/Brooklyn	CSO/Charlotte	CSO/Denver	DSO/Detroit	FWP/Fort Wayne	KCS/Kansas City	LBSO/Long Beach	LPO/New Orleans	NWS/Miami (Dade)	OS/Portland	TPO/Philadelphia	SLSO/Saint Louis	SPCO/Saint Paul	SAS/San Antonio	WSO/Wichita
All Respondents (Public Telephone Surveys)	Visiting art museums or galleries	5.0	5.2	5.3	4.7	5.3	5.1	4.6	5.1	5.7	5.3	5.4	5.0	5.4	5.5	5.1	5.1	4.8
	Attending jazz concerts	3.9	4.3	4.1	4.0	4.4	4.4	3.5	4.0	4.7	5.2	4.8	4.4	4.4	4.2	4.0	4.5	4.1
	Attending non-musical stage plays	5.4	5.0	4.7	4.6	5.2	5.3	4.7	4.8	4.9	5.3	5.3	4.8	5.3	5.0	5.4	4.7	4.9
	Attending musical theatre performances	5.6	5.8	6.2	5.4	5.7	5.8	5.3	5.4	5.7	6.1	6.0	5.6	6.2	6.1	6.1	5.7	5.6
	Attending opera performances	2.9	3.0	3.1	2.7	3.2	2.8	2.3	2.6	3.3	3.3	3.9	3.3	2.9	3.5	3.2	3.2	2.5
	Attending ballet performances	3.1	3.4	3.4	3.1	3.6	2.9	2.6	2.9	3.7	3.6	4.4	3.6	3.3	3.3	3.2	3.5	3.0
	Attending classical music concerts	4.3	4.4	4.3	4.2	4.4	4.2	3.9	4.0	4.7	4.4	5.1	4.7	4.0	4.5	4.7	4.4	4.2
Current Subscribers	Visiting art museums or galleries	N/A	8.2	8.8	7.7	8.2	8.3	7.4	7.8	8.1	8.5	8.6	8.3	8.6	8.2	8.3	8.1	8.2
	Attending jazz concerts	N/A	5.8	6.2	5.7	5.9	5.7	5.9	6.0	5.6	6.0	5.9	5.8	5.1	5.9	5.7	5.8	5.4
	Attending non-musical stage plays	N/A	8.0	8.8	8.1	7.8	8.0	7.5	7.9	8.1	8.1	8.5	7.7	8.0	7.9	8.2	7.8	7.6
	Attending musical theatre performances	N/A	8.2	7.2	8.4	8.2	8.5	8.6	8.3	8.6	8.2	8.4	8.0	8.1	8.1	7.6	8.4	8.6
	Attending opera performances	N/A	6.6	8.2	5.8	7.1	6.7	5.5	5.9	6.0	6.9	7.2	6.0	7.3	6.7	6.4	6.6	6.6
	Attending ballet performances	N/A	6.6	7.3	6.1	6.6	6.5	5.5	6.0	6.1	6.9	8.0	6.3	6.8	6.5	6.5	6.8	6.7
	Attending classical music concerts	N/A	9.1	9.3	8.7	9.2	8.9	8.3	9.0	8.5	9.6	9.5	8.8	9.5	9.1	9.6	8.8	9.5
% of Former Subscribers	Visiting art museums or galleries	N/A	8.0	9.1	7.3	8.0	8.2	7.4	8.0	8.1	8.2	8.5	7.9	8.3	7.8	7.9	8.0	8.0
	Attending jazz concerts	N/A	5.9	6.2	6.6	5.9	5.7	5.6	6.3	5.4	6.6	6.0	5.9	5.3	5.8	5.8	5.8	5.4
	Attending non-musical stage plays	N/A	7.7	8.3	8.2	7.8	7.9	7.4	7.6	7.4	7.9	8.3	7.3	7.6	7.5	7.7	7.8	7.5
	Attending musical theatre performances	N/A	8.0	6.0	8.3	7.9	8.2	8.6	8.1	8.3	8.5	8.0	7.5	7.8	8.2	7.2	8.6	8.8
	Attending opera performances	N/A	6.3	7.9	5.8	6.6	6.3	5.1	5.7	6.2	7.2	7.2	5.7	7.1	5.8	6.6	6.6	5.7
	Attending ballet performances	N/A	6.4	7.1	5.8	6.2	6.4	5.8	6.0	6.5	6.6	7.7	6.0	7.1	6.2	6.5	6.6	6.4
	Attending classical music concerts	N/A	8.8	9.3	8.4	9.1	8.8	8.2	8.5	8.5	9.2	9.5	8.3	9.2	8.6	9.2	8.6	9.0
Single Ticket Buyers	Visiting art museums or galleries	N/A	7.9	9.0	7.2	7.8	7.9	7.3	7.8	8.0	8.5	8.7	7.9	8.2	7.8	8.0	7.8	7.4
	Attending jazz concerts	N/A	6.0	6.7	5.5	6.5	6.1	5.6	6.4	6.1	6.5	6.4	6.0	5.7	6.0	5.5	5.9	5.8
	Attending non-musical stage plays	N/A	7.7	8.5	8.0	7.8	7.5	7.0	7.6	7.9	8.0	8.2	7.7	7.4	7.6	7.8	7.5	7.1
	Attending musical theatre performances	N/A	8.1	6.2	8.3	8.3	8.2	8.0	8.4	8.6	8.3	8.4	8.1	7.8	8.1	7.6	8.4	8.4
	Attending opera performances	N/A	5.9	7.5	5.3	6.1	5.8	4.4	5.6	6.3	7.1	7.4	6.0	6.2	5.5	5.9	5.8	4.8
	Attending ballet performances	N/A	6.3	7.1	5.8	6.4	6.0	5.1	6.1	6.6	7.0	7.6	6.6	6.4	5.9	6.0	7.2	5.5
	Attending classical music concerts	N/A	8.5	8.5	8.0	8.9	8.2	8.0	8.3	8.2	9.2	9.2	8.4	8.7	8.3	8.9	8.1	8.0

NOTES:

All figures from the national and local area telephone surveys are weighted. See the methodology section for details on weighting procedures.

Figures for subscribers, former subscribers, and single ticket buyers derive from the postal surveys of ticket buyers and are not weighted

TABLE 1D

PARTICIPATION RATES FOR CERTAIN ARTS ACTIVITIES, PAST 12 MONTHS

		NATL SURVEY	AVERAGE OF 15 MARKET SURVEYS	BPO/Brooklyn	CSO/Charlotte	CSO/Denver	DSO/Detroit	FWP/Fort Wayne	KCS/Kansas City	LBSO/Long Beach	LPO/New Orleans	NWS/Miami (Dade)	OS/Portland	TPO/Philadelphia	SLSO/Saint Louis	SPCO/Saint Paul	SAS/San Antonio	WSO/Wichita
All Respondents (Public Telephone Surveys)	Visited an Art Museums or Gallery	37%	43%	43%	38%	53%	36%	33%	38%	44%	40%	46%	42%	45%	55%	50%	43%	43%
	Attended a Jazz Concert	18%	22%	18%	20%	23%	23%	13%	21%	26%	32%	19%	24%	23%	21%	21%	26%	21%
	Attended a Non-musical Stage Play	N/A	30%	30%	27%	33%	29%	23%	30%	27%	28%	37%	28%	31%	32%	41%	22%	28%
	Attended a Musical Theater Performance	24%	30%	38%	26%	34%	28%	23%	29%	29%	29%	32%	26%	34%	39%	33%	26%	33%
	Attended an Opera Performance	5%	7%	7%	6%	7%	6%	2%	5%	8%	7%	14%	7%	6%	12%	7%	5%	3%
	Attended a Ballet Performance	8%	10%	11%	8%	12%	6%	5%	10%	9%	11%	20%	13%	9%	8%	9%	9%	8%
	Attended a Classical Music Concert	17%	20%	15%	19%	23%	15%	20%	18%	21%	19%	17%	22%	18%	25%	24%	17%	21%
Current Subscribers	Visited an Art Museums or Gallery	N/A	83%	94%	81%	84%	81%	73%	82%	79%	89%	86%	83%	86%	87%	86%	76%	77%
	Attended a Jazz Concert	N/A	30%	33%	28%	40%	27%	30%	36%	28%	35%	32%	28%	20%	29%	25%	27%	26%
	Attended a Non-musical Stage Play	N/A	72%	87%	70%	72%	71%	71%	77%	71%	68%	82%	63%	71%	69%	81%	67%	64%
	Attended a Musical Theater Performance	N/A	66%	72%	70%	66%	62%	67%	67%	72%	56%	74%	55%	62%	65%	48%	71%	78%
	Attended an Opera Performance	N/A	37%	66%	31%	51%	33%	12%	34%	22%	49%	49%	34%	47%	39%	34%	30%	27%
	Attended a Ballet Performance	N/A	27%	47%	32%	28%	18%	17%	24%	16%	29%	65%	25%	29%	22%	18%	21%	20%
	Attended a Classical Music Concert	N/A	91%	97%	88%	94%	87%	79%	91%	78%	98%	97%	86%	97%	92%	99%	83%	98%
Former Subscribers	Visited an Art Museums or Gallery	N/A	81%	97%	75%	84%	75%	72%	78%	89%	83%	81%	82%	89%	79%	85%	74%	73%
	Attended a Jazz Concert	N/A	30%	32%	37%	32%	34%	20%	35%	30%	47%	29%	24%	20%	34%	30%	23%	27%
	Attended a Non-musical Stage Play	N/A	67%	83%	79%	68%	64%	60%	66%	67%	65%	74%	51%	67%	64%	79%	61%	60%
	Attended a Musical Theater Performance	N/A	59%	62%	69%	60%	58%	59%	63%	68%	56%	65%	36%	53%	71%	46%	62%	72%
	Attended an Opera Performance	N/A	32%	75%	32%	39%	32%	8%	21%	31%	43%	48%	18%	43%	32%	36%	38%	14%
	Attended a Ballet Performance	N/A	26%	59%	25%	24%	15%	14%	23%	21%	24%	53%	24%	33%	18%	24%	19%	22%
	Attended a Classical Music Concert	N/A	86%	96%	99%	89%	85%	80%	81%	73%	88%	91%	70%	93%	87%	96%	73%	85%
Single Ticket Buyers	Visited an Art Museums or Gallery	N/A	76%	97%	64%	75%	75%	62%	74%	78%	84%	85%	80%	83%	82%	78%	66%	67%
	Attended a Jazz Concert	N/A	30%	45%	23%	36%	31%	23%	37%	22%	44%	34%	26%	29%	35%	18%	22%	28%
	Attended a Non-musical Stage Play	N/A	64%	87%	67%	71%	58%	52%	67%	62%	61%	73%	59%	63%	61%	72%	53%	54%
	Attended a Musical Theater Performance	N/A	58%	61%	65%	63%	55%	54%	60%	62%	54%	63%	44%	56%	61%	52%	59%	64%
	Attended an Opera Performance	N/A	26%	60%	19%	36%	20%	7%	26%	24%	42%	49%	19%	23%	17%	20%	17%	15%
	Attended a Ballet Performance	N/A	26%	54%	23%	30%	14%	13%	25%	23%	30%	49%	23%	25%	16%	16%	34%	13%
	Attended a Classical Music Concert	N/A	79%	86%	80%	86%	68%	76%	77%	70%	91%	84%	77%	76%	76%	91%	61%	73%

NOTES:

All figures from the national and local area telephone surveys are weighted. See the methodology section for details on weighting procedures.

Figures for subscribers, former subscribers, and single ticket buyers derive from the postal surveys of ticket buyers and are not weighted.

TABLE 1E

MEAN NUMBER OF LIVE PERFORMING ARTS EVENTS ATTENDED, LAST 12 MONTHS

	NAT'L SURVEY	AVERAGE OF 15 MARKET SURVEYS	BPO/Brooklyn	CSO/Charlotte	CSO/Denver	DSO/Detroit	FWP/Fort Wayne	KCS/Kansas City	LBSO/Long Beach	LPO/New Orleans	NWS/Miami (Dade)	OS/Portland	TPO/Philadelphia	SLSO/Saint Louis	SPCO/Saint Paul	SAS/San Antonio	WSO/Wichita
All Telephone Survey Respondents	3.4	4.0	4.3	3.2	4.3	3.0	2.9	3.8	3.7	4.5	5.0	4.4	3.7	4.3	5.2	3.7	4.1
Current Subscribers	N/A	18.7	31.0	14.9	20.4	15.8	15.2	18.0	15.8	19.9	23.6	15.5	19.0	19.1	19.7	16.1	18.9
Former Subscribers	N/A	14.3	33.6	13.0	12.8	10.5	12.3	13.4	13.6	13.6	20.3	10.0	15.5	13.7	16.7	10.7	11.6
Single Ticket Buyers	N/A	13.3	32.1	8.5	13.2	10.7	9.3	11.7	12.6	15.6	20.1	9.0	13.0	12.8	13.1	9.5	9.1

NOTES:

All figures from the national and local area telephone surveys are weighted. See the methodology section for details on weighting procedures.

Respondents who reported more than 125 attendances in the past year were classified as outliers (i.e., invalid responses).

MEAN NUMBER OF CLASSICAL MUSIC CONCERTS ATTENDED, PAST 12 MONTHS

	NAT'L SURVEY	AVERAGE OF 15 MARKET SURVEYS	BPO/Brooklyn	CSO/Charlotte	CSO/Denver	DSO/Detroit	FWP/Fort Wayne	KCS/Kansas City	LBSO/Long Beach	LPO/New Orleans	NWS/Miami (Dade)	OS/Portland	TPO/Philadelphia	SLSO/Saint Louis	SPCO/Saint Paul	SAS/San Antonio	WSO/Wichita
Telephone Survey Respondents Who Reported ANY Classical Attendance in Past Year (i.e., "Current" Attendees)	3.0	3.1	3.6	3.3	3.6	2.6	2.5	2.5	3.2	3.5	3.9	3.0	3.2	3.3	3.3	2.9	2.1
Current Subscribers	N/A	10.9	17.5	7.8	12.3	9.3	7.4	9.6	8.1	13.8	13.7	8.5	11.8	9.8	12.5	9.3	12.7
Former Subscribers	N/A	6.9	20.5	6.0	6.1	4.9	4.3	6.0	4.7	6.2	10.5	4.0	7.8	6.3	8.7	4.9	5.6
Single Ticket Buyers	N/A	5.5	9.7	3.6	6.4	3.6	3.7	4.4	5.3	7.8	9.9	3.7	5.6	5.4	5.6	4.1	3.4

NOTES:

All figures from the national and local area telephone surveys are weighted. See the methodology section for details on weighting procedures.

Figures for subscribers, former subscribers, and single ticket buyers derive from the postal surveys of ticket buyers and are not weighted.

Respondents who reported more than 125 attendances in the past year were classified as outliers (i.e., invalid responses).

TABLE 1F

PERCENTAGE OF RESPONDENTS WHO HAVE EVER VOLUNTEERED FOR A NON-PROFIT ARTS OR CULTURAL ORGANIZATION

	NAT'L SURVEY	AVERAGE OF 15 MARKET SURVEYS	BPO/Brooklyn	CSO/Charlotte	CSO/Denver	DSO/Detroit	FWP/Fort Wayne	KCS/Kansas City	LBSO/Long Beach	LPO/New Orleans	NWS/Miami (Dade)	OS/Portland	TPO/Philadelphia	SLSO/Saint Louis	SPCO/Saint Paul	SAS/San Antonio	WSO/Wichita
All Telephone Survey Respondents	16%	16%	15%	17%	18%	14%	17%	15%	18%	18%	16%	17%	14%	15%	16%	16%	16%
Current Subscribers	N/A	47%	49%	48%	49%	42%	46%	47%	52%	50%	45%	45%	44%	41%	43%	47%	55%
Former Subscribers	N/A	43%	52%	39%	48%	37%	46%	46%	35%	56%	42%	36%	34%	37%	43%	48%	41%
Single Ticket Buyers	N/A	38%	49%	34%	40%	35%	30%	36%	44%	51%	48%	41%	35%	28%	37%	35%	31%

NOTES:

All figures from the national and local area telephone surveys are weighted. See the methodology section for details on weighting procedures.

Figures for subscribers, former subscribers, and single ticket buyers derive from the postal surveys of ticket buyers and are not weighted.

TABLE 1G

PERCENT OF RESPONDENTS WHO WOULD LIKE TO ATTEND LIVE PERFORMANCES OF MUSIC, DANCE, OR THEATER MORE OFTEN THAN THEY DO NOW

	NAT'L SURVEY	AVERAGE OF 15 MARKET SURVEYS	BPO/Brooklyn	CSO/Charlotte	CSO/Denver	DSO/Detroit	FWP/Fort Wayne	KCS/Kansas City	LBSO/Long Beach	LPO/New Orleans	NWS/Miami (Dade)	OS/Portland	TPO/Philadelphia	SLSO/Saint Louis	SPCO/Saint Paul	SAS/San Antonio	WSO/Wichita
All Telephone Survey Respondents	65%	59%	60%	60%	63%	56%	53%	57%	65%	58%	61%	62%	61%	60%	62%	58%	56%
Current Subscribers	N/A	71%	69%	67%	65%	77%	74%	71%	69%	73%	68%	74%	73%	70%	69%	76%	71%
Former Subscribers	N/A	85%	73%	78%	92%	87%	90%	84%	82%	90%	83%	92%	86%	80%	81%	92%	84%
Single-Ticket Buyers	N/A	87%	71%	88%	87%	92%	90%	84%	90%	90%	89%	89%	87%	88%	83%	86%	87%

NOTES:

All figures from the national and local area telephone surveys are weighted. See the methodology section for details on weighting procedures.

Figures for subscribers, former subscribers, and single ticket buyers derive from the postal surveys of ticket buyers and are not weighted.

TABLE 1H

PERCENTAGE OF RESPONDENTS WHO WOULD ACCEPT A FREE TICKET TO A CLASSICAL MUSIC CONCERT, IF OFFERED BY A FRIEND OR FAMILY MEMBER

All Telephone Survey Respondents	NAT'L SURVEY	AVERAGE OF 15 MARKET SURVEYS	BPO/Brooklyn	CSO/Charlotte	CSO/Denver	DSO/Detroit	FWP/Fort Wayne	KCS/Kansas City	LBSO/Long Beach	LPO/New Orleans	NWS/Miami (Dade)	OS/Portland	TPO/Philadelphia	SLSO/Saint Louis	SPCO/Saint Paul	SAS/San Antonio	WSO/Wichita
Yes	66%	56%	51%	56%	54%	55%	50%	55%	61%	58%	54%	60%	54%	60%	63%	51%	55%
Maybe/Depends	11%	13%	12%	14%	13%	13%	13%	14%	12%	9%	17%	15%	10%	10%	13%	10%	14%
No	23%	32%	37%	31%	33%	33%	37%	31%	27%	33%	29%	25%	37%	30%	24%	39%	31%

NOTES:

All figures from the national and local area telephone surveys are weighted. See the methodology section for details on weighting procedures.

1H

TABLE 2A-1

INFORMATION ACQUISITION - LEVEL OF AGREEMENT WITH THE STATEMENT: "I'M ALWAYS LOOKING FOR INFORMATION ABOUT CULTURAL ACTIVITIES TO DO"

		NAT'L SURVEY	AVERAGE OF 15 MARKET SURVEYS	BPO/Brooklyn	CSO/Charlotte	CSO/Denver	DSO/Detroit	FWP/Fort Wayne	KCS/Kansas City	LBSO/Long Beach	LPO/New Orleans	NWS/Miami (Dade)	OS/Portland	TPO/Philadelphia	SLSO/Saint Louis	SPCO/Saint Paul	SAS/San Antonio	WSO/Wichita
Potential Classical Music Consumers*	Agree a lot	27%	30%	36%	25%	31%	33%	22%	26%	34%	38%	38%	29%	33%	31%	25%	30%	21%
	Agree a little	40%	40%	33%	42%	41%	38%	45%	42%	37%	36%	32%	41%	44%	39%	40%	41%	46%
	Disagree a little	25%	21%	23%	21%	20%	21%	22%	19%	19%	19%	24%	22%	16%	22%	25%	21%	20%
	Disagree a lot	9%	9%	8%	12%	8%	8%	11%	13%	10%	8%	5%	9%	7%	7%	10%	9%	13%
Current Subscribers	Agree a lot	N/A	48%	65%	49%	47%	42%	38%	49%	47%	52%	70%	47%	50%	50%	43%	45%	48%
	Agree a little	N/A	42%	30%	43%	45%	48%	49%	42%	40%	38%	26%	41%	40%	36%	46%	45%	41%
	Disagree a little	N/A	8%	3%	7%	6%	8%	11%	8%	11%	7%	3%	11%	7%	11%	9%	7%	9%
	Disagree a lot	N/A	2%	2%	2%	1%	2%	3%	1%	2%	3%	1%	1%	4%	4%	3%	3%	2%
Former Subscribers	Agree a lot	N/A	49%	67%	54%	49%	43%	39%	45%	46%	54%	81%	37%	46%	40%	51%	40%	49%
	Agree a little	N/A	40%	26%	37%	38%	45%	47%	42%	45%	35%	17%	46%	38%	47%	38%	48%	44%
	Disagree a little	N/A	9%	5%	8%	11%	10%	11%	8%	7%	10%	1%	13%	12%	10%	8%	8%	6%
	Disagree a lot	N/A	2%	1%	2%	1%	2%	3%	6%	3%	0%	1%	4%	4%	3%	3%	5%	2%
Single Ticket Buyers	Agree a lot	N/A	49%	73%	53%	48%	48%	33%	41%	50%	62%	74%	39%	44%	40%	41%	37%	46%
	Agree a little	N/A	39%	23%	36%	41%	42%	48%	47%	40%	28%	21%	46%	40%	40%	45%	46%	41%
	Disagree a little	N/A	10%	4%	9%	8%	10%	14%	9%	7%	8%	3%	11%	15%	15%	11%	13%	10%
	Disagree a lot	N/A	3%	1%	3%	3%	1%	5%	3%	4%	2%	1%	3%	1%	5%	4%	5%	2%

NOTES:

**"Potential Classical Music Consumers" are defined as the sub-set of respondents in each area who qualified for an extended interview, based on their responses to an initial series of questions.

All figures from the national and local area telephone surveys are weighted. See the methodology section for details on weighting procedures.

Figures for subscribers, former subscribers, and single ticket buyers derive from the postal surveys of ticket buyers and are not weighted.

TABLE 2A-2

PLANNING MODE - LEVEL OF AGREEMENT WITH THE STATEMENT: "I'M THE KIND OF PERSON WHO LIKES TO ORGANIZE CULTURAL OUTINGS FOR MY FRIENDS"

		NAT'L SURVEY	AVERAGE OF 15 MARKET SURVEYS	BPO/Brooklyn	CSO/Charlotte	CSO/Denver	DSO/Detroit	FWP/Fort Wayne	KCS/Kansas City	LBSO/Long Beach	LPO/New Orleans	NWS/Miami (Dade)	OS/Portland	TPO/Philadelphia	SLSO/Saint Louis	SPCO/Saint Paul	SAS/San Antonio	WSO/Wichita
Potential Classical Music Consumers*	Agree a lot	18%	16%	23%	15%	16%	17%	14%	14%	19%	23%	23%	10%	16%	16%	13%	21%	8%
	Agree a little	25%	27%	26%	24%	29%	25%	21%	25%	31%	28%	24%	28%	32%	30%	25%	30%	25%
	Disagree a little	27%	28%	27%	26%	23%	31%	25%	29%	23%	25%	29%	30%	27%	27%	34%	24%	34%
	Disagree a lot	31%	29%	24%	35%	31%	27%	40%	32%	27%	25%	24%	32%	25%	28%	28%	25%	34%
Current Subscribers	Agree a lot	N/A	11%	14%	12%	13%	12%	9%	11%	11%	11%	15%	10%	13%	11%	12%	10%	8%
	Agree a little	N/A	31%	32%	33%	27%	31%	34%	28%	33%	31%	34%	30%	30%	34%	34%	29%	32%
	Disagree a little	N/A	27%	28%	34%	28%	27%	25%	27%	31%	23%	22%	34%	22%	22%	27%	28%	28%
	Disagree a lot	N/A	30%	27%	22%	32%	31%	31%	34%	25%	35%	29%	26%	36%	33%	27%	33%	32%
Former Subscribers	Agree a lot	N/A	13%	19%	11%	11%	15%	11%	15%	8%	14%	20%	14%	13%	12%	11%	13%	11%
	Agree a little	N/A	30%	36%	37%	28%	32%	30%	29%	24%	25%	33%	24%	24%	36%	36%	19%	34%
	Disagree a little	N/A	28%	24%	25%	32%	27%	25%	27%	35%	29%	24%	30%	29%	23%	26%	39%	32%
	Disagree a lot	N/A	29%	21%	28%	31%	26%	34%	28%	33%	32%	23%	33%	35%	29%	26%	29%	24%
Single Ticket Buyers	Agree a lot	N/A	13%	15%	13%	11%	15%	7%	10%	16%	14%	30%	10%	14%	10%	8%	17%	11%
	Agree a little	N/A	31%	39%	32%	33%	33%	31%	32%	28%	34%	32%	30%	30%	26%	29%	26%	29%
	Disagree a little	N/A	27%	23%	27%	24%	27%	31%	33%	24%	25%	14%	34%	27%	26%	36%	24%	25%
	Disagree a lot	N/A	29%	24%	28%	32%	25%	30%	26%	33%	27%	25%	26%	29%	38%	26%	33%	37%

NOTES:

**"Potential Classical Music Consumers" are defined as the sub-set of respondents in each area who qualified for an extended interview, based on their responses to an initial series of questions.

All figures from the national and local area telephone surveys are weighted. See the methodology section for details on weighting procedures.

Figures for subscribers, former subscribers, and single ticket buyers derive from the postal surveys of ticket buyers and are not weighted.

TABLE 2A-3

PLANNING MODE - LEVEL OF AGREEMENT WITH THE STATEMENT: "I'M MUCH MORE LIKELY TO ATTEND CULTURAL OUTINGS IF SOMEONE ELSE INVITES ME"

Group	Response	NAT'L SURVEY	AVERAGE OF 15 MARKET SURVEYS	BPO/Brooklyn	CSO/Charlotte	CSO/Denver	DSO/Detroit	FWP/Fort Wayne	KCS/Kansas City	LBSO/Long Beach	LPO/New Orleans	NWS/Miami (Dade)	OS/Portland	TPO/Philadelphia	SLSO/Saint Louis	SPCO/Saint Paul	SAS/San Antonio	WSO/Wichita
Potential Classical Music Consumers*	Agree a lot	56%	52%	60%	54%	47%	50%	56%	49%	54%	54%	50%	46%	51%	54%	50%	54%	49%
	Agree a little	29%	30%	25%	25%	33%	32%	29%	32%	28%	28%	29%	34%	27%	26%	35%	29%	34%
	Disagree a little	10%	13%	10%	14%	14%	14%	10%	11%	12%	14%	13%	13%	17%	15%	10%	11%	13%
	Disagree a lot	4%	6%	6%	7%	6%	4%	5%	8%	7%	4%	9%	7%	6%	5%	6%	6%	5%
Current Subscribers	Agree a lot	N/A	11%	7%	8%	8%	14%	13%	13%	23%	12%	9%	17%	9%	12%	8%	9%	10%
	Agree a little	N/A	30%	23%	32%	26%	32%	36%	31%	31%	31%	25%	37%	28%	30%	29%	36%	31%
	Disagree a little	N/A	30%	28%	26%	32%	29%	32%	31%	29%	24%	27%	24%	33%	33%	38%	33%	31%
	Disagree a lot	N/A	28%	42%	34%	35%	25%	19%	25%	17%	33%	39%	22%	30%	25%	26%	22%	28%
Former Subscribers	Agree a lot	N/A	15%	10%	11%	13%	19%	20%	13%	15%	15%	14%	23%	18%	10%	13%	20%	10%
	Agree a little	N/A	34%	25%	35%	27%	35%	41%	40%	44%	34%	24%	38%	31%	30%	31%	25%	48%
	Disagree a little	N/A	28%	26%	34%	33%	25%	20%	25%	21%	30%	23%	23%	26%	37%	36%	34%	27%
	Disagree a lot	N/A	23%	39%	20%	27%	22%	19%	22%	21%	21%	29%	17%	26%	23%	20%	21%	14%
Single Ticket Buyers	Agree a lot	N/A	17%	8%	14%	10%	16%	25%	18%	20%	20%	13%	17%	20%	23%	16%	16%	19%
	Agree a little	N/A	35%	25%	42%	36%	37%	35%	32%	34%	34%	34%	39%	33%	39%	36%	34%	39%
	Disagree a little	N/A	28%	32%	25%	32%	34%	29%	29%	27%	23%	21%	29%	30%	20%	26%	30%	29%
	Disagree a lot	N/A	20%	36%	19%	22%	14%	11%	21%	19%	23%	32%	15%	16%	18%	21%	20%	14%

NOTES:

**"Potential Classical Music Consumers" are defined as the sub-set of respondents in each area who qualified for an extended interview, based on their responses to an initial series of questions.

All figures from the national and local area telephone surveys are weighted. See the methodology section for details on weighting procedures.

Figures for subscribers, former subscribers, and single ticket buyers derive from the postal surveys of ticket buyers and are not weighted.

TABLE 2B

RESPONDENT'S TYPICAL ROLE IN THE PROCESS OF DECIDING WHETHER OR NOT TO ATTEND LIVE PERFORMANCES

		NAT'L SURVEY	AVERAGE OF 15 MARKET SURVEYS	BPO/Brooklyn	CSO/Charlotte	CSO/Denver	DSO/Detroit	FWP/Fort Wayne	KCS/Kansas City	LBSO/Long Beach	LPO/New Orleans	NWS/Miami (Dade)	OS/Portland	TPO/Philadelphia	SLSO/Saint Louis	SPCO/Saint Paul	SAS/San Antonio	WSO/Wichita
Potential Classical Music Consumers*	I am the primary decision-maker	N/A	25%	21%	22%	24%	22%	21%	24%	29%	31%	34%	26%	26%	29%	21%	27%	24%
	I participate in a joint decision process	N/A	56%	51%	59%	56%	56%	57%	61%	50%	52%	53%	59%	62%	53%	57%	54%	58%
	Someone else usually decides and I go along	N/A	19%	28%	20%	20%	22%	23%	15%	22%	17%	13%	16%	11%	19%	22%	20%	18%
Current Subscribers	I am the primary decision-maker	N/A	44%	58%	N/A	43%	39%	37%	41%	36%	48%	44%	45%	50%	49%	42%	41%	43%
	I participate in a joint decision process	N/A	55%	42%	N/A	56%	60%	62%	59%	61%	51%	56%	55%	49%	49%	58%	59%	56%
	Someone else usually decides and I go along	N/A	1%	0%	N/A	1%	1%	1%	1%	3%	1%	1%	0%	1%	2%	1%	1%	1%
Former Subscribers	I am the primary decision-maker	N/A	47%	66%	N/A	48%	44%	45%	35%	50%	50%	51%	45%	52%	43%	43%	48%	43%
	I participate in a joint decision process	N/A	52%	32%	N/A	50%	55%	55%	65%	47%	50%	47%	54%	43%	56%	57%	52%	55%
	Someone else usually decides and I go along	N/A	1%	2%	N/A	2%	1%	0%	0%	3%	1%	2%	1%	5%	1%	0%	0%	2%
Single Ticket Buyers	I am the primary decision-maker	N/A	45%	63%	N/A	48%	48%	40%	38%	41%	50%	54%	40%	42%	42%	46%	38%	38%
	I participate in a joint decision process	N/A	52%	36%	N/A	50%	51%	55%	59%	54%	47%	44%	60%	57%	56%	51%	57%	59%
	Someone else usually decides and I go along	N/A	3%	1%	N/A	2%	2%	6%	3%	4%	4%	1%	1%	1%	1%	3%	5%	2%

NOTES:

*"Potential Classical Music Consumers" are defined as the sub-set of respondents in each area who qualified for an extended interview, based on their responses to an initial series of questions.

All figures from the national and local area telephone surveys are weighted. See the methodology section for details on weighting procedures.

Figures for subscribers, former subscribers, and single ticket buyers derive from the postal surveys of ticket buyers and are not weighted.

TABLE 2C

RESPONDENTS' TYPICAL PLANNING HORIZON FOR LEISURE ACTIVITIES LIKE GOING OUT TO LIVE PERFORMANCES

		NAT'L SURVEY	AVERAGE OF 15 MARKET SURVEYS	BPO/Brooklyn	CSO/Charlotte	CSO/Denver	DSO/Detroit	FWP/Fort Wayne	KCS/Kansas City	LBSO/Long Beach	LPO/New Orleans	NWS/Miami (Dade)	OS/Portland	TPO/Philadelphia	SLSO/Saint Louis	SPCO/Saint Paul	SAS/San Antonio	WSO/Wichita
Potential Classical Music Consumers*	A month or more beforehand	26%	25%	22%	21%	28%	34%	20%	25%	31%	15%	17%	33%	37%	29%	29%	23%	13%
	Several weeks beforehand	23%	24%	22%	23%	26%	27%	28%	26%	25%	23%	24%	23%	28%	27%	23%	21%	20%
	A week to ten days beforehand	31%	29%	29%	33%	28%	27%	29%	30%	26%	32%	36%	28%	20%	23%	25%	31%	34%
	Several days to a week beforehand	18%	18%	23%	17%	15%	11%	21%	17%	14%	25%	20%	14%	12%	16%	17%	17%	27%
	The day of the event	3%	4%	5%	5%	4%	3%	3%	3%	4%	6%	3%	2%	4%	5%	6%	9%	5%
Current Subscribers	A month or more beforehand	N/A	50%	63%	51%	61%	44%	39%	49%	54%	36%	56%	50%	56%	53%	61%	43%	27%
	Several weeks beforehand	N/A	33%	24%	27%	30%	39%	38%	35%	34%	37%	29%	35%	33%	32%	29%	36%	35%
	A week to ten days beforehand	N/A	11%	6%	13%	6%	12%	14%	11%	6%	17%	10%	10%	7%	9%	6%	15%	22%
	Several days to a week beforehand	N/A	7%	7%	9%	3%	5%	8%	5%	5%	10%	5%	6%	5%	5%	4%	6%	15%
	The day of the event	N/A	0%	0%	1%	0%	0%	1%	0%	1%	0%	0%	0%	0%	8%	0%	3%	0%
Former Subscribers	A month or more beforehand	N/A	33%	48%	35%	34%	35%	26%	34%	37%	23%	44%	27%	47%	28%	36%	28%	16%
	Several weeks beforehand	N/A	37%	24%	32%	38%	39%	42%	36%	45%	28%	29%	45%	31%	44%	38%	37%	37%
	A week to ten days beforehand	N/A	19%	19%	25%	17%	16%	26%	18%	12%	26%	15%	18%	12%	19%	12%	25%	29%
	Several days to a week beforehand	N/A	11%	9%	8%	11%	10%	7%	8%	5%	22%	10%	9%	9%	8%	13%	6%	18%
	The day of the event	N/A	1%	0%	0%	0%	0%	0%	4%	1%	1%	1%	1%	1%	1%	1%	0%	0%
Single Ticket Buyers	A month or more beforehand	N/A	28%	39%	31%	34%	27%	27%	25%	37%	16%	27%	29%	37%	29%	31%	25%	15%
	Several weeks beforehand	N/A	37%	30%	35%	35%	41%	36%	44%	39%	25%	29%	39%	39%	36%	37%	47%	40%
	A week to ten days beforehand	N/A	20%	12%	21%	13%	21%	21%	17%	10%	26%	25%	25%	12%	23%	20%	20%	27%
	Several days to a week beforehand	N/A	15%	18%	13%	18%	12%	17%	14%	13%	30%	18%	8%	12%	13%	11%	9%	18%
	The day of the event	N/A	1%	1%	1%	0%	0%	0%	1%	1%	3%	1%	0%	0%	0%	2%	0%	1%

NOTES:

**"Potential Classical Music Consumers" are defined as the sub-set of respondents in each area who qualified for an extended interview, based on their responses to an initial series of questions.

All figures from the national and local area telephone surveys (top three rows) are weighted. See the methodology section for details on weighting procedures. Figures for subscribers, former subscribers, and single ticket buyers derive from the postal surveys of ticket buyers and are not weighted.

TABLE 2F

% OF RESPONDENTS WHO'VE EVER PURCHASED TICKETS ONLINE, AND LIKELIHOOD OF PURCHASING TICKETS ONLINE IN THE FUTURE, IF NOT

	NAT'L SURVEY	AVERAGE OF 15 MARKET SURVEYS	BPO/Brooklyn	CSO/Charlotte	CSO/Denver	DSO/Detroit	FWP/Fort Wayne	KCS/Kansas City	LBSO/Long Beach	LPO/New Orleans	NWS/Miami (Dade)	OS/Portland	TPO/Philadelphia	SLSO/Saint Louis	SPCO/Saint Paul	SAS/San Antonio	WSO/Wichita
Potential Classical Music Consumers[1]																	
% Who've EVER Purchased Online	N/A	25%	17%	23%	38%	23%	12%	24%	31%	26%	24%	34%	29%	21%	22%	24%	17%
If not, how likely are you to purchase tickets online in the future?																	
Very Likely	N/A	10%	9%	10%	6%	11%	10%	9%	13%	11%	10%	16%	12%	12%	9%	8%	6%
Somewhat Likely	N/A	29%	33%	32%	28%	31%	27%	30%	30%	28%	29%	31%	31%	20%	30%	29%	26%
Not Very Likely	N/A	61%	58%	58%	66%	59%	63%	62%	57%	60%	61%	53%	57%	68%	62%	64%	69%
Subscribers: % Who've EVER Purchased Online	N/A	25%	34%	29%	26%	26%	17%	24%	26%	30%	31%	26%	30%	25%	22%	24%	14%
Former Subscribers: % Who've EVER Purchased Online	N/A	32%	40%	22%	34%	35%	22%	35%	38%	35%	35%	34%	38%	38%	36%	23%	17%
Single Ticket Buyers: % Who've EVER Purchased Online	N/A	38%	54%	43%	36%	43%	21%	40%	31%	51%	43%	39%	44%	34%	34%	39%	22%

NOTES:

[1]"Potential Classical Music Consumers" are defined as the sub-set of respondents in each area who qualified for an extended interview, based on their responses to an initial series of questions.

All figures from the national and local area telephone surveys are weighted. See the methodology section for details on weighting procedures.

Figures for subscribers, former subscribers, and single ticket buyers derive from the postal surveys of ticket buyers and are not weighted.

TABLE 2G

MEAN RATING OF INCLINATION TO SUBSCRIBE
(SCALE: 0="NOT AT ALL INCLINED"; 10="EXTREMELY INCLINED")

	NAT'L SURVEY	AVERAGE OF 15 MARKET SURVEYS	BPO/Brooklyn	CSO/Charlotte	CSO/Denver	DSO/Detroit	FWP/Fort Wayne	KCS/Kansas City	LBSO/Long Beach	LPO/New Orleans	NWS/Miami (Dade)	OS/Portland	TPO/Philadelphia	SLSO/Saint Louis	SPCO/Saint Paul	SAS/San Antonio	WSO/Wichita
Potential Classical Music Consumers *	N/A	3.6	3.4	3.9	3.4	3.1	3.4	3.6	3.9	3.8	4.1	3.3	3.8	3.6	3.6	3.3	3.3
Current Subscribers	N/A	8.7	8.4	8.7	9.1	8.5	8.3	8.8	8.1	8.8	8.9	8.5	8.7	8.6	8.6	8.7	8.6
Former Subscribers	N/A	6.5	6.9	6.8	6.8	6.1	6.1	6.6	6.2	6.0	7.3	6.1	6.2	6.5	7.0	6.0	6.2
Single Ticket Buyers	N/A	4.7	6.2	4.9	4.7	4.0	4.0	5.1	5.2	5.0	5.6	4.2	4.5	4.4	4.3	4.7	4.2

NOTES:

*"Potential Classical Music Consumers" are defined as the sub-set of respondents in each area who qualified for an extended interview, based on their responses to an initial series of questions.

All figures from the national and local area telephone surveys are weighted. See the methodology section for details on weighting procedures.

TABLE 3A

RATE OF ATTENDANCE AT DIFFERENT TYPES OF CLASSICAL CONCERTS - LIFETIME

		NAT'L SURVEY	AVERAGE OF 15 MARKET SURVEYS	BPO/Brooklyn	CSO/Charlotte	CSO/Denver	DSO/Detroit	FWP/Fort Wayne	KCS/Kansas City	LBSO/Long Beach	LPO/New Orleans	NWS/Miami (Dade)	OS/Portland	TPO/Philadelphia	SLSO/Saint Louis	SPCO/Saint Paul	SAS/San Antonio	WSO/Wichita
Potential Classical Music Consumers*	Pops Concert by a Symphony Orchestra	48%	55%	41%	61%	57%	49%	64%	54%	54%	56%	53%	51%	47%	62%	61%	51%	63%
	Classical Concert by a Symphony Orchestra	53%	65%	50%	64%	75%	63%	63%	64%	59%	62%	62%	68%	63%	71%	70%	66%	67%
	Chamber Music Concert	37%	36%	33%	37%	40%	29%	35%	38%	36%	30%	39%	38%	37%	32%	55%	29%	34%
	Classical Music Recital by a Singer or Instrumentalist	46%	47%	50%	43%	48%	44%	39%	48%	50%	47%	54%	48%	53%	43%	45%	44%	48%
	Classical Concert by a Choir or Vocal Ensemble	52%	52%	49%	58%	57%	46%	53%	55%	46%	54%	46%	53%	49%	52%	56%	47%	56%
	Performance of Classical Music by a Concert or Symphonic Band	45%	N/A	N/A	N/A	N/A	N/A	N/A	N/A	N/A	N/A	N/A	N/A	N/A	N/A	N/A	N/A	N/A
	Special Holiday Performance of Classical Music	53%	56%	48%	62%	57%	49%	61%	61%	48%	55%	46%	55%	53%	59%	63%	63%	60%
	Classical Concert Geared for Children or Families	43%	43%	43%	45%	45%	43%	42%	43%	43%	49%	35%	37%	45%	48%	40%	48%	45%
Current Subscribers	Pops Concert by a Symphony Orchestra	N/A	81%	55%	94%	81%	85%	90%	81%	83%	81%	72%	82%	66%	80%	77%	88%	87%
	Classical Concert by a Symphony Orchestra	N/A	93%	97%	94%	96%	92%	86%	96%	88%	94%	94%	88%	95%	94%	94%	92%	97%
	Chamber Music Concert	N/A	76%	94%	73%	75%	72%	62%	76%	68%	76%	82%	67%	77%	75%	96%	70%	75%
	Classical Music Recital by a Singer or Instrumentalist	N/A	79%	89%	78%	76%	76%	71%	84%	70%	79%	82%	72%	80%	78%	85%	79%	84%
	Classical Concert by a Choir or Vocal Ensemble	N/A	83%	89%	90%	83%	81%	78%	87%	78%	84%	73%	79%	82%	86%	89%	80%	89%
	Performance of Classical Music by a Concert or Symphonic Band	N/A	80%	75%	84%	78%	80%	84%	83%	83%	77%	78%	76%	72%	84%	79%	84%	82%
	Special Holiday Performance of Classical Music	N/A	83%	78%	90%	86%	82%	85%	88%	81%	82%	72%	80%	76%	86%	89%	85%	87%
	Classical Concert Geared for Children or Families	N/A	64%	55%	70%	70%	62%	62%	69%	63%	64%	59%	63%	61%	57%	62%	66%	72%
Former Subscribers	Pops Concert by a Symphony Orchestra	N/A	80%	48%	94%	76%	87%	94%	84%	85%	79%	74%	79%	66%	78%	77%	86%	93%
	Classical Concert by a Symphony Orchestra	N/A	93%	95%	99%	96%	94%	87%	91%	91%	95%	91%	88%	94%	95%	96%	94%	96%
	Chamber Music Concert	N/A	73%	93%	74%	71%	67%	66%	70%	73%	69%	72%	67%	71%	68%	95%	62%	75%
	Classical Music Recital by a Singer or Instrumentalist	N/A	80%	86%	77%	81%	77%	67%	81%	77%	83%	84%	76%	80%	78%	85%	73%	84%
	Classical Concert by a Choir or Vocal Ensemble	N/A	83%	89%	97%	85%	81%	80%	84%	83%	85%	76%	75%	78%	84%	91%	74%	86%
	Performance of Classical Music by a Concert or Symphonic Band	N/A	80%	69%	89%	79%	84%	83%	84%	77%	79%	70%	76%	64%	87%	83%	80%	84%
	Special Holiday Performance of Classical Music	N/A	83%	69%	91%	84%	81%	89%	86%	81%	81%	64%	77%	82%	86%	89%	86%	91%
	Classical Concert Geared for Children or Families	N/A	64%	49%	69%	64%	59%	67%	71%	51%	70%	51%	63%	59%	61%	75%	62%	75%
Single Ticket Buyers	Pops Concert by a Symphony Orchestra	N/A	75%	42%	88%	80%	75%	88%	80%	78%	70%	70%	78%	61%	78%	68%	72%	83%
	Classical Concert by a Symphony Orchestra	N/A	89%	93%	93%	96%	89%	85%	87%	82%	86%	90%	90%	92%	90%	91%	83%	84%
	Chamber Music Concert	N/A	66%	89%	61%	69%	62%	51%	64%	57%	71%	73%	71%	61%	56%	88%	54%	60%
	Classical Music Recital by a Singer or Instrumentalist	N/A	71%	84%	68%	75%	72%	58%	72%	70%	70%	77%	76%	69%	68%	83%	61%	66%
	Classical Concert by a Choir or Vocal Ensemble	N/A	75%	84%	76%	81%	76%	70%	75%	71%	74%	70%	80%	74%	75%	80%	69%	73%
	Performance of Classical Music by a Concert or Symphonic Band	N/A	78%	68%	84%	79%	79%	80%	80%	78%	79%	80%	78%	74%	84%	73%	72%	77%
	Special Holiday Performance of Classical Music	N/A	80%	68%	87%	81%	80%	82%	85%	74%	80%	72%	83%	79%	81%	84%	81%	79%
	Classical Concert Geared for Children or Families	N/A	57%	43%	56%	67%	56%	55%	63%	54%	62%	54%	60%	52%	54%	60%	60%	57%

NOTES:

**"Potential Classical Music Consumers" are defined as the sub-set of respondents in each area who qualified for an extended interview, based on their responses to an initial series of questions.

All figures from the national and local area telephone surveys (top three rows) are weighted. See the methodology section for details on weighting procedures. Figures for subscribers, former subscribers, and single ticket buyers derive from the postal surveys of ticket buyers and are not weighted.

TABLE 3B

	NAT'L SURVEY	AVERAGE OF 15 MARKET SURVEYS	BPO/Brooklyn	CSO/Charlotte	CSO/Denver	DSO/Detroit	FWP/Fort Wayne	KCS/Kansas City	LBSO/Long Beach	LPO/New Orleans	NWS/Miami (Dade)	OS/Portland	TPO/Philadelphia	SLSO/Saint Louis	SPCO/Saint Paul	SAS/San Antonio	WSO/Wichita
Potential Classical Music Consumers*																	
Pops Concert by a Symphony Orchestra	12%	14%	13%	14%	11%	11%	19%	9%	14%	14%	11%	12%	9%	18%	15%	13%	22%
Classical Concert by a Symphony Orchestra	22%	27%	22%	28%	31%	24%	27%	23%	27%	28%	30%	28%	28%	34%	30%	25%	27%
Chamber Music Concert	13%	12%	11%	10%	11%	7%	9%	11%	12%	15%	15%	12%	11%	11%	19%	11%	9%
Classical Music Recital by a Singer or Instrumentalist	17%	19%	22%	18%	17%	13%	12%	19%	20%	27%	21%	18%	21%	20%	19%	19%	17%
Classical Concert by a Choir or Vocal Ensemble	23%	26%	26%	34%	24%	22%	22%	21%	20%	33%	21%	21%	21%	26%	29%	22%	29%
Performance of Classical Music by a Concert or Symphonic Band	16%	N/A	N/A	N/A	N/A	N/A	N/A	N/A	N/A	N/A	N/A	N/A	N/A	N/A	N/A	N/A	N/A
Special Holiday Performance of Classical Music	22%	24%	21%	27%	21%	21%	24%	25%	22%	25%	21%	26%	22%	28%	25%	34%	25%
Classical Concert Geared for Children or Families	18%	19%	18%	22%	18%	19%	18%	17%	21%	24%	15%	15%	21%	19%	15%	23%	17%
Current Subscribers																	
Pops Concert by a Symphony Orchestra	N/A	43%	11%	74%	39%	52%	75%	49%	46%	36%	32%	37%	21%	47%	20%	44%	64%
Classical Concert by a Symphony Orchestra	N/A	81%	92%	86%	86%	83%	70%	74%	68%	88%	88%	63%	87%	86%	89%	74%	85%
Chamber Music Concert	N/A	37%	79%	29%	29%	21%	24%	29%	26%	33%	50%	29%	32%	25%	83%	22%	32%
Classical Music Recital by a Singer or Instrumentalist	N/A	40%	62%	39%	37%	33%	29%	45%	26%	38%	59%	30%	44%	38%	44%	35%	44%
Classical Concert by a Choir or Vocal Ensemble	N/A	46%	65%	55%	43%	42%	50%	46%	40%	49%	39%	30%	39%	50%	58%	38%	51%
Performance of Classical Music by a Concert or Symphonic Band	N/A	38%	55%	49%	34%	45%	47%	41%	41%	45%	39%	30%	23%	45%	30%	32%	42%
Special Holiday Performance of Classical Music	N/A	44%	29%	65%	45%	38%	63%	46%	30%	43%	25%	38%	37%	44%	52%	48%	48%
Classical Concert Geared for Children or Families	N/A	18%	11%	28%	21%	20%	13%	21%	10%	23%	13%	19%	7%	22%	23%	22%	21%
Former Subscribers																	
Pops Concert by a Symphony Orchestra	N/A	46%	13%	71%	50%	53%	73%	45%	61%	35%	31%	54%	17%	42%	23%	61%	54%
Classical Concert by a Symphony Orchestra	N/A	87%	95%	84%	92%	86%	72%	91%	77%	92%	91%	79%	95%	90%	83%	80%	96%
Chamber Music Concert	N/A	44%	33%	33%	36%	30%	32%	37%	33%	44%	64%	32%	41%	33%	91%	32%	45%
Classical Music Recital by a Singer or Instrumentalist	N/A	46%	61%	40%	44%	35%	38%	49%	36%	49%	57%	37%	48%	42%	51%	41%	58%
Classical Concert by a Choir or Vocal Ensemble	N/A	54%	60%	60%	61%	48%	51%	58%	44%	59%	35%	18%	48%	55%	60%	52%	63%
Performance of Classical Music by a Concert or Symphonic Band	N/A	40%	34%	60%	37%	41%	51%	47%	51%	44%	35%	34%	24%	42%	29%	46%	39%
Special Holiday Performance of Classical Music	N/A	47%	43%	43%	37%	47%	62%	51%	45%	46%	30%	46%	36%	43%	50%	46%	45%
Classical Concert Geared for Children or Families	N/A	19%	29%	25%	26%	18%	16%	19%	19%	16%	17%	22%	14%	17%	14%	23%	21%
Single-Ticket Buyers																	
Pops Concert by a Symphony Orchestra	N/A	40%	7%	63%	44%	37%	70%	44%	45%	33%	29%	31%	29%	46%	20%	34%	57%
Classical Concert by a Symphony Orchestra	N/A	70%	76%	75%	85%	68%	55%	67%	65%	78%	79%	64%	76%	70%	74%	52%	63%
Chamber Music Concert	N/A	31%	57%	20%	31%	22%	15%	23%	23%	35%	48%	22%	29%	20%	68%	22%	25%
Classical Music Recital by a Singer or Instrumentalist	N/A	35%	51%	27%	41%	28%	25%	37%	34%	37%	48%	34%	32%	32%	37%	32%	35%
Classical Concert by a Choir or Vocal Ensemble	N/A	39%	52%	43%	51%	39%	28%	38%	30%	42%	40%	30%	38%	33%	40%	34%	39%
Performance of Classical Music by a Concert or Symphonic Band	N/A	38%	23%	41%	36%	39%	43%	42%	38%	43%	45%	29%	22%	46%	28%	37%	44%
Special Holiday Performance of Classical Music	N/A	46%	24%	55%	52%	49%	61%	50%	41%	51%	37%	36%	48%	46%	50%	49%	44%
Classical Concert Geared for Children or Families	N/A	19%	8%	24%	25%	16%	16%	24%	17%	22%	18%	14%	14%	15%	17%	30%	21%

NOTES:

*"Potential Classical Music Consumers" are defined as the sub-set of respondents in each area who qualified for an extended interview, based on their responses to an initial series of questions.

All figures from the national and local area telephone surveys (top three rows) are weighted. See the methodology section for details on weighting procedures. Figures for subscribers, former subscribers, and single ticket buyers derive from the postal surveys of ticket buyers and are not weighted.

TABLE 3C

RATE OF USE OF DIFFERENT TYPES OF VENUES FOR CLASSICAL MUSIC CONCERTS OVER THE PAST YEAR

		NAT'L SURVEY	AVERAGE OF 15 MARKET SURVEYS	BPO/Brooklyn	CSO/Charlotte	CSO/Denver	DSO/Detroit	FWP/Fort Wayne	KCS/Kansas City	LBSO/Long Beach	LPO/New Orleans	NWS/Miami (Dade)	OS/Portland	TPO/Philadelphia	SLSO/Saint Louis	SPCO/Saint Paul	SAS/San Antonio	WSO/Wichita
Potential Classical Music Consumers*	Church or Synagogue	25%	27%	26%	34%	25%	25%	26%	30%	25%	33%	20%	25%	24%	28%	31%	28%	26%
	School Auditorium or Gymnasium	31%	27%	25%	33%	25%	25%	24%	28%	28%	28%	24%	24%	26%	29%	30%	30%	31%
	Concert Hall, Theater or Opera House	35%	40%	34%	38%	43%	39%	38%	32%	37%	42%	36%	41%	39%	48%	47%	40%	44%
	Outdoor Amphitheater	22%	23%	21%	31%	24%	23%	22%	22%	27%	27%	22%	20%	17%	29%	15%	24%	21%
	Private Residence	5%	6%	10%	6%	6%	4%	4%	4%	6%	6%	7%	6%	7%	4%	4%	7%	7%
Current Subscribers	Church or Synagogue	N/A	44%	47%	46%	43%	41%	41%	45%	35%	47%	35%	49%	40%	42%	64%	41%	41%
	School Auditorium or Gymnasium	N/A	18%	12%	13%	16%	20%	18%	17%	16%	22%	13%	22%	18%	12%	19%	20%	26%
	Concert Hall, Theater or Opera House	N/A	91%	96%	90%	95%	88%	79%	91%	81%	94%	97%	84%	94%	91%	96%	87%	96%
	Outdoor Amphitheater	N/A	37%	43%	50%	34%	43%	48%	36%	46%	39%	29%	32%	46%	36%	30%	16%	26%
	Private Residence	N/A	9%	15%	6%	9%	4%	6%	6%	8%	15%	11%	7%	9%	8%	10%	10%	10%
Former Subscribers	Church or Synagogue	N/A	40%	45%	43%	40%	36%	40%	40%	37%	28%	39%	33%	44%	40%	61%	35%	37%
	School Auditorium or Gymnasium	N/A	21%	20%	11%	14%	21%	17%	18%	26%	25%	19%	24%	21%	14%	23%	20%	31%
	Concert Hall, Theater or Opera House	N/A	87%	93%	91%	92%	86%	74%	82%	81%	91%	91%	80%	89%	90%	96%	78%	91%
	Outdoor Amphitheater	N/A	37%	40%	57%	43%	37%	48%	31%	42%	41%	32%	33%	44%	34%	31%	15%	24%
	Private Residence	N/A	8%	14%	6%	5%	6%	4%	5%	90%	9%	14%	8%	6%	8%	12%	4%	8%
Single-Ticket Buyers	Church or Synagogue	N/A	34%	32%	36%	34%	26%	30%	32%	33%	39%	38%	35%	33%	26%	50%	36%	26%
	School Auditorium or Gymnasium	N/A	19%	10%	17%	17%	18%	19%	24%	18%	20%	18%	22%	21%	15%	24%	19%	22%
	Concert Hall, Theater or Opera House	N/A	80%	85%	82%	88%	76%	76%	81%	72%	86%	86%	75%	78%	84%	91%	67%	72%
	Outdoor Amphitheater	N/A	37%	53%	44%	41%	43%	42%	38%	47%	41%	30%	26%	39%	36%	24%	17%	30%
	Private Residence	N/A	6%	9%	3%	6%	5%	2%	3%	6%	13%	10%	8%	6%	6%	4%	8%	4%

NOTES:

**"Potential Classical Music Consumers" are defined as the sub-set of respondents in each area who qualified for an extended interview, based on their responses to an initial series of questions.

All figures from the national and local area telephone surveys (top three rows) are weighted. See the methodology section for details on weighting procedures. Figures for subscribers, former subscribers, and single ticket buyers derive from the postal surveys of ticket buyers and are not weighted.

TABLE 3D

LEVEL OF KNOWLEDGE ABOUT CLASSICAL MUSIC (SELF-REPORTED)

		NAT'L SURVEY	AVERAGE OF 15 MARKET SURVEYS	BPO/Brooklyn	CSO/Charlotte	CSO/Denver	DSO/Detroit	FWP/Fort Wayne	KCS/Kansas City	LBSO/Long Beach	LPO/New Orleans	NWS/Miami (Dade)	OS/Portland	TPO/Philadelphia	SLSO/Saint Louis	SPCO/Saint Paul	SAS/San Antonio	WSO/Wichita
Potential Classical Music Consumers*	Very Knowledgeable	6%	6%	7%	4%	9%	5%	6%	6%	6%	7%	14%	3%	8%	5%	4%	8%	6%
	Somewhat Knowledgeable	44%	45%	43%	42%	45%	41%	44%	47%	47%	49%	40%	47%	47%	42%	45%	45%	43%
	Not Very Knowledgeable	51%	49%	50%	54%	46%	55%	50%	47%	47%	44%	47%	50%	44%	53%	51%	47%	52%
Current Subscribers	Very Knowledgeable	N/A	23%	36%	24%	27%	20%	15%	16%	17%	29%	24%	22%	30%	22%	23%	20%	25%
	Somewhat Knowledgeable	N/A	60%	52%	55%	62%	58%	58%	64%	57%	60%	67%	57%	60%	59%	68%	61%	62%
	Not Very Knowledgeable	N/A	16%	12%	21%	11%	23%	27%	20%	26%	11%	9%	21%	10%	19%	9%	19%	13%
Former Subscribers	Very Knowledgeable	N/A	21%	44%	22%	23%	15%	13%	16%	15%	20%	34%	22%	23%	20%	29%	21%	14%
	Somewhat Knowledgeable	N/A	61%	47%	49%	65%	68%	64%	55%	59%	59%	59%	65%	71%	55%	60%	56%	65%
	Not Very Knowledgeable	N/A	19%	9%	29%	12%	18%	23%	30%	26%	21%	7%	26%	6%	25%	11%	23%	21%
Single Ticket Buyers	Very Knowledgeable	N/A	17%	20%	12%	23%	14%	10%	16%	20%	21%	27%	19%	19%	10%	20%	13%	11%
	Somewhat Knowledgeable	N/A	56%	68%	59%	60%	53%	49%	55%	53%	60%	58%	53%	51%	58%	60%	53%	53%
	Not Very Knowledgeable	N/A	27%	13%	30%	17%	33%	41%	29%	27%	19%	15%	28%	30%	32%	20%	33%	37%

NOTES:

*"Potential Classical Music Consumers" are defined as the sub-set of respondents in each area who qualified for an extended interview, based on their responses to an initial series of questions.

All figures from the national and local area telephone surveys (top three rows) are weighted. See the methodology section for details on weighting procedures. Figures for subscribers, former subscribers, and single ticket buyers derive from the postal surveys of ticket buyers and are not weighted.

TABLE 3E

LEVEL OF INTEREST IN LEARNING MORE ABOUT CLASSICAL MUSIC

		NAT'L SURVEY	AVERAGE OF 15 MARKET SURVEYS	BPO/Brooklyn	CSO/Charlotte	CSO/Denver	DSO/Detroit	FWP/Fort Wayne	KCS/Kansas City	LBSO/Long Beach	LPO/New Orleans	NWS/Miami (Dade)	OS/Portland	TPO/Philadelphia	SLSO/Saint Louis	SPCO/Saint Paul	SAS/San Antonio	WSO/Wichita
Potential Classical Music Consumers*	Very Interested	13%	14%	19%	13%	12%	11%	9%	13%	15%	21%	19%	14%	18%	9%	12%	16%	9%
	Somewhat Interested	53%	51%	48%	52%	56%	48%	54%	48%	52%	53%	51%	53%	53%	55%	50%	58%	50%
	Not Very Interested	33%	34%	34%	36%	32%	40%	38%	39%	33%	26%	30%	33%	30%	36%	38%	26%	41%
Current Subscribers	Very Interested	N/A	38%	51%	38%	40%	35%	23%	37%	32%	48%	47%	33%	48%	34%	37%	33%	40%
	Somewhat Interested	N/A	54%	45%	52%	54%	57%	60%	53%	56%	47%	49%	55%	49%	58%	58%	58%	52%
	Not Very Interested	N/A	8%	5%	10%	8%	8%	17%	10%	13%	4%	5%	12%	4%	8%	6%	9%	8%
Former Subscribers	Very Interested	N/A	34%	51%	31%	34%	30%	25%	33%	24%	37%	56%	25%	43%	32%	35%	38%	28%
	Somewhat Interested	N/A	56%	44%	55%	56%	59%	59%	54%	63%	56%	41%	61%	55%	56%	60%	46%	62%
	Not Very Interested	N/A	10%	4%	14%	10%	11%	15%	14%	13%	7%	3%	14%	2%	13%	5%	17%	11%
Single Ticket Buyers	Very Interested	N/A	30%	35%	29%	34%	29%	16%	25%	30%	45%	54%	32%	38%	17%	26%	23%	16%
	Somewhat Interested	N/A	57%	58%	57%	57%	55%	62%	62%	57%	48%	40%	55%	53%	67%	65%	56%	66%
	Not Very Interested	N/A	13%	8%	14%	9%	17%	22%	14%	13%	7%	6%	13%	9%	16%	8%	21%	19%

NOTES:

*"Potential Classical Music Consumers" are defined as the sub-set of respondents in each area who qualified for an extended interview, based on their responses to an initial series of questions.

All figures from the national and local area telephone surveys (top three rows) are weighted. See the methodology section for details on weighting procedures. Figures for subscribers, former subscribers, and single ticket buyers derive from the postal surveys of ticket buyers and are not weighted.

TABLE 3F

PERCENT OF RESPONDENTS WITH "CLOSE FRIENDS" OR "IMMEDIATE FAMILY" WHO ATTEND CLASSICAL MUSIC CONCERTS

	Single Ticket Buyers		Former Subscribers		Current Subscribers		Potential Classical Music Consumers*	
	Immediate Family that Attend	Close Friends that Attend	Immediate Family that Attend	Close Friends that Attend	Immediate Family that Attend	Close Friends that Attend	Immediate Family that Attend	Close Friends that Attend
NAT'L SURVEY	N/A	N/A	N/A	N/A	N/A	N/A	35%	45%
AVERAGE OF 15 MARKET SURVEYS	59%	74%	66%	81%	69%	85%	38%	50%
BPO/Brooklyn	56%	88%	74%	90%	74%	89%	37%	55%
CSO/Charlotte	54%	75%	69%	77%	66%	81%	40%	50%
CSO/Denver	68%	76%	72%	75%	72%	85%	41%	54%
DSO/Detroit	62%	69%	63%	74%	63%	79%	41%	46%
FWP/Fort Wayne	43%	61%	60%	80%	56%	75%	41%	52%
KCS/Kansas City	60%	73%	59%	78%	60%	79%	33%	43%
LBSO/Long Beach	52%	75%	49%	88%	60%	86%	40%	49%
LPO/New Orleans	61%	82%	64%	75%	75%	91%	39%	50%
NWS/Miami (Dade)	71%	87%	79%	94%	80%	90%	41%	46%
OS/Portland	62%	81%	56%	75%	64%	83%	37%	52%
TPO/Philadelphia	69%	78%	70%	89%	77%	91%	37%	54%
SLSO/Saint Louis	51%	67%	68%	71%	65%	81%	37%	52%
SPCO/Saint Paul	73%	72%	77%	85%	78%	88%	42%	53%
SAS/San Antonio	50%	63%	62%	76%	65%	79%	38%	40%
WSO/Wichita	53%	75%	63%	83%	76%	90%	33%	48%

NOTES:

*"Potential Classical Music Consumers" are defined as the sub-set of respondents in each area who qualified for an extended interview, based on their responses to an initial series of questions.

All figures from the national and local area telephone surveys (top three rows) are weighted. See the methodology section for details on weighting procedures. Figures for subscribers, former subscribers, and single ticket buyers derive from the postal surveys of ticket buyers and are not weighted.

TABLE 3G

PERCENT OF RESPONDENTS WHO PREFER OTHER ART FORMS OVER CLASSICAL MUSIC

	NAT'L SURVEY	AVERAGE OF 15 MARKET SURVEYS	BPO/Brooklyn	CSO/Charlotte	CSO/Denver	DSO/Detroit	FWP/Fort Wayne	KCS/Kansas City	LBSO/Long Beach	LPO/New Orleans	NWS/Miami (Dade)	OS/Portland	TPO/Philadelphia	SLSO/Saint Louis	SPCO/Saint Paul	SAS/San Antonio	WSO/Wichita
Potential Classical Music Consumers*																	
Prefer Jazz over C.M.	43%	46%	52%	48%	47%	54%	37%	46%	43%	58%	52%	43%	44%	44%	36%	48%	45%
Prefer Non-musical Stage Plays over C.M.	62%	44%	47%	48%	47%	46%	40%	44%	46%	41%	43%	42%	49%	38%	43%	38%	40%
Prefer Musical Theater over C.M.	60%	61%	69%	67%	62%	71%	58%	61%	61%	61%	53%	54%	62%	59%	60%	55%	59%
Prefer Opera over C.M.	12%	14%	24%	12%	10%	13%	5%	9%	15%	21%	21%	15%	13%	11%	10%	16%	11%
Prefer Ballet over C.M	22%	22%	30%	23%	16%	20%	14%	18%	23%	29%	38%	20%	26%	15%	15%	26%	18%
Prefer Popular Music over C.M.	63%	59%	62%	62%	60%	68%	58%	65%	57%	59%	45%	61%	56%	54%	59%	59%	61%
Current Subscribers																	
Prefer Jazz over C.M.	N/A	9%	4%	16%	7%	13%	20%	13%	14%	2%	4%	9%	2%	7%	2%	17%	4%
Prefer Non-musical Stage Plays over C.M.	N/A	17%	15%	26%	11%	22%	32%	23%	34%	11%	13%	21%	8%	14%	7%	23%	9%
Prefer Musical Theater over C.M.	N/A	20%	11%	33%	15%	25%	37%	24%	34%	12%	14%	25%	9%	16%	7%	32%	14%
Prefer Opera over C.M.	N/A	5%	13%	2%	5%	4%	4%	2%	4%	8%	4%	7%	5%	5%	3%	7%	3%
Prefer Ballet over C.M	N/A	5%	7%	7%	3%	4%	5%	7%	9%	5%	9%	7%	2%	5%	2%	9%	4%
Prefer Popular Music over C.M.	N/A	11%	7%	18%	6%	13%	23%	11%	19%	5%	3%	13%	4%	9%	4%	21%	5%
Former Subscribers																	
Prefer Jazz over C.M.	N/A	12%	2%	28%	8%	10%	16%	18%	20%	13%	4%	17%	8%	14%	6%	15%	4%
Prefer Non-musical Stage Plays over C.M.	N/A	24%	11%	32%	17%	22%	33%	37%	33%	19%	15%	28%	13%	28%	12%	33%	27%
Prefer Musical Theater over C.M.	N/A	26%	6%	39%	19%	32%	44%	36%	35%	23%	16%	27%	14%	30%	14%	37%	27%
Prefer Opera over C.M.	N/A	7%	13%	6%	7%	7%	2%	4%	8%	12%	14%	5%	9%	5%	7%	16%	1%
Prefer Ballet over C.M	N/A	8%	8%	9%	3%	12%	8%	8%	12%	1%	8%	8%	6%	12%	8%	17%	5%
Prefer Popular Music over C.M.	N/A	16%	3%	23%	12%	17%	25%	26%	19%	15%	3%	20%	11%	19%	7%	28%	15%
Single Ticket Buyers																	
Prefer Jazz over C.M.	N/A	18%	12%	21%	14%	24%	26%	20%	27%	9%	9%	16%	16%	19%	8%	27%	21%
Prefer Non-musical Stage Plays over C.M.	N/A	33%	37%	41%	24%	33%	35%	35%	38%	23%	23%	35%	33%	37%	24%	41%	43%
Prefer Musical Theater over C.M.	N/A	35%	17%	48%	30%	36%	41%	39%	40%	22%	24%	34%	37%	38%	22%	47%	51%
Prefer Opera over C.M.	N/A	7%	17%	7%	7%	5%	1%	6%	7%	11%	6%	8%	9%	5%	5%	9%	3%
Prefer Ballet over C.M	N/A	11%	16%	9%	9%	11%	7%	15%	12%	9%	12%	15%	16%	8%	6%	17%	10%
Prefer Popular Music over C.M.	N/A	26%	19%	35%	17%	30%	38%	30%	27%	18%	11%	26%	26%	30%	16%	38%	34%

NOTES:

*"Potential Classical Music Consumers" are defined as the sub-set of respondents in each area who qualified for an extended interview, based on their responses to an initial series of questions.

All figures from the national and local area telephone surveys (top three rows) are weighted. See the methodology section for details on weighting procedures. Figures for subscribers, former subscribers, and single ticket buyers derive from the postal surveys of ticket buyers and are not weighted.

TABLE 3H

TYPE OF CLASSICAL MUSIC LISTENER (SELF-REPORTED)

		NAT'L SURVEY	AVERAGE OF 15 MARKET SURVEYS	BPO/Brooklyn	CSO/Charlotte	CSO/Denver	DSO/Detroit	FWP/Fort Wayne	KCS/Kansas City	LBSO/Long Beach	LPO/New Orleans	NWS/Miami (Dade)	OS/Portland	TPO/Philadelphia	SLSO/Saint Louis	SPCO/Saint Paul	SAS/San Antonio	WSO/Wichita
Potential Classical Music Consumers*	Critical Listener	10%	11%	13%	10%	15%	11%	7%	8%	12%	13%	17%	10%	11%	11%	7%	9%	8%
	Casual Listener	78%	76%	74%	78%	73%	76%	81%	73%	75%	76%	67%	76%	76%	79%	81%	79%	79%
	Uninterested Listener	11%	13%	13%	11%	12%	13%	12%	20%	12%	11%	16%	14%	13%	10%	11%	12%	13%
Current Subscribers	Critical Listener	N/A	42%	58%	41%	47%	37%	26%	34%	35%	45%	54%	38%	53%	39%	40%	36%	45%
	Casual Listener	N/A	57%	41%	58%	52%	60%	70%	63%	62%	55%	45%	60%	47%	59%	60%	63%	55%
	Uninterested Listener	N/A	1%	1%	1%	1%	3%	4%	3%	3%	0%	1%	2%	0%	2%	0%	1%	0%
Former Subscribers	Critical Listener	N/A	35%	68%	29%	38%	37%	17%	29%	30%	37%	55%	24%	46%	32%	39%	30%	28%
	Casual Listener	N/A	63%	32%	71%	63%	62%	79%	66%	67%	64%	45%	74%	54%	66%	61%	66%	72%
	Uninterested Listener	N/A	2%	0%	0%	0%	2%	4%	5%	4%	0%	0%	2%	0%	2%	0%	5%	1%
Single Ticket Buyers	Critical Listener	N/A	28%	46%	21%	36%	24%	15%	24%	35%	34%	41%	27%	33%	21%	30%	25%	19%
	Casual Listener	N/A	68%	53%	76%	62%	67%	79%	73%	58%	66%	59%	71%	66%	75%	67%	69%	75%
	Uninterested Listener	N/A	4%	1%	4%	3%	9%	5%	3%	7%	1%	0%	2%	1%	5%	3%	7%	6%

NOTES:

*"Potential Classical Music Consumers" are defined as the sub-set of respondents in each area who qualified for an extended interview, based on their responses to an initial series of questions.

All figures from the national and local area telephone surveys (top three rows) are weighted. See the methodology section for details on weighting procedures. Figures for subscribers, former subscribers, and single ticket buyers derive from the postal surveys of ticket buyers and are not weighted.

TABLE 31

PERCENT OF RESPONDENTS WHO HAVE A FAVORITE COMPOSER/COMPOSITION

% of Potential Classical Music Consumers*	NAT'L SURVEY	AVERAGE OF 15 MARKET SURVEYS	BPO/Brooklyn	CSO/Charlotte	CSO/Denver	DSO/Detroit	FWP/Fort Wayne	KCS/Kansas City	LBSO/Long Beach	LPO/New Orleans	NWS/Miami (Dade)	OS/Portland	TPO/Philadelphia	SLSO/Saint Louis	SPCO/Saint Paul	SAS/San Antonio	WSO/Wichita
Favorite Classical Composer	43%	46%	45%	41%	53%	40%	47%	42%	52%	46%	52%	48%	47%	46%	47%	44%	47%
Favorite Classical Composition	24%	35%	35%	29%	43%	33%	29%	33%	38%	32%	43%	37%	35%	33%	30%	33%	37%

NOTES:

*"Potential Classical Music Consumers" are defined as the sub-set of respondents in each area who qualified for an extended interview, based on their responses to an initial series of questions.

All figures from the national and local area telephone surveys (top three rows) are weighted. See the methodology section for details on weighting procedures.

TABLE 3K

AVERAGE RATING OF LIKELIHOOD OF VARIOUS INDUCEMENTS TO STIMULATE INCREASED ATTENDANCE AT SYMPHONY ORCHESTRA CONCERTS
(SCALE: 0=NOT ANY MORE LIKELY; 10=MUCH MORE LIKELY)

% of Potential Classical Music Consumers*	NAT'L SURVEY	AVERAGE OF 15 MARKET SURVEYS	BPO/Brooklyn	CSO/Charlotte	CSO/Denver	DSO/Detroit	FWP/Fort Wayne	KCS/Kansas City	LBSO/Long Beach	LPO/New Orleans	NWS/Miami (Dade)	OS/Portland	TPO/Philadelphia	SLSO/Saint Louis	SPCO/Saint Paul	SAS/San Antonio	WSO/Wichita
If more people invited you to go with them	6.2	6.0	6.3	6.2	5.8	5.8	5.6	5.9	6.3	6.4	6.1	5.7	6.3	6.2	5.7	6.7	5.7
If tickets were less expensive	6.6	6.3	6.9	6.4	6.2	6.0	5.8	6.2	6.8	6.5	6.1	6.2	6.5	6.2	6.3	6.7	6.3
If there was more opportunity to socialize	5.0	4.6	5.5	5.0	3.8	4.3	4.1	4.3	5.4	5.3	5.0	3.8	4.3	4.4	3.9	5.4	4.3
If orchestras played more familiar music	5.7	5.2	6.0	5.3	4.8	5.2	4.6	5.0	5.9	5.4	5.3	4.5	5.4	5.6	4.8	5.7	5.1
If you could get half price tickets on the day of the concert	6.6	6.0	6.3	6.1	6.0	5.4	5.4	5.8	6.5	6.1	6.0	5.9	6.2	5.9	5.9	6.7	6.2
If someone else did the driving	4.9	4.3	5.4	4.6	3.8	4.2	2.8	4.2	5.3	4.9	4.6	3.7	4.6	4.0	3.8	5.1	3.5
If the concerts weren't so long	4.6	4.0	4.9	4.2	3.8	3.9	3.5	4.0	4.6	4.6	4.2	3.6	3.7	3.5	3.6	4.6	3.9
If tickets were always available at the last minute	5.6	5.1	5.6	5.3	5.1	4.3	4.4	4.8	5.5	5.2	5.3	4.7	5.1	5.0	5.1	6.0	5.1
If the quality of the performance was higher	5.8	5.2	5.6	5.5	5.1	4.9	4.5	5.2	5.9	5.6	5.9	4.6	5.3	4.5	4.3	6.3	4.8
If getting tickets online was fast and easy	4.7	3.8	4.6	4.0	3.6	3.5	2.8	3.4	4.3	4.2	4.3	3.7	4.1	3.4	3.5	4.7	3.3
If conductors talked to the audience more	4.4	4.1	4.9	3.9	3.7	3.9	3.7	3.8	4.8	4.3	4.2	3.9	3.8	4.1	3.8	4.6	4.0

NOTES:

**"Potential Classical Music Consumers" are defined as the sub-set of respondents in each area who qualified for an extended interview, based on their responses to an initial series of questions.

All figures from the national and local area telephone surveys (top three rows) are weighted. See the methodology section for details on weighting procedures.

The actual wording of this questions was: "How likely would you be to attend symphony orchestra concerts more often than you do now if..."

TABLE 3L

RATE OF CONSUMPTION OF CLASSICAL MUSIC VIA ELECTRONIC MEDIA - LIFETIME

		NAT'L SURVEY	AVERAGE OF 15 MARKET SURVEYS	BPO/Brooklyn	CSO/Charlotte	CSO/Denver	DSO/Detroit	FWP/Fort Wayne	KCS/Kansas City	LBSO/Long Beach	LPO/New Orleans	NWS/Miami (Dade)	OS/Portland	TPO/Philadelphia	SLSO/Saint Louis	SPCO/Saint Paul	SAS/San Antonio	WSO/Wichita
Potential Classical Music Consumers*	Radio	72%	70%	65%	72%	75%	61%	64%	71%	71%	73%	72%	75%	68%	75%	73%	74%	67%
	Records, Tapes or CDs	66%	68%	68%	62%	71%	67%	73%	66%	65%	66%	69%	70%	72%	63%	72%	66%	66%
	Internet	5%	7%	11%	5%	7%	5%	5%	9%	6%	6%	5%	9%	8%	4%	4%	10%	6%
	Television or VCR	64%	60%	68%	61%	53%	62%	59%	57%	57%	59%	68%	57%	68%	62%	53%	61%	61%
Current Subscribers	Radio	N/A	94%	95%	94%	96%	92%	88%	90%	93%	98%	89%	92%	98%	95%	100%	91%	93%
	Records, Tapes or CDs	N/A	95%	96%	93%	96%	96%	90%	93%	93%	96%	97%	96%	97%	93%	99%	95%	94%
	Internet	N/A	10%	13%	9%	7%	10%	8%	11%	9%	9%	11%	11%	14%	9%	9%	10%	9%
	Television or VCR	N/A	71%	64%	68%	71%	69%	69%	72%	67%	71%	79%	74%	81%	67%	64%	72%	81%
Former Subscribers	Radio	N/A	93%	97%	86%	92%	91%	87%	93%	91%	94%	94%	90%	97%	98%	99%	89%	91%
	Records, Tapes or CDs	N/A	96%	97%	94%	96%	95%	90%	95%	95%	96%	99%	95%	94%	95%	99%	95%	96%
	Internet	N/A	10%	16%	8%	7%	10%	4%	8%	8%	11%	18%	12%	9%	7%	11%	11%	14%
	Television or VCR	N/A	65%	64%	43%	66%	71%	68%	66%	58%	72%	75%	60%	70%	55%	55%	77%	73%
Single-Ticket Buyers	Radio	N/A	88%	90%	90%	95%	84%	75%	91%	87%	94%	94%	88%	88%	93%	95%	82%	80%
	Records, Tapes or CDs	N/A	91%	97%	88%	94%	90%	84%	89%	88%	98%	96%	92%	95%	85%	98%	86%	90%
	Internet	N/A	10%	13%	8%	7%	10%	9%	6%	10%	19%	19%	12%	15%	7%	10%	11%	5%
	Television or VCR	N/A	60%	48%	55%	64%	57%	58%	56%	71%	64%	75%	55%	58%	59%	55%	65%	65%

NOTES:

**Potential Classical Music Consumers" are defined as the sub-set of respondents in each area who qualified for an extended interview, based on their responses to an initial series of questions.

All figures from the national and local area telephone surveys (top three rows) are weighted. See the methodology section for details on weighting procedures. Figures for subscribers, former subscribers, and single ticket buyers derive from the postal surveys of ticket buyers and are not weighted.

TABLE 3M-1

FREQUENCY OF CONSUMPTION OF CLASSICAL MUSIC VIA ELECTRONIC MEDIA: PERCENT WHO LISTEN "DAILY"

		NAT'L SURVEY	AVERAGE OF 15 MARKET SURVEYS	BPO/Brooklyn	CSO/Charlotte	CSO/Denver	DSO/Detroit	FWP/Fort Wayne	KCS/Kansas City	LBSO/Long Beach	LPO/New Orleans	NWS/Miami (Dade)	OS/Portland	TPO/Philadelphia	SLSO/Saint Louis	SPCO/Saint Paul	SAS/San Antonio	WSO/Wichita
Potential Classical Music Consumers*	Radio	9%	12%	11%	11%	17%	9%	5%	9%	13%	17%	19%	11%	11%	14%	12%	10%	8%
	Records, Tapes or CDs	5%	6%	6%	3%	6%	6%	7%	7%	9%	8%	12%	5%	7%	7%	5%	6%	5%
	Internet	0%	1%	1%	0%	1%	1%	0%	0%	0%	1%	1%	1%	1%	1%	1%	1%	0%
	Television or VCR	1%	1%	1%	0%	1%	0%	1%	1%	1%	1%	1%	1%	2%	1%	0%	0%	3%
Current Subscribers	Radio	N/A	41%	44%	36%	47%	30%	29%	37%	35%	52%	30%	41%	47%	42%	57%	38%	43%
	Records, Tapes or CDs	N/A	15%	17%	10%	15%	16%	10%	17%	8%	19%	27%	17%	22%	11%	14%	12%	16%
	Internet	N/A	1%	1%	0%	0%	1%	1%	1%	0%	1%	1%	1%	0%	0%	1%	1%	0%
	Television or VCR	N/A	2%	1%	2%	1%	2%	1%	1%	1%	1%	4%	3%	2%	1%	0%	2%	3%
Former Subscribers	Radio	N/A	38%	39%	32%	42%	28%	25%	33%	42%	51%	42%	31%	38%	37%	52%	31%	39%
	Records, Tapes or CDs	N/A	14%	14%	9%	15%	12%	13%	17%	7%	14%	26%	12%	22%	12%	17%	8%	12%
	Internet	N/A	1%	0%	0%	1%	1%	1%	1%	1%	1%	2%	1%	0%	0%	0%	0%	1%
	Television or VCR	N/A	2%	0%	2%	1%	2%	3%	1%	2%	0%	2%	1%	5%	1%	1%	0%	3%
Single Ticket Buyers	Radio	N/A	27%	30%	22%	33%	15%	16%	20%	39%	44%	43%	21%	22%	23%	36%	25%	16%
	Records, Tapes or CDs	N/A	13%	19%	7%	16%	10%	7%	9%	15%	17%	29%	10%	18%	8%	11%	13%	36%
	Internet	N/A	1%	2%	0%	0%	1%	0%	0%	1%	1%	2%	0%	1%	1%	1%	1%	0%
	Television or VCR	N/A	1%	1%	1%	1%	0%	0%	0%	1%	4%	6%	0%	3%	1%	1%	0%	2%

NOTES:

*"Potential Classical Music Consumers" are defined as the sub-set of respondents in each area who qualified for an extended interview, based on their responses to an initial series of questions.

All figures from the national and local area telephone surveys (top three rows) are weighted. See the methodology section for details on weighting procedures. Figures for subscribers, former subscribers, and single ticket buyers derive from the postal surveys of ticket buyers and are not weighted. Tables 3M1 through 3M4 are additive. To figure the percentage of respondents who listen to classical radio daily or several times per week, add the figures from Table 3M1 and 3M2.

FREQUENCY OF CONSUMPTION OF CLASSICAL MUSIC VIA ELECTRONIC MEDIA:
PERCENT WHO LISTEN "SEVERAL TIMES PER WEEK"

TABLE 3M-2

		NAT'L SURVEY	AVERAGE OF 15 MARKET SURVEYS	BPO/Brooklyn	CSO/Charlotte	CSO/Denver	DSO/Detroit	FWP/Fort Wayne	KCS/Kansas City	LBSO/Long Beach	LPO/New Orleans	NWS/Miami (Dade)	OS/Portland	TPO/Philadelphia	SLSO/Saint Louis	SPCO/Saint Paul	SAS/San Antonio	WSO/Wichita
Potential Classical Music Consumers*	Radio	19%	22%	18%	24%	24%	16%	19%	25%	24%	17%	25%	24%	23%	14%	25%	24%	22%
	Records, Tapes or CDs	17%	20%	17%	17%	29%	14%	17%	17%	19%	18%	18%	25%	25%	18%	18%	21%	20%
	Internet	1%	2%	5%	1%	2%	2%	0%	4%	1%	2%	2%	2%	4%	1%	1%	3%	1%
	Television or VCR	5%	6%	8%	3%	7%	3%	5%	7%	7%	5%	13%	3%	5%	7%	16%	7%	5%
Current Subscribers	Radio	N/A	26%	25%	30%	28%	25%	23%	25%	27%	23%	30%	23%	26%	29%	24%	22%	28%
	Records, Tapes or CDs	N/A	33%	36%	27%	36%	27%	24%	28%	32%	35%	38%	31%	42%	36%	32%	29%	33%
	Internet	N/A	1%	3%	1%	1%	2%	1%	1%	1%	1%	2%	1%	3%	1%	0%	0%	1%
	Television or VCR	N/A	2%	2%	4%	4%	4%	6%	6%	6%	4%	4%	5%	5%	4%	2%	4%	1%
Former Subscribers	Radio	N/A	26%	32%	20%	25%	21%	28%	26%	20%	17%	27%	29%	21%	29%	26%	36%	25%
	Records, Tapes or CDs	N/A	34%	43%	28%	28%	31%	27%	27%	38%	36%	47%	38%	31%	30%	37%	31%	37%
	Internet	N/A	1%	2%	0%	1%	0%	0%	0%	1%	3%	1%	3%	4%	1%	0%	0%	0%
	Television or VCR	N/A	4%	0%	3%	3%	3%	4%	6%	3%	3%	6%	1%	4%	3%	0%	8%	10%
Single Ticket Buyers	Radio	N/A	23%	27%	29%	29%	22%	14%	25%	21%	22%	21%	21%	25%	27%	27%	18%	21%
	Records, Tapes or CDs	N/A	28%	35%	25%	33%	24%	23%	23%	28%	32%	37%	28%	30%	23%	30%	25%	20%
	Internet	N/A	1%	1%	1%	1%	0%	1%	1%	2%	3%	4%	1%	1%	1%	1%	2%	2%
	Television or VCR	N/A	4%	2%	4%	3%	2%	2%	4%	8%	4%	7%	3%	3%	2%	2%	5%	5%

NOTES:

***"Potential Classical Music Consumers" are defined as the sub-set of respondents in each area who qualified for an extended interview, based on their responses to an initial series of questions.

All figures from the national and local area telephone surveys (top three rows) are weighted. See the methodology section for details on weighting procedures. Figures for subscribers, former subscribers, and single ticket buyers derive from the postal surveys of ticket buyers and are not weighted. Tables 3M1 through 3M4 are additive. To figure the percentage of respondents who listen to classical radio daily or several times per week, add the figures from Table 3M1 and 3M2.

TABLE 3M-3

FREQUENCY OF CONSUMPTION OF CLASSICAL MUSIC VIA ELECTRONIC MEDIA: PERCENT WHO LISTEN "SEVERAL TIMES PER MONTH"

		NAT'L SURVEY	AVERAGE OF 15 MARKET SURVEYS	BPO/Brooklyn	CSO/Charlotte	CSO/Denver	DSO/Detroit	FWP/Fort Wayne	KCS/Kansas City	LBSO/Long Beach	LPO/New Orleans	NWS/Miami (Dade)	OS/Portland	TPO/Philadelphia	SLSO/Saint Louis	SPCO/Saint Paul	SAS/San Antonio	WSO/Wichita
Potential Classical Music Consumers*	Radio	27%	23%	21%	24%	21%	23%	24%	22%	24%	26%	20%	26%	22%	22%	23%	25%	23%
	Records, Tapes or CDs	24%	25%	28%	26%	21%	27%	28%	25%	25%	26%	20%	26%	25%	23%	28%	25%	23%
	Internet	2%	2%	3%	1%	2%	1%	3%	2%	4%	3%	1%	4%	3%	1%	1%	4%	2%
	Television or VCR	19%	20%	25%	22%	15%	22%	18%	20%	19%	17%	23%	15%	21%	18%	16%	23%	20%
Current Subscribers	Radio	N/A	14%	18%	15%	10%	20%	16%	16%	18%	12%	10%	15%	14%	14%	10%	15%	10%
	Records, Tapes or CDs	N/A	28%	25%	34%	28%	32%	31%	26%	30%	26%	22%	30%	23%	27%	36%	28%	27%
	Internet	N/A	2%	3%	3%	1%	3%	1%	2%	2%	2%	3%	3%	5%	1%	1%	2%	2%
	Television or VCR	N/A	14%	9%	11%	13%	9%	15%	13%	15%	10%	17%	5%	17%	12%	10%	15%	17%
Former Subscribers	Radio	N/A	15%	13%	20%	15%	25%	14%	12%	15%	16%	10%	25%	21%	15%	11%	17%	13%
	Records, Tapes or CDs	N/A	27%	24%	23%	31%	29%	23%	25%	22%	27%	21%	29%	30%	30%	32%	32%	24%
	Internet	N/A	2%	4%	2%	1%	1%	0%	2%	1%	2%	6%	2%	1%	1%	3%	3%	2%
	Television or VCR	N/A	11%	16%	10%	11%	20%	14%	11%	14%	12%	20%	5%	8%	7%	4%	15%	11%
Single Tticket Buyers	Radio	N/A	18%	17%	19%	12%	20%	17%	21%	13%	16%	16%	25%	24%	26%	21%	14%	17%
	Records, Tapes or CDs	N/A	27%	31%	29%	27%	27%	25%	30%	26%	30%	18%	33%	24%	27%	37%	18%	25%
	Internet	N/A	2%	3%	1%	2%	3%	4%	1%	1%	3%	4%	3%	6%	1%	1%	3%	0%
	Television or VCR	N/A	12%	11%	7%	15%	6%	10%	11%	2%	12%	19%	8%	16%	11%	9%	10%	12%

NOTES:

Potential Classical Music Consumers are defined as the sub-set of respondents in each area who qualified for an extended interview, based on their responses to an initial series of questions.

All figures from the national and local area telephone surveys (top three rows) are weighted. Figures for subscribers, former subscribers, and single ticket buyers derive from the postal surveys of ticket buyers and are not weighted. See the methodology section for details on weighting procedures. Tables 3M1 through 3M4 are additive. To figure the percentage of respondents who listen to classical radio daily or several times per week, add the figures from Table 3M1 and 3M2.

TABLE 3M-4

FREQUENCY OF CONSUMPTION OF CLASSICAL MUSIC VIA ELECTRONIC MEDIA: PERCENT WHO LISTEN "SEVERAL TIMES PER YEAR"

		NATL SURVEY	AVERAGE OF 15 MARKET SURVEYS	BPO/Brooklyn	CSO/Charlotte	CSO/Denver	DSO/Detroit	FWP/Fort Wayne	KCS/Kansas City	LBSO/Long Beach	LPO/New Orleans	NWS/Miami (Dade)	OS/Portland	TPO/Philadelphia	SLSO/Saint Louis	SPCO/Saint Paul	SAS/San Antonio	WSO/Wichita
Potential Classical Music Consumers*	Radio	17%	12%	14%	10%	12%	12%	15%	14%	9%	12%	5%	14%	11%	12%	12%	15%	18%
	Records, Tapes or CDs	19%	16%	17%	15%	14%	19%	20%	17%	11%	14%	14%	14%	14%	15%	21%	13%	17%
	Internet	5%	2%	3%	3%	2%	2%	1%	2%	1%	1%	1%	3%	1%	2%	1%	2%	2%
	Television or VCR	39%	32%	31%	33%	28%	37%	36%	30%	29%	29%	25%	37%	38%	35%	32%	30%	34%
Current Subscribers	Radio	N/A	13%	8%	13%	11%	17%	20%	13%	12%	10%	11%	13%	12%	10%	9%	16%	12%
	Records, Tapes or CDs	N/A	19%	18%	22%	17%	22%	25%	23%	24%	15%	9%	18%	11%	20%	16%	26%	18%
	Internet	N/A	6%	9%	6%	5%	4%	6%	8%	6%	6%	4%	7%	6%	6%	7%	6%	6%
	Television or VCR	N/A	51%	52%	52%	53%	51%	48%	49%	42%	49%	45%	54%	57%	49%	52%	55%	52%
Former Subscribers	Radio	N/A	14%	13%	14%	10%	17%	20%	22%	15%	14%	15%	14%	16%	18%	9%	5%	15%
	Records, Tapes or CDs	N/A	20%	14%	34%	23%	22%	27%	25%	28%	19%	5%	16%	11%	24%	14%	25%	23%
	Internet	N/A	7%	11%	7%	5%	8%	3%	6%	4%	4%	9%	7%	5%	4%	8%	8%	11%
	Television or VCR	N/A	49%	48%	30%	51%	58%	46%	47%	40%	59%	47%	52%	54%	44%	50%	54%	49%
Single Ticket Buyers	Radio	N/A	20%	17%	21%	22%	26%	28%	25%	13%	12%	14%	21%	18%	17%	11%	25%	26%
	Records, Tapes or CDs	N/A	24%	13%	26%	18%	28%	29%	28%	19%	19%	12%	21%	24%	27%	21%	30%	36%
	Internet	N/A	6%	8%	7%	4%	7%	4%	5%	7%	12%	9%	8%	7%	4%	8%	4%	3%
	Television or VCR	N/A	44%	34%	43%	45%	49%	47%	41%	43%	44%	43%	44%	37%	45%	43%	50%	46%

NOTES:

*"Potential Classical Music Consumers" are defined as the sub-set of respondents in each area who qualified for an extended interview, based on their responses to an initial series of questions.

All figures from the national and local area telephone surveys (top three rows) are weighted. See the methodology section for details on weighting procedures. Figures for subscribers, former subscribers, and single ticket buyers derive from the postal surveys of ticket buyers and are not weighted. Tables 3M1 through 3M4 are additive. To figure the percentage of respondents who listen to classical radio daily or several times per week, add the figures from Table 3M1 and 3M2.

TABLE 3N

PERCENT OF RESPONDENTS WHO USE DIFFERENT SETTINGS FOR LISTENING TO CLASSICAL MUSIC RADIO AND RECORDINGS

		NAT'L SURVEY	AVERAGE OF 15 MARKET SURVEYS	BPO/Brooklyn	CSO/Charlotte	CSO/Denver	DSO/Detroit	FWP/Fort Wayne	KCS/Kansas City	LBSO/Long Beach	LPO/New Orleans	NWS/Miami (Dade)	OS/Portland	TPO/Philadelphia	SLSO/Saint Louis	SPCO/Saint Paul	SAS/San Antonio	WSO/Wichita
Potential Classical Music Consumers*	At Home	46%	67%	69%	60%	74%	66%	63%	69%	68%	64%	68%	71%	69%	65%	69%	66%	62%
	In a Car	50%	59%	39%	60%	64%	56%	52%	63%	58%	62%	62%	62%	59%	60%	63%	63%	57%
	At Work	16%	19%	22%	15%	22%	20%	18%	21%	22%	19%	24%	17%	19%	18%	18%	19%	19%
Current Subscribers	At Home	N/A	85%	93%	81%	89%	85%	78%	81%	80%	85%	83%	86%	91%	87%	94%	80%	88%
	In a Car	N/A	84%	60%	88%	87%	85%	76%	84%	82%	88%	83%	80%	84%	88%	89%	83%	87%
	At Work	N/A	19%	22%	17%	15%	20%	14%	18%	13%	26%	14%	19%	20%	19%	24%	21%	20%
Former Subscribers	At Home	N/A	86%	94%	80%	87%	82%	78%	82%	89%	82%	89%	85%	91%	87%	93%	74%	91%
	In a Car	N/A	81%	47%	74%	85%	88%	76%	84%	80%	82%	84%	77%	86%	85%	91%	84%	85%
	At Work	N/A	22%	23%	22%	18%	25%	17%	22%	9%	27%	24%	21%	24%	24%	32%	25%	22%
Single Ticket Buyers	At Home	N/A	78%	92%	69%	84%	74%	73%	74%	74%	80%	82%	84%	81%	71%	88%	71%	70%
	In a Car	N/A	74%	44%	82%	82%	75%	64%	76%	77%	82%	76%	75%	77%	84%	86%	74%	66%
	At Work	N/A	24%	30%	20%	21%	27%	19%	26%	19%	29%	22%	25%	26%	28%	24%	21%	23%

NOTES:

*"Potential Classical Music Consumers" are defined as the sub-set of respondents in each area who qualified for an extended interview, based on their responses to an initial series of questions.

All figures from the national and local area telephone surveys (top three rows) are weighted. See the methodology section for details on weighting procedures. Figures for subscribers, former subscribers, and single ticket buyers derive from the postal surveys of ticket buyers and are not weighted.

TABLE 30

PERCENT OF RESPONDENTS WHO'VE EVER MADE A DONATION TO A NON-PROFIT RADIO STATION THAT PLAYS CLASSICAL MUSIC

	NAT'L SURVEY	AVERAGE OF 15 MARKET SURVEYS	BPO/Brooklyn	CSO/Charlotte	CSO/Denver	DSO/Detroit	FWP/Fort Wayne	KCS/Kansas City	LBSO/Long Beach	LPO/New Orleans	NWS/Miami (Dade)	OS/Portland	TPO/Philadelphia	SLSO/Saint Louis	SPCO/Saint Paul	SAS/San Antonio	WSO/Wichita
Potential Classical Music Consumers*	17%	19%	12%	21%	23%	17%	22%	14%	15%	20%	16%	23%	20%	21%	28%	15%	19%
Current Subscribers	N/A	70%	79%	76%	75%	55%	64%	53%	55%	77%	67%	68%	75%	56%	92%	66%	77%
Former Subscribers	N/A	65%	78%	59%	67%	51%	66%	54%	49%	73%	69%	66%	66%	45%	87%	53%	72%
Single Ticket Buyers	N/A	46%	52%	44%	56%	39%	32%	43%	38%	61%	60%	48%	45%	30%	64%	48%	38%

NOTES:

*"Potential Classical Music Consumers" are defined as the sub-set of respondents in each area who qualified for an extended interview, based on their responses to an initial series of questions.

All figures from the national and local area telephone surveys (top three rows) are weighted. See the methodology section for details on weighting procedures. Figures for subscribers, former subscribers, and single ticket buyers derive from the postal surveys of ticket buyers and are not weighted.

TABLE 3P

MEAN NUMBER OF CLASSICAL RECORDINGS OWNED, PURCHASED IN THE PAST YEAR

		NAT'L SURVEY	AVERAGE OF 15 MARKET SURVEYS	BPO/Brooklyn	CSO/Charlotte	CSO/Denver	DSO/Detroit	FWP/Fort Wayne	KCS/Kansas City	LBSO/Long Beach	LPO/New Orleans	NWS/Miami (Dade)	OS/Portland	TPO/Philadelphia	SLSO/Saint Louis	SPCO/Saint Paul	SAS/San Antonio	WSO/Wichita
Potential Classical Music Consumers*	Classical Music Recordings Owned	16	22	18	17	22	31	21	17	23	21	32	22	32	22	28	15	14
	# of Classical Recordings Purchased in the last 12 Months	2	2	3	2	2	2	2	2	2	2	2	2	2	1	2	1	1
Current Subscribers	Classical Music Recordings Owned	N/A	105	219	76	124	83	81	84	79	129	121	82	157	78	105	80	98
	# of Classical Recordings Purchased in the last 12 Months	N/A	8	14	6	8	8	5	6	5	9	10	6	11	6	8	6	7
Former Subscribers	Classical Music Recordings Owned	N/A	98	245	68	87	81	67	79	120	99	132	77	152	67	118	52	68
	# of Classical Recordings Purchased in the last 12 Months	N/A	7	15	4	7	5	4	6	6	7	7	5	9	6	8	6	5
Single Ticket Buyers	Classical Music Recordings Owned	N/A	63	145	40	66	49	42	50	83	67	85	51	62	42	83	54	32
	# of Classical Recordings Purchased in the last 12 Months	N/A	6	11	3	6	5	3	5	7	7	10	4	6	4	6	5	4

NOTES:

**"Potential Classical Music Consumers" are defined as the sub-set of respondents in each area who qualified for an extended interview, based on their responses to an initial series of questions.

All figures from the national and local area telephone surveys are weighted. See the methodology section for details on weighting procedures.

Figures for subscribers, former subscribers, and single ticket buyers derive from the postal surveys of ticket buyers and are not weighted.

Respondents who reported owning more than 1500 recordings were classified as outliers (i.e., invalid responses).

Respondents who reported purchasing more than 100 recordings in the past year were classified as outliers (i.e., invalid responses).

TABLE 4A

LENGTH OF RESIDENCE, IN YEARS

		AVERAGE OF 15 MARKET SURVEYS	BPO/Brooklyn	CSO/Charlotte	CSO/Denver	DSO/Detroit	FWP/Fort Wayne	KCS/Kansas City	LBSO/Long Beach	LPO/New Orleans	NWS/Miami (Dade)	OS/Portland	TPO/Philadelphia	SLSO/Saint Louis	SPCO/Saint Paul	SAS/San Antonio	WSO/Wichita
Potential Classical Music Consumers*	0-1 Years	6%	7%	7%	6%	2%	5%	7%	11%	4%	15%	7%	7%	4%	2%	7%	5%
	2-4 Years	9%	14%	13%	9%	6%	5%	11%	16%	5%	17%	9%	4%	5%	5%	11%	7%
	5-9 Years	10%	12%	14%	12%	7%	10%	9%	14%	8%	10%	14%	5%	5%	9%	9%	7%
	10+ Years	75%	67%	66%	73%	85%	81%	73%	59%	83%	58%	70%	84%	86%	84%	73%	81%
Current Subscribers	0-1 Years	2%	1%	2%	1%	1%	1%	2%	5%	1%	6%	1%	1%	2%	1%	1%	2%
	2-4 Years	4%	0%	9%	4%	2%	2%	4%	4%	2%	5%	6%	21%	4%	2%	7%	3%
	5-9 Years	7%	5%	17%	5%	4%	5%	8%	4%	6%	8%	11%	3%	6%	5%	12%	5%
	10+ Years	88%	94%	73%	91%	93%	92%	86%	87%	91%	81%	82%	94%	89%	91%	80%	90%
Former Subscribers	0-1 Years	2%	1%	2%	0%	1%	1%	1%	5%	1%	23%	1%	0%	1%	1%	0%	1%
	2-4 Years	4%	5%	12%	3%	2%	1%	4%	7%	4%	3%	8%	7%	4%	4%	7%	2%
	5-9 Years	8%	9%	12%	12%	5%	4%	8%	4%	3%	9%	11%	0%	7%	11%	17%	7%
	10+ Years	85%	85%	74%	85%	92%	93%	87%	84%	92%	65%	80%	93%	88%	85%	75%	90%
Single Ticket Buyers	0-1 Years	6%	2%	9%	2%	4%	3%	5%	19%	4%	19%	5%	3%	5%	7%	3%	5%
	2-4 Years	10%	8%	16%	6%	7%	4%	14%	7%	9%	15%	16%	11%	8%	14%	14%	8%
	5-9 Years	11%	16%	18%	13%	7%	7%	8%	8%	12%	13%	12%	11%	6%	13%	17%	7%
	10+ Years	73%	75%	57%	79%	82%	86%	74%	65%	76%	53%	67%	76%	81%	67%	65%	81%

NOTES:

**"Potential Classical Music Consumers" are defined as the sub-set of respondents in each area who qualified for an extended interview, based on their responses to an initial series of questions.

All figures from the national and local area telephone surveys are weighted. See the methodology section for details on weighting procedures.

Figures for subscribers, former subscribers, and single ticket buyers derive from the postal surveys of ticket buyers and are not weighted.

TABLE 4B

DRIVE TIME TO VENUE, IN MINUTES

	NAT'L SURVEY	AVERAGE OF 15 MARKET SURVEYS	BPO/Brooklyn	CSO/Charlotte	CSO/Denver	DSO/Detroit	FWP/Fort Wayne	KCS/Kansas City	LBSO/Long Beach	LPO/New Orleans	NWS/Miami (Dade)	OS/Portland	TPO/Philadelphia	SLSO/Saint Louis	SPCO/Saint Paul	SAS/San Antonio	WSO/Wichita
Potential Classical Music Consumers*																	
1-15 Minutes	N/A	33%	16%	21%	15%	52%	26%	50%	41%	26%	31%	11%	26%	32%	45%	64%	33%
16-30 Minutes	N/A	45%	45%	49%	48%	34%	50%	46%	38%	40%	51%	41%	56%	53%	44%	31%	45%
31-45 Minutes	N/A	16%	30%	25%	27%	11%	20%	2%	11%	22%	15%	33%	15%	13%	9%	5%	17%
46+ Minutes	N/A	6%	9%	4%	10%	3%	5%	2%	10%	12%	3%	15%	4%	2%	2%	0%	5%
Current Subscribers																	
1-15 Minutes	N/A	26%	41%	25%	N/A	5%	37%	9%	N/A	41%	N/A	N/A	N/A	19%	28%	18%	39%
16-30 Minutes	N/A	53%	36%	57%	N/A	58%	46%	71%	N/A	48%	N/A	N/A	N/A	54%	47%	67%	44%
31-45 Minutes	N/A	14%	13%	14%	N/A	31%	8%	16%	N/A	7%	N/A	N/A	N/A	19%	15%	8%	10%
46+ Minutes	N/A	7%	10%	3%	N/A	7%	9%	4%	N/A	4%	N/A	N/A	N/A	8%	10%	7%	7%
Former Subscribers																	
1-15 Minutes	N/A	25%	32%	17%	N/A	10%	29%	12%	N/A	38%	N/A	N/A	N/A	26%	24%	20%	38%
16-30 Minutes	N/A	50%	27%	69%	N/A	50%	52%	55%	N/A	48%	N/A	N/A	N/A	57%	52%	59%	42%
31-45 Minutes	N/A	16%	26%	8%	N/A	28%	10%	25%	N/A	7%	N/A	N/A	N/A	11%	18%	14%	13%
46+ Minutes	N/A	8%	14%	6%	N/A	11%	10%	8%	N/A	8%	N/A	N/A	N/A	6%	6%	8%	7%
Single Ticket Buyers																	
1-15 Minutes	N/A	24%	25%	23%	N/A	10%	35%	8%	N/A	39%	N/A	N/A	N/A	19%	24%	18%	38%
16-30 Minutes	N/A	48%	34%	51%	N/A	48%	50%	66%	N/A	40%	N/A	N/A	N/A	51%	44%	54%	39%
31-45 Minutes	N/A	16%	24%	16%	N/A	31%	8%	16%	N/A	10%	N/A	N/A	N/A	19%	16%	17%	9%
46+ Minutes	N/A	12%	18%	11%	N/A	12%	6%	10%	N/A	11%	N/A	N/A	N/A	11%	15%	11%	14%

NOTES:

**"Potential Classical Music Consumers" are defined as the sub-set of respondents in each area who qualified for an extended interview, based on their responses to an initial series of questions.

All figures from the national and local area telephone surveys are weighted. See the methodology section for details on weighting procedures.

TABLE 4C

LIFETIME INVOLVEMENT WITH LOCAL ORCHESTRA: POTENTIAL CLASSICAL CONSUMERS

Potential Classical Music Consumers*	NAT'L SURVEY	AVERAGE OF 15 MARKET SURVEYS	BPO/Brooklyn	CSO/Charlotte	CSO/Denver	DSO/Detroit	FWP/Fort Wayne	KCS/Kansas City	LBSO/Long Beach	LPO/New Orleans	NWS/Miami (Dade)	OS/Portland	TPO/Philadelphia	SLSO/Saint Louis	SPCO/Saint Paul	SAS/San Antonio	WSO/Wichita
% Unaware	N/A	12%	41%	10%	8%	6%	4%	8%	23%	12%	33%	6%	10%	5%	7%	10%	7%
% Aware, never considered attending	N/A	18%	30%	18%	15%	14%	11%	21%	28%	16%	17%	18%	15%	12%	27%	15%	12%
% Aware, considered attending but never have	N/A	25%	16%	25%	27%	25%	24%	29%	26%	23%	28%	28%	32%	20%	27%	30%	22%
% Ever attended, but not subscribed	N/A	38%	11%	42%	44%	47%	51%	38%	19%	43%	19%	38%	38%	51%	35%	41%	52%
% Have ever subscribed	N/A	7%	3%	5%	5%	9%	11%	5%	4%	6%	2%	11%	6%	13%	5%	5%	8%

NOTES:

*"Potential Classical Music Consumers" are defined as the sub-set of respondents in each area who qualified for an extended interview, based on their responses to an initial series of questions.

All figures from the national and local area telephone surveys are weighted. See the methodology section for details on weighting procedures.

Figures in each column total to 100% of potential classical consumers in that market. Percentages in the bottom two rows may be added to figure the percent of potential classical consumers in each market who've ever attended a concert by the local orchestra. For example, in Fort Wayne, 62% of potential classical consumers have ever attended a concert by the Fort Wayne Philharmonic.

TABLE 4D

SOCIAL CONTEXT FOR ATTENDING LOCAL ORCHSTRA CONCERTS

% WHO HAVE FRIENDS OR FAMILY WHO ATTEND THE.. [SPECIFIC LOCAL ORCHESTRA]

	Potential Classical Music Consumers*
NAT'L SURVEY	N/A
AVERAGE OF 15 MARKET SURVEYS	57%
BPO/Brooklyn	39%
CSO/Charlotte	56%
CSO/Denver	56%
DSO/Detroit	62%
FWP/Fort Wayne	68%
KCS/Kansas City	54%
LBSO/Long Beach	38%
LPO/New Orleans	59%
NWS/Miami (Dade)	37%
OS/Portland	61%
TPO/Philadelphia	60%
SLSO/Saint Louis	67%
SPCO/Saint Paul	49%
SAS/San Antonio	56%
WSO/Wichita	68%

NOTES:

*"Potential Classical Music Consumers" are defined as the sub-set of respondents in each area who qualified for an extended interview, based on their responses to an initial series of questions.

All figures from the national and local area telephone surveys are weighted. See the methodology section for details on weighting procedures.

TABLE 4G

RECENCY OF ATTENDANCE AT LOCAL ORCHESTRA
AMONG RESPONDENTS WHO'VE EVER ATTENDED A CONCERT BY THAT ORCHESTRA

Potential Classical Music Consumers*	NATL SURVEY	AVERAGE OF 15 MARKET SURVEYS	BPO/Brooklyn	CSO/Charlotte	CSO/Denver	DSO/Detroit	FWP/Fort Wayne	KCS/Kansas City	LBSO/Long Beach	LPO/New Orleans	NWS/Miami (Dade)	OS/Portland	TPO/Philadelphia	SLSO/Saint Louis	SPCO/Saint Paul	SAS/San Antonio	WSO/Wichita
Within The Past Year	N/A	38%	24%	52%	40%	33%	41%	35%	28%	39%	38%	38%	33%	46%	22%	34%	42%
About 1-2 Years Ago	N/A	21%	32%	23%	18%	19%	21%	18%	30%	24%	38%	18%	12%	19%	25%	24%	21%
About 2-3 Years Ago	N/A	17%	15%	11%	20%	17%	14%	17%	11%	15%	18%	18%	19%	13%	25%	18%	16%
About 4-5 Years Ago	N/A	10%	10%	6%	6%	13%	13%	15%	15%	10%	7%	13%	10%	5%	14%	9%	8%
About 6-10 Years Ago	N/A	8%	14%	5%	9%	10%	6%	8%	8%	8%	0%	8%	9%	10%	7%	7%	7%
More Than 10 Years Ago	N/A	7%	6%	4%	7%	8%	6%	8%	10%	4%	0%	5%	13%	6%	7%	7%	7%

NOTES:

*"Potential Classical Music Consumers" are defined as the sub-set of respondents in each area who qualified for an extended interview, based on their responses to an initial series of questions.

All figures from the national and local area telephone surveys are weighted. See the methodology section for details on weighting procedures.

TABLE 4H

MEAN NUMBER OF TIMES ATTENEDED CONCERTS BY SPECIFIC LOCAL ORCHESTRA, PAST YEAR

	NAT'L SURVEY	AVERAGE OF 15 MARKET SURVEYS	BPO/Brooklyn	CSO/Charlotte	CSO/Denver	DSO/Detroit	FWP/Fort Wayne	KCS/Kansas City	LBSO/Long Beach	LPO/New Orleans	NWS/Miami (Dade)	OS/Portland	TPO/Philadelphia	SLSO/Saint Louis	SPCO/Saint Paul	SAS/San Antonio	WSO/Wichita
Subset of Telephone Survey Respondents who Reported Attending At Least One Concert by Local Orchestra in the Past Year	N/A	2.8	2.4	2.4	2.2	2.7	2.7	2.5	3.7	2.8	2.5	3.2	2.4	3.6	3.1	2.7	2.5
Number of Cases		949	11	90	77	68	84	55	27	67	25	79	54	124	40	52	96
Current Subscribers	N/A		5.4	7.9	11.1	8.5	7.7	7.7	5.6	9.5	8.6	7.6	8.9	8.5	6.6	8.7	9.9
Former Subscribers	N/A		2.9	4.8	4.5	4.6	4.8	3.3	1.9	4.4	3.7	2.4	4.6	4.9	4.0	4.0	4.1
Single Ticket Buyers	N/A		1.6	3.0	4.5	2.5	4.5	2.9	2.0	4.8	3.2	2.4	3.4	3.4	2.3	3.3	3.3

NOTES:

All figures from the national and local area telephone surveys are weighted. See the methodology section for details on weighting procedures.

Figures for subscribers, former subscribers, and single ticket buyers derive from the postal surveys of ticket buyers and are not weighted.

Respondents who reported more than 30 attendances in the past year were classified as outliers (i.e., invalid responses).

TABLE 4I		DEMOGRAPHIC CHARACTERISTICS BY TYPE OF LOCAL ORCHESTRA CONCERT EVER ATTENDED (TICKET BUYER DATA)					
		Classical Concert (N=7,992)	Pops Concert (N=3,934)	Children's Concert (N=1,576)	Outdoor Concert (N=1,918)	Holiday Concert (N=4,035)	Chamber Concert (N=801)
Gender	Female	59%	64%	73%	61%	67%	58%
	Male	41%	36%	27%	39%	33%	42%
Marital Status	Married (or Partnered)	71%	73%	79%	73%	73%	67%
	Single/Never Married	11%	9%	6%	10%	10%	10%
	Divorced/Separated	9%	9%	10%	10%	10%	10%
	Widowed	10%	9%	7%	7%	8%	12%
Age Group	18-34	6%	4%	4%	5%	6%	3%
	35-44	10%	9%	21%	11%	12%	9%
	45-54	21%	23%	28%	24%	25%	21%
	55-64	25%	28%	23%	29%	27%	23%
	65-74	24%	25%	18%	22%	22%	29%
	75+	14%	11%	6%	9%	9%	16%
Children in the HH	% w/ANY CHILDREN	16%	15%	41%	19%	19%	10%
Education	Grade School	0%	0%	0%	0%	0%	0%
	Some High School	0%	0%	0%	0%	0%	0%
	High School Graduate	3%	4%	2%	2%	4%	2%
	Some College	13%	17%	11%	12%	16%	12%
	College Degree	26%	27%	28%	27%	28%	24%
	Post Graduate Study	59%	51%	58%	59%	52%	62%
Employment Status - Respondent	Working Full-Time (For Pay)	40%	39%	41%	44%	42%	35%
	Working Part-Time (For Pay)	8%	8%	11%	8%	8%	7%
	Self-employed	9%	8%	9%	10%	9%	10%
	In School Full-Time	1%	1%	0%	1%	1%	1%
	Not Employed, But Looking	1%	1%	1%	1%	1%	1%
	Full-Time Family Caregiver	5%	6%	13%	6%	6%	3%
	Retired	37%	39%	25%	31%	33%	43%
Race/Ethnicity	White/Anglo	95%	97%	95%	96%	96%	96%
	Black/African-American	1%	1%	2%	2%	2%	0%
	Asian	1%	1%	1%	1%	1%	1%
	Other Race	3%	2%	3%	2%	2%	3%
	Hispanic (Independent of Race)	3%	2%	3%	2%	2%	3%
Household Income	< $35,000	8%	9%	6%	6%	9%	9%
	$35,000-$49,999	13%	13%	13%	12%	13%	15%
	$50,000-$74,999	19%	22%	18%	19%	21%	19%
	$75,000-$99,999	17%	18%	19%	19%	18%	15%
	$100,000-$124,999	13%	13%	15%	14%	14%	13%
	$125,000-$149,999	7%	7%	7%	7%	7%	6%
	$150,000-$174,999	6%	5%	5%	5%	5%	5%
	$175,000-$199,999	4%	3%	3%	3%	3%	3%
	$200,000 +	13%	11%	15%	14%	11%	15%

NOTES:

Figures in this table represent averages for all respondents to the ticket buyer postal surveys. Respondents were allowed to select multiple product types.

TABLE 4K

% OF TICKET BUYERS WHO'VE EVER HAD AN UNSATISFACTORY EXPERIENCE ATTENDING A CONCERT BY THEIR LOCAL ORCHESTRA

	NAT'L SURVEY	AVERAGE OF 15 MARKET SURVEYS	BPO/Brooklyn	CSO/Charlotte	CSO/Denver	DSO/Detroit	FWP/Fort Wayne	KCS/Kansas City	LBSO/Long Beach	LPO/New Orleans	NWS/Miami (Dade)	OS/Portland	TPO/Philadelphia	SLSO/Saint Louis	SPCO/Saint Paul	SAS/San Antonio	WSO/Wichita
Current Subscribers	N/A	24%	26%	28%	32%	22%	24%	22%	21%	17%	16%	23%	29%	25%	19%	25%	24%
Former Subscribers	N/A	19%	31%	19%	21%	14%	14%	22%	21%	13%	13%	26%	21%	23%	12%	15%	18%
Single Ticket Buyers	N/A	7%	4%	9%	12%	10%	4%	6%	7%	10%	6%	11%	8%	10%	7%	6%	4%

NOTES:

Figures for subscribers, former subscribers, and single ticket buyers derive from the postal surveys of ticket buyers and are not weighted.

TABLE 4L-1

LOYALTY - LEVEL OF AGREEMENT WITH THE STATEMENT: "I BELIEVE THE [LOCAL ORCHESTRA] DESERVES MY LOYALTY"

		AVERAGE OF 15 MARKET SURVEYS	BPO/Brooklyn	CSO/Charlotte	CSO/Denver	DSO/Detroit	FWP/Fort Wayne	KCS/Kansas City	LBSO/Long Beach	LPO/New Orleans	NWS/Miami (Dade)	OS/Portland	TPO/Philadelphia	SLSO/Saint Louis	SPCO/Saint Paul	SAS/San Antonio	WSO/Wichita
Current Subscribers	Agree a lot	71%	76%	N/A	73%	69%	73%	65%	63%	83%	80%	60%	67%	68%	65%	75%	74%
	Agree a little	25%	22%	N/A	23%	28%	24%	31%	34%	15%	19%	37%	26%	28%	30%	22%	23%
	Disagree a little	3%	1%	N/A	3%	2%	3%	4%	2%	2%	1%	3%	6%	4%	5%	2%	3%
	Disagree a lot	1%	0%	N/A	1%	1%	1%	0%	1%	1%	0%	1%	2%	1%	0%	1%	0%
Former Subscribers	Agree a lot	42%	42%	N/A	53%	41%	56%	26%	33%	51%	61%	35%	35%	42%	29%	41%	42%
	Agree a little	43%	32%	N/A	37%	45%	39%	58%	47%	37%	29%	47%	40%	43%	55%	44%	43%
	Disagree a little	12%	15%	N/A	7%	12%	4%	12%	17%	11%	6%	15%	21%	14%	17%	12%	13%
	Disagree a lot	3%	11%	N/A	3%	2%	1%	4%	3%	2%	4%	3%	4%	0%	0%	3%	2%
Single Ticket Buyers	Agree a lot	35%	20%	N/A	41%	30%	43%	29%	24%	50%	42%	28%	34%	40%	21%	37%	36%
	Agree a little	48%	43%	N/A	49%	55%	42%	52%	56%	40%	46%	52%	45%	45%	51%	46%	50%
	Disagree a little	14%	27%	N/A	9%	13%	12%	16%	15%	10%	8%	16%	16%	12%	20%	15%	11%
	Disagree a lot	4%	10%	N/A	2%	3%	4%	4%	5%	0%	4%	4%	5%	3%	8%	2%	3%

NOTES:

Figures for subscribers, former subscribers, and single ticket buyers derive from the postal surveys of ticket buyers and are not weighted.

Questions pertaining to loyalty were added to the questionniare after the Charlotte Symphony mailing.

TABLE 4L-2

LOYALTY - LEVEL OF AGREEMENT WITH THE STATEMENT: "THE [LOCAL ORCHESTRA] REALLY CARES ABOUT BUILDING A RELATIONSHIP WITH ME."

		AVERAGE OF 15 MARKET SURVEYS	BPO/Brooklyn	CSO/Charlotte	CSO/Denver	DSO/Detroit	FWP/Fort Wayne	KCS/Kansas City	LBSO/Long Beach	LPO/New Orleans	NWS/Miami (Dade)	OS/Portland	TPO/Philadelphia	SLSO/Saint Louis	SPCO/Saint Paul	SAS/San Antonio	WSO/Wichita
Current Subscribers	Agree a lot	46%	58%	N/A	39%	48%	54%	40%	52%	66%	51%	46%	38%	35%	45%	48%	39%
	Agree a little	43%	36%	N/A	47%	41%	39%	53%	40%	29%	41%	46%	46%	48%	45%	46%	47%
	Disagree a little	8%	4%	N/A	11%	9%	6%	6%	6%	4%	7%	6%	11%	14%	9%	6%	10%
	Disagree a lot	3%	2%	N/A	3%	3%	2%	2%	2%	2%	2%	2%	6%	4%	1%	1%	4%
Former Subscribers	Agree a lot	39%	47%	N/A	30%	37%	56%	39%	41%	49%	46%	32%	37%	36%	40%	42%	28%
	Agree a little	45%	41%	N/A	49%	47%	37%	42%	47%	40%	43%	56%	35%	42%	49%	46%	53%
	Disagree a little	11%	5%	N/A	16%	12%	4%	17%	10%	5%	5%	10%	12%	17%	10%	6%	15%
	Disagree a lot	4%	7%	N/A	5%	4%	3%	3%	3%	5%	5%	2%	16%	5%	0%	6%	4%
Single Ticket Buyers	Agree a lot	34%	31%	N/A	36%	37%	38%	28%	42%	44%	29%	33%	27%	41%	29%	36%	30%
	Agree a little	52%	50%	N/A	51%	52%	51%	57%	48%	47%	55%	54%	50%	43%	57%	51%	55%
	Disagree a little	10%	17%	N/A	10%	8%	6%	11%	7%	9%	14%	9%	15%	9%	11%	10%	9%
	Disagree a lot	4%	3%	N/A	3%	3%	6%	5%	2%	1%	3%	4%	8%	6%	3%	2%	6%

NOTES:

Questions pertaining to loyalty were added to the questionnaire after the Charlotte Symphony mailing.

Figures for subscribers, former subscribers, and single ticket buyers derive from the postal surveys of ticket buyers and are not weighted.

TABLE 4L-3

LOYALTY - LEVEL OF AGREEMENT WITH THE STATEMENT: "I FEEL A STRONG CONNECTION WITH THE MUSICIANS OF THE [LOCAL ORCHESTRA]."

		AVERAGE OF 15 MARKET SURVEYS	BPO/Brooklyn	CSO/Charlotte	CSO/Denver	DSO/Detroit	FWP/Fort Wayne	KCS/Kansas City	LBSO/Long Beach	LPO/New Orleans	NWS/Miami (Dade)	OS/Portland	TPO/Philadelphia	SLSO/Saint Louis	SPCO/Saint Paul	SAS/San Antonio	WSO/Wichita
Current Subscribers	Agree a lot	30%	38%	N/A	31%	30%	21%	19%	24%	48%	36%	22%	33%	29%	29%	33%	29%
	Agree a little	44%	44%	N/A	47%	41%	47%	45%	45%	39%	43%	50%	40%	41%	46%	45%	43%
	Disagree a little	19%	15%	N/A	17%	19%	22%	23%	22%	11%	15%	21%	19%	21%	20%	17%	20%
	Disagree a lot	7%	4%	N/A	5%	10%	11%	14%	9%	3%	6%	7%	9%	9%	5%	5%	8%
Former Subscribers	Agree a lot	15%	21%	N/A	16%	11%	17%	8%	11%	20%	32%	5%	23%	17%	13%	13%	14%
	Agree a little	42%	36%	N/A	43%	43%	48%	35%	43%	44%	38%	37%	33%	48%	43%	40%	47%
	Disagree a little	26%	25%	N/A	25%	29%	22%	34%	20%	25%	21%	35%	18%	22%	29%	27%	23%
	Disagree a lot	17%	19%	N/A	16%	17%	14%	24%	26%	12%	9%	22%	26%	13%	15%	21%	16%
Single Ticket Buyers	Agree a lot	11%	2%	N/A	15%	6%	13%	8%	14%	21%	18%	6%	9%	10%	6%	9%	10%
	Agree a little	33%	26%	N/A	36%	30%	33%	34%	28%	42%	41%	28%	29%	40%	30%	36%	29%
	Disagree a little	33%	39%	N/A	26%	44%	33%	37%	35%	24%	22%	38%	34%	32%	33%	28%	39%
	Disagree a lot	23%	34%	N/A	23%	19%	21%	21%	23%	13%	19%	28%	27%	18%	31%	27%	21%

NOTES:

Figures for subscribers, former subscribers, and single ticket buyers derive from the postal surveys of ticket buyers and are not weighted.

Questions pertaining to loyalty were added to the questionniare after the Charlotte Symphony mailing.

TABLE 4L-4

LOYALTY - LEVEL OF AGREEMENT WITH THE STATEMENT: "I HAVE CONFIDENCE IN THE [LOCAL ORCHESTRA] ORGANIZATION."

		AVERAGE OF 15 MARKET SURVEYS	BPO/Brooklyn	CSO/Charlotte	CSO/Denver	DSO/Detroit	FWP/Fort Wayne	KCS/Kansas City	LBSO/Long Beach	LPO/New Orleans	NWS/Miami (Dade)	OS/Portland	TPO/Philadelphia	SLSO/Saint Louis	SPCO/Saint Paul	SAS/San Antonio	WSO/Wichita
Current Subscribers	Agree a lot	61%	60%	N/A	45%	72%	75%	56%	61%	81%	78%	59%	46%	35%	74%	50%	73%
	Agree a little	31%	32%	N/A	43%	26%	23%	39%	32%	17%	21%	39%	39%	35%	22%	40%	26%
	Disagree a little	6%	7%	N/A	10%	2%	1%	3%	5%	2%	2%	2%	12%	23%	3%	7%	1%
	Disagree a lot	2%	2%	N/A	2%	1%	1%	1%	1%	0%	0%	0%	4%	7%	1%	2%	1%
Former Subscribers	Agree a lot	51%	38%	N/A	41%	62%	67%	41%	38%	61%	65%	49%	46%	33%	53%	51%	60%
	Agree a little	39%	41%	N/A	48%	33%	33%	53%	52%	33%	31%	39%	35%	33%	43%	30%	38%
	Disagree a little	8%	14%	N/A	8%	4%	1%	5%	7%	4%	3%	12%	12%	26%	3%	17%	2%
	Disagree a lot	2%	7%	N/A	3%	1%	0%	1%	3%	2%	1%	0%	7%	7%	0%	1%	1%
Single Ticket Buyers	Agree a lot	45%	28%	N/A	41%	45%	61%	32%	41%	59%	51%	43%	44%	41%	43%	44%	49%
	Agree a little	47%	56%	N/A	50%	51%	35%	61%	51%	37%	42%	50%	47%	42%	50%	47%	48%
	Disagree a little	6%	12%	N/A	8%	3%	2%	6%	6%	3%	5%	6%	5%	11%	6%	9%	2%
	Disagree a lot	2%	5%	N/A	1%	1%	0%	1%	2%	1%	2%	2%	4%	7%	2%	0%	1%

NOTES:

Figures for subscribers, former subscribers, and single ticket buyers derive from the postal surveys of ticket buyers and are not weighted.

Questions pertaining to loyalty were added to the questionniare after the Charlotte Symphony mailing.

TABLE 4M

% WHO HAVE EVER PERSONALLY BOUGHT TICKETS TO THE LOCAL ORCHESTRA, AMONG THE SUBSET OF RESPONDENTS WHO'VE EVER ATTENDED

	NATL SURVEY	AVERAGE OF 15 MARKET SURVEYS	BPO/Brooklyn	CSO/Charlotte	CSO/Denver	DSO/Detroit	FWP/Fort Wayne	KCS/Kansas City	LBSO/Long Beach	LPO/New Orleans	NWS/Miami (Dade)	OS/Portland	TPO/Philadelphia	SLSO/Saint Louis	SPCO/Saint Paul	SAS/San Antonio	WSO/Wichita
% of Public Survey Respondents who have ever purchased tickets, among those who have EVER attended a concert by their Local Orchestra	N/A	60%	22%	46%	66%	60%	58%	62%	55%	63%	62%	67%	63%	73%	53%	50%	58%
Number of Cases		2553	51	177	187	212	212	161	100	179	66	206	152	270	187	157	236

NOTES:

All figures from the national and local area telephone surveys are weighted. See the methodology section for details on weighting procedures.

TABLE 4N

ANTICIPATED CHANGE IN ATTENDANCE LEVEL IF LOCAL ORCHESTRA PLAYED MORE CLASSICAL MUSIC COMPOSITIONS BY CONTEMPORARY COMPOSERS

		AVERAGE OF 15 MARKET SURVEYS	BPO/Brooklyn	CSO/Charlotte	CSO/Denver	DSO/Detroit	FWP/Fort Wayne	KCS/Kansas City	LBSO/Long Beach	LPO/New Orleans	NWS/Miami (Dade)	OS/Portland	TPO/Philadelphia	SLSO/Saint Louis	SPCO/Saint Paul	SAS/San Antonio	WSO/Wichita
Potential Classical Music Consumers*	Less Often	12%	N/A	9%	13%	15%	9%	12%	9%	8%	26%	12%	11%	11%	17%	8%	10%
	About As Often As I Do Now	68%	N/A	73%	67%	64%	74%	64%	59%	70%	45%	74%	67%	67%	68%	68%	71%
	More Often	21%	N/A	18%	20%	21%	18%	24%	32%	22%	29%	15%	22%	23%	15%	24%	19%
Current Subscribers	Less Often	29%	N/A	24%	32%	27%	22%	28%	22%	27%	30%	28%	34%	36%	39%	21%	28%
	About As Often As I Do Now	66%	N/A	69%	62%	67%	78%	66%	73%	67%	64%	67%	60%	61%	57%	69%	66%
	More Often	6%	N/A	7%	6%	6%	0%	7%	4%	6%	6%	5%	6%	4%	4%	11%	6%
Former Subscribers	Less Often	33%	N/A	34%	30%	31%	21%	33%	29%	34%	33%	32%	44%	44%	42%	30%	28%
	About As Often As I Do Now	58%	N/A	59%	55%	57%	79%	56%	61%	61%	58%	61%	46%	48%	52%	53%	60%
	More Often	9%	N/A	8%	15%	12%	0%	12%	9%	5%	9%	8%	11%	9%	6%	17%	12%
Single Ticket Buyers	Less Often	23%	N/A	20%	28%	25%	22%	19%	18%	21%	28%	21%	25%	25%	36%	14%	15%
	About As Often As I Do Now	64%	N/A	63%	63%	59%	78%	63%	61%	61%	55%	72%	62%	62%	57%	71%	67%
	More Often	14%	N/A	18%	9%	17%	0%	18%	21%	18%	17%	8%	12%	14%	8%	16%	18%

NOTES:

**"Potential Classical Music Consumers" are defined as the sub-set of respondents in each area who qualified for an extended interview, based on their responses to an initial series of questions.

All figures from the national and local area telephone surveys are weighted. See the methodology section for details on weighting procedures.

Figures for subscribers, former subscribers, and single ticket buyers derive from the postal surveys of ticket buyers and are not weighted.

TABLE 40

MEAN RATING OF ORCHESTRA'S QUALITY OF PLAYING
(SCALE: 0="POOR QUALITY"; 10="EXCELLENT QUALITY")

	AVERAGE OF 15 MARKET SURVEYS	BPO/Brooklyn	CSO/Charlotte	CSO/Denver	DSO/Detroit	FWP/Fort Wayne	KCS/Kansas City	LBSO/Long Beach	LPO/New Orleans	NWS/Miami (Dade)	OS/Portland	TPO/Philadelphia	SLSO/Saint Louis	SPCO/Saint Paul	SAS/San Antonio	WSO/Wichita
Subset of Public Survey Respondents Who Have EVER Attended a Concert By Their Local Orchestra	8.6	8.9	8.3	8.0	8.8	8.7	8.3	8.3	8.6	8.1	8.5	9.2	9.2	8.7	8.6	8.4
Current Subscribers	9.2	8.9	8.7	9.0	9.5	9.3	8.4	8.9	9.1	9.4	9.0	9.6	9.6	9.6	9.1	9.0
Former Subscribers	8.9	8.2	8.4	8.8	9.0	9.4	8.3	8.4	9.1	9.2	8.8	9.5	9.4	9.3	8.7	8.7
Single Ticket Buyers	8.8	8.0	8.5	8.8	9.0	9.2	8.2	8.5	8.9	8.8	8.7	9.4	9.4	9.1	8.8	8.8
"Critical Listeners"	9.0	8.4	8.2	8.9	9.3	9.2	8.2	8.5	8.9	9.3	8.6	9.6	9.5	9.5	8.9	8.9
"Casual Listeners"	9.1	8.6	8.8	9.0	9.2	9.3	8.3	8.8	9.1	9.1	8.9	9.5	9.6	9.3	9.1	8.9
"Very Knowledgeable" About C.M.	8.9	8.5	8.1	8.9	9.3	9.1	8.2	8.4	8.7	9.3	8.6	9.6	9.4	9.5	8.8	8.8
"Somewhat Knowledgeable" About C.M.	9.0	8.4	8.6	8.9	9.3	9.3	8.2	8.8	9.1	9.2	8.8	9.6	9.6	9.4	9.0	8.9
"Not Very Knowledgeable" About C.M.	9.1	9.0	8.8	9.0	9.1	9.3	8.4	8.8	9.2	9.3	9.1	9.5	9.5	9.3	9.1	8.9

NOTES:

*"Potential Classical Music Consumers" are defined as the sub-set of respondents in each area who qualified for an extended interview, based on their responses to an initial series of questions.

All figures from the national and local area telephone surveys are weighted. See the methodology section for details on weighting procedures.

Figures for subscribers, former subscribers, and single ticket buyers derive from the postal surveys of ticket buyers and are not weighted.

TABLE 4P

ATTITUDES ABOUT FUTURE ATTENDANCE AT CONCERTS BY LOCAL ORCHESTRA

Which of the following statements best describes your current attitude about attending concerts by the [specific local orchestra]?

Potential Classical Music Consumers*

	AVERAGE OF 15 MARKET SURVEYS	BPO/Brooklyn	CSO/Charlotte	CSO/Denver	DSO/Detroit	FWP/Fort Wayne	KCS/Kansas City	LBSO/Long Beach	LPO/New Orleans	NWS/Miami (Dade)	OS/Portland	TPO/Philadelphia	SLSO/Saint Louis	SPCO/Saint Paul	SAS/San Antonio	WSO/Wichita
I'm NOT AT ALL INTERESTED in attending a concert	8%	15%	7%	7%	10%	4%	11%	6%	8%	13%	5%	8%	6%	9%	6%	6%
I'm OPEN TO ATTENDING, but it's not a high priority	71%	66%	70%	74%	71%	77%	69%	74%	67%	65%	73%	66%	67%	76%	69%	73%
I'm VERY INTERESTED in attending a concert	22%	19%	24%	19%	18%	20%	21%	21%	25%	22%	23%	26%	27%	16%	24%	21%

In the future, do you anticipate attending [specific local orchestra] concerts...

	AVERAGE OF 15 MARKET SURVEYS	BPO/Brooklyn	CSO/Charlotte	CSO/Denver	DSO/Detroit	FWP/Fort Wayne	KCS/Kansas City	LBSO/Long Beach	LPO/New Orleans	NWS/Miami (Dade)	OS/Portland	TPO/Philadelphia	SLSO/Saint Louis	SPCO/Saint Paul	SAS/San Antonio	WSO/Wichita
Current Subscribers																
More often	10%	7%	18%	18%	13%	15%	8%	5%	11%	9%	9%	12%	11%	11%	13%	4%
About as often as I do now	88%	91%	78%	78%	86%	82%	91%	92%	88%	89%	88%	85%	89%	88%	86%	94%
Less often	2%	1%	5%	5%	1%	3%	1%	3%	1%	2%	3%	2%	1%	0%	2%	2%
Former Subscribers																
More often	29%	15%	31%	31%	32%	31%	28%	19%	34%	40%	34%	34%	18%	23%	23%	27%
About as often as I do now	59%	65%	52%	52%	54%	61%	65%	57%	64%	47%	60%	56%	71%	63%	59%	61%
Less often	11%	20%	17%	17%	14%	8%	7%	23%	2%	13%	6%	10%	11%	14%	17%	12%
Single Ticket Buyers																
More often	30%	20%	36%	36%	34%	28%	25%	32%	40%	42%	31%	33%	24%	24%	30%	28%
About as often as I do now	67%	77%	62%	62%	61%	69%	72%	64%	60%	56%	67%	63%	73%	74%	69%	70%
Less often	3%	3%	3%	3%	5%	3%	3%	4%	1%	2%	3%	4%	3%	3%	1%	2%

NOTES:

*"Potential Classical Music Consumers" are defined as the sub-set of respondents in each area who qualified for an extended interview, based on their responses to an initial series of questions.

All figures from the national and local area telephone surveys are weighted. See the methodology section for details on weighting procedures.

Figures for subscribers, former subscribers, and single ticket buyers derive from the postal surveys of ticket buyers and are not weighted.

TABLE 5A

MARITAL STATUS

		NAT'L SURVEY	AVERAGE OF 15 MARKET SURVEYS	BPO/Brooklyn	CSO/Charlotte	CSO/Denver	DSO/Detroit	FWP/Fort Wayne	KCS/Kansas City	LBSO/Long Beach	LPO/New Orleans	NWS/Miami (Dade)	OS/Portland	TPO/Philadelphia	SLSO/Saint Louis	SPCO/Saint Paul	SAS/San Antonio	WSO/Wichita
Potential Classical Music Consumers[1]	Married (or Partnered)	58%	51%	38%	56%	52%	48%	59%	58%	42%	45%	43%	60%	55%	54%	54%	48%	54%
	Single/Never Married	23%	30%	44%	27%	32%	27%	23%	23%	37%	32%	35%	25%	31%	28%	33%	34%	27%
	Divorced/Separated	12%	12%	13%	11%	11%	14%	9%	14%	15%	14%	15%	10%	8%	11%	7%	12%	14%
	Widowed	7%	7%	6%	7%	4%	11%	9%	6%	6%	9%	8%	5%	6%	8%	7%	6%	5%
NOT Potential Classical Music Consumers[2]	Married (or Partnered)	55%	53%	42%	62%	58%	49%	68%	54%	50%	43%	51%	50%	55%	53%	53%	51%	60%
	Single/Never Married	20%	28%	42%	25%	30%	27%	16%	26%	32%	28%	34%	31%	26%	26%	34%	27%	21%
	Divorced/Separated	12%	10%	6%	8%	8%	13%	9%	13%	11%	15%	8%	10%	7%	12%	8%	12%	11%
	Widowed	13%	9%	9%	5%	4%	11%	8%	7%	7%	14%	7%	8%	12%	9%	5%	11%	8%
Current Subscribers	Married	N/A	68%	55%	78%	65%	71%	74%	72%	65%	61%	62%	63%	67%	65%	72%	72%	69%
	Partnered/Not Married	N/A	3%	10%	1%	4%	2%	1%	2%	4%	6%	6%	5%	3%	3%	3%	3%	1%
	Single/Never Married	N/A	9%	20%	5%	8%	11%	6%	7%	6%	11%	6%	5%	9%	11%	12%	8%	8%
	Divorced/Separated	N/A	9%	10%	8%	11%	7%	7%	10%	9%	8%	8%	12%	7%	11%	8%	10%	8%
	Widowed	N/A	11%	5%	8%	12%	8%	12%	8%	16%	14%	19%	16%	13%	10%	6%	7%	15%
Former Subscribers	Married	N/A	67%	42%	62%	71%	67%	74%	75%	59%	71%	59%	70%	67%	68%	70%	82%	66%
	Partnered/Not Married	N/A	4%	15%	2%	4%	1%	4%	3%	6%	3%	8%	5%	8%	2%	4%	0%	3%
	Single/Never Married	N/A	9%	27%	19%	8%	13%	9%	5%	10%	10%	3%	7%	7%	12%	8%	6%	5%
	Divorced/Separated	N/A	10%	12%	12%	9%	10%	5%	12%	10%	11%	12%	10%	8%	14%	12%	10%	12%
	Widowed	N/A	9%	3%	6%	8%	9%	9%	6%	14%	6%	18%	9%	10%	3%	6%	7%	15%
Single Ticket Buyers	Married	N/A	65%	39%	73%	68%	72%	68%	72%	62%	60%	59%	62%	67%	59%	70%	67%	67%
	Partnered/Not Married	N/A	6%	17%	3%	4%	4%	3%	3%	7%	6%	9%	13%	8%	4%	5%	7%	4%
	Single/Never Married	N/A	13%	32%	13%	11%	12%	12%	10%	9%	15%	12%	8%	18%	17%	14%	5%	13%
	Divorced/Separated	N/A	9%	9%	9%	10%	8%	12%	8%	9%	13%	9%	13%	5%	12%	5%	13%	8%
	Widowed	N/A	7%	3%	3%	7%	3%	6%	7%	13%	6%	12%	5%	3%	7%	6%	9%	9%

NOTES:

[1] "Potential Classical Music Consumers" are defined as the sub-set of respondents in each area who qualified for an extended interview, based on their responses to an initial series of questions.

[2] "NOT Potential Classical Music Consumers" are defined as the sub-set of respondents in each area who DID NOT qualified for an extended interview, based on their responses to an initial series of questions.

All figures from the national and local area telephone surveys are weighted. See the methodology section for details on weighting procedures.

Figures for subscribers, former subscribers, and single ticket buyers derive from the postal surveys of ticket buyers and are not weighted.

TABLE 5C

PRESENCE OF CHILDREN IN THE HOUSEHOLD

Segment	Measure	NAT'L SURVEY	AVERAGE OF 15 MARKET SURVEYS	BPO/Brooklyn	CSO/Charlotte	CSO/Denver	DSO/Detroit	FWP/Fort Wayne	KCS/Kansas City	LBSO/Long Beach	LPO/New Orleans	NWS/Miami (Dade)	OS/Portland	TPO/Philadelphia	SLSO/Saint Louis	SPCO/Saint Paul	SAS/San Antonio	WSO/Wichita
Potential Classical Music Consumers[1]	% w/Children Under Age 7	19%	48%	51%	47%	47%	46%	44%	50%	40%	47%	54%	47%	45%	56%	40%	53%	59%
	% w/Children Ages 7-12	19%	46%	37%	50%	44%	55%	45%	55%	54%	42%	42%	47%	51%	48%	46%	42%	35%
	% w/Children Ages 13-17	16%	39%	39%	34%	39%	33%	45%	35%	37%	34%	34%	43%	43%	31%	36%	42%	40%
	% w/ANY CHILDREN	44%	40%	41%	39%	40%	43%	39%	46%	40%	39%	41%	38%	44%	37%	36%	42%	41%
NOT Potential Classical Music Consumers[2]	% w/Children Under Age 7	20%	47%	44%	53%	47%	52%	43%	55%	58%	42%	33%	48%	47%	41%	34%	57%	43%
	% w/Children Ages 7-12	19%	46%	46%	54%	39%	44%	52%	45%	46%	44%	51%	51%	45%	42%	46%	46%	51%
	% w/Children Ages 13-17	15%	39%	38%	24%	42%	38%	35%	39%	36%	41%	40%	42%	41%	45%	57%	37%	40%
	% w/ANY CHILDREN	43%	40%	36%	41%	40%	36%	40%	44%	48%	39%	46%	36%	38%	38%	35%	44%	40%
Current Subscribers	% w/Children Ages 13-17	N/A	10%	13%	7%	6%	11%	11%	10%	9%	7%	5%	13%	9%	12%	14%	15%	10%
	% w/Children Ages 6-12	N/A	10%	8%	12%	7%	14%	8%	7%	7%	9%	7%	13%	9%	14%	12%	12%	6%
	% w/Children Under Age 6	N/A	6%	6%	10%	3%	7%	5%	2%	6%	8%	4%	7%	5%	6%	7%	7%	2%
	% w/ANY CHILDREN	N/A	12%	14%	21%	7%	14%	10%	10%	9%	10%	8%	13%	11%	14%	15%	15%	8%
Former Subscribers	% w/Children Ages 13-17	N/A	10%	8%	12%	13%	23%	4%	5%	6%	12%	6%	11%	6%	16%	11%	10%	6%
	% w/Children Ages 6-12	N/A	19%	12%	6%	19%	26%	17%	15%	7%	26%	12%	30%	2%	31%	33%	23%	12%
	% w/Children Under Age 6	N/A	10%	5%	6%	17%	31%	16%	19%	12%	21%	11%	23%	8%	24%	24%	28%	17%
	% w/ANY CHILDREN	N/A	21%	14%	26%	21%	31%	16%	18%	15%	28%	12%	29%	9%	29%	34%	19%	14%
Single Ticket Buyers	% w/Children Ages 13-17	N/A	13%	6%	13%	12%	18%	16%	13%	12%	20%	4%	19%	20%	13%	12%	17%	10%
	% w/Children Ages 6-12	N/A	20%	14%	16%	15%	25%	29%	30%	14%	22%	12%	20%	12%	23%	16%	28%	17%
	% w/Children Under Age 6	N/A	19%	10%	14%	19%	26%	18%	29%	14%	14%	13%	22%	26%	23%	28%	16%	21%
	% w/ANY CHILDREN	N/A	23%	13%	30%	24%	29%	25%	28%	20%	24%	13%	25%	23%	24%	27%	29%	21%

NOTES:

[1] "Potential Classical Music Consumers" are defined as the sub-set of respondents in each area who qualified for an extended interview, based on their responses to an initial series of questions.

[2] "NOT Potential Classical Music Consumers" are defined as the sub-set of respondents in each area who DID NOT qualified for an extended interview, based on their responses to an initial series of questions.

All figures from the national and local area telephone surveys are weighted. See the methodology section for details on weighting procedures.

Figures for subscribers, former subscribers, and single ticket buyers derive from the postal surveys of ticket buyers and are not weighted.

TABLE 5D

HIGHEST LEVEL OF EDUCATIONAL ATTAINMENT

		NATL SURVEY	AVERAGE OF 15 MARKET SURVEYS	BPO/Brooklyn	CSO/Charlotte	CSO/Denver	DSO/Detroit	FWP/Fort Wayne	KCS/Kansas City	LBSO/Long Beach	LPO/New Orleans	NWS/Miami (Dade)	OS/Portland	TPO/Philadelphia	SLSO/Saint Louis	SPCO/Saint Paul	SAS/San Antonio	WSO/Wichita
Potential Classical Music Consumers[1]	Grade School	3%	1%	3%	2%	1%	1%	2%	1%	1%	0%	1%	0%	0%	1%	1%	0%	0%
	Some High School	10%	6%	6%	6%	5%	2%	8%	5%	8%	3%	14%	4%	5%	2%	4%	9%	5%
	High School Graduate	27%	34%	47%	30%	27%	40%	35%	30%	26%	39%	39%	30%	31%	40%	26%	36%	30%
	Some College	31%	22%	17%	26%	19%	19%	26%	24%	24%	21%	13%	23%	22%	19%	24%	25%	27%
	College Degree	19%	25%	18%	28%	30%	25%	20%	28%	29%	24%	19%	29%	26%	24%	28%	20%	25%
	Post Graduate Study	10%	13%	10%	9%	18%	13%	10%	13%	13%	13%	15%	14%	17%	13%	17%	10%	13%
NOT Potential Classical Music Consumers[2]	Grade School	11%	2%	5%	2%	1%	3%	1%	1%	1%	3%	1%	1%	1%	5%	4%	2%	2%
	Some High School	13%	12%	18%	18%	5%	16%	12%	10%	9%	17%	15%	5%	8%	9%	9%	9%	12%
	High School Graduate	42%	49%	51%	43%	44%	47%	58%	50%	40%	50%	53%	46%	57%	51%	46%	49%	52%
	Some College	21%	18%	15%	18%	19%	19%	17%	19%	26%	16%	7%	20%	15%	20%	19%	23%	15%
	College Degree	10%	14%	8%	17%	22%	12%	11%	16%	18%	11%	12%	20%	13%	10%	16%	13%	12%
	Post Graduate Study	3%	6%	4%	3%	8%	5%	2%	4%	6%	3%	12%	9%	6%	5%	6%	5%	7%
Current Subscribers	Grade School	n/a	0%	0%	0%	0%	0%	0%	0%	0%	0%	0%	0%	0%	0%	0%	0%	1%
	Some High School	n/a	0%	0%	0%	0%	0%	1%	0%	0%	1%	0%	0%	0%	0%	0%	0%	1%
	High School Graduate	n/a	3%	1%	3%	1%	6%	7%	1%	3%	3%	2%	3%	4%	4%	2%	3%	2%
	Some College	n/a	13%	5%	11%	13%	12%	19%	15%	17%	13%	15%	15%	8%	14%	10%	14%	15%
	College Degree	n/a	24%	23%	36%	22%	23%	25%	29%	22%	26%	26%	23%	20%	24%	23%	20%	24%
	Post Graduate Study	n/a	59%	71%	50%	64%	59%	50%	56%	57%	58%	57%	60%	68%	58%	65%	63%	58%
Former Subscribers	Grade School	n/a	0%	0%	0%	0%	0%	0%	0%	0%	0%	0%	0%	0%	0%	0%	0%	0%
	Some High School	n/a	0%	0%	0%	0%	0%	1%	0%	3%	1%	0%	4%	0%	4%	1%	0%	0%
	High School Graduate	n/a	3%	1%	3%	3%	4%	7%	1%	3%	2%	5%	4%	3%	12%	8%	15%	3%
	Some College	n/a	14%	3%	12%	13%	14%	20%	18%	28%	7%	13%	20%	12%	12%	8%	15%	21%
	College Degree	n/a	26%	23%	32%	28%	22%	25%	33%	18%	26%	26%	26%	19%	30%	25%	31%	25%
	Post Graduate Study	n/a	57%	74%	52%	56%	60%	48%	48%	51%	65%	56%	50%	67%	55%	66%	54%	52%
Single Ticket Buyers	Grade School	n/a	0%	0%	0%	0%	0%	0%	0%	0%	0%	0%	0%	0%	0%	0%	0%	0%
	Some High School	n/a	0%	0%	0%	0%	0%	1%	0%	1%	1%	5%	5%	5%	1%	3%	1%	1%
	High School Graduate	n/a	4%	1%	3%	2%	2%	11%	2%	3%	2%	5%	5%	5%	5%	3%	4%	10%
	Some College	n/a	17%	9%	13%	10%	15%	23%	18%	19%	16%	12%	25%	17%	17%	14%	24%	27%
	College Degree	n/a	32%	26%	40%	29%	33%	32%	35%	25%	29%	31%	31%	35%	37%	36%	29%	27%
	Post Graduate Study	n/a	47%	64%	46%	58%	51%	33%	45%	52%	52%	52%	50%	43%	40%	48%	43%	36%

NOTES:

[1] "Potential Classical Music Consumers" are defined as the sub-set of respondents in each area who qualified for an extended interview, based on their responses to an initial series of questions.

[2] "NOT Potential Classical Music Consumers" are defined as the sub-set of respondents in each area who DID NOT qualified for an extended interview, based on their responses to an initial series of questions.

All figures are from the national and local area telephone surveys are weighted. See the methodology section for details on weighting procedures.

Figures for subscribers, former subscribers, and single ticket buyers derive from the postal surveys of ticket buyers and are not weighted.

5D

TABLE 5E

AGE

Category	Age	NAT'L SURVEY	AVERAGE OF 15 MARKET SURVEYS	BPO/Brooklyn	CSO/Charlotte	CSO/Denver	DSO/Detroit	FWP/Fort Wayne	KCS/Kansas City	LBSO/Long Beach	LPO/New Orleans	NWS/Miami (Dade)	OS/Portland	TPO/Philadelphia	SLSO/Saint Louis	SPCO/Saint Paul	SAS/San Antonio	WSO/Wichita
Potential Classical Music Consumers [1]	18-34	34%	33%	43%	35%	32%	28%	26%	30%	37%	34%	35%	35%	30%	28%	31%	39%	33%
	35-44	20%	20%	22%	19%	25%	19%	22%	19%	20%	19%	14%	20%	16%	17%	21%	18%	23%
	45-54	17%	18%	12%	16%	19%	19%	19%	18%	17%	20%	12%	16%	16%	22%	20%	16%	15%
	55-64	12%	16%	12%	18%	13%	17%	12%	12%	15%	14%	21%	19%	20%	17%	21%	16%	23%
	65-74	9%	9%	9%	7%	8%	10%	14%	7%	17%	11%	12%	11%	10%	11%	11%	11%	9%
	75+	6%	5%	3%	4%	2%	6%	8%	5%	6%	8%	6%	4%	6%	8%	7%	1%	5%
NOT Potential Classical Music Consumers [2]	18-34	28%	31%	39%	35%	33%	28%	24%	28%	36%	31%	37%	35%	27%	25%	31%	35%	29%
	35-44	21%	19%	15%	21%	22%	19%	19%	20%	19%	18%	15%	19%	15%	17%	20%	16%	21%
	45-54	19%	17%	13%	13%	19%	17%	21%	19%	14%	17%	17%	19%	19%	19%	20%	16%	20%
	55-64	11%	16%	16%	19%	19%	19%	22%	18%	19%	20%	11%	16%	20%	22%	21%	20%	15%
	65-74	11%	10%	10%	16%	8%	10%	12%	7%	6%	7%	21%	6%	16%	17%	20%	18%	11%
	75+	10%	7%	7%	8%	2%	6%	8%	5%	6%	5%	6%	4%	6%	8%	7%	1%	5%
Current Subscribers	18-34	N/A	2%	4%	4%	4%	8%	2%	3%	1%	4%	1%	0%	2%	4%	1%	2%	1%
	35-44	N/A	7%	11%	13%	0%	8%	5%	6%	5%	16%	5%	9%	7%	9%	8%	7%	4%
	45-54	N/A	18%	13%	21%	22%	23%	21%	19%	19%	18%	12%	17%	15%	18%	26%	16%	16%
	55-64	N/A	27%	15%	35%	33%	24%	29%	31%	34%	31%	24%	35%	27%	25%	33%	29%	30%
	65-74	N/A	29%	39%	28%	25%	28%	29%	30%	28%	28%	35%	35%	25%	26%	25%	31%	36%
	75+	N/A	17%	14%	18%	22%	15%	15%	20%	22%	20%	24%	20%	21%	18%	24%	31%	21%
Former Subscribers	18-34	N/A	5%	10%	8%	4%	8%	1%	5%	8%	4%	1%	0%	8%	6%	7%	5%	3%
	35-44	N/A	13%	11%	13%	7%	18%	12%	14%	8%	16%	5%	9%	9%	21%	16%	7%	4%
	45-54	N/A	27%	24%	22%	25%	23%	21%	25%	20%	20%	20%	29%	24%	26%	26%	33%	30%
	55-64	N/A	26%	25%	36%	25%	25%	30%	25%	38%	31%	18%	29%	28%	26%	33%	34%	27%
	65-74	N/A	20%	23%	16%	31%	20%	23%	27%	24%	29%	28%	26%	33%	22%	26%	18%	22%
	75+	N/A	10%	9%	8%	9%	7%	9%	10%	13%	17%	24%	11%	8%	12%	11%	9%	14%
Single Ticket Buyers	18-34	N/A	14%	21%	16%	18%	18%	17%	17%	18%	20%	16%	18%	24%	16%	17%	9%	9%
	35-44	N/A	18%	24%	23%	18%	18%	12%	27%	19%	24%	16%	18%	18%	19%	18%	25%	16%
	45-54	N/A	25%	20%	26%	26%	34%	32%	25%	24%	24%	18%	24%	20%	23%	25%	23%	26%
	55-64	N/A	20%	19%	16%	26%	20%	19%	21%	21%	19%	18%	23%	18%	19%	22%	17%	21%
	65-74	N/A	15%	9%	13%	18%	7%	12%	18%	28%	15%	28%	11%	14%	15%	11%	14%	13%
	75+	N/A	9%	7%	7%	7%	3%	9%	8%	13%	6%	12%	7%	6%	9%	7%	13%	16%

NOTES:

[1] "Potential Classical Music Consumers" are defined as the sub-set of respondents in each area who qualified for an extended interview, based on their responses to an initial series of questions.

[2] "NOT Potential Classical Music Consumers" are defined as the sub-set of respondents in each area who DID NOT qualified for an extended interview, based on their responses to an initial series of questions.

All figures from the national and local area telephone surveys are weighted. See the methodology section for details on weighting procedures.

Figures for subscribers, former subscribers, and single ticket buyers derive from the postal surveys of ticket buyers and are not weighted.

TABLE 5F-1

EMPLOYMENT STATUS - RESPONDENT

Group	Status	NAT'L SURVEY	AVERAGE OF 15 MARKET SURVEYS	BPO/Brooklyn	CSO/Charlotte	CSO/Denver	DSO/Detroit	FWP/Fort Wayne	KCS/Kansas City	LBSO/Long Beach	LPO/New Orleans	NWS/Miami (Dade)	OS/Portland	TPO/Philadelphia	SLSO/Saint Louis	SPCO/Saint Paul	SAS/San Antonio	WSO/Wichita
Potential Classical Music Consumers[1]	Working Full-Time (For Pay)	55%	51%	51%	58%	58%	46%	47%	56%	48%	51%	41%	59%	48%	50%	48%	48%	56%
	Working Part-Time (For Pay)	13%	13%	12%	10%	11%	13%	13%	12%	18%	9%	14%	9%	13%	11%	17%	14%	13%
	In School Full-Time	5%	5%	8%	4%	4%	7%	4%	2%	8%	8%	8%	4%	7%	4%	4%	6%	4%
	Not Employed, But Looking	5%	5%	8%	4%	5%	5%	4%	4%	8%	3%	8%	6%	6%	4%	5%	9%	2%
	Full-Time Family Caregiver	9%	7%	7%	6%	8%	6%	9%	10%	5%	11%	5%	7%	6%	8%	6%	10%	8%
	Retired	15%	18%	15%	18%	15%	24%	23%	17%	13%	19%	24%	15%	19%	23%	21%	13%	17%
NOT Potential Classical Music Consumers[2]	Working Full-Time (For Pay)	49%	46%	41%	55%	54%	40%	43%	50%	50%	40%	42%	47%	41%	43%	53%	49%	47%
	Working Part-Time (For Pay)	9%	9%	6%	7%	11%	10%	10%	8%	9%	9%	5%	13%	9%	7%	16%	6%	10%
	In School Full-Time	3%	4%	4%	3%	6%	4%	2%	5%	4%	4%	13%	3%	5%	4%	4%	3%	4%
	Not Employed, But Looking	6%	6%	13%	5%	4%	6%	7%	5%	5%	7%	9%	6%	6%	5%	5%	3%	6%
	Full-Time Family Caregiver	10%	8%	8%	8%	7%	10%	9%	10%	9%	9%	7%	10%	8%	8%	3%	9%	8%
	Retired	24%	26%	28%	22%	18%	31%	30%	23%	23%	31%	24%	22%	31%	33%	19%	31%	25%
Current Subscribers	Working Full-Time (For Pay)	n/a	33%	50%	37%	24%	37%	34%	37%	26%	32%	27%	26%	35%	32%	40%	37%	28%
	Working Part-Time (For Pay)	n/a	8%	7%	3%	6%	8%	10%	7%	10%	9%	8%	9%	7%	9%	8%	6%	4%
	Self-Employed	n/a	9%	14%	11%	10%	9%	6%	7%	12%	12%	11%	7%	11%	9%	7%	8%	6%
	In School Full-Time	n/a	0%	0%	0%	0%	0%	1%	0%	1%	0%	1%	0%	1%	2%	0%	0%	0%
	Not Employed, But Looking	n/a	1%	1%	1%	1%	1%	1%	1%	1%	1%	0%	1%	1%	0%	1%	0%	0%
	Full-Time Family Caregiver	n/a	5%	3%	13%	2%	4%	5%	6%	2%	7%	3%	4%	3%	6%	6%	5%	6%
	Retired	n/a	45%	26%	32%	57%	41%	44%	41%	50%	39%	51%	54%	43%	45%	39%	43%	57%
Former Subscribers	Working Full-Time (For Pay)	n/a	44%	45%	58%	40%	49%	45%	39%	33%	43%	34%	44%	46%	44%	52%	46%	41%
	Working Part-Time (For Pay)	n/a	9%	9%	3%	7%	7%	9%	13%	6%	7%	4%	8%	10%	8%	15%	3%	13%
	Self-Employed	n/a	9%	18%	5%	11%	10%	6%	11%	7%	13%	14%	8%	5%	9%	6%	5%	5%
	In School Full-Time	n/a	1%	2%	0%	1%	0%	2%	3%	1%	0%	0%	1%	1%	3%	0%	0%	2%
	Not Employed, But Looking	n/a	1%	2%	0%	1%	2%	0%	1%	1%	1%	1%	2%	1%	1%	1%	0%	1%
	Full-Time Family Caregiver	n/a	5%	1%	6%	5%	5%	5%	4%	3%	8%	3%	7%	1%	7%	6%	9%	4%
	Retired	n/a	32%	22%	28%	35%	28%	34%	29%	48%	29%	43%	31%	35%	29%	20%	37%	35%
Single Ticket Buyers	Working Full-Time (For Pay)	n/a	49%	55%	53%	43%	68%	48%	46%	37%	58%	36%	42%	52%	54%	49%	52%	46%
	Working Part-Time (For Pay)	n/a	8%	10%	8%	6%	11%	10%	13%	8%	5%	5%	9%	7%	8%	14%	6%	6%
	Self-Employed	n/a	9%	16%	6%	11%	4%	6%	8%	10%	12%	14%	6%	10%	8%	6%	8%	9%
	In School Full-Time	n/a	2%	3%	1%	2%	3%	2%	1%	2%	3%	2%	2%	4%	3%	2%	1%	1%
	Not Employed, But Looking	n/a	1%	2%	0%	3%	1%	1%	0%	0%	1%	1%	2%	1%	1%	1%	1%	1%
	Full-Time Family Caregiver	n/a	7%	1%	14%	7%	4%	8%	6%	6%	9%	2%	12%	6%	5%	7%	6%	6%
	Retired	n/a	24%	13%	19%	28%	11%	26%	27%	37%	13%	40%	27%	20%	22%	20%	25%	31%

NOTES:

[1]"Potential Classical Music Consumers" are defined as the sub-set of respondents in each area who qualified for an extended interview, based on their responses to an initial series of questions.

[2]"NOT Potential Classical Music Consumers" are defined as the sub-set of respondents in each area who DID NOT qualified for an extended interview, based on their responses to an initial series of questions.

All figures from the national and local area telephone surveys are weighted. See the methodology section for details on weighting procedures.

Figures for subscribers, former subscribers, and single ticket buyers derive from the postal surveys of ticket buyers and are not weighted.

TABLE 5F-2

EMPLOYMENT STATUS - RESPONDENT'S SPOUSE

		NAT'L SURVEY	AVERAGE OF 15 MARKET SURVEYS	BPO/Brooklyn	CSO/Charlotte	CSO/Denver	DSO/Detroit	FWP/Fort Wayne	KCS/Kansas City	LBSO/Long Beach	LPO/New Orleans	NWS/Miami (Dade)	OS/Portland	TPO/Philadelphia	SLSO/Saint Louis	SPCO/Saint Paul	SAS/San Antonio	WSO/Wichita
Potential Classical Music Consumers[1]	Working Full-Time (For Pay)	66%	68%	66%	74%	69%	65%	66%	70%	69%	64%	64%	70%	64%	60%	70%	61%	56%
	Working Part-Time (For Pay)	8%	8%	8%	7%	7%	7%	7%	8%	10%	9%	8%	12%	7%	11%	9%	4%	13%
	Self-Employed	8%	9%	13%	13%	9%	7%	11%	8%	11%	12%	11%	9%	9%	10%	9%	9%	9%
	In School Full-Time	1%	1%	0%	0%	0%	1%	0%	1%	0%	0%	0%	0%	1%	1%	0%	1%	0%
	Not Employed, But Looking	1%	3%	2%	2%	3%	5%	2%	2%	1%	3%	3%	6%	2%	6%	3%	3%	2%
	Full-Time Family Caregiver	8%	7%	6%	6%	6%	4%	7%	6%	10%	5%	6%	4%	7%	5%	3%	9%	6%
	Retired	15%	17%	19%	16%	9%	21%	21%	14%	10%	15%	15%	24%	21%	23%	18%	24%	34%
NOT Potential Classical Music Consumers[2]	Working Full-Time (For Pay)	63%	60%	48%	71%	69%	55%	52%	67%	59%	51%	56%	68%	51%	60%	70%	61%	62%
	Working Part-Time (For Pay)	5%	7%	12%	6%	6%	4%	11%	6%	10%	4%	8%	7%	7%	10%	9%	8%	8%
	Self-Employed	0%	9%	13%	13%	9%	7%	11%	8%	11%	12%	11%	9%	9%	9%	9%	9%	9%
	In School Full-Time	1%	1%	0%	0%	0%	1%	0%	1%	0%	0%	0%	0%	0%	1%	1%	1%	0%
	Not Employed, But Looking	2%	3%	5%	2%	3%	5%	2%	2%	1%	3%	3%	6%	2%	6%	3%	3%	4%
	Full-Time Family Caregiver	10%	7%	8%	5%	9%	8%	8%	8%	15%	19%	15%	10%	10%	6%	3%	9%	5%
	Retired	20%	23%	24%	20%	16%	28%	28%	20%	17%	29%	25%	22%	31%	25%	19%	24%	24%
Current Subscribers	Working Full-Time (For Pay)	N/A	47%	46%	58%	46%	48%	40%	58%	44%	56%	24%	52%	41%	51%	58%	44%	43%
	Working Part-Time (For Pay)	N/A	7%	4%	7%	6%	7%	6%	5%	7%	6%	0%	8%	5%	6%	9%	6%	6%
	Self-Employed	N/A	11%	13%	13%	9%	7%	11%	8%	11%	18%	18%	8%	10%	9%	11%	12%	9%
	In School Full-Time	N/A	1%	1%	0%	0%	1%	0%	1%	0%	0%	0%	0%	1%	1%	0%	0%	0%
	Not Employed, But Looking	N/A	1%	0%	0%	1%	1%	0%	1%	1%	0%	0%	1%	2%	0%	1%	0%	1%
	Full-Time Family Caregiver	N/A	6%	8%	8%	6%	8%	6%	5%	7%	8%	6%	6%	5%	6%	4%	7%	3%
	Retired	N/A	41%	26%	30%	51%	40%	39%	44%	47%	17%	41%	48%	41%	40%	41%	40%	48%
Former Subscribers	Working Full-Time (For Pay)	N/A	52%	47%	61%	49%	59%	59%	47%	44%	63%	34%	56%	52%	54%	56%	44%	48%
	Working Part-Time (For Pay)	N/A	7%	9%	4%	14%	7%	5%	9%	6%	2%	4%	4%	8%	9%	10%	5%	6%
	Self-Employed	N/A	11%	20%	9%	10%	12%	0%	8%	7%	18%	14%	7%	10%	5%	11%	15%	13%
	In School Full-Time	N/A	0%	1%	1%	1%	1%	0%	0%	0%	0%	0%	2%	1%	1%	3%	1%	0%
	Not Employed, But Looking	N/A	1%	5%	1%	1%	0%	1%	1%	1%	2%	2%	4%	0%	1%	2%	0%	0%
	Full-Time Family Caregiver	N/A	6%	0%	8%	4%	8%	5%	5%	5%	6%	3%	2%	9%	5%	3%	10%	4%
	Retired	N/A	23%	18%	16%	21%	12%	20%	25%	36%	15%	44%	24%	21%	25%	19%	24%	31%
Single Ticket Buyers	Working Full-Time (For Pay)	N/A	52%	47%	61%	49%	59%	59%	47%	44%	63%	34%	56%	52%	54%	56%	44%	48%
	Working Part-Time (For Pay)	N/A	7%	9%	4%	14%	7%	5%	9%	6%	2%	4%	4%	8%	9%	10%	5%	6%
	Self-Employed	N/A	10%	20%	9%	10%	8%	12%	8%	8%	13%	14%	7%	10%	5%	11%	15%	13%
	In School Full-Time	N/A	1%	1%	1%	1%	0%	1%	0%	0%	1%	1%	2%	1%	1%	3%	1%	0%
	Not Employed, But Looking	N/A	0%	5%	9%	4%	11%	5%	11%	7%	6%	11%	4%	9%	1%	2%	10%	0%
	Full-Time Family Caregiver	N/A	6%	0%	8%	4%	0%	0%	0%	5%	5%	3%	2%	0%	5%	3%	0%	0%
	Retired	N/A	23%	18%	16%	21%	12%	20%	25%	36%	15%	44%	24%	21%	25%	19%	24%	31%

NOTES:

[1] "Potential Classical Music Consumers" are defined as the sub-set of respondents in each area who qualified for an extended interview, based on their responses to an initial series of questions.

[2] "NOT Potential Classical Music Consumers" are defined as the sub-set of respondents in each area who DID NOT qualified for an extended interview, based on their responses to an initial series of questions.

All figures from the national and local area telephone surveys are weighted. See the methodology section for details on weighting procedures.

Figures for subscribers, former subscribers, and single ticket buyers derive from the postal surveys of ticket buyers and are not weighted.

TABLE 5G

RACIAL / ETHNIC BACKGROUND

		NAT'L SURVEY	AVERAGE OF 15 MARKET SURVEYS	BPO/Brooklyn	CSO/Charlotte	CSO/Denver	DSO/Detroit	FWP/Fort Wayne	KCS/Kansas City	LBSO/Long Beach	LPO/New Orleans	NWS/Miami (Dade)	OS/Portland	TPO/Philadelphia	SLSO/Saint Louis	SPCO/Saint Paul	SAS/San Antonio	WSO/Wichita
Potential Classical Music Consumers[1]	White/Anglo	75%	71%	39%	74%	81%	68%	94%	82%	56%	61%	39%	88%	69%	81%	90%	46%	84%
	Black/African-American	13%	14%	38%	16%	4%	25%	4%	11%	9%	34%	19%	2%	21%	15%	5%	11%	6%
	Asian	4%	3%	3%	1%	2%	2%	1%	1%	14%	1%	4%	1%	4%	1%	3%	2%	3%
	Other Race	8%	12%	20%	9%	13%	5%	1%	7%	22%	5%	38%	8%	6%	4%	3%	40%	7%
	Hispanic (Independent of Race)	10%	12%	18%	4%	15%	3%	2%	5%	22%	9%	43%	3%	5%	3%	4%	51%	7%
NOT Potential Classical Music Consumers[2]	White/Anglo	81%	67%	41%	76%	76%	69%	88%	80%	44%	60%	27%	84%	68%	77%	85%	46%	82%
	Black/African-American	11%	18%	40%	21%	4%	19%	9%	14%	16%	33%	26%	5%	26%	22%	5%	16%	12%
	Asian	2%	3%	5%	0%	2%	2%	0%	1%	9%	3%	2%	3%	2%	1%	6%	2%	1%
	Other Race	6%	13%	14%	3%	18%	9%	3%	6%	31%	4%	45%	8%	5%	1%	4%	36%	5%
	Hispanic (Independent of Race)	6%	14%	11%	4%	20%	4%	2%	5%	34%	8%	52%	10%	3%	2%	5%	41%	10%
Current Subscribers	White/Anglo	n/a	97%	94%	99%	99%	94%	99%	96%	98%	95%	93%	97%	96%	97%	99%	92%	97%
	Black/African-American	n/a	1%	3%	1%	0%	4%	0%	1%	0%	1%	0%	0%	1%	0%	0%	2%	1%
	Asian	n/a	1%	1%	0%	1%	0%	1%	1%	1%	0%	0%	1%	1%	1%	0%	2%	1%
	Other	n/a	2%	2%	1%	0%	2%	1%	2%	1%	3%	7%	2%	2%	2%	1%	5%	2%
	Hispanic (Independent of Race)	n/a	2%	1%	1%	0%	2%	0%	1%	2%	4%	6%	1%	1%	1%	0%	8%	1%
Former Subscribers	White/Anglo	n/a	95%	90%	92%	97%	89%	99%	96%	93%	97%	90%	95%	92%	96%	95%	87%	99%
	Black/African-American	n/a	1%	1%	5%	0%	6%	1%	1%	0%	1%	0%	0%	3%	1%	0%	2%	0%
	Asian	n/a	1%	6%	2%	1%	3%	0%	1%	4%	0%	0%	3%	1%	1%	2%	0%	1%
	Other	n/a	3%	3%	1%	3%	3%	3%	3%	3%	2%	10%	2%	3%	2%	3%	12%	0%
	Hispanic (Independent of Race)	n/a	3%	5%	1%	1%	1%	1%	2%	5%	3%	9%	2%	4%	1%	0%	12%	0%
Single Ticket Buyers	White/Anglo	n/a	93%	90%	92%	97%	86%	97%	96%	88%	91%	85%	99%	92%	94%	98%	92%	99%
	Black/African-American	n/a	2%	1%	5%	1%	8%	0%	1%	1%	2%	1%	0%	3%	2%	0%	1%	1%
	Asian	n/a	2%	6%	2%	2%	3%	0%	1%	4%	2%	3%	0%	1%	2%	1%	1%	1%
	Other	n/a	3%	3%	1%	1%	4%	3%	3%	6%	5%	11%	1%	3%	2%	1%	6%	1%
	Hispanic (Independent of Race)	n/a	4%	5%	1%	3%	1%	1%	2%	8%	7%	18%	3%	1%	2%	0%	13%	2%

NOTES:

[1] "Potential Classical Music Consumers" are defined as the sub-set of respondents in each area who qualified for an extended interview, based on their responses to an initial series of questions.

[2] "NOT Potential Classical Music Consumers" are defined as the sub-set of respondents in each area who DID NOT qualified for an extended interview, based on their responses to an initial series of questions.

All figures from the national and local area telephone surveys are weighted. See the methodology section for details on weighting procedures.

Figures for subscribers, former subscribers, and single ticket buyers derive from the postal surveys of ticket buyers and are not weighted.

TABLE 5K-1

	NAT'L SURVEY	AVERAGE OF 15 MARKET SURVEYS	BPO/Brooklyn	CSO/Charlotte	CSO/Denver	DSO/Detroit	FWP/Fort Wayne	KCS/Kansas City	LBSO/Long Beach	LPO/New Orleans	NWS/Miami (Dade)	OS/Portland	TPO/Philadelphia	SLSO/Saint Louis	SPCO/Saint Paul	SAS/San Antonio	WSO/Wichita
Potential Classical Music Consumers[1]																	
< $35,000	41%	24%	30%	17%	17%	21%	25%	24%	23%	37%	41%	22%	20%	27%	15%	31%	24%
$35,000-$49,999	15%	25%	33%	25%	17%	20%	25%	25%	24%	24%	18%	23%	28%	27%	24%	26%	32%
$50,000-$74,999	19%	21%	12%	26%	29%	29%	20%	19%	18%	15%	19%	24%	18%	23%	23%	18%	22%
$75,000-$99,999	11%	16%	17%	18%	16%	20%	16%	21%	18%	14%	10%	18%	13%	11%	20%	14%	14%
$100,000-$124,999	7%	7%	3%	7%	11%	5%	6%	8%	9%	3%	6%	7%	14%	7%	12%	5%	3%
$125,000-$149,999	3%	3%	2%	2%	3%	1%	2%	0%	5%	1%	3%	1%	3%	3%	3%	3%	2%
$150,000-$174,999	1%	1%	2%	1%	3%	1%	2%	0%	2%	2%	1%	1%	2%	0%	1%	0%	2%
$175,000-$199,999	1%	1%	1%	0%	1%	0%	0%	0%	0%	1%	0%	1%	1%	1%	1%	0%	1%
$200,000 +	2%	2%	1%	4%	3%	0%	0%	0%	1%	3%	2%	1%	1%	1%	2%	1%	1%
NOT Potential Classical Music Consumers[2]																	
< $35,000	50%	30%	37%	23%	20%	26%	29%	30%	30%	47%	43%	27%	29%	30%	19%	37%	29%
$35,000-$49,999	16%	25%	33%	26%	20%	23%	27%	25%	22%	22%	18%	25%	26%	26%	23%	28%	27%
$50,000-$74,999	16%	20%	11%	21%	24%	25%	22%	20%	18%	14%	21%	20%	16%	20%	23%	16%	22%
$75,000-$99,999	9%	14%	13%	18%	19%	17%	15%	17%	15%	10%	10%	16%	11%	12%	17%	11%	14%
$100,000-$124,999	4%	6%	3%	5%	8%	6%	4%	5%	7%	4%	4%	7%	10%	7%	10%	4%	4%
$125,000-$149,999	2%	3%	2%	3%	5%	2%	3%	2%	4%	1%	2%	3%	2%	1%	3%	2%	1%
$150,000-$174,999	0%	1%	1%	1%	2%	1%	1%	1%	2%	1%	1%	1%	2%	1%	2%	0%	2%
$175,000-$199,999	1%	1%	5%	0%	1%	0%	0%	0%	0%	1%	1%	0%	1%	2%	2%	1%	0%
$200,000 +	1%	1%	1%	3%	2%	1%	0%	0%	1%	2%	2%	1%	1%	1%	2%	1%	1%

NOTES:

[1] "Potential Classical Music Consumers" are defined as the sub-set of respondents in each area who qualified for an extended interview, based on their responses to an initial series of questions.

[2] "NOT Potential Classical Music Consumers" are defined as the sub-set of respondents in each area who DID NOT qualified for an extended interview, based on their responses to an initial series of questions.

All figures from the national and local area telephone surveys are weighted. See the methodology section for details on weighting procedures.

TABLE 5K-2

HOUSEHOLD INCOME: TICKET BUYER SURVEY DATA

Group	Income	AVERAGE OF 15 MARKET SURVEYS	BPO/Brooklyn	CSO/Charlotte	CSO/Denver	DSO/Detroit	FWP/Fort Wayne	KCS/Kansas City	LBSO/Long Beach	LPO/New Orleans	NWS/Miami (Dade)	OS/Portland	TPO/Philadelphia	SLSO/Saint Louis	SPCO/Saint Paul	SAS/San Antonio	WSO/Wichita
Current Subscribers	< $35,000	8%	6%	2%	9%	6%	13%	9%	8%	8%	6%	13%	6%	12%	6%	5%	12%
	$35,000-$49,999	12%	8%	7%	13%	11%	13%	9%	15%	10%	10%	14%	10%	11%	13%	10%	17%
	$50,000-$74,999	19%	16%	15%	21%	21%	20%	18%	18%	18%	13%	24%	15%	21%	22%	23%	23%
	$75,000-$99,999	16%	14%	17%	16%	14%	16%	16%	14%	14%	12%	14%	18%	20%	17%	21%	18%
	$100,000-$124,999	13%	17%	16%	12%	14%	13%	14%	13%	15%	9%	15%	15%	11%	13%	12%	11%
	$125,000-$149,999	7%	9%	4%	10%	6%	7%	9%	9%	8%	8%	8%	6%	6%	7%	8%	5%
	$150,000-$174,999	6%	4%	8%	5%	5%	4%	8%	4%	6%	6%	4%	7%	5%	7%	5%	5%
	$175,000-$199,999	4%	4%	6%	3%	4%	3%	6%	4%	5%	3%	3%	3%	3%	3%	5%	1%
	$200,000 +	16%	22%	25%	12%	18%	12%	14%	14%	18%	33%	5%	20%	12%	12%	11%	9%
Former Subscribers	< $35,000	8%	7%	3%	6%	6%	13%	6%	10%	6%	2%	11%	4%	7%	4%	5%	17%
	$35,000-$49,999	15%	19%	17%	18%	7%	19%	14%	13%	13%	24%	18%	16%	16%	10%	10%	15%
	$50,000-$74,999	21%	19%	19%	23%	26%	24%	19%	15%	19%	20%	19%	19%	18%	22%	17%	28%
	$75,000-$99,999	18%	20%	20%	13%	17%	20%	16%	26%	17%	13%	16%	19%	27%	19%	27%	16%
	$100,000-$124,999	14%	9%	12%	14%	14%	11%	24%	10%	15%	12%	19%	11%	11%	17%	20%	13%
	$125,000-$149,999	6%	8%	2%	6%	8%	6%	8%	5%	6%	5%	6%	7%	11%	6%	3%	5%
	$150,000-$174,999	4%	1%	3%	3%	7%	0%	6%	7%	3%	2%	2%	8%	1%	12%	3%	3%
	$175,000-$199,999	3%	2%	3%	6%	3%	0%	2%	3%	6%	3%	2%	1%	1%	3%	5%	2%
	$200,000 +	11%	14%	20%	11%	12%	7%	7%	13%	14%	20%	8%	16%	8%	8%	10%	2%
Single Ticket Buyers	< $35,000	11%	11%	7%	12%	5%	21%	5%	9%	13%	6%	18%	11%	14%	10%	13%	18%
	$35,000-$49,999	15%	8%	12%	11%	11%	20%	13%	11%	14%	14%	23%	12%	19%	14%	13%	24%
	$50,000-$74,999	21%	19%	22%	20%	23%	23%	21%	26%	19%	17%	18%	17%	27%	18%	29%	20%
	$75,000-$99,999	18%	14%	22%	20%	18%	16%	23%	17%	13%	19%	24%	13%	17%	21%	18%	15%
	$100,000-$124,999	13%	15%	10%	17%	22%	9%	15%	12%	15%	11%	10%	16%	10%	17%	9%	12%
	$125,000-$149,999	6%	6%	10%	7%	7%	6%	5%	6%	6%	9%	2%	10%	5%	5%	6%	3%
	$150,000-$174,999	5%	7%	7%	4%	3%	3%	8%	6%	6%	7%	1%	6%	2%	8%	5%	2%
	$175,000-$199,999	3%	5%	4%	1%	3%	1%	2%	6%	4%	7%	4%	4%	2%	2%	2%	1%
	$200,000 +	7%	15%	7%	8%	9%	3%	7%	6%	9%	11%	2%	12%	5%	3%	8%	6%

NOTES:

Figures for subscribers, former subscribers, and single ticket buyers derive from the postal surveys of ticket buyers and are not weighted.

5K-2

Audience Insight LLC

TABLE 5M

GENDER

		NAT'L SURVEY	AVERAGE OF 15 MARKET SURVEYS	BPO/Brooklyn	CSO/Charlotte	CSO/Denver	DSO/Detroit	FWP/Fort Wayne	KCS/Kansas City	LBSO/Long Beach	LPO/New Orleans	NWS/Miami (Dade)	OS/Portland	TPO/Philadelphia	SLSO/Saint Louis	SPCO/Saint Paul	SAS/San Antonio	WSO/Wichita
Potential Classical Music Consumers[1]	Female	57%	55%	53%	52%	54%	56%	54%	53%	58%	56%	59%	54%	55%	55%	56%	59%	53%
	Male	44%	45%	48%	48%	46%	44%	46%	47%	42%	44%	41%	47%	45%	45%	44%	41%	47%
NOT Potential Classical Music Consumers[2]	Female	55%	51%	56%	47%	52%	51%	48%	51%	55%	52%	51%	51%	51%	52%	53%	54%	52%
	Male	45%	49%	44%	53%	48%	49%	52%	49%	45%	48%	49%	50%	49%	49%	47%	46%	48%
Current Subscribers	Female	N/A	60%	49%	63%	60%	57%	61%	56%	63%	58%	57%	75%	51%	63%	68%	54%	60%
	Male	N/A	40%	51%	37%	40%	43%	39%	45%	37%	42%	43%	25%	49%	37%	32%	46%	40%
Former Subscribers	Female	N/A	64%	51%	72%	63%	58%	69%	64%	55%	68%	60%	73%	52%	66%	65%	67%	74%
	Male	N/A	36%	49%	28%	37%	42%	31%	36%	45%	32%	40%	27%	48%	34%	35%	33%	26%
Single Ticket Buyers	Female	N/A	63%	51%	66%	56%	63%	67%	61%	66%	67%	55%	73%	63%	63%	65%	64%	67%
	Male	N/A	37%	50%	34%	44%	37%	33%	39%	34%	34%	45%	27%	37%	37%	35%	36%	33%

NOTES:

[1] "Potential Classical Music Consumers" are defined as the sub-set of respondents in each area who qualified for an extended interview, based on their responses to an initial series of questions.

[2] "NOT Potential Classical Music Consumers" are defined as the sub-set of respondents in each area who DID NOT qualified for an extended interview, based on their responses to an initial series of questions.

All figures from the national and local area telephone surveys are weighted. See the methodology section for details on weighting procedures.

Figures for subscribers, former subscribers, and single ticket buyers derive from the postal surveys of ticket buyers and are not weighted.

TABLE S1-A

SEGMENTATION RESULTS: ART FORM RELATIONSHIP
% OF POTENTIAL CLASSICAL CONSUMERS IN EACH SEGMENT
(BASED ON A CLUSTER ANALYSIS OF NATIONAL SURVEY DATA)

Potential Classical Music Consumers*	NAT'L SURVEY	AVERAGE OF 15 MARKET SURVEYS	BPO/Brooklyn	CSO/Charlotte	CSO/Denver	DSO/Detroit	FWP/Fort Wayne	KCS/Kansas City	LBSO/Long Beach	LPO/New Orleans	NWS/Miami (Dade)	OS/Portland	TPO/Philadelphia	SLSO/Saint Louis	SPCO/Saint Paul	SAS/San Antonio	WSO/Wichita
1. Educated Classical Audience	6.5%	8.7%	6.1%	5.9%	11.0%	5.2%	7.9%	6.4%	10.5%	10.6%	9.4%	13.5%	7.5%	10.2%	9.6%	6.0%	8.8%
2. Classical Ghosts (Low-Yield Sophisticates)	8.9%	11.9%	9.2%	9.6%	15.6%	10.0%	15.2%	12.2%	11.8%	9.1%	10.8%	12.0%	14.5%	11.8%	13.6%	12.8%	10.8%
3. Aspiring Classical Enthusiasts	5.8%	6.0%	10.4%	5.8%	5.5%	6.7%	3.3%	5.4%	6.1%	10.4%	11.2%	3.8%	4.8%	3.4%	4.2%	6.9%	4.0%
4. Casual Listeners	9.2%	9.1%	8.8%	12.3%	7.9%	8.1%	7.8%	9.6%	5.4%	9.5%	6.9%	5.9%	9.3%	12.7%	11.5%	10.2%	10.2%
5. Classical Lite	10.7%	10.6%	14.9%	11.1%	12.4%	10.3%	14.2%	8.4%	10.8%	8.9%	8.4%	10.2%	9.8%	11.3%	10.2%	8.6%	10.1%
6. Out-of-Reach	13.2%	12.7%	11.9%	12.0%	9.7%	11.9%	12.9%	14.3%	15.9%	10.6%	9.1%	13.1%	15.4%	10.6%	13.6%	12.4%	15.9%
7. Blue Moon	10.8%	8.8%	5.6%	9.6%	8.8%	9.4%	8.8%	7.8%	8.0%	7.3%	6.9%	9.7%	7.8%	11.4%	9.7%	9.6%	10.6%
8. Family Occasion	7.6%	7.1%	7.7%	9.9%	6.6%	6.9%	5.4%	5.9%	6.0%	8.6%	9.1%	3.7%	8.9%	8.1%	4.6%	8.5%	8.0%
9. Disinclined	11.5%	11.1%	13.3%	10.2%	8.2%	11.8%	8.7%	10.7%	11.7%	14.7%	18.7%	12.9%	11.3%	7.0%	9.4%	11.9%	8.1%
10. Least Interested	15.8%	13.9%	12.2%	13.4%	14.2%	19.6%	15.7%	19.3%	13.7%	10.3%	9.4%	15.2%	10.7%	13.5%	13.8%	13.2%	13.5%

NOTES:

*"Potential Classical Music Consumers" are defined as the sub-set of respondents in each area who qualified for an extended interview, based on their responses to an initial series of questions.

All figures from the national and local area telephone surveys are weighted. See the methodology section for details on weighting procedures.

High and low figures for each segment are in **bold** type.

TABLE S1-B

SEGMENTATION RESULTS: ART FORM RELATIONSHIP
% OF ORCHESTRA SUBSCRIBERS IN EACH SEGMENT
(BASED ON A CLUSTER ANALYSIS OF NATIONAL SURVEY DATA)

% of Orchestra Subscribers

	NAT'L SURVEY	AVERAGE OF 15 MARKET SURVEYS	BPO/Brooklyn	CSO/Charlotte	CSO/Denver	DSO/Detroit	FWP/Fort Wayne	KCS/Kansas City	LBSO/Long Beach	LPO/New Orleans	NWS/Miami (Dade)	OS/Portland	TPO/Philadelphia	SLSO/Saint Louis	SPCO/Saint Paul	SAS/San Antonio	WSO/Wichita
1. Educated Classical Audience	N/A	59.6%	75.1%	54.3%	63.3%	49.3%	44.8%	51.4%	47.5%	64.7%	76.6%	51.1%	66.8%	51.2%	75.6%	50.0%	69.6%
2. Classical Ghosts (Low-Yield Sophisticates)	N/A	19.3%	12.4%	12.6%	21.9%	24.3%	15.0%	21.3%	17.6%	20.5%	13.3%	23.3%	23.2%	32.1%	15.6%	18.0%	17.3%
3. Aspiring Classical Enthusiasts	N/A	1.4%	0.6%	1.6%	0.7%	1.7%	1.6%	2.0%	3.1%	0.7%	2.0%	1.7%	1.1%	1.3%	0.3%	2.1%	0.9%
4. Casual Listeners	N/A	11.5%	7.9%	20.2%	9.3%	14.2%	19.0%	15.8%	13.7%	10.6%	6.0%	13.6%	4.9%	8.0%	6.8%	14.1%	9.4%
5. Classical Lite	N/A	2.8%	2.8%	3.0%	1.4%	2.1%	2.9%	4.0%	7.8%	2.1%	1.6%	4.0%	2.3%	2.7%	0.8%	5.6%	0.9%
6. Out-of-Reach	N/A	0.6%	0.0%	0.3%	0.2%	1.0%	0.7%	0.0%	0.8%	0.0%	0.0%	1.1%	1.1%	1.3%	0.3%	1.1%	0.9%
7. Blue Moon	N/A	1.4%	1.1%	2.7%	0.7%	2.1%	5.2%	1.2%	1.2%	0.3%	0.0%	1.7%	0.0%	0.7%	0.3%	1.4%	0.6%
8. Family Occasion	N/A	1.7%	0.0%	3.5%	1.8%	1.0%	5.6%	2.4%	3.1%	0.7%	0.0%	0.0%	0.6%	1.0%	0.3%	3.9%	0.3%
9. Disinclined	N/A	1.2%	0.0%	1.3%	0.5%	3.1%	3.3%	1.2%	2.0%	0.3%	0.4%	2.8%	0.0%	1.3%	0.0%	2.5%	0.0%
10. Least Interested	N/A	0.5%	0.0%	0.5%	0.2%	1.0%	2.0%	0.8%	0.8%	0.0%	0.0%	0.6%	0.0%	0.3%	0.0%	1.4%	0.0%

NOTES:

Figures represent the percentage of orchestra subscribers (from the pool of respondents to the postal surveys of ticket buyers) who were classified into each segment.

The segmentation model is based on a cluster analysis of over 30 variables from the national survey of classical music consumers, 2000

TABLE S1-C

SEGMENTATION RESULTS: ART FORM RELATIONSHIP
% OF FORMER SUBSCRIBERS IN EACH SEGMENT
(BASED ON A CLUSTER ANALYSIS OF NATIONAL SURVEY DATA)

% of Former Subscribers

	NAT'L SURVEY	AVERAGE OF 15 MARKET SURVEYS	BPO/Brooklyn	CSO/Charlotte	CSO/Denver	DSO/Detroit	FWP/Fort Wayne	KCS/Kansas City	LBSO/Long Beach	LPO/New Orleans	NWS/Miami (Dade)	OS/Portland	TPO/Philadelphia	SLSO/Saint Louis	SPCO/Saint Paul	SAS/San Antonio	WSO/Wichita
1. Educated Classical Audience	N/A	49.7%	83.1%	48.4%	44.8%	40.0%	48.0%	37.6%	35.1%	48.1%	72.9%	33.9%	51.4%	36.4%	74.6%	37.5%	50.4%
2. Classical Ghosts (Low-Yield Sophisticates)	N/A	20.4%	11.3%	9.7%	27.6%	25.0%	10.6%	22.6%	29.8%	22.1%	20.0%	26.6%	31.4%	23.4%	10.0%	21.4%	19.1%
3. Aspiring Classical Enthusiasts	N/A	3.0%	1.4%	3.2%	3.7%	2.0%	1.6%	4.3%	3.5%	1.3%	1.4%	3.7%	4.3%	3.9%	1.5%	12.5%	0.9%
4. Casual Listeners	N/A	13.2%	0.0%	25.8%	13.4%	19.0%	19.5%	17.2%	14.0%	9.1%	1.4%	9.2%	5.7%	19.5%	8.5%	8.9%	20.0%
5. Classical Lite	N/A	5.4%	1.4%	4.8%	4.5%	5.0%	2.4%	9.7%	10.5%	7.8%	2.9%	10.1%	7.1%	2.6%	0.8%	5.4%	7.8%
6. Out-of-Reach	N/A	1.6%	0.0%	0.0%	2.2%	2.0%	3.3%	0.0%	0.0%	2.6%	0.0%	6.4%	0.0%	2.6%	0.8%	0.0%	0.0%
7. Blue Moon	N/A	1.9%	1.4%	0.0%	2.2%	3.0%	1.6%	1.1%	0.0%	2.6%	1.4%	4.6%	0.0%	2.6%	2.3%	3.6%	0.0%
8. Family Occasion	N/A	2.6%	0.0%	4.8%	1.5%	1.0%	5.7%	3.2%	3.5%	5.2%	0.0%	1.8%	0.0%	6.5%	0.8%	5.4%	1.7%
9. Disinclined	N/A	1.6%	1.4%	1.6%	0.0%	1.0%	4.1%	2.2%	3.5%	1.3%	0.0%	2.8%	0.0%	2.6%	0.8%	5.4%	0.0%
10. Least Interested	N/A	0.7%	0.0%	1.6%	0.0%	2.0%	3.3%	2.2%	0.0%	0.0%	0.0%	0.9%	0.0%	0.0%	0.0%	0.0%	0.0%

NOTES:

Figures represent the percentage of former subscribers/current single ticket buyers (from the pool of respondents to the postal surveys of ticket buyers) who were classified into each segment.

The segmentation model is based on a cluster analysis of over 30 variables from the national survey of classical music consumers, 2000

TABLE S1-D

SEGMENTATION RESULTS: ART FORM RELATIONSHIP
% OF SINGLE TICKET BUYERS IN EACH SEGMENT
(BASED ON A CLUSTER ANALYSIS OF NATIONAL SURVEY DATA)

% of Single Ticket Buyers

	NAT'L SURVEY	AVERAGE OF 15 MARKET SURVEYS	BPO/Brooklyn	CSO/Charlotte	CSO/Denver	DSO/Detroit	FWP/Fort Wayne	KCS/Kansas City	LBSO/Long Beach	LPO/New Orleans	NWS/Miami (Dade)	OS/Portland	TPO/Philadelphia	SLSO/Saint Louis	SPCO/Saint Paul	SAS/San Antonio	WSO/Wichita
1. Educated Classical Audience	N/A	36.1%	47.6%	29.4%	43.9%	30.3%	22.3%	33.0%	34.0%	47.9%	53.7%	32.8%	40.5%	20.8%	50.7%	25.5%	28.5%
2. Classical Ghosts (Low-Yield Sophisticates)	N/A	20.5%	25.7%	17.4%	22.8%	19.9%	19.7%	16.2%	19.0%	22.9%	22.9%	25.4%	19.6%	31.2%	16.4%	17.9%	14.5%
3. Aspiring Classical Enthusiasts	N/A	2.6%	6.4%	0.0%	2.6%	2.0%	0.4%	2.1%	5.2%	2.7%	4.6%	2.5%	4.6%	1.2%	1.9%	3.4%	1.9%
4. Casual Listeners	N/A	16.2%	9.1%	23.9%	15.9%	19.4%	16.6%	21.5%	10.5%	12.2%	9.7%	12.3%	10.5%	16.2%	17.9%	17.9%	24.2%
5. Classical Lite	N/A	7.6%	6.4%	7.5%	4.2%	10.0%	8.7%	7.9%	9.8%	3.7%	4.6%	12.3%	11.1%	10.4%	5.3%	6.2%	8.2%
6. Out-of-Reach	N/A	2.8%	0.0%	3.5%	3.2%	2.5%	5.7%	2.6%	2.6%	3.7%	1.1%	2.5%	1.3%	2.9%	2.9%	3.4%	2.4%
7. Blue Moon	N/A	3.7%	1.6%	6.0%	1.1%	3.5%	7.0%	3.7%	2.6%	2.1%	1.1%	4.9%	3.9%	4.6%	0.5%	5.5%	7.2%
8. Family Occasion	N/A	4.5%	1.1%	7.5%	3.2%	4.5%	8.7%	8.4%	4.6%	1.6%	1.7%	4.9%	3.3%	5.2%	1.9%	6.2%	3.9%
9. Disinclined	N/A	3.7%	2.1%	2.0%	1.6%	5.0%	3.9%	3.7%	9.2%	3.2%	0.6%	2.5%	3.9%	4.0%	1.4%	8.3%	5.3%
10. Least Interested	N/A	2.3%	0.0%	3.0%	1.6%	3.0%	7.0%	1.0%	2.6%	0.0%	0.0%	0.0%	1.3%	3.5%	1.0%	5.5%	3.9%

NOTES:

Figures represent the percentage of orchestra single ticket buyers (from the pool of respondents to the postal surveys of ticket buyers) who were classified into each segment.

The segmentation model is based on a cluster analysis of over 30 variables from the national survey of classical music consumers, 2000

TABLE S2-A

SEGMENTATION RESULTS: LOCAL ORCHESTRA RELATIONSHIP
% OF POTENTIAL CLASSICAL CONSUMERS IN EACH SEGMENT
(BASED ON A CLUSTER ANALYSIS OF DATA FROM 15 LOCAL TELEPHONE SURVEYS)

% of Potential Classical Music Consumers*	NATL SURVEY	AVERAGE OF 15 MARKET SURVEYS	BPO/Brooklyn	CSO/Charlotte	CSO/Denver	DSO/Detroit	FWP/Fort Wayne	KCS/Kansas City	LBSO/Long Beach	LPO/New Orleans	NWS/Miami (Dade)	OS/Portland	TPO/Philadelphia	SLSO/Saint Louis	SPCO/Saint Paul	SAS/San Antonio	WSO/Wichita
1. High Involvement Subscribers	N/A	3.3%	0.4%	2.8%	2.7%	3.7%	4.9%	1.5%	2.0%	1.8%	1.4%	6.0%	2.6%	10.1%	2.3%	1.9%	3.3%
2. Current, High Frequency Single Ticket Buyers (STB)	N/A	5.3%	1.4%	7.5%	7.1%	5.3%	8.5%	5.2%	1.6%	7.5%	1.5%	5.6%	3.5%	8.2%	2.6%	5.5%	8.2%
3. Low Frequency & Former Subscribers	N/A	3.5%	2.3%	2.8%	2.8%	5.8%	5.8%	3.3%	2.5%	4.1%	1.0%	5.1%	3.3%	3.0%	2.2%	3.4%	4.4%
4. Very Interested STB & Ghosts	N/A	9.7%	5.6%	11.2%	8.7%	7.8%	7.9%	13.4%	6.2%	11.5%	6.9%	11.2%	14.3%	12.3%	7.6%	11.6%	9.0%
5. Low Involvement STB & Ghosts	N/A	23.5%	5.7%	24.4%	27.7%	33.1%	34.7%	21.6%	12.1%	25.0%	13.8%	22.3%	20.0%	29.9%	23.7%	24.6%	32.6%
6. Non-Users with Social Context	N/A	15.1%	12.0%	13.7%	14.1%	18.6%	14.8%	18.9%	13.4%	11.9%	9.3%	16.7%	19.5%	11.6%	17.7%	16.4%	16.4%
7. No History, Not Interested	N/A	29.3%	33.8%	29.5%	30.4%	22.8%	19.9%	30.2%	41.2%	28.0%	36.7%	27.8%	28.8%	21.9%	37.7%	28.3%	20.8%
8. Unaware of Local Orchestra	N/A	10.4%	38.8%	8.2%	6.6%	3.0%	3.5%	5.8%	21.0%	10.2%	29.4%	5.3%	8.1%	3.1%	6.2%	8.2%	5.4%

NOTES:

*"Potential Classical Music Consumers" are defined as the sub-set of respondents in each area who qualified for an extended interview, based on their responses to an initial series of questions.

All figures from the national and local area telephone surveys are weighted. See the methodology section for details on weighting procedures.

TABLE S2-B

SEGMENTATION RESULTS: LOCAL ORCHESTRA RELATIONSHIP
% OF ORCHESTRA SUBSCRIBERS IN EACH SEGMENT
(BASED ON A CLUSTER ANALYSIS OF DATA FROM 15 LOCAL TELEPHONE SURVEYS)

% of Subscribers	NAT'L SURVEY	AVERAGE OF 15 MARKET SURVEYS	BPO/Brooklyn	CSO/Charlotte	CSO/Denver	DSO/Detroit	FWP/Fort Wayne	KCS/Kansas City	LBSO/Long Beach	LPO/New Orleans	NWS/Miami (Dade)	OS/Portland	TPO/Philadelphia	SLSO/Saint Louis	SPCO/Saint Paul	SAS/San Antonio	WSO/Wichita
1. High Involvement Subscribers	N/A	94.7%	89.7%	90.7%	98.7%	95.9%	91.9%	95.6%	93.8%	92.7%	94.5%	93.4%	95.8%	96.8%	95.2%	95.6%	95.9%
2. Current, High Frequency Single Ticket Buyers (STB)	N/A	0.0%	0.0%	0.0%	0.0%	0.0%	0.0%	0.0%	0.0%	0.0%	0.0%	0.0%	0.0%	0.0%	0.0%	0.0%	0.0%
3. Low Frequency & Former Subscribers	N/A	5.3%	10.3%	9.3%	1.3%	4.1%	8.1%	4.4%	6.2%	7.3%	5.5%	6.6%	4.2%	3.2%	4.8%	4.4%	4.1%
4. Very Interested STB & Ghosts	N/A	0.0%	0.0%	0.0%	0.0%	0.0%	0.0%	0.0%	0.0%	0.0%	0.0%	0.0%	0.0%	0.0%	0.0%	0.0%	0.0%
5. Low Involvement STB & Ghosts	N/A	0.0%	0.0%	0.0%	0.0%	0.0%	0.0%	0.0%	0.0%	0.0%	0.0%	0.0%	0.0%	0.0%	0.0%	0.0%	0.0%
6. Non-Users with Social Context	N/A	0.0%	0.0%	0.0%	0.0%	0.0%	0.0%	0.0%	0.0%	0.0%	0.0%	0.0%	0.0%	0.0%	0.0%	0.0%	0.0%
7. No History, Not Interested	N/A	0.0%	0.0%	0.0%	0.0%	0.0%	0.0%	0.0%	0.0%	0.0%	0.0%	0.0%	0.0%	0.0%	0.0%	0.0%	0.0%
8. Unaware of Local Orchestra	N/A	0.0%	0.0%	0.0%	0.0%	0.0%	0.0%	0.0%	0.0%	0.0%	0.0%	0.0%	0.0%	0.0%	0.0%	0.0%	0.0%

NOTES:

Figures represent the percentage of orchestra subscribers (from the pool of respondents to the postal surveys of ticket buyers) who were classified into each segment.

The segmentation model is based on a cluster analysis of eight variables from the combined data from 15 local telephone surveys, 2001 - 2002

TABLE S2-C

SEGMENTATION RESULTS: LOCAL ORCHESTRA RELATIONSHIP
% OF FORMER SUBSCRIBERS IN EACH SEGMENT
(BASED ON A CLUSTER ANALYSIS OF DATA FROM 15 LOCAL TELEPHONE SURVEYS)

% of Former Subscribers	NAT'L SURVEY	AVERAGE OF 15 MARKET SURVEYS	BPO/Brooklyn	CSO/Charlotte	CSO/Denver	DSO/Detroit	FWP/Fort Wayne	KCS/Kansas City	LBSO/Long Beach	LPO/New Orleans	NWS/Miami (Dade)	OS/Portland	TPO/Philadelphia	SLSO/Saint Louis	SPCO/Saint Paul	SAS/San Antonio	WSO/Wichita
1. High Involvement Subscribers	N/A	76.6%	68.1%	92.3%	82.6%	83.1%	85.2%	79.3%	52.6%	81.3%	63.5%	56.3%	74.4%	86.6%	81.9%	73.9%	82.7%
2. Current, High Frequency Single Ticket Buyers (STB)	N/A	0.0%	0.0%	0.0%	0.0%	0.0%	0.0%	0.0%	0.0%	0.0%	0.0%	0.0%	0.0%	0.0%	0.0%	0.0%	0.0%
3. Low Frequency & Former Subscribers	N/A	23.4%	31.9%	7.7%	17.4%	16.9%	14.8%	20.7%	47.4%	18.8%	36.5%	43.8%	25.6%	13.4%	18.1%	26.1%	17.3%
4. Very Interested STB & Ghosts	N/A	0.0%	0.0%	0.0%	0.0%	0.0%	0.0%	0.0%	0.0%	0.0%	0.0%	0.0%	0.0%	0.0%	0.0%	0.0%	0.0%
5. Low Involvement STB & Ghosts	N/A	0.0%	0.0%	0.0%	0.0%	0.0%	0.0%	0.0%	0.0%	0.0%	0.0%	0.0%	0.0%	0.0%	0.0%	0.0%	0.0%
6. Non-Users with Social Context	N/A	0.0%	0.0%	0.0%	0.0%	0.0%	0.0%	0.0%	0.0%	0.0%	0.0%	0.0%	0.0%	0.0%	0.0%	0.0%	0.0%
7. No History, Not Interested	N/A	0.0%	0.0%	0.0%	0.0%	0.0%	0.0%	0.0%	0.0%	0.0%	0.0%	0.0%	0.0%	0.0%	0.0%	0.0%	0.0%
8. Unaware of Local Orchestra	N/A	0.0%	0.0%	0.0%	0.0%	0.0%	0.0%	0.0%	0.0%	0.0%	0.0%	0.0%	0.0%	0.0%	0.0%	0.0%	0.0%

NOTES:

Figures represent the percentage of former subscribers/current single ticket buyers (from the pool of respondents to the postal surveys of ticket buyers) who were classified into each segment.

The segmentation model is based on a cluster analysis of eight variables from the combined data from 15 local telephone surveys, 2001 - 2002.

TABLE S2-D

SEGMENTATION RESULTS: LOCAL ORCHESTRA RELATIONSHIP
% OF SINGLE TICKET BUYERS IN EACH SEGMENT
(BASED ON A CLUSTER ANALYSIS OF DATA FROM 15 LOCAL TELEPHONE SURVEYS)

% of Single Ticket Buyers	NAT'L SURVEY	AVERAGE OF 15 MARKET SURVEYS	BPO/Brooklyn	CSO/Charlotte	CSO/Denver	DSO/Detroit	FWP/Fort Wayne	KCS/Kansas City	LBSO/Long Beach	LPO/New Orleans	NWS/Miami (Dade)	OS/Portland	TPO/Philadelphia	SLSO/Saint Louis	SPCO/Saint Paul	SAS/San Antonio	WSO/Wichita
1. High Involvement Subscribers	N/A	0.0%	0.0%	0.0%	0.0%	0.0%	0.0%	0.0%	0.0%	0.0%	0.0%	0.0%	0.0%	0.0%	0.0%	0.0%	0.0%
2. Current, High Frequency Single Ticket Buyers (STB)	N/A	0.0%	0.0%	0.0%	0.0%	0.0%	0.0%	0.0%	0.0%	0.0%	0.0%	0.0%	0.0%	0.0%	0.0%	0.0%	0.0%
3. Low Frequency & Former Subscribers	N/A	0.0%	0.0%	0.0%	0.0%	0.0%	0.0%	0.0%	0.0%	0.0%	0.0%	0.0%	0.0%	0.0%	0.0%	0.0%	0.0%
4. Very Interested STB & Ghosts	N/A	58.2%	23.2%	70.9%	73.4%	56.9%	68.2%	55.4%	38.9%	72.2%	62.6%	52.6%	59.4%	70.2%	46.2%	53.5%	63.2%
5. Low Involvement STB & Ghosts	N/A	41.8%	76.8%	29.1%	26.6%	43.1%	31.8%	44.6%	61.1%	27.8%	37.4%	47.4%	40.6%	29.8%	53.8%	46.5%	36.8%
6. Non-Users with Social Context	N/A	0.0%	0.0%	0.0%	0.0%	0.0%	0.0%	0.0%	0.0%	0.0%	0.0%	0.0%	0.0%	0.0%	0.0%	0.0%	0.0%
7. No History, Not Interested	N/A	0.0%	0.0%	0.0%	0.0%	0.0%	0.0%	0.0%	0.0%	0.0%	0.0%	0.0%	0.0%	0.0%	0.0%	0.0%	0.0%
8. Unaware of Local Orchestra	N/A	0.0%	0.0%	0.0%	0.0%	0.0%	0.0%	0.0%	0.0%	0.0%	0.0%	0.0%	0.0%	0.0%	0.0%	0.0%	0.0%

NOTES:

Figures represent the percentage of orchestra single ticket buyers (from the pool of respondents to the postal surveys of ticket buyers) who were classified into each segment.

The segmentation model is based on a cluster analysis of eight variables from the combined data from 15 local telephone surveys, 2001 - 2002

THE PROSPECT UNIVERSE FOR 15 ORCHESTRAS
% OF ADULTS IN EACH PROSPECT SEGMENT

TABLE S3-A

		AVERAGE OF 15 MARKET SURVEYS	BPO/Brooklyn	CSO/Charlotte	CSO/Denver	DSO/Detroit	FWP/Fort Wayne	KCS/Kansas City	LBSO/Long Beach	LPO/New Orleans	NWS/Miami (Dade)	OS/Portland	TPO/Philadelphia	SLSO/Saint Louis	SPCO/Saint Paul	SAS/San Antonio	WSO/Wichita
Captured Prospects	1. Sophisticated Active Audience	1.7%	0.3%	1.5%	2.4%	1.5%	1.7%	1.2%	0.8%	2.5%	0.5%	3.3%	0.9%	4.5%	1.9%	1.4%	1.6%
	2. Casually-Involved Active Audience	2.0%	0.5%	2.2%	2.2%	2.3%	3.3%	2.0%	0.9%	1.4%	0.6%	2.3%	1.5%	4.7%	1.0%	1.6%	3.6%
	Sub-Total, Captured Prospects	**3.7%**	**0.8%**	**3.8%**	**4.6%**	**3.7%**	**5.0%**	**3.2%**	**1.7%**	**4.0%**	**1.1%**	**5.6%**	**2.4%**	**9.2%**	**2.9%**	**3.0%**	**5.3%**
Low/No Involvement Alumni	3. Sophisticated Low-Frequency Alumni	1.7%	0.5%	1.4%	2.2%	1.0%	1.4%	1.5%	2.1%	2.2%	1.9%	3.4%	1.4%	0.9%	2.8%	0.8%	2.2%
	4. Interested STB & Ghosts	4.4%	2.3%	3.6%	6.2%	4.9%	4.0%	4.2%	2.8%	5.2%	3.3%	4.3%	4.8%	4.9%	5.1%	4.6%	5.1%
	5. Low-Interest Dabblers	4.8%	1.2%	6.9%	3.9%	5.6%	5.6%	5.1%	2.7%	4.6%	1.4%	4.8%	5.2%	8.0%	6.0%	4.7%	6.6%
	6. Special Occasion Only	4.6%	1.3%	4.3%	4.3%	5.9%	6.6%	5.0%	2.3%	4.2%	1.1%	5.9%	3.9%	8.2%	3.2%	4.8%	7.6%
	Sub-Total, Low Frequency Alumni	**15.5%**	**5.3%**	**16.1%**	**16.6%**	**17.4%**	**17.6%**	**15.9%**	**9.9%**	**16.1%**	**7.8%**	**18.5%**	**15.2%**	**21.9%**	**17.1%**	**14.9%**	**21.5%**
No Trial Experience	7. Uninitiated Prospects without Social Context	2.5%	5.4%	2.1%	1.6%	1.8%	1.2%	2.4%	4.9%	1.7%	4.3%	1.8%	2.4%	0.6%	4.5%	1.5%	0.7%
	8. Uninitiated Prospects with Social Context	1.7%	1.9%	1.1%	2.0%	0.7%	1.8%	1.9%	1.8%	1.2%	1.5%	2.4%	1.7%	1.0%	3.1%	1.9%	1.1%
	9. Uninitiated Suspects	3.7%	2.3%	3.5%	3.6%	5.2%	2.7%	3.8%	3.7%	3.0%	1.7%	4.3%	4.7%	2.5%	5.4%	3.2%	5.4%
	Sub-Total, Uninitiated Prospects	**7.8%**	**9.6%**	**6.7%**	**7.2%**	**7.7%**	**5.6%**	**8.0%**	**10.4%**	**5.9%**	**7.6%**	**8.4%**	**8.7%**	**4.1%**	**12.9%**	**6.6%**	**7.2%**
	Sub-Total, The Prospect Universe	**27.0%**	**15.7%**	**26.6%**	**28.3%**	**28.8%**	**28.2%**	**27.1%**	**22.0%**	**25.9%**	**16.4%**	**32.5%**	**26.3%**	**35.2%**	**32.9%**	**24.5%**	**34.0%**
Unclassified	10. Non-Prospects & Unaware	20.5%	27.6%	20.0%	20.5%	18.4%	13.9%	20.5%	30.2%	19.2%	22.2%	21.0%	16.5%	16.0%	25.8%	18.7%	16.6%
	11. Other Adults (Unclassified)	52.6%	56.7%	53.4%	51.2%	52.8%	57.9%	52.4%	47.8%	54.9%	61.4%	46.5%	57.2%	48.8%	41.3%	56.8%	49.4%
	Total - All Adults	**100.0%**	**100.0%**	**100.0%**	**100.0%**	**100.0%**	**100.0%**	**100.0%**	**100.0%**	**100.0%**	**100.0%**	**100.0%**	**100.0%**	**100.0%**	**100.0%**	**100.0%**	**100.0%**

NOTES:

Source: National survey of classical music consumers (2000), and 15 random sample public telephone surveys, 2001 - 2002

This segmentation model is an integration of two separate consumer models developed in the study: 1) relationship with the art form of classical music, and 2) relationship with the specific local orchestra.

TABLE S3-B

PROSPECT SEGMENTS - KEY CHARACTERISTICS

	1. Sophisticated Active Audience	2. Casually-Involved Active Audience	3. Sophisticated Low-Frequency Alumni	4. Interested STB & Ghosts	5. Low-Interest Dabblers	6. Special Occasion Only	7. Uninitiated Prospects without Social Context	8. Uninitiated Prospects with Social Context	9. Uninitiated Suspects	10. Non-Prospects & Unaware	11. Other Adults (Unclassified)
Average Preference Rating for Attending Classical Music Concerts (Scale: 0 = 'Dislike a lot', 10 = 'like a lot')	9.2	9.3	8.5	7.5	6.7	6.1	7.7	7.0	6.0	5.6	5.6
Average Number of Live Performing Arts Events Attended, Last 12 Months	16.1	9.3	12.4	6.1	6.8	3.9	9.0	6.8	4.8	3.8	5.0
Average Number of Classical Music Concerts Attended, Last 12 Months	8.6	4.0	4.4	2.2	2.1	1.5	2.9	2.7	1.4	2.2	3.0
Average Number of Local Orchestra Concerts Attended, Last 12 Months	5.3	3.9	0.4	0.3	0.3	0.3	0.0	0.0	0.0	0.1	1.9
Average Drive Time to Local Orchestra's Primary Venue, in Minutes	20.6	21.5	25.3	23.4	23.0	24.9	26.6	25.0	26.0	26.0	23.4
Level of Knowledge About Classical Music (Self Reported) Very Knowledgeable	34%	8%	21%	11%	5%	1%	13%	10%	2%	3%	1%
Somewhat Knowledgeable	56%	56%	70%	69%	56%	42%	70%	63%	38%	31%	36%
Not Very Knowledgeable	11%	36%	9%	20%	40%	57%	17%	27%	61%	66%	63%
Type of Classical Music Listener (Self Reported) Critical Listener	49%	13%	37%	20%	7%	5%	25%	17%	5%	5%	1%
Casual Listener	51%	85%	63%	79%	89%	90%	75%	81%	87%	71%	81%
Uninterested Listener	0%	2%	0%	0%	3%	5%	1%	2%	9%	24%	18%
Statement Best Describing Current Attitude About Attending Concerts by the Local Orchestra I'm NOT AT ALL INTERESTED in attending a concert	0%	0%	2%	2%	2%	3%	3%	2%	4%	14%	0%
I'm OPEN TO ATTENDING, but it's not a high priority	23%	42%	53%	59%	69%	75%	69%	97%	95%	78%	60%
I'm VERY INTERESTED in attending a concert	77%	58%	45%	40%	28%	22%	27%	1%	1%	8%	40%
	CAPTURED PROSPECTS		LOW FREQUENCY ALUMNI				UNINITIATED PROSPECTS			NOT PROSPECTS	

NOTES:

Source: National survey of classical music consumers (2000), and 15 random sample public telephone surveys, 2001 - 2002

This segmentation model is an integration of two separate consumer models developed in the study: 1) relationship with the art form of classical music, and 2) relationship with the specific local orchestra.

TABLE F

ANALYSIS OF COMBINED FREQUENCY DATA FROM TICKET BUYER SURVEYS: CLASSICAL ATTENDANCE AS A PERCENTAGE OF ALL LIVE PERFORMANCE ATTENDANCE SPECIFIC ORCHESTRA ATTENDANCE AS A PERCENTAGE OF ALL CLASSICAL ATTENDANCE

		AVERAGE OF 15 MARKET SURVEYS	BPO/Brooklyn	CSO/Charlotte	CSO/Denver	DSO/Detroit	FWP/Fort Wayne	KCS/Kansas City	LBSO/Long Beach	LPO/New Orleans	NWS/Miami (Dade)	OS/Portland	TPO/Philadelphia	SLSO/Saint Louis	SPCO/Saint Paul	SAS/San Antonio	WSO/Wichita
SUBSCRIBERS	Average Frequency, All Live Performing Arts Events, Past Year	18.7	31.0	14.9	20.4	15.8	15.2	18.0	15.8	19.9	23.6	15.5	19.0	19.1	19.7	16.1	18.9
	Average Frequency, All Classical Music Attendance, Past Year	10.9	17.5	7.8	12.3	9.3	7.4	9.6	8.1	13.8	13.7	8.5	11.8	9.8	12.5	9.3	12.7
	% Classical of Total Performing Arts "Diet"	58%	56%	52%	60%	58%	49%	53%	51%	69%	58%	55%	62%	51%	63%	58%	67%
	Average Frequency, Specific Local Orchestra Attendance, Past Year	8.4	5.4	7.9	11.1	8.5	7.7	7.7	5.6	9.5	8.6	7.6	8.9	8.5	6.6	8.7	9.9
	% Specific Orchestra of Total Classical "Diet"	77%	31%	101%	90%	92%	104%	80%	69%	69%	63%	90%	76%	87%	53%	94%	78%
FORMER SUBSCRIBERS	Average Frequency, All Live Performing Arts Events, Past Year	14.3	33.6	13.0	12.8	10.5	12.3	13.4	13.6	13.6	20.3	10.0	15.5	13.7	16.7	10.7	11.6
	Average Frequency, All Classical Music Attendance, Past Year	6.9	20.5	6.0	6.1	4.9	4.3	6.0	4.7	6.2	10.5	4.0	7.8	6.3	8.7	4.9	5.6
	% Classical of Total Performing Arts "Diet"	48%	61%	46%	48%	46%	35%	45%	35%	45%	52%	40%	50%	46%	52%	46%	48%
	Average Frequency, Specific Local Orchestra Attendance, Past Year	4.0	2.9	4.8	4.5	4.6	4.8	3.3	1.9	4.4	3.7	2.4	4.6	4.9	4.0	4.0	4.1
	% Specific Orchestra of Total Classical "Diet"	57%	14%	81%	73%	94%	110%	55%	40%	72%	35%	61%	60%	78%	46%	82%	73%
SINGLE TICKET BUYERS	Average Frequency, All Live Performing Arts Events, Past Year	13.3	32.1	8.5	13.2	10.7	9.3	11.7	12.6	15.6	20.1	9.0	13.0	12.8	13.1	9.5	9.1
	Average Frequency, All Classical Music Attendance, Past Year	5.5	9.7	3.6	6.4	3.6	3.7	4.4	5.3	7.8	9.9	3.7	5.6	5.4	5.6	4.1	3.4
	% Classical of Total Performing Arts "Diet"	41%	30%	42%	48%	33%	40%	38%	43%	50%	49%	41%	43%	42%	42%	44%	37%
	Average Frequency, Specific Local Orchestra Attendance, Past Year	3.2	1.6	3.0	4.5	2.5	4.5	2.9	2.0	4.8	3.2	2.4	3.4	3.4	2.3	3.3	3.3
	% Specific Orchestra of Total Classical "Diet"	58%	16%	83%	71%	71%	121%	65%	37%	61%	33%	65%	60%	63%	41%	80%	98%

NOTES:

Respondents who reported more than 125 attendances in the past year were classified as outliers (i.e., invalid responses).

TABLE B1-A (Subscribers)

AVERAGE RATING OF LEVEL OF AGREEMENT WITH STATEMENTS ABOUT CLASSICAL MUSIC: CURRENT SUBSCRIBERS
(SCALE: 0=STRONGLY DISAGREE; 10=STRONGLY AGREE)

Category	Statement	AVERAGE OF 14 TICKET BUYER SURVEYS	BPO/Brooklyn	CSO/Charlotte	CSO/Denver	DSO/Detroit	FWP/Fort Wayne	KCS/Kansas City	LBSO/Long Beach	LPO/New Orleans	NWS/Miami (Dade)	OS/Portland	TPO/Philadelphia	SLSO/Saint Louis	SPCO/Saint Paul	SAS/San Antonio	WSO/Wichita
Artistic/Educational	Hearing specific artists and repertoire is what I value most about the concert experience.	6.8	6.3	N/A	7.0	6.9	6.8	6.8	6.3	6.3	6.9	6.9	7.0	6.8	6.2	7.0	6.8
	I carefully read program notes and enjoy the educational aspects of a classical music concert.	7.8	7.9	N/A	7.9	7.9	7.3	7.5	7.3	7.8	8.3	7.5	7.9	8.0	7.9	7.9	8.0
Spiritual	Classical music connects me with a higher power.	5.1	4.3	N/A	5.2	4.9	4.8	5.0	4.9	5.8	5.4	5.0	5.1	5.0	5.2	5.1	5.3
	Attending classical concerts is an important way that I nourish my soul.	6.3	6.5	N/A	6.5	5.8	5.2	6.0	5.5	6.9	6.7	6.2	6.6	6.1	6.8	6.0	6.5
Therapeutic/Healing	Listening to classical music helps me make it through difficult times.	6.6	6.7	N/A	6.6	6.4	6.0	6.2	6.0	6.9	6.7	6.2	6.8	6.7	6.9	6.6	6.8
	Classical music is an important healing force in my life.	5.9	5.9	N/A	6.1	5.4	5.3	5.7	5.4	6.4	6.2	5.8	6.2	5.7	6.4	5.9	6.2
Ritual/Ambience	People should dress up and look sharp when they go to classical music concerts.	6.3	4.5	N/A	5.9	5.8	6.8	6.5	7.1	5.6	6.4	5.9	6.7	6.6	5.7	6.0	6.7
	The ambience and architectural setting is an important part of the concert experience.	6.8	6.5	N/A	6.2	7.3	6.8	6.5	6.2	6.6	6.7	6.4	7.3	7.3	7.3	6.9	6.6
Social Interaction	I wish there were more opportunities to socialize at concerts.	3.6	3.4	N/A	3.2	3.5	3.7	4.0	4.0	3.7	4.2	3.2	3.8	3.3	3.4	3.8	3.5
	For me, going out to dinner beforehand is an essential part of the experience.	3.6	2.7	N/A	3.6	3.6	3.7	3.5	4.0	2.4	4.7	3.5	4.5	2.7	3.2	4.0	3.4
Relationship Enhancement	Going to classical music concerts is a great way to strengthen personal relationships.	4.7	4.2	N/A	4.7	4.6	4.4	4.7	4.7	4.8	4.9	4.9	4.9	4.8	5.3	4.6	4.9
	I nurture people that I care about by taking them to classical music concerts.	4.5	4.1	N/A	4.5	4.4	4.2	4.1	4.1	4.5	5.2	4.3	4.9	4.6	4.7	4.6	4.8
Occasion	I go to classical concerts to celebrate birthdays, anniversaries and other special occasions.	2.9	2.5	N/A	2.9	2.9	3.0	2.5	2.7	2.5	3.1	2.9	2.9	2.9	3.4	2.9	2.8
	I am very likely to take visiting friends and family to classical concerts.	5.4	5.2	N/A	5.3	5.0	5.1	4.9	5.2	5.4	6.6	5.1	5.8	5.5	5.3	5.5	5.6

NOTES:

Protocol for this question was tested on Charlotte Symphony Orchestra ticket buyers. After the pre-test, a different scale was used for the other 14 orchestras. Results for CSO buyers are not comparable.

TABLE B1-B (Former Subscribers)

AVERAGE RATING OF LEVEL OF AGREEMENT WITH STATEMENTS ABOUT CLASSICAL MUSIC: FORMER SUBSCRIBERS
(SCALE: 0=STRONGLY DISAGREE; 10=STRONGLY AGREE)

		AVERAGE OF 14 TICKET BUYER SURVEYS	BPO/Brooklyn	CSO/Charlotte	CSO/Denver	DSO/Detroit	FWP/Fort Wayne	KCS/Kansas City	LBSO/Long Beach	LPO/New Orleans	NWS/Miami (Dade)	OS/Portland	TPO/Philadelphia	SLSO/Saint Louis	SPCO/Saint Paul	SAS/San Antonio	WSO/Wichita
Artistic/Educational	Hearing specific artists and repertoire is what I value most about the concert experience.	7.0	7.8	N/A	7.2	7.3	6.7	6.8	6.2	6.6	7.1	6.6	7.3	7.1	7.2	7.3	6.6
	I carefully read program notes and enjoy the educational aspects of a classical music concert.	7.7	8.2	N/A	7.7	7.8	7.5	7.4	7.0	7.7	8.3	7.4	7.6	7.3	7.8	7.4	8.1
Spiritual	Classical music connects me with a higher power.	5.0	5.2	N/A	5.2	4.4	5.0	4.7	4.8	5.2	5.1	4.5	5.7	5.0	5.2	5.0	5.6
	Attending classical concerts is an important way that I nourish my soul.	6.0	7.1	N/A	6.0	5.4	5.5	5.7	5.3	6.1	6.9	5.4	6.4	5.7	6.4	5.6	6.1
Therapeutic/Healing	Classical music is an important healing force in my life.	5.7	6.3	N/A	5.6	5.4	5.4	5.3	5.0	5.9	6.6	5.3	6.1	5.5	6.1	5.3	6.2
	Listening to classical music helps me make it through difficult times.	6.5	7.0	N/A	6.5	6.2	6.2	6.5	6.2	6.5	7.2	6.4	6.6	6.4	6.4	6.3	6.7
Ritual/Ambience	People should dress up and look sharp when they go to classical music concerts.	6.2	4.7	N/A	6.4	6.9	6.6	6.5	7.1	5.9	6.2	5.7	6.7	6.0	5.0	6.5	6.8
	The ambience and architectural setting is an important part of the concert experience for me.	6.6	6.7	N/A	6.4	6.9	6.6	6.3	6.1	6.7	6.4	6.2	7.1	6.9	6.9	6.7	6.6
Social Interaction	I wish there were more opportunities to socialize at concerts.	3.5	4.0	N/A	3.2	3.7	3.7	3.2	3.6	3.3	4.0	2.8	4.2	3.6	3.3	3.2	3.3
	For me, going out to dinner beforehand is an essential part of the experience.	3.5	3.0	N/A	3.3	3.4	3.5	3.8	4.1	2.8	3.9	3.5	4.0	3.6	3.5	4.1	3.3
Relationship Enhancement	Going to classical music concerts is a great way to strengthen personal relationships.	4.6	4.6	N/A	4.7	4.8	4.5	4.2	3.8	4.3	4.7	4.2	5.2	4.5	4.7	4.8	4.5
	I nurture people that I care about by taking them to classical music concerts.	4.2	5.0	N/A	4.1	4.3	3.8	3.9	3.7	4.3	5.0	3.5	4.5	4.3	4.5	4.2	4.2
Occasion	I go to classical concerts to celebrate birthdays, anniversaries and other special occasions.	3.3	3.0	N/A	3.5	3.7	3.4	3.1	2.6	2.6	3.0	3.2	3.7	3.8	3.3	3.3	3.5
	I am very likely to take visiting friends and family to classical concerts.	5.0	5.4	N/A	4.8	4.9	4.9	4.6	4.7	4.6	6.3	4.6	5.5	5.3	5.3	5.3	4.9

NOTES:

Protocol for this question was tested on Charlotte Symphony Orchestra ticket buyers. After the pre-test, a different scale was used for the other 14 orchestras. Results for CSO buyers are not comparable.

TABLE B1-C (Single Ticket Buyers)

AVERAGE RATING OF LEVEL OF AGREEMENT WITH STATEMENTS ABOUT CLASSICAL MUSIC: SINGLE-TICKET BUYERS
(SCALE: 0=STRONGLY DISAGREE; 10=STRONGLY AGREE)

Category	Statement	AVERAGE OF 14 TICKET BUYER SURVEYS	BPO/Brooklyn	CSO/Charlotte	CSO/Denver	DSO/Detroit	FWP/Fort Wayne	KCS/Kansas City	LBSO/Long Beach	LPO/New Orleans	NWS/Miami (Dade)	OS/Portland	TPO/Philadelphia	SLSO/Saint Louis	SPCO/Saint Paul	SAS/San Antonio	WSO/Wichita
Artistic/Educational	Hearing specific artists and repertoire is what I value most about the concert experience.	6.7	7.4	N/A	6.8	6.7	6.3	6.6	6.6	6.7	7.0	6.7	6.9	6.9	6.9	6.6	5.8
Artistic/Educational	I carefully read program notes and enjoy the educational aspects of a classical music concert.	7.2	7.1	N/A	7.6	7.2	6.7	6.9	7.4	7.8	8.0	7.1	7.3	6.7	7.4	7.0	7.0
Spiritual	Classical music connects me with a higher power.	4.7	4.8	N/A	5.3	4.2	4.1	4.6	4.3	5.4	6.0	4.5	4.7	4.4	4.8	4.4	4.3
Spiritual	Attending classical concerts is an important way that I nourish my soul.	5.2	5.8	N/A	5.7	4.7	4.4	4.6	4.9	5.9	6.8	5.5	5.3	5.0	5.7	4.8	4.3
Therapeutic/Healing	Classical music is an important healing force in my life.	5.1	4.2	N/A	5.3	4.6	4.1	4.6	5.0	5.8	6.5	4.9	5.1	5.0	5.2	4.5	4.4
Therapeutic/Healing	Listening to classical music helps me make it through difficult times.	6.0	6.3	N/A	6.1	5.6	5.5	5.8	6.0	6.7	7.1	5.6	6.0	5.9	6.1	5.9	5.4
Ritual/Ambience	The ambience and architectural setting is an important part of the concert experience for me.	6.6	6.2	N/A	6.6	6.8	6.7	6.5	6.7	7.1	7.0	6.4	7.2	6.9	6.7	7.2	5.8
Ritual/Ambience	People should dress up and look sharp when they go to classical music concerts.	3.6	4.2	N/A	3.5	3.4	3.7	3.3	3.7	3.9	4.8	3.0	3.8	3.4	3.1	3.7	2.8
Social Interaction	I wish there were more opportunities to socialize at concerts.	3.6	3.0	N/A	3.7	3.4	3.7	3.3	3.7	3.4	4.4	3.2	4.6	3.8	3.9	4.6	3.7
Social Interaction	For me, going out to dinner beforehand is an essential part of the experience.	3.8	3.5	N/A	4.8	3.8	3.9	4.1	4.3	4.8	5.2	4.5	4.8	4.4	4.6	4.8	4.1
Relationship Enhancement	Going to classical music concerts is a great way to strengthen personal relationships.	4.5	4.0	N/A	4.8	4.2	4.4	4.1	4.3	4.8	5.3	4.5	4.8	4.4	4.6	4.8	4.1
Relationship Enhancement	I nurture people that I care about by taking them to classical music concerts.	4.0	3.5	N/A	4.5	3.9	3.5	3.8	3.6	3.6	4.1	3.3	4.2	3.7	3.9	3.9	3.2
Occasion	I go to classical concerts to celebrate birthdays, anniversaries and other special occasions.	3.6	2.7	N/A	4.0	3.6	3.5	3.3	3.6	3.6	4.1	3.3	3.9	3.5	4.2	3.9	3.2
Occasion	I am very likely to take visiting friends and family to classical concerts.	4.9	4.2	N/A	5.2	4.9	4.7	4.7	4.4	5.3	6.2	4.4	5.5	4.7	4.8	5.2	4.4

NOTES:

Protocol for this question was tested on Charlotte Symphony Orchestra ticket buyers. After the pre-test, a different scale was used for the other 14 orchestras. Results for CSO buyers are not comparable.

TABLE B2

MEAN RANKINGS OF SEVEN "VALUE CLUSTERS" ASSOCIATED WITH CLASSICAL MUSIC
(1=HIGHEST RANKING; 7=LOWEST RANKING)

		AVERAGE OF 5 TICKET BUYER SURVEYS	CSO/Denver	LBSO/Long Beach	NWS/Miami (Dade)	OS/Portland	TPO/Philadelphia
Current Subscribers	Artistic or educational value	2.0	1.9	2.2	2.0	2.0	1.8
	Spiritual or self-enrichment value	2.9	2.9	3.2	2.8	2.7	2.8
	Therapeutic or healing value	4.3	4.2	4.5	4.3	4.2	4.3
	Social/community interaction	4.4	4.5	3.7	4.2	4.6	4.7
	Value of the ambience/architectural setting	4.5	4.7	4.6	4.5	4.7	4.0
	Opportunity to enhance your personal relationships	4.6	4.7	4.3	4.7	4.4	4.8
	Opportunity to celebrate special occasions	5.5	5.5	5.6	5.5	5.4	5.6
Former Subscribers	Artistic or educational value	2.0	1.9	2.1	2.0	2.2	2.0
	Spiritual or self-enrichment value	2.9	2.8	3.2	2.3	3.0	3.3
	Therapeutic or healing value	4.3	4.5	4.4	4.0	4.2	4.4
	Value of the ambience/architectural setting	4.5	4.6	4.4	4.5	4.8	4.1
	Opportunity to enhance your personal relationships	4.6	4.4	4.8	4.7	4.5	4.6
	Social/community interaction value	4.7	4.8	4.1	4.7	4.8	4.9
	Opportunity to celebrate special occasions	5.0	5.1	5.2	5.2	4.9	4.6
Single Ticket Buyers	Artistic or educational value	2.1	2.1	2.2	2.1	1.9	2.1
	Spiritual or self-enrichment value	3.1	3.0	3.6	2.8	2.9	3.5
	Value of the ambience/architectural setting	4.3	4.5	4.4	4.2	4.5	3.9
	Therapeutic or healing value	4.4	4.4	4.6	4.0	4.5	4.8
	Opportunity to enhance your personal relationships	4.6	4.5	4.7	4.5	4.5	4.7
	Social/community interaction value	4.6	5.0	4.3	4.6	4.8	4.6
	Opportunity to celebrate special occasions	4.8	4.8	4.3	5.3	4.9	4.4

NOTES:

Due to space constraints, this question was included in only five orchestras' ticket buyer surveys.

TABLE B3

DID YOU EVER/DO YOU SING OR PLAY A MUSICAL INSTRUMENT?

			AVERAGE OF 6 TICKET BUYER SURVEYS	BPO/Brooklyn	CSO/Charlotte	DSO/Detroit	FWP/Fort Wayne	SLSO/Saint Louis	SPCO/Saint Paul
Current Subscribers	Yes		74.0%	72.6%	71.4%	71.3%	74.1%	74.3%	79.5%
	No		26.0%	27.4%	28.6%	28.7%	25.9%	25.7%	20.5%
Former Subscribers	Yes		77.3%	73.3%	78.5%	74.1%	75.2%	75.3%	85.2%
	No		22.7%	26.7%	21.5%	25.9%	24.8%	24.7%	14.8%
Single Ticket Buyers	Yes		71.1%	64.6%	71.0%	71.0%	69.2%	69.2%	80.6%
	No		28.9%	35.4%	29.0%	29.0%	30.8%	30.8%	19.4%

NOTES:

Due to space constraints, this question was included in only six of the orchestra ticket buyer surveys.

TABLE FG-1

I WOULD PROBABLY GO TO DETROIT SYMPHONY CONCERTS MORE OFTEN IF...
(TOP FIVE INDUCEMENTS RANKED 1 THROUGH 5)

	The DSO did more things to make concerts more interesting to watch	Each piece was given a short introduction from the stage	I knew that I could always exchange my tickets for another date, even if I'm not a subscriber	The DSO played concerts at a venue closer to my home	I could buy tickets at the last minute	I knew that good seats were still available, without calling to ask	Concerts weren't so long and I could get home earlier	The DSO played more of the kind of music that I like	Someone else did the organizing, and I could just show up	There was always a group of friends to go with	Safety wasn't a concern	Tickets were less expensive	A friend of mine invited me to go	I could dress casually and feel more comfortable with that crowd
Uninitiated Prospects & Special Occasions Only (N=11)														
Ranked #1	1	0	0	1	0	0	0	1	1	1	0	2	3	0
Ranked #2	0	0	0	1	1	0	0	3	2	2	0	1	0	0
Ranked #3	3	1	0	0	0	0	0	0	1	2	1	1	1	0
Ranked #4	1	2	0	1	0	3	0	0	0	1	0	2	1	0
Ranked #5	0	1	0	1	1	1	0	0	1	0	0	1	1	0
Unranked	6	7	11	7	9	7	11	7	6	5	10	4	5	11
Sophisticated Low-Frequency Alumni & Interested STBs & Ghosts (N=10)														
Ranked #1	0	0	1	3	0	1	0	0	0	1	1	1	0	0
Ranked #2	0	0	0	1	2	1	0	0	0	2	3	0	0	0
Ranked #3	0	1	1	0	0	0	1	1	0	1	0	4	1	0
Ranked #4	0	2	1	2	1	1	0	0	1	0	0	4	0	0
Ranked #5	0	2	1	0	1	0	1	0	1	1	1	0	1	0
Unranked	10	5	6	4	7	7	8	9	9	5	5	1	8	10
Low Interest Dabblers (N=11)														
Ranked #1	1	0	0	0	2	0	0	1	0	1	0	4	1	0
Ranked #2	1	1	2	0	0	1	0	0	0	4	0	1	1	0
Ranked #3	0	3	1	0	3	1	0	1	0	0	0	0	1	1
Ranked #4	1	3	1	0	1	1	0	0	1	0	0	0	2	1
Ranked #5	0	3	1	3	0	1	1	0	0	1	0	0	0	1
Unranked	8	5	6	8	5	7	10	9	10	5	11	6	6	8

NOTES:
Data from focus groups conducted in Detroit, July 2002

FG-1